HOW EMOTIONS WORK

How EMOTIONS Work

JACK KATZ

THE UNIVERSITY OF CHICAGO PRESS
CHICAGO AND LONDON

JACK KATZ is professor of sociology at the University of
California, Los Angeles, and author of *Poor People's
Lawyers in Transition* (1982) and *Seductions of Crime:
Moral and Sensual Attractions in Doing Evil* (1988).

The University of Chicago Press, Chicago 60637
The University of Chicago Press, Ltd., London
© 1999 by Jack Katz
All rights reserved. Published 1999
Printed in the United States of America
08 07 06 05 04 03 02 01 00 99   1 2 3 4 5

ISBN: 0-226-42599-1 (cloth)

Library of Congress Cataloging-in-Publication Data

Katz, Jack, 1944–
    How emotions work / Jack Katz.
       p.   cm.
    Includes bibliographical references and index.
    ISBN 0-226-42599-1 (cloth : alk. paper)
    1. Emotions—Social aspects. I. Title.
BF531.K38   1999
152.4—dc21   99-32675
                                        CIP

To my children,
in the order in which they began shaping
the emotions of my everyday life:
Zac, Betty, Ric, and Alex.

And to Elena,
with whom, for twenty years now,
the metamorphoses have never
been mundane.

We think of ourselves as so intimately entwined in bodily life that a man is a complex unity—body and mind. But the body is part of the external world, continuous with it. In fact, it is just as much part of nature as anything else there—a river, or a mountain, or a cloud. Also, if we are fussily exact, we cannot define where a body begins and where external nature ends.
—Alfred North Whitehead, *Science and the Modern World*

[E]ven questions about gods saving us can be brought down to earth and must finally be settled . . . by looking to the extraordinarily subtle and varied way our everyday practices actually work to give us an understanding of what it means for us and everything else to be.
—Hubert Dreyfus and Harrison Hall, *Heidegger: A Critical Reader*

The object . . . [is] to describe the animation of the human body, not in terms of the descent into it of pure consciousness or reflection, but as a metamorphosis of life, and the body as the "body *of* the spirit" (Valéry).
—Maurice Merleau-Ponty, *Themes from the Lectures at the Collège de France, 1952–1960*

CONTENTS

ACKNOWLEDGMENTS

Questions from audiences, some anticipated and some unexpected, some uttered and others emphatically implied through polite but labored restraint, were indispensable for sustaining and repeatedly redirecting this project over a period of many years. My perspective on emotions was first worked out in interaction with students in seminar discussions. I am very grateful for the patient collaboration of several cohorts of Ph.D. students at UCLA, and to Prof. Alain Coulon, who, after wandering into my seminar in Los Angeles, set up a seminar course at the University of Paris VIII, where I first tried out a format for this book. For other challenging opportunities, I would like to thank Keith Oatley and a session in Würzburg, Germany, of the International Society for Research on Emotions; George Psathas and a meeting of the M.I.D.A.S. society at Harvard; Martin Jay and the "Experience" group of the German and European Study Center at Berkeley; and several sessions organized through the University of Lund, Sweden, by Malin Åkerström, Kajsa Ekholm Friedman, and Jonathan Friedman.

I was fortunate to receive comments on drafts of one or more sections from Howard S. Becker, Alain Coulon, Jeff Coulter, Lori Cronyn, Mitchell Duneier, Robert M. Emerson, Michael Flaherty, Robert Garot, Calin Goina, John Heritage, David Johnson, Gail Kligman, Margarethe Kusenbach, Melvin Lansky, Richard Leo, Dan Marks, Aundra Saa Meroe, Keith Oatley, Melvin Pollner, Fred Prichard, Suzanne Retzinger, Ted Sarbin, Thomas Scheff, Melvin Seeman, Lakshmi Srinivas, and Diane Vaughan. Loïc Wacquant digested the whole manuscript and offered extraordinarily incisive criticism and very usable advice. I thank Ricardo Halpern for producing the video images in chapter 2; Scott Galbraith for the illustrations in chapter 5, which he made from video stills; and both Scott Galbraith and Naomi Fujimoto for cheerful and painstaking research assistance. The Academic

Senate at UCLA helped with modest but essential research funds. Because of Doug Mitchell's enthusiasm, Michael Koplow's attention to detail, and Martin White's work on the index, it has been a pleasure to make the book with Chicago.

My appreciation for contributions of data is expressed in the chapters, but because of the need to make the subjects anonymous, my biggest debt cannot be properly paid. In a sense my job has been simply to haul barriers of artificial ideas and inappropriate methods out of the way so that we can see the intimate innovations that people make in their everyday lives. This book fails if it is not obvious that its creativity has been ripped off from its subjects.

For permission to reprint parts of chapters 2 and 3 that were previously published, I thank, respectively, the *American Journal of Sociology* and Analytic Press. For permission to use the photograph by André Kertész in chapter 2, I thank the Kertész estate and its curator, Robert Gurbo.

INTRODUCTION

Every day our emotions confront us with an abiding enigma. On the one hand, emotions come to us seemingly beyond our control. We may be possessed by anger, drenched in shame, taken by something we find hysterically funny, or surprised to find ourselves crying from joy. On the other hand, emotions make up a part of our lives that is intimately subjective. When a person laughs, the form of expression is remarkably idiosyncratic. Virtually everyone can recall a song, a sunset, or an appreciation of a child's innocence that brought him to tears even when others at his side were unmoved. A person knows that her shame is something she owns; the visibility of that self-knowledge is how a blush leads to further shame. And no matter how unjust another's action, an angry response is not inevitable. We understand that how a person emotionally responds uniquely defines who that person is.[1]

Because it postures the individual dialectically, indicating that he is both an object taken and a subjectivity in the process of defining himself, emotional experience raises two questions. If emotions are not just done to but also done by a person, how does he or she create them? How do we manage to produce the tears that emerge in moments of joy? Why does it make natural sense to shout when we are angry, cover our faces in shame, and make rough exhale sounds that instantly can be recognized as laughter? The first question is about emotional expression. How is it that we all possess the competence to shape and perform emotional behavior in such profoundly aesthetic ways?[2]

A second question closely follows. How is it that people do not sense that they are creating their emotions? The tickle behind laughter seems to come from without, but where, if not from oneself, does the tickle come from when we are not physically touched? When shame or rage flood through experience, where is the source of the inundation, where are the gates that let the rush of feelings come through, if they are not within? If we idiosyncratically own our emotions, why can't we fully own up to them? By what fine legerdemain does a person hide from himself the artful process in which he shapes his emotional experience?

Left in a general form, the mysteries of emotions might be considered problems for philosophers or grist for poets. But if we collect experiences rich in the specifics of everyday life, we can transform the mysteries of emotions into problems for sociological investigation. With good sets of data in hand, we can ask such empirically researchable questions as the following.

Why is it that drivers so often get ferociously mad at each other one moment, only to feel like fools for having done so the next?

How does it happen that, even when people politely laugh to acknowledge a corny joke, the laughter sometimes appears to set loose spirits of humor that soon do them in?

Everyone seems to have had memorable experiences with shame. What does the apparently universal vulnerability to shame indicate about us? If shame is always potential in social life, is this emotion the hidden inner lining of the selves we present to others? If so, is shame also the basis of our anger, our laughter, even of our crying? Is a personal strategy for avoiding shame somehow the basis of the individual identities we fashion? Or more perversely, are we masochistic beings, always seeking to live, if not right on the edge, just a few short and quickly traversed steps from the wells of shame?

As to crying, each of its many forms restates the enigma of emotions in distinctive ways. How can a three-year-old child, after being continuously consumed by whining for five minutes, jump into speech instantly and without showing any residue of distress? Was that whining "just manipulative"? Even if it produced real tears?

The study of crying can reveal the dialectics of emotions as they change over the life course. Crying starts life as a noisily willful production. Later on, despite or perhaps ironically because one has arrived at a mature stage of control over conventional practical problems, one's eyes can begin to well up in unexpected moments of powerlessness as they never did in youth. When people cry in awe, the dialectics of emotions are present as themes of bittersweet interplay. Mortality is highlighted by immortality, the eternal mocks the evanescent, endings are implied in beginnings, and oppression sets the background for the triumphant resistance it can inspire.

Whatever crying essentially is, it is richly varied expressive behavior. The mourner's wail and the child's whine may be sustained on and on, but crying also exists in the fleeting moment when a tear quietly drops. People cry in both the worst and the best moments of their lives. Can we reach any general understanding of what people are doing when they are crying? Until we can say what it means to cry, are we not missing something of great importance about how people live and relate to each?

The causes of crying are not only academic questions. In many lines of work, they are recurrent problems. Occupational specialists develop effective folk theories of the emotion's workings. What do preschool teachers know that enables them to get young children to stop crying? And what is it that police interrogators know that enables them to elicit spates of crying that will lubricate confessions from both amateur and career criminals? Is there some inversely related craft knowledge by which they induce their role partners respectively to shape up and to unravel?

The enigma of emotions has always provoked its investigation, at least since Freud's focus on the interrelation of the manifest and subconscious meanings of dreams. In the last twenty years, studies of emotions have mushroomed across academic fields and across continents, often in protest against exclusively rational models of action. This broad and encouraging movement in social thought invites a more direct approach to the phenomena of concern than methodological and interpretive commitments have usually allowed.

Research on static and decontextualized phenomena, such as studies of how people perceive photographs of facial expressions, have produced significant evidence of limited universals in emotional culture. We can take encouragement from such studies for developing a cross-cultural theory of emotions. A next challenge is to develop empirically grounded explanations of emotions as they rise and decline in the vibrant flow of social life.[3]

Too often, the reader of research on emotions must become preoccupied more with comprehending an author's elaborate interpretive scheme and rigorous methodology than with understanding the subtleties of emotional life. Sociologists have used questionnaires to seek reports on decontextualized emotional experiences and to elicit responses to hypothetical narratives. In either case, the researcher routinely leaves it to the reader to guess how respondents understood the situations in which they supplied responses, and how if at all they considered the relationship between the research situation and emotional experiences as they occur in the practical settings of their social lives. But it is also possible to study rigorously how people construct their understandings of emotional behavior in natural settings.[4]

Repeatedly, anthropologists have called readers to examine emotions in non-Western cultural worlds, but the studies almost always have ended up analyzing how people *talk about* their emotions. If there is anything distinctive about emotions, it is that, even if they commonly occur in the course of speaking, they are not talk, not even just forms of expression. Indeed, to the extent emotions are forms of expression, they are ways of expressing that something is going on that talk cannot grasp. Historical and cultural studies similarly elide the challenge of understanding emotional experience when they analyze texts, symbols, material objects, and ways of life as *representations* of emotions.[5]

This book is an invitation to search for an empirically grounded explanation of some of the common emotional patterns in everyday life. If we start with dreams or with troublesome cases of pathological development, everyone lacking clinical access and expertise will remain shut out of the inquiry. If we start with undergraduates in university laboratories where experimental conditions can be controlled, social life will seem artificially thin. If we use survey questionnaires, we will have to preconceive and preanalyze the thing we want to study. Why not for once start by giving priority to the things we want to understand, structuring methods and allowing theory to take shape to fit the contours of what we find? What will our ideas about emotions become if we start with some vivid emotional experiences that people have as they go about their daily activities?[6]

If we want to develop some measure of general understanding about emotions, we want to examine more than just one emotion. On the other hand we cannot look at a sample of all emotions, and not just because time and textual space are limited but because at the start of the project we cannot assume we already know what "all emotions" could mean. A convenient way to finesse the problem of definition, at least long enough to get the inquiry under way, is to focus initially not on emotional states or feelings but on what people, as they expressively relate their conduct to each other, recognize as emotions. Thus I propose that we begin by trying to explain some common forms of laughter, crying, shame, and anger.

We will need qualitative data if we are to avoid presetting limits on our ability to pursue exceptions and nuances in emotional experience, but in order to hedge our bets, we should probably not rely on any one method of qualitative investigation or any one form of qualitative data. Although our focus will be on vivid and colorful scenes of everyday life, what happens in those scenes will usually be inconsequential to everyone but the people immediately involved, and even for them, only for a few brief moments. If we change the kinds of materials as we go along, it should also help to make the inquiry less tedious.

We can use videotapes to study a few types of emotional phenomena, such as laughter in a fun house and crying in day care centers and rooms dedicated to police interrogations. For a good look at anger, we can review conversational interviews about experiences of getting mad when driving around Los Angeles. For examining shame, we have diverse sources. They include painful self-reports, great fictional descriptions and philosophers' examples, ethnographic passages written by academic researchers, interviews with friends of middle-aged executives who are being prosecuted for white-collar crime, and videotapes of what seven- and eight-year-old boys do after they strike out at the baseball plate.

Although the focus in this book will be on familiar experiences, the substantive topics have not before been made the focus of inquiry by students of emotions. The way I propose to make connections with prior investigations is more by appreciating how different research perspectives dovetail than by citing the findings of previous research. Three traditions of inquiry guide these studies. The first is related to the Freudian exercise of double interpretation but with the phenomenological twist that both meanings must be grounded in evidence of the subject's own doubly resonant experience.[7] I will not try to describe any "subconscious" meanings but I will describe meanings that are sensually and tacitly understood by each participant (meanings that are "preconscious," as Freud sometimes used the term), as well as meanings that are made manifest to the others who are immediately present.

The second line of investigation joins the sociological tradition of examining how emotional expressions are shaped in anticipation of how they will be perceived.[8] The third line of inquiry joins the currently emerging movement of research on the embodiment of conduct.[9] Here is a preview of how these lines of inquiry are applied to everyday emotions in the chapters that follow.

1. *Situation-responsive and situation-transcendent narrative projects.* What is the socially visible sense that a person is trying to make in the immediate situation of his action, and what is the current sense that the situation acquires within his awareness that his life reaches beyond the current situation? For example, I will ask, first, In what ways does one's provocation of laughter in the fun house create an immediate bond with another family member?; and then, In what ways does the ensuing laughter shape one's understanding of what it means

to be in a family? I will analyze how a killer cries in his confession so that his crying, on the one hand, serves his immediate interests in dealing with his police interrogators, and also, on the other hand, grasps the implications of the interrogation episode for his quickly narrowing future. When looking at angry drivers, I will examine "flippings off" and other narratives for getting revenge on the car in the next lane, but also how creating such minidramas figures into where the gesturing driver is coming from and where he is trying to get to.

2. *Interaction processes.* How does a person shape his emotional conduct with regard to the readings and responses that others will give? I will ask how one exploits unique equipment in the setting, such as distorting mirrors in a fun house or the expressive possibilities of automobiles in highway traffic, in order to produce what friends will recognize as humor or what enemies will appreciate as moral indignation. In shaping emotional conduct, the subject also exploits resources for interaction that she finds in her own body. I will describe how a three-year-old in preschool, working to hold the attentions of her teacher, manages her respiratory tract to explore the communicative possibilities of vocalizations that move in fine steps between crying and talking. In each case we will see people creatively mining the resources they find at hand in order to shape the impressions that others take of their emotions.

3. *Sensual metamorphoses.* Emotional experience is not only a matter of shaping the meaning of the moment for others in the here and now and of simultaneously grasping the implications for one's life in other places and times. As a person moves into and out of laughter, shame, crying, and anger, the sensual framework of his action changes. These experiences are transformations of the embodied vehicle of conduct. In the following analyses, I take seriously what might at first glance seem to be hyperbole or surreal images. For example, I treat drivers' complaints that they have been "cut off" as literal descriptions; I then look for evidence of what in their corporeal experience was amputated. In examining shame, I will argue that a desire that "the earth open up and swallow me whole" is not an artificial description nor a figure borrowed from mythology; the imagery naturally tracks the experience of shame. And we will see that the critical stage in moving out from crying and into an unperturbed line of conversation occurs when the person effaces her body, rubbing out an awareness of her three-dimensional, corporeal existence.

The distinctions between these three lines of inquiry are not ontological. We do not "present a self" by some means or in some time and place that is separate from "the embodiment of our conduct," in turn separate from developing our "construction of the meanings" of the situation. But neither are these distinctions simply matters of convenient exposition. In these studies I treat experience in social life as three-dimensional. Our selves are best summarized as prisms, not as looking glasses. Any given action is the result of a person's integration of three simultaneously sustained processes. A moment's doings in social life entail maneuvering in detailed ways to make recognizable sense of one's situated behavior, even while one senses how the current situation fits into one's ongoing life, and even as the metaphoric vehicle of one's conduct is being transformed, often seemingly beyond one's control.

The overall understanding that this volume produces is that emotions, which have so often been treated as opposed to thinking,[10] are paradoxically self-reflective actions and experiences. But the self-reflection in emotions is corporeal rather than a matter of discursive reasoning. Through our emotions, we reach back sensually to grasp the tacit, embodied foundations of our selves. We are artful in producing our emotions because through them we seek to articulate the corporeal metaphors that operate implicitly at the foundations of all of our conduct.

In the concluding chapter I use the empirical ground that has been covered to elaborate the underlying, tripartite social-psychological theory. Throughout, I exploit complementarities among what, in the twentieth century, have been independently inspiring but, for the most part, mutually hostile forms of inquiry: the dualistic hermeneutics of depth psychology and Heideggerian philosophy; social interaction analysis as inspired by George Herbert Mead and Alfred Schutz; and the phenomenology of the body that Michael Polanyi suggested and that Maurice Merleau-Ponty independently and more faithfully developed.[11]

It turns out that each of these traditions of inquiry has been preoccupied with a common riddle, the enigma that underlies the substantively narrow, colloquially put questions that are addressed chapter by chapter in this volume: What is it that, being itself invisible, is responsible for all that is visible? They provide different essential elements of the answer. By interweaving their insights, we can resolve the opening enigma about emotions and obtain a new standpoint for social psychology. Our emotions are dialectical in nature, something we artfully produce and yet experience as forces that take us over independent of our will, because what we are reaching for through our emotions are sensual resources that operate as a foundation for our conduct only when they remain outside of the foreground of our self-awareness. The study of emotions in everyday life helps remedy the failure of the social and psychological sciences to appreciate the hidden sensual and aesthetic foundations of the self.

Methodological Commitments

How are we to find empirical data on a process that produces socially visible emotions if much of that process is itself invisible? A common understanding by psychoanalysts, interactionists, and phenomenologists is that one should not trust methods that ask subjects to point directly to the causes of their conduct, to identify the social contingencies of their behavior, or to represent the lived meaning of their experience. Although people are intimately familiar with and vividly touched by the forces that shape their lived experiences, the critical shaping processes work like habitually worn eyeglasses: they are transparent to the person even while, by structuring perception, they critically influence the person's response to his/her environment. But if many of the forces, mechanisms, and conditions that shape a person's emotional conduct must be invisible to that person while he or she acts, that limitation still leaves open many routes of direct inquiry. Several methodological strategies have guided the following studies.

1. These studies are of *naturally occurring* conduct and experience. The data are in situ in nature. While the data, whether interviews, ethnographic field notes, or videotapes, can always be questioned as possibly shaped by the recording process, the objective was to minimize the chance of studying research artifacts. The ethnographic character of the materials follows through on that commitment.

2. These studies are about forms of *emotional behavior enacted in face-to-face social situations*. Much of emotional life is a matter of mood that persists in solitude and of characteristic styles of behaving that cut across settings for action. But for methodological reasons this inquiry takes situations of interaction practices as a focal point for restarting a sociology of emotions.

The data focus on things people do with others when they are emotional. When people *generalize* about what they do, much less try to explain *why* they do it, what they say is extremely suspect as anything other than an artifact of the inquiry. On the other hand, when people *describe* what they were doing at times when the stakes for them were both high and independent of the current inquiry, we have reason to have more faith in reading what they say as evidence about what they have lived.[12] In the following chapters, virtually all of the data are about what a person did and experienced in a particular time and place, and in immediately responsive interaction with someone else. This is so whether the data take the form of interviews, transcribed videotape, or ethnographic field notes written originally by the author, by other researchers, or by "lay" observers.

When the data come from interviews, the interviewees are asked to give a sequential narrative describing a recent instance of a certain kind of emotional experience, and they are pressed for details, especially about what happened at turning points in the events. (As an example, the interview guide used for collecting the data in chapter 1 is available in the appendix.) Perceptions—the subject's description of what the scene was and what others were doing—are especially useful. A person's perceptions are both the product of the posture he or she has tacitly taken up and the immediate provocation of his or her next actions.

Interviewees who are guided to stick with situation-specific reports on relations with others are led to describe what they witnessed and did in time- and space-focused, sensually vivid, and socially responsive ways. It is painfully obvious when data about socially situated emotions are weak. In colloquial terms, this is recognized when people try to retell humorous events and, unable to conjure up the specifics of what the parties were doing or the embodied sense of the situation, they throw up their hands with a "you had to be there." The data in these chapters should themselves provoke a range of emotions because they try to take the reader "there."

3. I often construct sets of data that *emphasize personal idiosyncrasy* in perception, conduct, and forms of expression. Chapter 1, for example, is built on hundreds of interviews in which drivers describe their experience in getting mad. Chapter 2 is based on hundreds of incidents of people passing before distorting mirrors in an amusement park. Chapter 4 draws on many incidents of people crying when speaking before mass audiences. Such personally colorful data sets enable the analyst to "hold constant" competing explanatory factors, or rival hypotheses in the form of personality, ethnicity, sex, social class status, situational environmental conditions, etc.

4. I *supplement people's own accounts* of their emotional experiences *with the perceptions of others* present. When a data set is mostly based on interviews, it is complemented by observer accounts. We obtain key insights into the contingencies of a driver's anger, for example, by getting an account of what happened from the perspective of a passenger who, seated inches away, had a markedly different experience of the event.

5. I use *videotape* extensively. Videotape is the main source of data

for three chapters: on laughter in the fun house, on an episode of whining in preschool, and on a murder suspect under interrogation who breaks into crying as his story is broken down by the police. Videotape provides supplementary data on shame and on crying in many different types of social situations. I personally videotaped in a Parisian fun house and in several other settings examined in this volume, including Little League baseball games, preschool activity, and retirement parties. Other researchers supplied videotapes that they had made on social life in preschools, karate classes, greetings in public places, southern California street gangs, etc. I also transcribed and analyzed videotapes made by commercial broadcasters (e.g., of awards ceremonies), by participants in social occasions such as weddings and retirement parties, and by people in positions of authority who regularly record behavior in work settings for purposes such as documenting police interrogations.

Videotape is no miracle cure for the methodological problems flowing from the inherently invisible side of emotional processes, but it can be very helpful. Without relying on hidden recording devices (none of the material in this book was produced by hidden cameras or microphones), we can tape regions of individuals' embodied conduct that lie behind and below their own perceptive reach. By maintaining a fixed focus, we can record changes in a person's conduct as another person arrives, allowing us to watch how our subject moves into a social interaction. And by reviewing a given passage numerous times, we can bring eternally back into focus what was transparent and audibly fleeting to the participants even as they expressed and responded to it. We can rewind and replay, endlessly framing what they, in the inexorable ongoingness of everyday life, had to see, hear, and instantly work through.

6. I *take subjects' metaphors seriously* as providing elements of explanation. At the most fundamental level of emotional experience and conduct, there is no nonmetaphoric, nonfigurative, "literal" level of reality to address.[13] We can, for example, run an audiotape of a two-year-old's whining through a meter and produce a graph that describes some of its audible dimensions. But those lines and readings are not what the child and others who are present hear and respond to. The whining child draws on her body in a distinctive way; she is creating a unique corporeal vehicle for her conduct, and she knows what she is doing in some holistic, proprioceptive sense.[14] The metaphors I choose are, of course, not inevitably right; the reader will have a free hand to substitute his/her own. But I submit that if we insist on trying to capture emotional phenomena in their natural state, we social scien-

tists will have to risk being lousy poets because our subjects are constantly obliged to take on more immediate aesthetic risks.[15]

7. I use the methodology of *analytic induction* to organize and analyze the data. An extensive discussion of this method as applied to ethnographic data is available elsewhere,[16] but some of its distinguishing features can be briefly noted. The definitions of the emotions addressed by the analysis were developed as hypotheses on explanatory conditions were tested. This accounts for the colloquial description of the emotions explained. Drivers are angry about many things, some being things that haunt them whether or not they are driving, but when they get cut off they get "pissed off." Anger in other social relationships, for example about a national leader's betrayal of trust, might have to be described in other terms and explained in other ways.

Some of the classic products of analytic induction lay out the step-by-step changes that the researcher made in the definition of the explanandum and the explanans as he confronted negative cases and was forced to revise theory.[17] The author explicitly shows the rival hypotheses that were rejected. An alternative and I think more palatable way of doing the same thing is by writing a richly nuanced ethnographic account. For example, by describing many different approaches that people make to distorting mirrors in order to make them funny, we can define the essential contingencies of appreciating humor in the situation. That each of many ways of "working" the mirrors is sufficient to elicit laughter enables us to discount explanations that would cite any one way as crucial. Or, again, by showing that the enunciation of the word "heart" brings tears to a Samoan-American gang member giving an interview to a friend in Long Beach, a Holocaust survivor receiving an Academy Award, and a man released from prison for rape after DNA evidence indicated that he had been falsely accused, I argue that it is not the distinguishing aspects of any of these situations (e.g., whether they are stressful or not), but (inter alia) the self-reflective three-dimensionality of the word, both sensually and metaphorically, that explains the crying. It is not necessary to label the rival hypotheses formally in order to discount them (e.g., that the horror of having been a Holocaust victim sets one up for this crying). The process of ruling out rival hypotheses is made available to the reader in the thick and closely differentiated character of the data.

Analytic induction is a causal inquiry; it seeks the necessary and sufficient conditions of a phenomenon that develops sequentially and that enters and leaves or rises and falls in lives and experiences. Positive data, showing the coincidence of the explanans and the explanandum, are useful when they take an atemporal, correlational, or cross-sectional form. But data are especially useful when they describe closely related but negative cases in atemporal data (the result does not occur, the cause is not present), and, even more, when they describe the decline and disappearance of the hypothesized phenomenon in a strip of action. For example, a key point in chapter 1 comes when we see that people sitting next to an angry driver often do not themselves get mad. In chapter 3, the foundations of shame are significantly indicated by how people work to get out of shame by arranging things when they get home. And in chapter 5, the analysis of whining is developed not just by showing what happens in the interaction while the whining persists but what happens in the brief moments when whining stops and speech begins.[18]

8. Data and analysis are arranged to construct a *triangular relationship between subject, author, and reader.* The data were first created in sets of interviews, field notes, and videotapes. In the text, the reader is given as much independent access to the data as is feasible in print form. The author's Web page, <http://www.sscnet.ucla.edu/soc/faculty/katz/>, should be consulted for access to audio-video strips of data. The subject of the volume itself facilitates the reader's independent verification of the analysis insofar as he or she has traveled through the settings examined here. The objective is to promote a democratic process of inquiry, a sociology without clubs in which the reader is as enfranchised as is the author in developing and judging explanations.[19]

Plan of the Book

Chapters differ by types of emotions and by social settings as well as by types of data. The first chapter is the longest because interviews with once-angry drivers are especially useful for fully introducing both the theory of emotions and the logic of explanation that run throughout the volume. In later chapters, especially in the case studies of whining in chapter 5 and of a police suspect breaking down in chapter 6, the data require a more patient reading. Differences in the social structuring of emotional experience call for differences in the researcher's methodology for gathering data, in the author's style of writing, and in the work required of the reader.

When emotional experience can be captured by interviews, the author can ground analysis in the folk metaphors that subjects expressly use. As part of their everyday social lives and quite independent of the occasions for sociological research, people like to tell stories about what happened to make them angry when they were driving. Indeed, in Los Angeles, the recounting of "road rage" is for many people virtually an everyday ritual. Drivers, reporting on their anger, can anticipate that their listeners will have had similar experiences and can vividly imagine the provocation of their emotions. But most emotional experience is not of a similarly transportable narrative nature.

Interview materials are not especially helpful for examining humor and laughter in the fun house nor for explaining the crying examined in chapters 5 and 6. What three-year-olds can say about their crying is a fascinating but largely separate subject for study. And what adults will say about their emotions is often unreliable for adult reasons. Unlike the pissed-off driver, the murderer described in chapter 6 would be well advised to assume that his listeners will not identify with his perspective on his story. As a professional criminal suspect, he knows that interviewers, whether policemen or social researchers, are not idly enjoying an entertaining story but are listening to gain a basis for working up a portrait of him that may not be to his advantage. As we will see, when he cries he quickly offers a self-serving explanation of why.

Another reason that the road rage reported in chapter 1 is especially accessible through interviews is that part of what makes people angry when they drive is that driving makes them mute. They know what they want to say to the others who cut them off, but the logistics of their communicative situation limit them to rough gestures. When they are interviewed, they often virtually burst with details of perception and indignant response that they were forced to repress just under the surface of their situated experience. The same cannot be said about the vast majority of emotional life. The humor examined in chapter 2, for example, essentially consists of gesticulations and guttural responses. The fun house is fun in part because what happens there transpires so quickly, so lightly, and in such a uniquely embodied way that amused visitors have little interest in and even less capacity for recounting the mechanics of their experience.

Once we start examining people's emotions as they occur outside of cars, it is not so easy to identify the vehicles of their experience. The vehicle of one's conduct is more typically an instrumentation of one's body and of immobile objects at hand. While car culture is a rich part of contemporary civilization, we lack figures of speech for the more ubiquitous grounds of our conduct. We need materials that go beyond what is grasped by everyday culture if we want to describe techniques of the body that are matters of the ways we use chairs, how we audibly mark our respiratory system, and the tricks we employ to generate metaphoric meanings by opposing one of our body parts to another.

Videotape is an invaluable resource for grasping the interplay of emotion, language, and embodied metaphor in the fun house, in the preschool, and in police interrogations. In order to appreciate the corporeal instrumentation of a toddler's whine and see how it is shaped by child and teacher to weave a bond between them, we must look at an emotional expression that willfully resists language. A whining child cannot tell you that her crying is fuguelike, but we need that image, in both the psychological and musical senses of the term, to trace the course and the contingencies of the emotional experience. Whining is in a way recognizably "obsessive" and, like a musical fugue in which a melodic line points to its subsequent reappearance, whining carries the promise of endless repetition of a recognizable motif. The participants in chapter 5 orient to the fuguelike character of the whine, but never explicitly. Indeed, the two interact for about five minutes, constantly negotiating a transition from whining to speech, until the teacher, in the frustrating moment when the whining, having finally stopped, emphatically starts up again, turns to the child and asks directly, "And Rachel, why are you crying?" The child's explicit answer clearly, pointedly, and significantly makes no sense.

A criminal suspect cannot tell you that, just before he cried, he made a fateful admission and then said "I know I'm getting the electric chair for this." Nor could he report that just before using this figure of speech he raised and repositioned his bottom in his chair as if he were already in a hot seat. His grasping for a means to organize himself is too desperate, too existentially compelled, too raw to be simply spoken. The metaphors in his speech, his emotional expression, and his corporeal gesture are part of a frantic search for a serviceable vehicle for situated action. After the fact, he will not be able to articulate how, following a particularly fateful admission, he found a figure of speech, a revised image of himself, and a line of emotional action that would enable him simultaneously to reassure himself and lend a touch of verisimilitude to a new line of self-defense.

Nor is it likely that anyone would be able to explain to an interviewer what happens when his polite laughter starts to do him in. Often when a person is intensely involved in laughter, his eyes are forced to close, his posture is pressed into doubling up, and he may even be compelled to turn away from others in order to save what little remains of his composure. The process of laughing itself blocks the perception of self and surrounds.

If we could understand everything about emotions that we need to by studying angry drivers, the writing and reading experience would be much more fun than the bulk of what follows. But as the chapters differ in materials, so also do they differ in the contributions they make to the overall presentation of the theory of emotions that unites the volume. Chapter 1, "Pissed Off in L.A." presents perhaps the most balanced treatment of each of the three conditions of emotions that make up the theory. Chapter 2, on laughter in the fun house, takes advantage of the documentation on videotape of the transition from "doing" emotions, here in the form of using laughter to show another person that one thinks something is funny, to being "done by" emotions, in the sense of being overcome by the humor of the moment. That transition is especially important because it shows that, in studying emotions, one can combine what has been kept separate by different traditions of social-psychological research, namely an analysis of emotional expression and an analysis of the sensuality of emotional experience.

Chapter 3, "Shameful Moments," is unique within the volume in addressing a kind of emotional experience that is rich in narrative content but that frequently occurs without producing the strips of distinctive, interaction-shaped conduct that describe many bouts of crying, riffs of laughter, and spates of anger. As a behavior, shame is often little more than a moment's experience and part of what is experienced in shame is impotence to organize conventional behavior. Materials on shame invite an analysis of the emotion's elemental structure.

That analysis shows the emotion to be both dialectical and dualistic: there are two complementary forms of shame, each being an experience of dynamic tension. Having grasped this complex composition in experiences of shame, we are better prepared to see that there are two complementary forms of crying, two forms of laughter, and two forms of anger, and that each emotional experience is dialectical in nature. That analysis in turn sets up an effort to explain the social-psychological basis for the dualistic, dialectical nature of emotional experience in social life.

Chapter 4, "What Is Crying?" combines ethnographic observation, videotape analysis, and interview materials on a given emotion as it unfolds in a range of social settings. Like all emotions, I will argue, crying is the presentation of a mystery, but crying presents the mystery of emotions in unique ways. In contrast to shame, crying often presents its mystery in a sustained strip of conventionally recognizable, distinctive conduct. Unlike anger, in which the person attempts to shift the focus of attention to another, crying keeps the mystery focused on oneself. And while laughter is commonly polite and superficial, crying more routinely resonates with dimensions of profound experience even when it is as brief as a single silent tear.

What the study of the variety of crying perhaps most distinctively reveals is the natural poetry of emotional experience. Interviews and ethnographic observations indicate that, as an appreciative response to what they experience as sacred, precious, or beautiful, adults spontaneously humble themselves by becoming quietly tearful. Videotape shows that the enunciation of the word "heart" in a variety of bittersweet circumstances appears to have a power that is surprisingly moving to both speaker and audience. Audiotapes reveal how, in case after case of hearings to decide whether to parole murderers from prison, relatives of long-deceased victims can regularly and easily underscore their demands for continued confinement with the dramatic power of sincere tears. In crying, people often give themselves up to be taken by aesthetic and dramaturgical forms that they have themselves invoked.

The two extended case studies of videotaped crying provide resources for clarifying what is at once perhaps the most obvious and most elusive social-psychological truth about emotions: that they are emphatically three-dimensional ways of making explicit what is usually the invisible reality of our being interlaced with the world. Dramatic alterations of respiration figure especially clearly in crying. Some actors get themselves into crying by punctuating their inhales into short gasps of breath. Children whine by marking each exhale with sound. Respiration is the most constant proof of our natural intertwining with the world.

But we usually do not notice that the breath that distinguishes life from death proves that there is no ontological separation between subject and environment, self and other. The prevailing folk and scientific cultures for considering our identities doggedly refuse to acknowledge that there is no point of separation between what is "outside" and what is "inside," no definable limit to the penetration of self into world and world into self, no place where one's identity neatly ends and the social environment obdurately begins. By turning on respiration to mark it expressively, crying defines the intertwining of self and other as a social problem. In chapter 5, we can see that as the child's whining ends, the opposite occurs: individual and joint awareness of the body of each participant is effaced, and there is born the mundane and locally invisible, intertwined collective body of ordinary, everyday social action.

On Theory

A final note about the kind of theory to anticipate. Most social psychologists are dedicated to a version of science that would allow one to know emotions much as one finds places with the aid of a map. Looking for a particular site, one finds its name in an index, the index gives coordinates, and one can then see what is described at the indicated intersection. Someday, the aspiration seems to be, one will be able to use a map to find out if, say, women in powerful positions smile more or less than do powerless women. An inventory of research findings would describe what the map displays at the intersections represented by B1 and B3, 1 and 3 being at the lower and upper districts of Power Street and B indicating the female side of Gender Boulevard.

The present studies offer a different vision of what social-psychological research might accomplish. The strategy is to enter some densely populated and lively part of social life, get lost, and then use local resources in a scramble to get home. You wander about for some time while noticing interesting things, and then you try to find a way out by listening for what the natives suggest, even though you know that in the singularity of your own experience, you will always remain an outsider, even though the natives often can't give directions to the major landmarks in their own hometown, and even though you can never wipe out your own accent or ignore theirs, with the result that, when you are finally ready to restate what you think they are saying, you know you still might be led astray.

What can one hope to get out of such a process of inquiry? Minimally one should be able to map with great intricacy some small islands of social life. After reading these studies, one should end up with substantial confidence that this is how laughter works in the fun house, how drivers get angry on the road, how parents come to cry at children's first music recitals, how eight-year-olds handle the shame of striking out, etc. At a middle-range level, one will have leads on what to look for wherever one tries to map out the workings of the four emotions treated in these studies. And if one accepts that emotions are inherently labyrinthine, this volume most generally offers up a series of theoretical threads that should be helpful for exploring any foreign emotional place without ever denying its exotic character.

If one expects inevitably to be wandering repeatedly in the dark, worrying how to distinguish good leads from false but also willing to take pleasure in unexpected sights found on the way, what one wants is not a map to a fixed location but a few principles of inquiry that, if resolutely pursued, should reliably lead to daylight. At the very least, the ethnographic research strategy of throwing oneself into some field of blooming, buzzing confusion, then scrambling for points of orientation and efficient routes around, should avoid the worst of all travelers' nightmares, that of having taken a long and costly trip only to find out in the end that one has never really left home.

ONE

PISSED OFF IN L.A.

Behind a Los Angeles preschool, a three-year-old boy is using his feet to propel a bottomless plastic car around a crowded playground. As he maneuvers he shouts, "move, fucking asshole" and "go away, fucking asshole." Occasionally he turns his car sharply to a child who had not been interacting with him and yells, "I don't know, fucking asshole." Soon a scatological epidemic has entered the classrooms and is raging throughout the school. The parents of the original cursing child are called to the director's office and they appear sincerely surprised, insisting that "he could not have picked up the phrase in our house." Just before addressing a remedial talk to the child, the director thinks to ask the child if he knows what the phrase means. "Yes," he says brightly, "bad driver."

Becoming "pissed off" when driving may be an unfortunately inescapable fact of public life in many places, but in Los Angeles it is a naturally occurring cornucopia for social psychology. Because this form of anger is known in memorably dramatic instances by virtually everyone who drives in L.A., because it is a brief and infinitely recurring experience, and because angry responses to other motorists are typically felt to be so deeply justified that they can be recounted readily to strangers without concern for loss of face, the experience of becoming "pissed off" while driving provides extraordinarily useful data for exploring fundamental issues about the nature and contingencies of anger as it emerges and declines in social interaction. The near universality of the experience means that we can examine its workings across a wide range of ethnic, gender, socioeconomic, age, and personality divides, in a diverse set of driving circumstances, and at very different moments in drivers' quotidian routines and life histories.

My materials come primarily from about 150 detailed reports in which people, mostly thirty years of age or older, were asked by an equal number of college student interviewers to recount one or more experiences of becoming pissed off while driving around Los Angeles.

When emotions are studied in their naturally occurring contexts, it is useful to kick off the search for relevant ideas by highlighting what initially seem to be absurdities in the phenomena. The search for explanation can then be guided by patterns that, in the light of existing knowledge and upon self-reflection by the people studied, remain as haunting enigmas.

What, for example, is going on when solo drivers gesticulate emphatically and curse vociferously in cars with windows that are completely closed up? It is not as if they believe that their expressions are so powerful that they will pass through the glass, cut through the traffic noise, and penetrate the awareness of an offender who may have provoked their indignation.

> Mike, a thirty-one-year-old paralegal, recalls that he "usually yells at the other drivers from inside his car. At this point he laughed to himself and remarked that he knows that they can't hear him."

While the appearance of this madness may be striking, it is equally intriguing that, despite its absurdity, the practice seems to work to resolve emotional tension.

> Lori, who is originally from Georgia but has lived in L.A. for many years, prefers public transportation but must drive here routinely. When "a big new brown truck . . . decided to cut her off, Lori turns to the truck, 'What do you think you are doing? You know better than that!' She talks to herself and uses hand motions. She looks toward the driver in a sideways glance and then talks facing straight ahead. . . .' She does not want to lose her life over a driving dispute.' " But after she goes through scolding motions "she [can] drop it."

Also intriguing are incidents in which the participants make extraordinary commitments to secure what can only be articulated as the most minor aspects of personal advantage. One example is a battle between two mothers who compete for priority at a McDonald's restaurant while driving station wagons that are packed with kids. The drivers repeatedly tap bumpers and the battle ends only when the police arrive in response to a call from the "losing" mother, who managed to call 911 on her car phone while struggling for advantage in the queue. In another example, a fellow "came to his senses" after racing to "return the favor" to a driver who had cut him off, when he found his car straddling a cement lane divider.

To characterize such scenes as absurd is to take an outsider's perspective, and that would violate a primary rule for developing empirically grounded explanations. But what do we do about the fact that such a characterization is often made by the participants themselves a few moments beyond the heat of the struggle? Thus:

> Mrs. Minh, a Vietnamese immigrant who came to Los Angeles after living in Nebraska, is astonished at the rudeness of drivers in L.A. She is even more astonished, and deeply embarrassed as well, when, after a fellow cuts her off and she shakes her head at his rudeness, he gives her "the finger" and she finds herself saying "shit" in front of her children.

> Jan, who lives with her husband and two children in Orange County and works as an athletic coach at a major university, is late to a practice as she drives her red Corvette convertible with a stick shift along a curvy road in Palos Verdes. At a stop sign, a fellow in front of her who is slow to depart irritates her. As she drives behind him, she finds that he slows up. She waits for an opportunity to pass and as they approach a long curve she downshifts forcefully to second, accelerates, and pulls out into the lane of oncoming traffic, only to find that he speeds up, preventing her from passing until they have driven in parallel around a long curve. A few moments later, she stops her car, "dead in the road," forcing him to stop behind her. She walks briskly to his car, puts her head through his window and yells, " 'You ASSHOLE! You could have killed me!!!' " He responds with " 'Shut up, you stupid CUNT!' " Jan immediately "smacked him across the face." After speeding off, she "could not believe she hit the guy." " 'That guy could have chased me and pulled a gun on me and shot me.' "

Even when the theme of personal danger does not apply, there is something enigmatic in the effort of pissed-off drivers to "teach a lesson" to the offending other, for instance by tailgating a tailgater. Self-interest cannot make such responsive actions sensible; even if the lesson is well learned, the teacher is unlikely personally to reap the benefit of the student's progress. If the motivation is explicated as altruistic it is no less mysterious. Moving into the role of the teacher, the angry driver defines other drivers as students against their will. Perhaps there is a wisdom here that angry drivers share with university teachers who know that a class can be taught perfectly well even though no student learns anything of lasting value from it. But an aura of mystery trails after this wisdom.

That there is something tricky to explain about becoming pissed off on the road is indicated also by its frequently sudden dissipation. A driver who, in being cut off, had just rushed to the brink of madness, often will be pulled back by nothing more than a retrospective nod of acknowledgment. What requires explanation is a mysterious metamorphosis. Powerful forces develop against the drivers' wills, "taking" them against their better judgment. Just as suddenly, the disturbing forces may vanish.

A final paradox that helps orient the search for explanation is the routine production of a sense of incredulity. Accounts of experiences of anger while driving are full of such phrases as "I can't *believe* that asshole!" and "Would you look at that jerk? How can people *do* that?" What is astonishing is that these phrases pop incessantly into the same driving heads day after day. For many, no amount of experience with road "assholes" is sufficient to overcome this learning disability. It may be commendable that so many drivers avoid a hard-headed cynicism; a posture of incredulity, after all, professes faith in the possibility of collective improvement. But given that nothing has been done to reform the driving public since one confronted the last unpleasant incident, why be amazed when one confronts yet another asshole?

In addition to noting seemingly contradictory and absurd patterns in the phenomena, another strategy for orienting inquiry is to consider the inadequacies of prevailing explanations. One explanation that is very commonly invoked is that something awful happened to the angry driver before and independent of starting the drive in question, perhaps a fight with a spouse or child; maybe a conflict with clients, colleagues, superiors, or everyone at work; perhaps just the recognition at some time before getting on the road of a "bad hair day." This explanation fits some of the originating contexts of motorists' anger, but certainly not all. Thus the current sample of some 150 reports describes anger arising while:

- a psychoanalyst, who is returning to her Laguna Hills home, is enjoying nostalgic recollections of her son's recent bar mitzvah;
- a young man, driving home from his girlfriend's house, is enjoying a sustained reverie after "having finished sex";
- many drivers, listening to music on radio, tape, or CD, sing accompaniments in gay, earnest, or seductive voices.

Another very common explanation is that becoming pissed off while driving arises in reaction to fear. Again the facts sometimes but not always fit this hypothesis. People often become pissed off when there is little if any danger to them. At times their cars are not moving at all, as when another driver slips into a space while one is waiting to park. Often the response of the pissed-off driver creates far more danger than the precipitating event. And in any case it is not clear why anger should be a natural, sensible, or likely upshot of fear. If one looks closely at accounts that cite fear, the irritating elements are not necessarily connected closely to the fearful aspects. Thus Dana, a woman of thirty-four who was returning to Westwood from an overnight party in Fountain Valley, cited fear and the need to slam on her brakes as the provocation for her angry response to a driver who cut her off on the 405, but she also noted that what "great[ly] upset her was that the driver of the Infiniti drove off as if nothing had ever happened." Not simply fear but the other's driving off, in and to "infinity," left her stuck in anger.

Drivers often use a version of frustration-aggression theory to explain their anger. The accounts of pissed-off drivers may be divided into two numerically unequal but morally balanced moieties, those who emphasize prudence and a pragmatic attitude (a favorite expression of their philosophy: "driving is only a way of getting from point A to point B") and those who celebrate their tactics for cutting through and around obstacles. The frustration-aggression hypothesis roughly fits many of the former accounts but it does not handle well the following shark, a not uncommon type who appears to be delightedly aggressive in searching for driving challenges.

> Marc, who sells plastics and chemicals to petroleum and chemical companies over a sales territory stretching from his home in Orange County up to Santa Barbara, speaks of his driving anger almost as a kind of therapy. . . . He is self-conscious about his construction of his anger: " 'I'm always in a rush even if I don't have to be.' " Marc "repeatedly said 'I don't know why I get so mad. I just do,' at the same time clenching his fists and his teeth followed by a squeal of laughter."

Brad, a thirty-one-year-old loan officer, intended no humor when he confessed that "running lights and speeding are probably the only two major rules that he breaks." With such driving habits, it is likely that aggression will often produce frustration, rather than the other way around. Lena, a hotel manager, was driving while she was being interviewed. At one point in the ride,

> a driver began to run a stop sign in front of us. Lena did not have a stop sign and decided that since she had the right of way, she did not have to stop or even slow down. "It's his problem," was all she had to say. . . . The other driver slammed on his brakes and swerved to the right to avoid hitting us as we went around. Lena said, "What an idiot"

and "Hah! I bet he thought I would stop!" And Lena even honked for a lengthy period of time. The other driver looked completely shocked and clueless as well as amazed at what had just transpired.

In addition to psychological theories of frustration and fear, drivers invoke sociological explanations, pointing to various background factors in standard demographic as well as in culturally distinctive forms. "Machismo" or "testosterone" is blamed, but so also are "women drivers." Bad driving is sometimes attributed to the diminished capacities of the elderly, but carefree youth are also damned. Racial and ethnic identities are blamed, but at one time or another virtually all variations of such identities are cited. As we will see, *some* form of pejorative generalization is inherent in the causal process of becoming pissed off while driving; but that is quite a different matter from taking such background factors at face value as determining forces.

Finally, it is possible that a few aberrant drivers cause all the problematic situations, that the 150 or so subjects in this sample are indeed the impeccable drivers they claim to be, and that they have all had the extraordinarily coincidental bad luck of running across a small core of incorrigibly incompetent motorists. Fortunately the data before us include observational accounts by researchers who conducted their interviews while sitting next to drivers like Lena.

We are left with something of a mystery, not only about how and why people so often get so angry while driving, but also about the kind of causal understanding that could explain these emotional phenomena. It seems that pre-anger background factors, such as frustration at work or gendered driving styles, do not lodge causal forces in the driver, where they wait ready to spring out when the provocation is right. It seems also that no particular configurations of the driving situation create fear, frustration, or other dynamics that always shape the process of becoming pissed off. If we can't look *inside* the actor for reliable explanatory factors, and if we can't look *outside* the actor to identify objective features of the driver's environment that would consistently provoke anger, where *can* we look? We can look closely at the phenomena themselves, and in ways that do not require that we divide "inside" from "outside," "subjective" from "objective" factors, psychology from sociology.

Three lines of inquiry will prove fruitful in this chapter, and they will reappear each time an emotion is examined in this book. First, we will look at the distinctive features of the social interaction of driving, by which I mean the special problems that drivers have in managing their identities as they are perceived by other drivers. Second, we can examine the embodied qualities of the experience of anger, which requires that we take seriously the idea of metamorphosis, a sensual transformation in which the body of the person becomes a new vehicle for experience. Third, we must understand how becoming "pissed off" is not simply a "release of tension" or some other negatively defined phenomenon but is a positive effort to construct a new meaning for the situation. In the next three sections, I argue that a distinctive process of interactive interpretation, a specific experience of metamorphosis, and a focused narrative project are the individually necessary and jointly sufficient conditions for becoming pissed off when driving.

A final section of this chapter asks how drivers' anger may be different in L.A. Almost every reader, having already recollected similar events in other places, will be prepared to contest a claim that drivers get more angry, more often get angry, or get angry in some unique way in Los Angeles. Nevertheless, I will suggest that these phenomena deserve special attention in understanding social life in Los Angeles.

1. Driving as Dumb Behavior: The Emotional Provocations of Asymmetrical Interaction

With the exception of some narrow lanes that run through woods, small towns, and countryside, the space that is covered by public roads usually is defined as heading in one of two diametrically opposed directions. The signaling of the direction of travel may be achieved by lines painted on the ground, by arrows displayed on signage at on-ramps, by greenery that divides the land on which pavement is laid, by vacant space that separates pavement held up or hung in the air, or by physical barriers that impede passage from one to the other side of a road. In each case road culture requires drivers to sort themselves into two sets, one they travel "with," the other they travel "against." Once sorted out, drivers relate very peacefully to each other across these opposed moieties. It is a technico-sociological marvel of our civilization that people routinely whiz by each other in massive numbers and at fantastic rates of speed, only very rarely suffering accidents or even insults from those whose lives are headed in precisely opposite directions. Anger at other drivers is very systematically limited to only certain patterns of spatial interrelationship.

If accidents occur most often at intersections, the routine aggravations in driving occur within directional worlds that are more perfectly segregated. On the highway, and on local streets outside of intersections, what is happening among vehicles traveling in the opposite direction usually need not be of immediate concern. Drivers comfortably limit their horizons of perception to lanes traveling in the same rather than the opposite direction. The result is that drivers are most commonly gazing at the rear ends of others' vehicles, a perspective that is not incidentally related to the fact that the most common invective that emerges spontaneously in moments of anger, on L.A. roads at least, is "asshole."

The motorists' pattern of face-to-tail interaction makes for a major distinction with pedestrian passings, which are rich in face-to-face interactions. Exceptional moments of borderline embarrassment, in which people halt and hop around each other, indicate that as a rule, pedestrian passings are negotiated unproblematically. Pedestrians have relatively less reason or opportunity to perceive each other's rear ends, even though, as tortuous tactics indicate, they may have substantial motivations to observe along those lines.[1] In contrast, drivers have relatively little reason or opportunity to gaze for long at the "faces" of oncoming cars. Even when they look into rearview mirrors to perceive the faces in cars traveling "with" but behind them, drivers readily focus on whether and how much pressure is being placed on their own "tails."

This roughly inverse structure of pedestrian and driving interaction creates roughly inverse forms of personal incompetence. Just because other pedestrians can so readily monitor one's visual perception, one walks in public more or less in the manner of a horse fitted with blinders. In pedestrian passings, the line between a glance and a gaze is morally significant; aware of the social accountability of their vision, pedestrians routinely encumber it.[2] In contrast, drivers are relatively free to look wherever and however they practically can just because their vision is itself relatively invisible to other drivers.

When a person moves from being a pedestrian to being a driver, he or she trades in one dialectical complex of interaction competencies and incompetencies for another. For the same reason that the vision of drivers is relatively unencumbered, the driver's ability to speak and, more generally, to express his or her understanding and intentions to other drivers is severely impaired. The figurative uses of dumbness as a common line of insult among drivers ("idiot," "jerk," "*pendejo*") is an upshot of the exceptional and more literal inarticulateness of motorists in social interaction. In effect, drivers project onto each other, in accusations of idiosyncratic personal incompetence, the systematic incapacity that driving, as a method of going about in public, constructs for all. If the pedestrian is, relative to the driver, made blind, the driver relative to the pedestrian is rendered dumb.[3]

That the social interaction of driving makes drivers dumb is not a matter of an outsider's moral judgment[4] but something that motorists themselves take into account in the elaborate and inventive strategies with which they seek to compensate for the insult that the automobile imposes on their expressive capacities. Through personal inventiveness, the mute character of the automobile is confronted and partially transcended. One driver interviewed for this study keeps a stack of cardboard signs next to her so that she can flash messages of reprimand ("You cut me off, you &*@#%!") and of appreciation ("xxxGod bless!xxx").

For some, the effort to overcome the relatively inexpressive nature of cars begins with a restructuring of the vehicle. Jill, an executive assistant to the vice-president of a construction firm, recalls vividly the original horn in her prior car, a Toyota: "Wimpy. I mean, 'peep, peep.' You couldn't even hear it." Jill's husband delighted her by putting an "air horn" in her Toyota. Now she drives a Mercedes, which "has a *greaat* horn." At a more extravagant level, people may buy a Jeep-like vehicle that will never be driven off of smoothly paved streets but that in any case gives its driver a currently fashionable way of looming large in the sights of others. Drivers of such vehicles, praising the sense of "control" they obtain, often self-consciously enjoy their exceptional resources to project themselves into others' experience.

The aggravating dumbness of driving is exacerbated by the asymmetry of communicative interaction among drivers. Whether stuck in traffic or watching cars freely speed by, each driver has reason to sense that his or her own vivid awareness of other cars is not reciprocated. Shouting at other drivers with one's windows rolled up is a common phenomenon, but not because angry drivers fear violent responses from the object of their aggression. The pattern is common in Sweden as well as in the United States. More fundamentally, people shout in closed cars because the practice re-presents the animating problem, which is the challenge of being effectively appreciated by other drivers about whom one has become all too aware.

Drivers struggle to make communicative interaction more symmetrical. Horns are often insufficient, whether because their use is restricted by local ordinance, because the direction of their intentions can get clouded in a din of collective overuse, or because the target is so well insulated in his or her car and "sound system" that often the sole predictable effect of blowing one's horn is that it will pollute one's own audible environment. An alternative is to adapt the car's lighting system for expressive purposes, as by flashing high beams, but although the appropriate stick may be readily at hand, the driver often will have reason to believe that the message of the flash will not be "read" accurately unless he or she highlights the lighting by projecting it from a specific background, for example by tailgating the target.

Like the use of high beams to send signals, hand gestures also acknowledge the inadequacy of sound as a channel of effective expression. It is common to see a driver attempt to deliver a commentary by first maneuvering around other cars in order to get parallel to an offending driver, and then to launch into some idiosyncratic sign language. For example Carolina, a twenty-four-year-old college student, reports that if another driver has offended her and does not appear to be too intimidating, she will drive alongside and "give a dirty look and wave my hands all over the place with 'what the hell are you doing?' gestures." And Marc, a thirty-one-year-old salesman, employs the device of "shaking his hand in the air when driving by a driver which has made him mad to simulate the motion of masturbation." Marc and his female university student interviewer laughed heartily at this display, which they took as a message to "go fuck yourself."[5]

When used as a means of expression among motorists, headlights tend to be used in a relatively gentle manner. Drivers direct bright headlights at a car ahead in their own side of the road or to an oncoming car on the other side of the road in order to say "Move aside" or "Drop your beams." But when *brake lights* are used to send planned messages, they usually become instruments of perverse intention. Usually employed as devices that unwittingly signal a car is slowing down, brake lights can be strategic devices for, in effect, putting one's rear in another's face. By getting in front of an offending driver and then hitting the brakes unnecessarily, an offended driver literally and figuratively gets back at a driver who blocked an effort to pass. This is a common way of registering a complaint along the lines: you didn't pay attention to me before, but now you certainly will! Used in this manner, brake lights reflect backward in temporal as well as spatial senses, calling attention to an offense that has already been suffered.

At times frantically, offended drivers search the environment in order to find a way of forcing another driver to acknowledge their existence. One small window of opportunity is afforded by the necessity, felt by most if not all drivers, to glance periodically at their rearview mirrors. Tara, a forty-year-old woman, recalled an incident from some years before when she had to brake with all her strength to avoid hitting a car that had suddenly cut her off. When she caught the miscreant glancing at his rearview mirror, she glared at him in order to express her indignation:

My eyebrows came down and how I wish I could blink him into a tiny little frog, small and ugly. Yeah, I was really frustrated. Then I made sure I pronounced each cursed, angry word clearly so the guy could read them through the rearview mirror.

I have reviewed a few ways that drivers, when becoming angry on the road, acknowledge the expressive limitations of their vehicles in the actions they take to overcome them. It remains to demonstrate, however, that the relationship between pissed-off driving and the dumbing asymmetry of communication among motorists is causally significant. Is an awareness of this interaction dilemma a necessary condition for the experience of anger? In fact drivers precisely and elaborately appreciate the causal relevance to their anger of asymmetry in their communicative interactions with other drivers. What drivers get mad about is their own dumbness, experienced as a sensed inability to get other drivers to take them into account. An emphatic instance was provided by Philip, a twenty-five-year-old rock band musician. He reported that when he is behind someone who is driving slowly and who does not pull over so that he can pass, he will at times "get in front of the person and slow down, to say 'you fucking see me now, bitch!' "

Los Angelenos often disparage other drivers as "unconscious" even though those others are obviously sufficiently conscious to avoid driving off the road. The narcissistic demand in this labeling of others is left implicit; what is essentially disturbing is that the other driver appears to be deaf to one's own concerns. For the angry driver, the disturbance provoked by the apparently impenetrable insulation of other drivers sometimes takes on existential dimensions. Jim, a forty-three-year-old realtor who was suffering from a heart condition and a weak real estate market, had just lost a deal because a home buyer had failed to qualify for a loan. A Mercedes approached from his rear and irritated him by speedily changing lanes to pass other cars and then cutting in front of him. Jim remarks: "I get really mad when other drivers weave in and out and cut you off. They think they own the road and that you don't exist."

"Idiot," "unconscious," and similar insults overtly label others as incompetent, but they are the upshot of an energetic sensitivity to one's own incompetence. For all practical purposes, the other's deafness makes oneself dumb. Indeed, there is an irony here that is experienced as a bitter truth. The better you are as a driver, in the sense of being dutifully attentive to the movements of other cars, the more you are aware how circumscribed are the attentions of others. Your courtly efforts to accommodate the less competent run up against their failure to see, much less appreciate, what you are trying to do. Conscientiously monitoring others' awareness, superior drivers come to appreciate how, on the road, ignorance is power. Their appreciation of the incompetence of other drivers is at once evidence of their own superior driving competence and an explanation of the frustrating futility of their superiority.

I am arguing that a perception of asymmetrical awareness is a condition of becoming pissed off while driving. Acting as folk sociologists, drivers tacitly analyze the structure of their interaction with other drivers as part of the process of becoming angry with them. When undertaking this quick and dirty social research, drivers cannot easily ask other drivers about their orientations on the road. Instead they commonly use what sociologists call "unobtrusive measures" to infer subjective realities, in particular to characterize others as self-absorbed. Currently, two such measures are car phones and "Diet Coke." Philip, the young rock musician quoted above, bemoans drivers who are

> oblivious when they're in their car. They're always looking for a tape or doing something else rather than driving . . . [holding] their can of Diet Coke, they are in their own little world.

Other respondents referred disgustedly to drivers who continue past exits with their turn signals flashing on and on.

Some drivers create a characteristic emotional tone by employing a more advanced folk-sociological analysis of interaction asymmetry on the road. Just as sunglasses can be used to build a cool, "tough" image, so the windows of a car can be outfitted to put virtually the whole vehicle in "shades." The result in both cases is to create an aura of mystery rooted in a practical problem for interpretation: the reading of whether and where attentions may be directed becomes a unique problem for the person not sporting shades. Not uncommonly, a party in shades will be perceived as relatively indifferent to others, perhaps even disposed to at least small cruelties.

Because the person in shades does not as readily give off indications of his or her disposition but is presumably unimpaired in detecting the direction of others' gazes, an emotionally provocative potential for an asymmetrical uncertainty is built into street transactions. This became a serious problem for Rudi, a minister's son from Woodland Hills, as he traveled home one midnight on the Hollywood Freeway. After angrily cutting off a car that had cut him off, Rudi found himself surrounded by two cars working together to box in, chase, and fire gunshots at his car. Until almost too late, the tinted windows of the two cars impaired his ability to appreciate that the attentions of both were directed at him, and that their attentions to him were being organized through their attentions to each other.

Notably, the emotional course of this interaction ran close in relationship to its interpretive dynamics. At first believing that another driver was not considering his existence, Rudi was angry about being cut off. Then Rudi became fearful as he realized that he was confronting just the opposite problem, excessive attention to his existence. Drivers in Los Angeles today frequently struggle with defining the line between an oblivious and an overly concerned other, a line that runs on the slippery slope between anger and fear.

The close relationship of interaction asymmetry and anger in driving is revealed in particularly instructive ways when we follow out the emotional ramifications in those instances where the interpretive relationship reverses. It is not uncommon, for example, that a driver who has been angrily honking at a slowly moving, unresponsive car ahead, realizes that the target of his anger has not been ignoring him but has been frustrated by another obstacle further on. Denise, a computer analyst who works in Century City, had been honking at a Land Cruiser, urging the driver to speed up so that she could make a light, when she realized that there was a car in front of him. At this point "she silently fell back into her seat, rolled up the window, wished she could disappear, and mentally cursed herself for being so stupid." What had been humiliation became transformed into shame as Denise realized that she had not in fact been "dumb" in the sense of being unable to get the other driver to take her perspective, but "stupid" in being blind to what the other driver could see.

Embarrassment is the common upshot when one realizes that there is an interpretive asymmetry in the current interaction but that the failure to take the other's perspective is one's own fault alone. Brad, the owner of an export-import business, recalled his growing anger as he was being tailgated on his way to a choir performance:

> I could see the headlights glaring in my mirror, so I motioned him to pass by me but he doesn't. . . . Every single turn I make he's following. I start to think, "Where does this guy live? I mean why does this guy keep following me? Can't he see I'm lost?" . . . I told my wife, "Why does this stupid ass keep tailgating me?" . . . Later the guy who drove the car comes up to me and thanks me for leading him to the presentation. I was kind of embarrassed, so I just said, "No problem."

In effect, the limited expressive possibility in drivers' social interaction creates an infinite series of ambiguous moments. As a social practice, driving is a kind of endless Rorschach test in which, unless the driver finds interpretive dilemmas fascinating as a subject for study, he or she must impute a taken-for-granted descriptive sense of other drivers' social awareness. It is only by appreciating how driving is a "dumb" way of moving through public space that we can appreciate why the emotional results of motorists' interaction are so routinely appalling.

2. Getting Cut Off: The Metamorphosis of the Angered Body

Within some traditions in sociology, the sole focus of analysis would be on the *interactions* through which anger arises in driving. But getting pissed off while driving is also very much a matter of feeling. Accordingly we must now appreciate a part of social action that is consistently missed by social science: the *sensual* and *aesthetic* dimensions of the experience.

Note first that passengers typically do not have the same emotional experience as drivers. Sitting next to the driver, a passenger may observe the same rudeness, feel frustrated by the same traffic, be startled by the same aggressive conduct on the part of other drivers, but watch with amusement or fear as the driver of his or her own car gets mad. Sprinkled through the interviews in our data set are recollections by interviewer-observers of occasions in which they struggled to calm down their research subjects as the latter responded with frightful ferocity to the "idiots" and "assholes" of the road.

> Barry, a fifty-four-year-old attorney practicing in Orange County, is cruising down Rosecrans Avenue at fifty-five mph in his black Lexus, listening to soft music, with his wife and two others in the car. As he slows to merge into the left-turn lane, he spots a car behind him, "a white Integra with five Asians," that is crossing over the double yellow line in an attempt to enter the left-turn lane before Barry gets there. Angry that "this little shit wouldn't let me in," Barry maneuvers toward the left lane as if he is intent on hitting the other car. The Integra screeches to a stop, and as its driver bolts from his car, Barry stops and rushes out to "confront the confrontation." The passengers are "stunned and startled," not by the Integra but by Barry's rage.

Drivers themselves often realize the contrast between their rage and a passenger's fear. There is a significant clue to the causal contingencies of anger in the fact that drivers' realization of this contrast does not necessarily stem their anger. Ralph, an employee of a Beverly Hills architectural firm, is driving his girlfriend and his brother to

Las Vegas. Going seventy on a steep mountain incline, he finds a van pressing from behind with its high beams. When the road gets too narrow for the van to pass, he slows down to piss off its driver. As the van driver succeeds in passing him, he throws Ralph a finger and then cuts in close. Next Ralph uses his high beams on the van, then passes the van and again purposively slows dramatically. Ralph recalls how his girlfriend and brother urged him to calm down, to let it go.

> I didn't respond to their comments. I looked at my girlfriend to the right and noticed that she was holding on to the handle on the passenger door. I didn't care though. I didn't care if I was scaring her and my brother. I felt my face really flushed as I kept trying to catch up to the van. As I was driving, I was cussing the guy out at the top of my lungs. I said things like, "You fucking asshole! Who do you think you are? You don't own the fucking road! I'll show you who owns the fucking road!" Immediately after the incident, I looked at my girlfriend. She was shaking her head in disapproval and told me that my temper is exactly like my father's temper.

There is a crucial difference between the situation of the passenger and that of the driver. Even though both are in the same car, it is only the driver who is cut off. For the driver, being "cut off" is not only a figure of speech. In contrast to the passenger, the driver, in order to drive, must embody and be embodied by the car. The sensual vehicle of the driver's action is fundamentally different from that of the passenger's, because the driver, as part of the praxis of driving, dwells in the car, feeling the bumps on the road as contacts with his or her body not as assaults on the tires, swaying around curves as if the shifting of his or her weight will make a difference in the car's trajectory, loosening and tightening the grip on the steering wheel as a way of interacting with other cars.

Being a passenger is more a matter of being taken around, of hanging on rather than guiding the car through turns, and of orienting oneself to other cars through the driver in the next seat rather than through manipulating the body of the car. Not only are passengers unlikely to share the driver's emotions, but when passengers do get irritated they are more likely to focus on the faults of their own driver than on the drivers of other cars. Note the reference in the following classic complaint about a backseat driver to the very different physical disposition of the passenger-critic. When Ann's husband is her passenger, he often criticizes her. Her interviewer paraphrases her characterization of his attitude:

First she is going too fast, then too slow. Why doesn't she go now? Why didn't she go then? She demonstrates his position as he lies back in the passenger seat, like a lounge chair.

The structuring and the contingencies of the emotions of driver and passenger cannot be explained without taking into account the fact that, although they are only inches from each other and are in essentially the same perceptual position to witness interaction with other cars, their manners of embodying understanding and literally incorporating the scene, are radically different.[6]

Language describing the embodiment of action and the incorporation of personal identity brings us close to the philosophies of Michael Polanyi and Maurice Merleau-Ponty.[7] If we are to explain more satisfactorily the contingencies of the driver's anger we must appreciate how driving requires and occasions a metaphysical merger, an intertwining of the identities of driver and car that generates a distinctive ontology in the form of a person-thing, a humanized car or alternatively, an automobilized person.[8] If we insist on seeing only human "subjects" on one side of an ontological divide and "objective" conditions or the material circumstances for behavior on the other, we will fail to appreciate fully the difference in the perspectives of driver and passenger, and we will not be able to grasp just what is "cut off" that provokes anger while driving.

With regard to the driver's relationship with other cars, being cut off is a richly varied event. But what all such experiences have in common is a kind of amputation, a loss of a previously engaged, tacit use of the car and a loss of the transcendent body that the driver, in the process of driving, had been taking for granted as naturally available. While nothing happens to his or her physiological body—to that body as a thing described in isolation from its use in context—the driver does not doubt the sensual reality of the fact that *he or she,* i.e., his or her lived or phenomenological body, has been cut off. By attempting to describe the driver's tacit embodiment of the car, we will prepare the way to understand, in the next section, something that otherwise is very elusive: how becoming angry is a practical project in which the driver attempts to regain a taken-for-granted intertwining with the environment.

The Naturally Transcendent Body of the Driver

What is it that the driver senses so vividly and yet senses in ways so well hidden that intimate companions do not share the sensuality? What the driver senses in anger are transcendent meanings of the moment. From the passenger's side of the car, or when the driver is using discursive reason to talk with an interviewer about the event, only the specific situational meanings of the event are apparent, and they do not justify the anger. Looking narrowly at the socially situated interaction among cars, all that is at stake is:

- as a spatial matter, the necessity for the driver to move one foot a few inches from accelerator to brake;
- on a temporal dimension, the "loss" of a moment's time;
- and from a publicly visible perspective, a change in the relationship of cars, not people's lives.

But emotions are doubly resonant; through his or her emotions a person both attends to the immediate situation and orients to transcendent dimensions of the moment's experience. The feeling, the sensual reality of emotions, *is* this double resonance.

People run into, hit upon, discover or find emotional dynamics in their experience. Like things discovered or found, the significance that an emotion registers is regarded, by the person experiencing it, as already there but previously beyond the boundaries of awareness. Put colloquially, we find ourselves "taken" by emotions. In emotional experience, a person attends corporeally to temporal, spatial, and private meanings that reflect on and transcend whatever he or she is doing at the moment with others. Emotions are a paradoxical kind of turning on the embodied self, a sensual form of self-consciousness that brings into awareness, in the palpably aesthetic medium of the body, commitments that previously were tacitly engaged.

Given the familiar assertion of an opposition between reflection and emotions, it is perhaps ironic to note that, when they are emotional, people are engaged in bringing previously tacit dimensions into their awareness. *But this self-reflection does not take the form of thought.* Drivers usually do not *perceive* themselves being cut off *and then decide* to construct their anger; rather, it is in seeing themselves cut off that they first find themselves angry. What makes the self-conscious nature of emotions difficult to see is that the turn on the self is done sensually and aesthetically, through a kind of living poetry, and not in the form of discursive reason that commentaries about "reflection" have traditionally evoked.

How does becoming angry when driving bring previously tacit, transcendent dimensions of action into vivid corporeal awareness? First of all, driving is itself essentially a means of transcending space, of getting from here to there. When traffic or a "rude" driver cuts one off, the experience is of falling out of a flow and being stuck or held back. In the sense of confinement that anger brings to them, cut-off drivers sense the firmness of the boundary between the overall trajectory of their current trip and the local situation in which they interact with other cars. As cars in traffic start and stop, one responds by inching ahead, starting and stopping, in the process drawing an increasingly thick line describing the bounded nature of one's action. When traffic flows smoothly, if a rude driver cuts in close, one must fall out of the flow by hitting the brake or at least lifting off of the accelerator, in the process physically pulling oneself out of a previously tacit intertwining of body and machine.

Each driver usually will have no way of appreciating where other drivers are going and why, unless traffic stops completely and drivers exit their cars to converse with each other.[9] Each knows that he or she alone knows how the interaction "here" carries implications for the activities and relationships he or she maintains in some other setting, "there," and that what happens in the interaction with another driver "now" is meaningful with regard to situations "then," that is, with regard to what he or she has lived before and is likely to experience later on. As drivers relate the movements of their cars to each other, each has a necessarily private awareness of the transcendent meanings of his or her actions.

In some of the incidents of becoming angry, drivers are clearly frustrated in their attempts to "get there" and they imagine clear pictures of themselves as they once were or might soon be in other places. Note how anger arises as the following driver situates himself with reference to unpleasant versions of himself that he projects into the future and recalls from the recent past.

> Torrential rains in Malibu have slowed traffic to a crawl as Clarence, a tax accountant with a public accounting firm in Santa Monica, bangs his fists on the steering wheel, lights a cigarette, then repeatedly bangs his head against the side window. Aware that he is already late for work and aware that his job performance has recently come under question, Clarence observes a stream of cars moving freely on the shoulder and recalls the ticket he received a week ago for the same maneuver. Observing a police car up in the shoulder up ahead, he moves to block the attempt of a minivan to come off the shoulder into his lane: "Shaking his fists angrily at the minivan, he yelled, 'I am not going to let this fucking bitch in front of me.' "

In other experiences of drivers' becoming angry, a spatial rather than a temporal dimension of transcendence is most emphatic. For Dita, talking on a cellular phone as she drives "is a form of therapy"

in that it allows her to be in two social places at the same time, interacting with other drivers and with her phone correspondent. If another
driver acts rudely, what may be cut off is her ability to remain attentive
to her phone call. A set of observational field notes on Francine, a
forty-five-year-old travel agent and mother of two, show how she once
became angry in close relationship to her discussion with her daughter-
passenger about a dress that she, Francine, had tried on at the mall
and was considering buying. Her conversation continued as a white
car from the left put on his blinker and moved into her lane. Francine
"was not angry, she just slowed down and continued talking about
the dress." But as the white car progressively slowed down to well
below the speed limit, Francine repeatedly had to hit her brakes.

> Her anger heated up as she glanced at the speedometer and noticed that
> we were only going forty miles per hour. She stopped talking about that
> dress she was going to buy and looked over her shoulder to go around
> the white Camry.

Rude and inconsiderate drivers do not injure only in a symbolic manner, for example by showing disrespect; they strip dimensions from
one's social existence, in these cases undermining the drivers' ability
to be in two places at once.

As forms of sensuality, emotions render the body a prism, lighting
up otherwise invisible, transcendent meanings that in each interaction
always pass through the participants. Even for drivers who are not
headed toward a pressing engagement and who are focused exclusively
on the road, driving may have a series of other temporal and spatial
implications that reach beyond and lend emotional significance to particular encounters with other drivers. Driving is a prime field for the
study of what Michel de Certeau referred to as the "tactics" of contemporary everyday life.[10] Many people develop what they regard as particularly shrewd ways of moving around society.[11] These include carefully choosing streets that one knows carry little traffic, sneakily
cutting across corner gas stations to beat traffic lights, discreetly using
another car as a "screen" in order to merge onto a highway, passing
through an intersection and brazenly doubling back to avoid the queue
in a left-turn lane, and such triumphs of motoring chutzpah as following in the smooth-flowing wake of an ambulance as it cuts through
bottled-up traffic. Variations in motoring cunning are endless.

> Eddie keeps his speed between certain levels because to go too slow
> would put him in an inefficient gear and if he goes too fast "his gas
> mileage would decrease by 20 percent, due to excess wind resistance."

Bob, thirty-seven years old, a drug store employee who drives a recent-model Toyota truck, has his eight-mile round-trip between home and work all worked out. He knows the way the lights normally go, and which lanes to avoid because he could be blocked by "unprotected left turns."

For such shrewd drivers, what is at stake in any given interaction with another car is a trans-situational strategy of which other drivers on the road must be completely unaware. What can be cut off here is an overall game plan and a more or less grand conception of self.

All encounters in social life build their emotional meanings from the juxtaposition between a local situation, one to which the participants collaboratively respond as they construct its sense and boundaries in the "here and now," and the privately known destinations for which the local situation is for each but a way station. Chance meetings on the street, an episode of sexual interaction, an afternoon spent on a crew doing a roofing job, or a meeting of middle managers and lawyers to discuss security concerns at a shopping mall . . . for each participant what is collectively treated as locally transpiring will have unshared, transcendent implications in the form of sensed relevancies for other encounters in some other time and place. The emotional meanings of everyday life are naturally and necessarily hidden because selves, although they are always presented in forms that are tailored to a social time and place, are always produced by bodies, and what having a body most fundamentally means for a person is that he or she lives an ongoing continuity beyond the social situations passed through in everyday life. Bodies make us mortal in the long run, but until they do they are vehicles of situational immortality, constantly conferring the gift, unwanted or not, of signifying life beyond the deaths of the localized interactions that constitute our mundane social lives.

When a driver gets cut off, what occurs is an instantaneous and exceptionally pristine confrontation, not simply with other drivers but with the existential challenge of interminably working out the relationship between isolated social situations and a transcendent life course. Driving produces conflicts that are at once an unwanted therapeutic challenge, an undesired introduction to the social-psychological structure of everyday life, and a tiresome obligation to try to make sense of one's life.

Who needs this aggravation? Perhaps only drivers who happen to be social psychologists. Most people have other hobbies and occupational concerns. So, as is generally the case with anger, pissed-off drivers are angry that they are angry, that they must give so much importance to working out the relationship between their petty interactions with other drivers and the inescapably compelling themes of their lives.

Because cars are so naturally literal/figurative vehicles for transcendence in spatial and temporal senses, they are ready vehicles for a third dimension of transcendence. Cars as objects, and driving as an activity, are given private meanings that transcend what others—other drivers and the driver's own passengers—can observe. Thus each driver not only does not know where any other driver is going and how long it may be before he or she gets there, but each is unaware of the symbolic meaning that the others may have built into their relationships to their cars. Cars are treated like private living rooms that are driven about in public; secure in their privacy, drivers take for granted that others won't be successful Peeping Toms. Thus Ernie, a used-car salesman at Galpin Ford who lives in the Valley, does not need to change out of his pajamas when he leaves his home at 10:30 P.M. to drive a friend home. As he explains to his wife, "no one's going to see me. I don't have to impress anybody."

Usually, however, what privacy covers is not so much the driver's physical body as the folk philosophy that he or she has developed for his or her car and for driving. What makes driving so richly provocative of emotions is not simply or even primarily that situated interactions with other drivers impede one's progress to a given destination; it is that the sociophenomenological structure of driving interaction crystallizes a challenge common to all of social life. Because the meanings of driving build up from the naturally metaphoric character of the activity, they are especially subtle in their seductive power and doubly hidden, not only from other drivers but from oneself as well. If railroad trips figured prominently in Freud's dreams, narratives of driving play a richly hermeneutic role as contemporary adults dream nightmares of being eternally stalled in traffic, careening around sharp downhill curves while driving family members in a stuffy little car with faulty brakes, or being hauled around by some reckless driver in the company of utter strangers.[12]

When drivers are cut off, their anger may respond to one or both of two possible forms of embodied loss. First, the driver may have to pull out of a previously taken-for-granted corporeal involvement that is specific to the current trip. A given interaction with another driver may interrupt the phone conversation that one is sustaining with a friend, break the flow of strategic maneuvers that had been making the trip a testament to one's extraordinary urban cunning, or require that one remove a hand from lightly stroking a girlfriend's thigh in order to grip a steering wheel tightly.

Second, independent of the driver's machinations as they may be specific to any particular trip, driving a car may symbolize one's overall way of passing through society.[13] The postures and airs in the following examples demonstrate how some drivers habitually intertwine their identities and the bodies of their cars. The crucible that produces the extraordinary emotional power of the driving experience is the routine juxtaposition of immediately situated interaction with other drivers and situationally transcendent meanings of driving. This juxtaposition is a constant in episodes of road rage, even as situational dilemmas and transcendent meanings vary widely from one incident to the next.

Rick, a college student, keeps his 1994 Ford Probe gleaming. It is

> more than just a means to get from point A to point B; I take pride in keeping it looking good, it is a place I go to escape from the pressures of school and work.

Getting stuck in traffic as he is driving from Glendale to the Malibu Sea Lion to celebrate his fiancée's birthday "make it painfully clear that I am not the master of my destiny that I thought I was."

> When it became apparent that the traffic was not going to clear up and that no matter what I did, we were going to be late, I got pissed—I mean REALLY PISSED. I . . . basically just lost it in terms of self-control.

Because his car represents a shiny version of his future, traffic turns him to shameful memories of his past. Rick recalled that "my mother drilled it into me as a child that it is bad to be late; it makes you look irresponsible."

If for Rick his car is a pristine body that other drivers threaten to soil, Mark owns the car of Rick's nightmares, but its symbolic meaning is no less capable of generating enraging implications for its owner. Mark's car has 170,000 miles, its wheels are badly out of alignment, and driving it hurts his back. Far from symbolizing that at this stage of his life he is on a rapid trip to a bright future, Mark's car serves him less reliably when it is in motion than when it is functioning as his bedroom. A frequently unemployed roofer who states that he is often underbid on jobs by Mexican illegals, Mark finds that even when he works a forty-hour week he can't pay all of his bills. "My life is more fragile than it's ever been." When other cars cut him off, what they are cutting off often seems to be his last tie to respectable membership in the community. Ugly encounters with other drivers stimulate deep resentments that often take social-class directions. "Sometimes I'll fantasize about running a tailgater off the road or destroying a rich person's car."

The way that a person lives philosophical orientations to his or her car shapes his or her corporeal disposition when driving. Thus when Jill got her Mercedes, it meant "growing up" and being "an adult," which for her means driving cautiously. The "gutless" Toyota she had before was like driving "the ashtray of the Mercedes, very tinny." The heaviness of the car conveys to her an aspect of stability, which she enhances by braking far in advance of the spot at which she will come to rest and by taking corners slowly enough that the car avoids any tilt. If some "asshole" cuts in front of her, what is cut off is likely to be the faith that she is now secure and immune from the surprises and foolishness that threaten to bring uncertainty into a life.

Cars obviously can be outfitted to reflect the desired personal identities of their drivers with bumper stickers and accessories. But, what is more interesting, some drivers more discreetly *reshape themselves* to fit with the image that they expect the car to project. Brandy, "an attractive thirty-three-year-old Latina from East Los Angeles," is a middle-school teacher's aide who works with children with learning disorders and behavioral problems, work that "requires lots of patience." Interviewed by a female friend, Brandy reports that a " '95 jet-black Jeep Wrangler" is "her pride and joy." She labors elaborately to shape the car, passengers, and herself into a seamless version of self, which the interviewer characterizes as "the Jeep image of fun, adventure, wild youth, and excitement." The car has no radio, because Brandy does not want it to be broken into. On a trip to Tijuana, she parks on the California side of the border and she and her boyfriend walk across because the people there drive "like bats out of hell." The car and her body are mutually altered to create an ongoing, complementary whole. Brandy "would find something to do with herself each time we stopped at a light or slowed down in traffic," such as "smoothing down her hair and turning the mirror to inspect her face." The car elevates its driver, putting her on display, but she refrains from looking into other cars because it would be rude. She "always says that only a certain type of person can own a Jeep, like herself," and for that reason she "does not want to be seen in it with thick glasses on," even though, as the condition imposed on her driver's license indicates, she cannot see well without her glasses when she is driving at night.

On returning from a trip to Mexico one evening, the various elements that Brandy had built into her car-body identity came into conflict. When stopped by a CHP officer for speeding, she was given the choice to take a four hundred–dollar ticket, or put on her glasses, or turn the wheel over to her boyfriend-passenger. Not wanting to admit that she fails to wear glasses for the sake of appearance, she allowed him to drive, a choice that subjected her to endless humiliation as the story was told and retold in family and friendship circles.

Seductive Metaphori and Being Cut Off

Perhaps the most commonly visible indications that anger in driving emerges from an experience of being cut off from a tacit embodiment of and by one's car is the rise of tension in the driver's body. Interviews and participant observation field notes indicate changes in the rigidity and inclination of posture, in the grip on the wheel, and in the direction and intensity of the driver's visual focus. But to limit our appreciation of what is entailed in the loss of the tacit body to such surface aspects is to maintain a subject-object contrast of person and world, and this is precisely what is transcended in the natural course of driving. Driving is not a series of discrete touches on a machine and discrete sightings within a perceptual field, but an ongoing process in which one inevitably becomes sensually intertwined with mechanical tool and perceptual field.

The necessity of dwelling in objects in order to use them with an air of natural competence is not unique to driving. As Michael Polanyi noted in a memorable illustration of the point, when one writes by hand it is not possible to maintain a course of thought if one is attending to the shaping of each mark on the page; one must write strings of letters and words. Put another way, in order to write one must lose self-conscious attention to oneself by engaging in a kind of drawing (or, when typing, in a kind of keyboard playing).[14] Polanyi noted that if in moving over a glossy patch of the paper, the pen skips, the slippage is experienced *at the tip of the pen*. The writer dwells in the pen.

Similarly, in order to speak with an unbroken sense of natural coherence, one must engage unselfconsciously in a kind of singing that maintains a heard but unnoticed continuity of sound as the vehicle for enunciating individual words. Speech uttered in a way that its transcription usually appears on paper, with noticeable space between each word, much less with a clear silence between each letter, not only will sound weird, it will undermine the speaker's ability to speak to anything other than the enunciation project itself.

If there is a touch of the surreal in the image of the writer dwelling at the tip of the pen, or of speech creating the body that sustains thought, then we must acknowledge the practical necessity of the surreal. The surreal dimensions of the driving experience are not interview artifacts or analytical hyperbole but the foundations of any real driving conduct. Cartoonists who animate cars, and people who give names and recognize personality traits in their cars, are recognizing that people must in a sense "confuse" their identities with their cars in order to drive them. It is a fair question whether the person who gives a name to his or her car is sillier than someone who thinks that because cars are just lifeless, fungible tools, cartoon-animated cars are just silly conceits.

Cars are naturally seductive instruments. At the age of twenty-five, Alexander says that "his car gives him 'big balls' " and makes "his dick automatically grow three inches." When I reported this passage in class, one male student was moved to ask, with no apparent touch of irony, "What kind of car was he driving?" How drivers merge with their cars, and what is at stake for them when they are cut off, will not usually be so clear. But in ways so diverse they defy exhaustive listing, cars seduce by providing a new form that one must inhabit as if it were one's natural skin, if one is to drive with routine competence.

It is notable that in contemporary Athens, as Michel de Certeau liked to point out, public buses are *metaphori*. In L.A.'s culture, cars seduce drivers into a metamorphosis that is in many respects a literal process of transforming the practically useful vehicle of the self. Consider the perspectives of the following two retirees. They drive in contrasting styles but for both, other drivers are maddening when they compromise their treasured freedom.

Steve, fifty-eight years old, is a retired college professor. Recalling a recent experience of being cut off, he frames it against his recollections of taking public transportation when he was living in New York thirty-five years ago. A young man, apparently impatient with the rate at which Steve was exiting the freeway, shot in front and cut in to exit first. In contrast to public transportation, one's car offers the freedom of "not relying on somebody else or something else to get you where you need to go." What such events cut off is the pleasure of liberation Steve often feels when driving, a pleasure in which the car is so intimately part of the driver that it is not even, as he put it, "something else" that one relies on "to get you where you need to go." Unfortunately it sometimes turns out that driving means that what you do have to rely on are the narcissistic dispositions of other drivers.

Paco, who lived most of his life in the relatively tiny agricultural town of Salinas, is now seventy and a recent resident of L.A. When other drivers anger him,

> Los maltrato [I curse at them]. . . . If a young man cuts me off I yell at him, "Orale vato! Que no ves!" ["Hey punk! Can't you see!"]. . . . I might call someone "menzo" or "menza" [brainless]. . . . But the old folks are the worst. . . . I just say, look at this "viejito," he's too old to be driving.

Paco frames the displeasure of driving in L.A. against his small-city background. "Where I used to live people drove slower and there wasn't such a rush. . . . Here people drive too fast." In effect Paco insists on treating L.A. as if it were Salinas. He avoids the freeways, and as noted by the participant interviewer, Paco drives local streets at five miles below the speed limit. His interviewer paraphrases Paco's comments: "I feel too congested and as a result I may go slower just to go slower."

In these two cases, what is seductive about cars is their moment-by-moment evocation of a perspective that gives integrated meaning to huge stretches of personal biography. Steve and Paco indicate that at times they drive around in life metaphors that they defend against people who are rudely insensitive to what is at stake.

For other drivers, cars offer metamorphoses to states of moral perfection that they find difficult to manage elsewhere in their lives. Reina, a longtime L.A. resident who grew up in Guadalajara, now does morning volunteer work at the gift shop of a local hospital before going to work. For her the car offers a relatively restful passage between social situations that are routinely troublesome to get out of and into. One Wednesday morning, Reina got into her car in a flurry of small attentions, bouncing back to the house to pick up letters that had to be mailed that day, grabbing an Evian water bottle from the box that sits in the garage beside her car, figuring that although the tank was low she should have enough gas, and finally heading off on her twelve-mile trip to Pasadena. The concerns that flared up on entering the car were put into the background as the driving trip imposed its own integrity, up until she arrived at the hospital and found an "imbecile" moving to exit the parking lot in her lane, a lane marked for ingress. It may or may not be relevant to the shaping of Reina's emotions that the car serves as a vehicle for her altruistic work as a hospital volunteer. But even if her car does not promise to give moral purpose to her life on any grand scale, it does promise a kind of temporary perfection of orderliness for a short stretch of everyday life. Apart from the risk that the Evian bottle will spill as it rolls freely in the passenger well, the threats to coherence are displaced outside of the vehicle of her action and for a while she has a smooth and unambiguously focused drive.

The marketing of cars has long offered the potential of publicly displaying oneself to others in an enviable form[15] but also the promise of a private daily metamorphosis affording hands-on, real-world, sensual verification that one fits naturally into a peaceful, immortal, or transcendent form. Cars are increasingly designed in elaboration of this message. The button that will automatically lower the window happens to be just where the driver's hand naturally falls. His key is a bit different than hers, and when he begins to work it into the ignition, the driver's chair "knows" to adjust itself to a position that is tailored to his dimensions and sense of comfort. Cars have replaced watches (self-winding! shockproof! waterproof!) as the microengineered personal possession that, like a miniature world's fair exhibit, displays the latest technological achievements to the masses. Also like watches, cars can be readily consulted as a reassuring touchstone for the assessment of messier segments of one's life.[16]

That emotions flow most directly from an initially sensual being in the social world and not from personality traits appears in relief in Morgan's experience. For him the metaphoric dimensions of vehicles have an exceptionally high profile. Morgan drives a fourteen-wheeler to deliver beer in Culver City and Santa Monica. In his truck, cars

> look puny; kinda like ants, in a funny sort of way. Whenever I'm driving, I don't worry about how reckless I drive because I know that I won't get hurt. My truck is way too strong to sustain any damage. I've run into a few telephone poles, a fire hydrant or two, and even the side of a building. Other than a dent or two, nothing happened to my truck, Not only that, but the company takes care of it all. . . . So, yeah, I do feel a little more powerful than everyone else on the road.

The form of the vehicle gives rise to a fitting personality. When Morgan drives his BMW, "I'm not as invincible then, and I try to drive a little more carefully, since I know we really can't afford another car if I smash this one up."

Does a truck bring out a different style of driving than does a BMW? It will not do to substitute mysticism about the nature of different vehicles for mysticism about values and character. If the driver's emotions do not spring from his or her personality, neither does the form he or she embodies for action determine them. Both views are inadequate because both are static. When driving, a person takes a vehicular form to interact with others, and his or her emotions are the upshot of this corporeal process.

Max is a six-foot-six-inch, 250-pound resident of "mellow" Rancho Cucamonga who works out of a truck yard in Ontario. As he drives his diesel in Beverly Hills to pick up hazardous waste at the Hilton his truck becomes a monstrosity that threatens him more than other drivers. When he had to make a U-turn on Wilshire because he had gone too far, the other drivers wouldn't give him the space; they would speed up and cut him off.

> He said that it got so bad and was taking such a long time that . . . he started yelling and honking not only at the drivers around him, but also at some of the pedestrians who would not wait to let him complete his U-turn, before crossing the street.

The truckers, Max and Morgan, make it relatively easy to see something that is usually obscured, that the driver's emotions follow from sensing how his or her vehicle-form fits into the social environment. At one moment a truck-body makes the driver immune from concerns about fitting into community. At another it makes him emotionally vulnerable by isolating him from the surrounding community.

Drivers monitor the interaction contours of the vehicular form that they inhabit, managing their thing-selves from within and without. What the angry driver seeks to defend, when he or she is cut off, is not the trajectory of the car, but the intertwining of the body and the car. Anger's energy is in the first instance an effort to hold onto an inhabited form. When one is cut off, the offense lies precisely in the understanding that other drivers would treat one's car as an impersonal thing, without honoring the fact, of which the driver is intimately aware, that what is cut off is the driver. Drivers don't imagine that the "idiots" who piss them off are insulting them as individuals; that's one of the reasons they are idiots. The problem is that they *don't* "make it personal." The offense as commonly stated is that the other is acting "as if I'm not even there." The outraged driver addresses him- or herself with the impersonal perspective that the offending driver has manifested, and from that vantage point slips effortlessly into the indifferent and disrespectful perspectives of others encountered earlier in the day.

It is not possible to come up with a formula specifying the distance, speed, and timing of lane changes that will predict being cut off. The problem is not that there are too many factors to put into the formula but that the driver's body is not located where one might suspect it to be, either in the driver's seat, at the vehicle's metal skin, or indeed at any stable location. The driver operates from a moving point in a terrain for interaction, and that terrain is defined in part by the driver's current style of driving.

An enraging experience of being thrown out of one's car-body by others' insensitivities can occur even before the car starts moving. Parents of adolescent drivers are familiar with the assault that occurs when they turn the key in the ignition and find the seat position straining their backs, their feet stumbling on empty drink containers, music blasting in their ears, and the fuel gauge pointing to empty. It is relatively easy to see how anger arises in such circumstances from sensual beginnings, but the same sort of analysis is necessary to understand how drivers become angry when relating to each other through the interacting trajectories of their cars.

There is a common dimension in experiences of being cut off, whether the assault is on a moving or a stationary body. It is a matter of being reduced to a raw state of being. This is a kind of fall, an awakening to a self-conscious awareness of nakedness. The car-body, as a form of active social clothing, is stripped away and one is left exposed, vulnerable, without any persona with which one can relate respectably to others. Along with the sacrifice of these cartoonlike dimensions of ordinarily competent action, what ordinarily passes for civility and mundane rationality instantly, if only momentarily, disappears as well.

3. Flipping Off and Other Narrative Practices of Anger: On Righteous Indignation, Prejudicial Stereotyping, and the Socioemotional Logic of Revenge Scenarios

Mehdi, driving his black Porsche to represent his father's luxury car dealership at a car auction, did not get pissed when he was cut off by "an incredibly bright 911" Porsche driven by "one of the hottest females" he had ever seen. Instead he took the surprise encounter as an opportunity for a flirtatious "cat and mouse" game and for fantasizing about what winning might mean.

In order that anger may develop when one is cut off by others who seem to be indifferent to one's existence, some further work of sense making is necessary. The two aspects of social action that we have reviewed are never sufficient to explain conduct. People do not "perceive" their relations to others while standing outside the world of practical action; perception and response are joined in a seamless whole. Nor do people undergo sensual transformations without trying somehow to make sense of the experience. We will not have a complete explanation of becoming pissed off driving until we have determined how the experience is a practical project of making sense of a dynamic situation.

We already have one clue as to where to look for additional factors. If the driver's anger arises as he experiences being cut off from a tacit use of his automobilized body, perhaps the implicit practical and self-serving logic in anger is as an attempt to recover a taken-for-granted intertwining with the world. Surely there is something along these lines yet to explain, because drivers in L.A. do not just "get" angry, they "do" their anger, in all of the surprising and seemingly absurd ways we have already reviewed: yelling at other drivers over great distances, in the midst of deafening traffic noise, and with one's windows rolled up; getting back at the offender through risky maneuvers that don't seem worth it a few moments later; and perhaps the most common response of all, "giving the finger" or "flipping the other off."

We have come all this way in the analysis of a familiar phenomenon of everyday anger only to arrive at what may be its greatest enigma. The angry driver seeks to enact a drama that tells a story about the animating interaction, and if the story is told in an aesthetically satisfying fashion, anger fades quickly. Why is this an enigma? Because the way anger emerges in social interaction, it virtually guarantees that no matter how well the story is told, it will not be understood by anyone else as the narrator wishes. The enigma is that, on the one hand, anger arises to fuel and indeed seeks its apotheosis in *a practical story-telling project,* but on the other, *anger doesn't seek audience approval.* In some sense it is obvious that the effort to "teach a lesson" is a pretense, but it is obviously not obvious to the narrator, at least not just then. A moment after anger fades, yes. But at the moment, the narrative performer effectively suspends disbelief and is routinely taken in by his teaching/story-telling performance.

How could the amputation, the cutoff, be repaired and the tacit body restored to its natural, taken-for-granted state through enacting a story of revenge? What kind of emotionally compelling, natural sense does this seemingly silly process of sense making make? And if the moral of the story is likely to be convincing only to the narrator, why isn't it sufficient, in order to serve and dispel anger, just to *think* a scenario of revenge?

The secret of the magical force of the enactment is in its sensual dimensions. In contrast to just thinking up a story, telling it requires that the driver enact it bodily, and the process of embodying the story in a dramatization produces a sensual resonance for the narrator. By conjuring up a script of action that attributes great significance to the events, the angry driver becomes a magician taken in by his or her own magic.

The driver's fury hides the secret of emotional magic even from him- or herself. The trouble with thinking revenge, as a strategy for the resolution of anger, is that it is only thinking. One still has to act, and if the revenge scenario is not enacted, it competes with the actions one does take, increasing tension and compounding the problem. When revenge is just a thought that is not acted upon, it is evidence of impotence, and that shows the angry person yet another way that he has been cut off from him- or herself. Thoughts of revenge lack the charm of enacting revenge because in acting the narrator reshapes the perceived world to fit the contours of his or her anger, reshaping him- or herself in the process.

There appears to be some kind of "subconscious" or "psychic" mechanism at work here. But such phrases just flag the issue; at best they put on hold the business of providing an explanation. The route to the hidden objective of the driver's anger is through taking seriously the actor's "manifest" meaning, which we do by analyzing its constituent elements.

Looking for the essential elements of the angry driver's narrative project, we find three distinguishable phases. First, moral meaning is given to the social situation as the driver takes the posture of a victim. This step is already sly. Defining him- or herself as victimized, the driver sneaks moral meaning into the situation before projecting a moralistic response.

Second, the meaning of the immediate social situation is generalized. The interaction is given transcendent significance by various devices, most notably by the invocation of prejudicial stereotypes. This is a key step in gaining a new grounding for the self, because the meaning of the situation now transcends what is in front of the driver, and by going beyond what is in front of him or her, the driver breaks open a path to recover what was behind, a body tacitly deployed as an unseen resource for shaping conduct.

By generalizing the meaning of the moment, the angry driver sets the stage for an attempt to reverse the moral and sensual process he or she has witnessed. Now the driver can perform as a ritual actor before the general audience whose presence he or she has invoked. If, once on this communal stage, the driver enters a battle that cannot be won, he or she may stay out of sorts for some time. But if he or she can enact a role of ritualized revenge that is successful at least in the aesthetics of the performance, the driver will briefly celebrate his or her heroic communal status and then, from the heights of that pleasant self-regard, come down to reengage the world unselfconsciously.

To summarize the angry driver's situation: The animating problem is a loss of the taken-for-granted basis of action, experienced bodily as a tacit way of being in the world. The dilemma is how to get back something that cannot been seen, a touchstone for conduct that by definition one cannot grab onto directly. Some sleight of hand is required. The trick is to call up moral energy to construct a drama of communal importance in the immediate situation, and then to clothe oneself in the role of avenging hero. Once the situation has been given morally transcendent meaning, it does not matter that no one else is watching, since the relevant audience is universal and could never physically be in attendance anyway. Nor does it matter that the offender may remain intransigent. The process of invoking the communal role itself inducts one back into a sense of competent involvement in a transcendent realm, and that is the animating objective in any case.

But it will not do just to think this logic through; it must be enacted in some form. Anger calls for a practical, embodied project, if only a curse that reverberates within a closed vehicle, because a curse, unlike a thought, achieves sensual resonance on which a double meaning may be registered. The curse has one meaning as a response to this other in this locally situated interaction drama, and more importantly, it is meaningful as a stirring of universal moral spirits that can embrace the self as a competent community member.

Assuming a Victim's Posture

Assuming the posture of a victim is a condition for becoming pissed off, but it is hard to predict the moral infractions that drivers will discover as proof of insensitive treatment. Driving in Santa Monica, Dita is pulled over by a police officer "because a pedestrian who was jaywalking had placed one foot in the street" and Dita "continued to drive by without stopping." Reinforcing her sense of being victimized by laws that humiliate because of their oppressive stupidity, Dita gave

> the example of children in car seats. If you have a child under four years old in the car they must be strapped in a child car seat. On the other hand, if you are driving your neighbor's child who is seven months old, they can just be laying on the seat, not even strapped in.

Idiosyncratic sensitivities to oppression on the road are not peculiar to Dita. George is on hard times, out of work and prohibited by court order from visiting his children. He feels especially vulnerable in many facets of his life, not the least when he is on the road. Because he lost his license he is not free to retaliate against bad drivers, who not only routinely break the rules of courtesy in driving but also can insult him with impunity. Virtually every time he drives now he vividly suffers this patent injustice!

Passengers are often unable to anticipate what will victimize a driver. Bang, a sixty-year-old Vietnamese immigrant businessman, is doing well economically. He drives "a new black Toyota 4-Runner," but to him it also feels that " 'other people target me and only cut me off, not anyone else.' " When the interviewer drove with him, she was surprised to find that "he even considered drivers who got in front of him from a distance [as] cutting him off." Craig, identified by his girl-friend as a Japanese-American "doctor of Chinese medicine" who practices as an acupuncturist and herbalist, is cut off by an "old man in a pickup truck." Despite the fact that Craig, complaining, "He didn't even look before he changed lanes!" acknowledges that the offender didn't see him, he cuts the fellow off in retaliation, remarking as he does, "Thought you got me, didn't you?"

One aspect of the self-definitional work entailed in becoming pissed off when driving is to feel personally victimized, and this may be accomplished even though one knows that the offending driver meant nothing personal, even when one is stuck with a mass of other drivers in a traffic jam. When there is no single other driver to blame, one may blame "those who are responsible." Cindy, for example, is having trouble pulling out of a "stack" parking lot because other cars are too close. A line of cars builds, waiting for her to exit, and the attendant looks on, laughing.

> I started to get angry then. I started thinking—why do they have this stupid stack parking anyway? . . . why did the people running UCLA have to give a thousand spaces in the students' garage to new medical personnel?

A second aspect of self-definition as victim is seeing one's suffering as the result of a violation of community standards. The victim does not demand any special privileges; by protesting he or she stands up for everyone's rights. Ellen, an "independent businesswoman," refers to the pattern of alternating ramp and highway cars in merger situations as " 'It's just the etiquette, you let one in, and then you go.' " When her turn came up and a woman on the highway kept inching up to block her entry, Ellen understood the offense, not just personally but as an attack on the community as a whole: " 'When she [cut me off], she let down the whole team.' " Many interviewees reflected the same spirit when, after describing a personal experience of victimization, they would add, "Now wouldn't that piss you off?"

A psychoanalyst driver showed the way to reconcile the apparent conflict between, on the one hand, feeling personally put upon by bad drivers and, on the other, perceiving drivers as bad when they appear to be unaware of the cars around them. Her phrase was that such drivers are "intentionally unconscious." It would follow that anyone standing up to such drivers would be directing the offender's attention to a failing that oppresses the entire driving public.

Just because the offense consists of an impersonal indifference to me, the offense is to everyone. With this understanding of self and other in place, an altruistic response starts to make sense. La Verne is mad at drivers who may be driving "fast" but do not get out of the "passing" lane when she presses from behind: " 'They're not following the rules, you know? so I start making a scene and yelling and honking.' " Bruce, a respiratory therapist, makes a point of cutting off people who cut him off, whether or not they did it on purpose, because "they should pay attention." His revenge isn't simply for personal satisfaction: "You wouldn't believe how many accidents are a result of people just not paying attention."

Bob, who is thirty-seven years old and works for a drug store, has an unusually worked-out moral philosophy to justify retaliation against miscreant drivers. He casts his responses as serving the interests that used to be served by social laws honoring natural selection, before society lost its disciplinary nerve.

> Civilization came about because we are beings who have evolved a social way of working together to keep our species going. As we evolved and changed through time, we worked out rules of living together . . . and the people who were incompetent and didn't follow those rules in the old days centuries ago got killed or kicked out of their society. That doesn't happen as much now, and it shouldn't, but California and Los Angeles drivers make me want to rethink that train of thought. I mean, we have rules now in our society, both formal and written, and others that are just as strong but unwritten, in all aspects of life in America. One of those areas is driving. . . . If you don't or can't follow those rules, you don't deserve to drive.

The interviewer, his girlfriend, caught the altruism in his aggressive views: "Bob is standing up for everyone when he yells at people, and cuts them off, and tailgates them, he is performing a public service. And he knows it." An optimist in the end, Bob goes out of his way to teach bad drivers lessons, even though he suspects all along that they are " 'fucking brain-dead.' "

Typifying and Signifying: The Moral Attractions of Prejudice

In the first moment of self-definition in the process of becoming angry, the driver casts him- or herself as a victim. In a second moment, the person-becoming-pissed must turn more directly toward characterizing the other in a way that can sustain angry spirits. The key challenge here is to give the other a doubly resonant identity, one that, while appreciating a specific person in fine detail, also describes the other as the representative of a type of moral incompetence that one might confront virtually anywhere in society.

As a matter of the logistics of social interaction among drivers, the act of self-definition is much easier to bring off than a description of the other. One always carries rich familiarity with the object of self-definition. But the other is available to a driver only for some fleeting moments, and then often only as a person glimpsed at oblique angles within a largely opaque metal box. His or her perceptive competence severely constrained, the pissed-off driver's gaze must scramble to pick up features that can trigger a generalizing characterization.

Thus just after being cut off, drivers often turn immediately to focus sharply on the other, picking up whatever information is available: the make and model of the other's car, its state of maintenance, the driver's face and dress. At times drivers who have been cut off will make tricky maneuvers around traffic to get parallel to the other so that additional information can be acquired.[17]

At the same time, the victimized driver sets in motion a frenetic generalizing process as he or she seeks to tag the offending party with a seemingly fitting label, one that need stick just long enough for anger to emerge and run through a quick metamorphosis. In order to accomplish their dualistic descriptive task, drivers make dizzying jumps between specifics and generalizations, between noting details about makes of cars and reflecting on the nature of people "out there," between describing what happened at a particular intersection at a particular time of day and offering sociologically formulated explanations of general pathologies in society. Common examples of the latter are that the instant incident shows: why people get shot on the freeways, how civility is rapidly vanishing from life in L.A., and the shortcomings of various ascriptively defined subgroups of the population.

By exploring the different types of generalizations that drivers make, we can see how the process of characterizing the other provides the vehicle in which anger can run its course. There is no one substantive set of dimensions that drivers invoke to define the incompetence of those who offend them. The only universal element is an analytic jump from a given moment or move in driving behavior to the person's character as a whole. For the members of the current sample, this is achieved perhaps most often through applying "idiot" to an otherwise heterogeneous set of putative driving insensitivities and errors.

> That idiot driver [recalled Tara about an incident in which she was cut off close] was just obnoxious and annoying. He was like someone who wanted to take up every inch he could get on the road. It's OK with me, but he's got to watch out for other drivers on the road. He should make sure what he's doing is safe for everyone. Not to scare other drivers, like me. From that incident, I learned to be more aware on the road and watch out for stupid drivers.

Generalizing from a given driving act to the overall character of the offender, Tara reads the immediate situation for a meaning that she will take beyond it as she shifts her orientation to stupid drivers in general.

Irate drivers perceive various subclasses of faulty driving characters. "Space hoppers" who try to get ahead of the pack by making strategic little jumps into empty spaces irritate Francine. Using her perception of one or more space hops to characterize the driver, Francine tracks their fate when she can, and her irritation is sometimes resolved when "she actually enjoys seeing these space hoppers fail and end up a mile farther back that when they started." Similarly the tailgater type irritates George; he dreams of giving them their comeuppance. "Sometimes I'll fantasize about running a tailgater off the road."

In lieu of particular driving acts, angry drivers may fix on features of the offending driver's vehicle to give an encounter generalized meaning. Truck drivers are often seen along the following lines. As Pablo, age sixty-one, whose commute involves a drive to Burbank and a shuttle to Palmdale, puts it, "These truck drivers think everyone is just going to stop in their tracks or risk getting crushed; just because they don't value themselves doesn't mean they have to go fucking with me."

Sometimes angry drivers create novel character types by mixing features of the other's physique and car. Patrick, at thirty-three a successful title insurance salesman who lives in the "upper-middle class neighborhood of Studio City," imputed a "Napoleon's complex" to a driver of small stature who, in his Mercedes Benz and "cool little sunglasses on his balding head . . . [was] a little man driving an expensive car in hopes of impressing people." When Patrick "encounters these people he tries to 'bring them back down to earth and show them that their shit stinks like everyone else's.' "

The interviewer wisely asked Patrick if it would have made a difference if the driver who had cut him off was a tall woman in a Toyota Tercel. "He thought for second and with some hesitation he claimed it would not have made a difference. He said that he would have reacted just the same." His anger may have been the same, but it is a good bet that his characterization would have been different. The other driver must be defined as having caused the problem because of his indifference to or inability to appreciate the details of the situation around him. A patently inaccurate characterization will not work. But it does not matter much which type of prejudice the angry driver uses. Pressed by the need to act quickly in a situation of limited investigative possibilities, the driver works with what he or she finds readily available.

This is important to keep in mind when we turn to the next set of stereotypes, those related to race, because their politically sensational character invites the misleading view that they are simple revelations of causally significant racist motives. These data show that angry drivers use race interchangeably with stereotypes about politically insignificant characteristics. For some angry drivers there probably is an order of priority in the preference of race criteria over others, along the lines of: when working up anger toward another driver, look first to the other's apparent race, and if that will not work, go to sex, then age, then to type of driving malfeasance, then to type of car, etc. The data at hand do not permit the verification of such priorities. But they do show that the Los Angeles area provides rich possibilities for using racial and ethnic stereotypes to generalize about offending drivers, and the data also show that, even if racial prejudices are not essential to the stereotyping work that sustains anger, many drivers take their racial stereotypes very seriously.

One way of taking prejudices seriously is to offer them in the eminently respectable form of a well-researched sociological theory. Thus Rod, a Latino ex-marine, described a "tacky oriental lady who must have been over a hundred years old" as the person who made an illegal turn and hit him. No indifferent scholar he, Rod provided a documenting footnote for this view: " 'I have been to Korea and Japan and they drive all crazy and in different sorts of ways over there.' " Philip, a young musician we have met before, became outraged when, driving eastbound on Melrose and listening to a Melvin's tape, he became stuck behind two cars that stopped in traffic to have a conversation.

> Philip honked and yelled and was "belligerent at the fucking Iranians. Furious, he reached into his ashtray and grabbed a handful of pennies . . ." which he "flung" at the cars in front of him.

If offensive drivers are sometimes characterized as selfish, cliquish Iranians, the most consistently abused ethnicity in this sample is "Asian," in which I include "Japanese," "Korean," "Chinese," and "Asian." Barry, a middle-aged Jewish lawyer interviewed by a Korean student, explained that "most Asians pass their driver's test because they are given answers to the written test from the Asian driving schools," and "they need more driving experience before [they] are put on the road by themselves." Barry's explanation appears to be popular. When Ursula, a Latina, is cut off and blurts out the question, "That stupid Chinese, why do they get licenses?" her daughter says, "They buy their licenses, don't you know?"

Asian drivers are not unaware of these prejudices, and in order to fight back, some share them. The following narrative was told to a Japanese-American student by Hugh, a third-generation Japanese-American who works as an accountant in downtown L.A. Hugh introduces the problematic situation with: "Can you believe those people that drive forty-five miles an hour on the freeway?"

> I got stuck behind a Honda. The rest of the cars were going at least seventy. I looked at my speedometer and I was going forty-five! I tried to pass . . . but . . . the other cars were going too fast. So I started to tailgate the car in front of me. You'd think they would get the hint! But the car just kept going at forty-five. So I decided to be rude and honk. The car did not speed up. Boy was I mad. I finally saw a break. . . . As I passed the Honda I saw an Asian driver. I was pretty upset so I flipped the guy off as I passed him. Man!

The interviewer asked him "why he was so upset." " 'Well, people are always making cracks about us Asian drivers. It's those kind of drivers that give us a bad name.' "

Whatever the stereotypes that prevail in other areas of social life in Los Angeles, on the road Asians apparently are not "the model minority." African-Americans were insulted only once in this sample (by a Latino yelling "chango"), while Mexicans (as such or as "beaners") received a few insults. As the reader will see below, several stereotypes commonly associated with, and perhaps code phrases for, whites, such as "yuppie," "suburban Volvo mother," "a Betty," and "rich punk kid," were damned far more often than blacks. Mars, one of the student interviewers and herself white, offered this example of a popular prejudice against a subtype of Caucasian:

> Immediately, when I saw the woman cut me off I made all kinds of generalizations about what kind of woman she was because she was a

"blond in a convertible in L.A." At that point every blond, bimbo stereo-
type came to my mind.

If "racism" is at work here, it is not by simple extension from patterns extrinsic to the driving situation. We may get a clearer view of
how racial stereotyping works in sustaining the driver's anger after we
review how other ascriptive criteria are used. Age is commonly taken
as a revealing indicator of driving incompetence. Hugh, in describing
being held up by a car that blocked two lanes, recalled,

> I tried to swerve around it but when I did, the car swerved the same
> direction as I did. I saw this old man behind the wheel, you know, they
> shouldn't be allowed to drive. . . . Those old people put everyone on
> the road in danger.

Even when elderly drivers go fast, their age may be cited to give generalized significance to an irritating incident. Mario, forty-two years old
and an export-import businessman, recalled being cut off close by a
woman who was driving a white Volvo aggressively: "you think older
people would be a little more subdued."

But if age is commonly cited, it is not any particular age category
that receives abuse. Young drivers are frequently singled out as reckless. "Businessmen" and "mothers," categories with age connotations
somewhere between "fucking geriatrics" and "wild punks," are also
damned, sometimes for being so self-contented or preoccupied with
their own presumably conservative concerns that they will not let
working people get quickly to their more oppressive responsibilities.
Tony, who works at a multitude of jobs (in his father's antique store,
installing car alarms, managing a children's swimming school), recalled getting angry driving on Coldwater Canyon, a one-lane (in each
direction) road that he drives daily. Referring to "dickheads" who
drive too slowly because of excessive caution, he described a "Volvo, a
woman toting around her kids" who, because she was driving slowly,
"shouldn't have taken Coldwater." The interviewer suggests: "Is it like
they shouldn't be there when you are late for work?" "Yeah." In another
interview, Marnie, an art teacher at a high school in the Valley who lives
in Malibu, had to brake sharply to avoid an accident with a car that
pulled out unexpectedly on a canyon road. Marnie spontaneously yelled,
"You stupid fucking bitch," and described the offender as a "housewife
in her ugly minivan" who had been "thinking she owned the road."

Like age, sex is also frequently used to give generalized meaning to
angering encounters, but as with age, sexual stereotyping is neither
unidirectional in target nor simply cross-sex in the relation of source

and target of insult. As the last example indicates, women often see the offender as a woman, and men often find that the enemy is male. Mark, the roofer noted earlier, voiced anger at many types of drivers, including a fellow driving "one of those macho bullshit, bigger-than-necessary trucks." Of course men in the sample voiced the classic "typical woman driver!," for example about a car that failed to exit although its directional light was blinking that message. In complementary fashion, some women saw "an excess of testosterone" behind bad driving manners.

The categories invoked by drivers to mobilize their anger read like an old-fashioned sociology textbook. In addition to ethnicity, race, sex, and age, social class is used to give folk-theoretical meaning to experiences of being cut off, where the proxy used to identify social class is the brand, year, and condition of the car. Drivers presumed to be wealthy because they drive expensive cars are very commonly abused with phrases ringing with a revolutionary passion of class resentment that would thrill the most despondent Marxist radical. Here are but a few of the many examples:

- Hilaria: "You have to go with the flow. I go with the flow. There are no exclusive rights. And it's always some asshole in a BMW. BMWs think that they own the road. But they can't just cut people off. Mercedes owners, the same."
- Darlene, who tried to cut off a driver who had cut her off, only to be cut off again: "She wanted to avenge herself and all of her fellow drivers against the BMW, and she felt that she had failed in her mission. She . . . recognized some jealousy—rich people always seem to come out ahead, on top, whatever. . . . [This incident] made her realize that she had been waiting for a chance to put a rich yuppie in his or her place."
- Catherine, a middle-aged housing inspector for the city, after just avoiding an accident with a sports car that ran a light, damns "little, rich, hotshot L.A. people."
- Drew, a CPA, focuses his anger on a range of privileged types, noting, "One can tell a lot about another individual by the automobile that they drive." Struggling to rank the offenders, he declares that he is most angry at "yuppies" in BMWs talking on car phones, or perhaps at "middle-aged women in Jaguars talking on the car phone with their poodles panting in the backseat"; but then he recalls "the worst . . . those little teenagers who go around driving their daddys' cars and sports cars with their cute little girlfriends and driving as if they owned the whole damn road."

Lest this rhetoric of class resentment be taken as a sign of a general-ized revolutionary outlook, it should be noted that substantial indigna-tion is also directed against those presumed, on the basis of the vehicles that they drive, to be poor. In recalling a time when she stopped off at Trader Joe's to pick up something quick for dinner, Dana notes: "I was waiting to pull into the parking lot when some woman in a beat-up old car pulled in front of me when it was clearly my turn." The shabby condition of the offender's car is invoked, I suggest, not as a feature compounding the offense but as an indication of the moral incompetence that lies behind it. Ellen, trying to merge onto the 405 after working out at a Sports Connection club, is frustrated by " 'this one chick in a Volkswagen or some other stupid-ass car [who] kept inching forward even though I was ahead of her.' "

Angry drivers invoke the same variables to describe the objects of their attentions as are commonly used by sociologists working with statistical data. Demographic characteristics are especially useful for explaining people's behavior when you must come up with an explana-tion based only on a quick glance at others' lives. Pissed-off drivers take for granted that, with a look at another car, they can quickly and accurately perceive such personal identifiers as race, ethnicity, age, sex, and social-class status. In focusing on demographic factors, angry driv-ers rely on a common folk culture that assumes that such factors are major ubiquitous determinants of people's behavior.

When labeling offenders, drivers are seriously concerned about the empirical grounding of their descriptions. While they must work quickly, they do not take that constraint as an excuse to be sloppy in their data gathering. Yolanda, a Latina, focuses intently as her RX7 is almost hit by a car speeding out of a parking lot: "As I looked through my rearview mirror, I could tell the driver was a young male, possibly of Filipino or Spanish descent, in his early twenties." If it appears that their initial descriptions are in error, they work quickly to make corrections. May, who is "half Asian," "takes great pride in not falling into the category of stereotypically absentminded Asian drivers." One recent night, as she is returning from her workout to "the ever-popular Juice Club in Brentwood," she finds herself behind "an old beat-up compact car of an unidentifiable make. The car, and therefore its driver, are failing to drive even close to the speed limit." First she says, " 'fucking geriatrics,' " then she sees that the driver is a young man. After tailgating him, she passes him on the right and "remembers recognizing the driver to be a Persian man in his early to midtwenties, with what she referred to as a 'giant unibrow.' " First using relatively superficial indicators like the status of the car and its failure to be an identifiable brand, May moves more closely in, trying an age characterization. Then she shows the discipline to drop that variable and switch to an ethnic dimension when the evidence rules out earlier hypotheses. May adds a kind of methodological footnote with the "unibrow" observation, as this in effect displays her coding procedures for attributing ethnic identity.

Considered as lay sociologists, drivers are often refreshingly humble about the grounds of their knowledge. Some respondents volunteered confessions of biases that would undermine the credibility of their favorite social portraits of bad drivers. Mark, the unemployed roofer, for example, told his interviewer:

> Once more he lost a position with a solid roofing company to a Mexican crew who will work for less. And he told me when he is driving and sees somebody driving poorly he tends to want that person to be Mexican so he can go off on them.

And Bob, the motorized Darwinian we met earlier, invokes sex and ethnicity whenever he can, but he acknowledges that he is

> an equal opportunity insulter. No one type of driver is safe from his derogatory remarks. He says "I match the insult to the person pissing me off."

Many of the respondents voiced a self-deprecating humor about the slim rational bases for their anger, discounting any extrasituational validity for what are delivered in situ as strongly held views.

What we have here most clearly is broad evidence of situational practices of characterizing others in demographic terms in order to achieve a generalizing sense within the specific moments of anger. It is just not enough for the angry driver to structure his or her experience within the limits of the view that "someone cut me off, damn it!" Nor is it enough to imagine the other in a way that would suit one's fantasies unrestrained by obdurate reality. A *dualistic* descriptive job is required. A perspective must be constructed that fits both the *specifics* at hand and casts the other as *representative* of some class of people.

By constructing a transcendent meaning that is tailored to the local situation, the enraged driver has a practical objective, that of discovering a way out of the oppressive moment itself. Now we can follow pissed-off drivers as they rush to seize the possibilities along that escape route.

Flippings Off, Domino Games, and Other Narrative Strategies to Recover the Tacitly Grounded Body

Will is a sixty-six-year-old college professor and a father of six. He lives in the Valley and teaches educational psychology at a Cal State campus. Representing the prevailing opinion in academic psychological and sociological circles, Will would explain the dynamics of anger in rational terms. Will admits to anger when he is cut off but states that his response is only to "give a look." He explicates this look as conveying a cool reasoning.

> I am mad and you have diminished me somewhat. I resent the manner in which you drove and I'm giving you some negative feedback about your style as it affects other people. Please change.

This message neatly points out Will's sense of victimization and explicitly generalizes the meaning of the encounter, which he treats as an opportunity to teach the offender a lesson that will benefit the community as a whole, not himself in particular.

But when called on to relate a specific incident of anger, Will describes a more metaphorically dramatized and emotionally animated response. A young man who thought that he, Will, had cut him off, would

> roar up along side me, yell, would cut in front of me and jam on his brakes. If I went slow, he would go slow right on my rear bumper. [When they were both stopped at a red light] . . . he pulled up next to me and I called out to him a rather unflattering name. [Which was?] I believe, if memory serves me correct, I called him an anal orifice, an asshole! . . . very quickly the anger diminished and I got back into my fear because my wife was with me at the time and it had frightened her a great deal and I realized my responsibility in it.

Will's insulting shout is an effort to humiliate the offender publicly. He wants to "teach a lesson" to the offender in the moralistic rather than the educational sense of the phrase. If anger in driving is virtually a universal experience, very few drivers are routinely acting as road knights sworn to defend the rules of the road against those who would flout them, coldly running personal risks to defend the community's honor as defined by the DMV (California's Department of Motor Vehicles). Instead, the angry driver wants to dramatize his or her relationship to the offender in a way that emphasizes the offender's extraordinarily inferior moral status and by inference, his or her own superiority. What Will's confession means for our inquiry is that we still must explain why drivers naturally, without self-reflective thinking, try to transcend their anger by *constructing moral dramas* about the provocative incident.

The extent to which angry drivers try to enact coherent multiact narratives in which they regain the higher moral ground vis-à-vis their driving enemies is striking. Sometimes frustrated drivers simply sigh or utter a single-syllable "shit," but there is a great variety of much more elaborated responses that angry drivers favor as ways of publicly making sense of the situation. They give the finger to the offender, swerve around intervening cars to reciprocate a cut off, tailgate tailgaters, etc.

How does expressing a moralistic understanding of the interaction serve the project of quelling anger? It is not enough to explain why angry drivers construct moralistic *understandings* about the others who provoke them. More specifically, we must explain why angry drivers spontaneously and *dramatically express* (e.g., by shouting in their enclosed cars) or go *public* with the stories that they create about the scene. Why isn't it enough that Will just *think* his moralistic interpretation of what has transpired? Just thinking insulting thoughts about the offender does not work, indeed, "just thinking" frustrates more than it resolves, because it heightens rather than transcends the very self-consciousness that spurs anger on.

The scenes that we are about to review are colorful and their color suggests that there is a motivating interest in sensationalism at work. Indeed there is, and for two reasons. First, angry people do sensational things because they are trying to create a sensuality through which they can overcome their anger. Second, people in rage want to express their understandings in the form of dramatic stories. The link between the sensual and moral dynamics of anger is at the heart of the causal career of this emotion.

The proof that moral and sensual dynamics are critical contingencies in the empirical careers of rage lies in the details of what people do when they get pissed off. Angry people may experience wild feelings but they do not act randomly or go berserk in their behavior. The patterned conduct of anger provides systematic resources for explanation. In these patterns we can glimpse the hidden dependence of the naturally enacted self on its silent embrace by a sacred community.

Notes on the Well-Flipped Finger

A finger well flipped at an offending driver routinely works to transform the emotions of the pissed-off party. There is no apparent social group limitation to the attractions of, much less to the ability to understand, the folk meaning of "flipping" (sometimes "flicking") someone "off." The drivers who recalled performing spontaneous acts of this sort include a truck driver from the Inland Empire, a Vietnamese refugee who came to L.A. after first living in Montana, middle-aged attorneys and accountants, a retired college professor, and, among several middle-aged mothers, a nurse, a psychoanalyst, and multiple homemakers. These data contain no instances in which the respondents doubt whether or not they have given or received "the finger," although it is not inconceivable that such an event would occur.[18] That a particular gesture is so widely and routinely understood as unambiguous suggests that it exploits mechanical properties that are reserved with some care from alternative uses.

Giving the finger requires the use of a particular finger held up from an otherwise closed hand: not the pinky, which hangs at an oblique angle off of a lazy wrist to suggest a fey character; nor the thumb, which when stuck up from a fist often conveys a hearty, friendly meaning; nor the index finger, which has vast experience in the precise work of focusing attentions away from the person behind the referencing hand; but the middle finger. As the longest finger of the hand, the middle finger reaches the farthest out into the world even while it retains a powerful tie to its base in the hand, which it roughly divides into two sections. Easily capable of a rapid, stiff erection that intersects and is juxtaposed against a balled hand, the middle finger is aesthetically unparalleled for suggesting an aggressive phallic penetration of another's world. When thrust upward rapidly and then stopped abruptly, the middle finger creates a stiffness that runs back through the arm to disappear at some ambiguous point in the body, at once manifesting an outward thrust and demonstrating that this projection is powerfully controlled from the center of its owner's being. It is in just this regard that the ring finger, which for most people can only weakly be extended in radical juxtaposition to a closed fist, fails in the intra-hand competition for selection as the finger's finger.[19]

In obscene gestures suggesting erotic sex, the middle finger may be moved languidly through or may trace the internal perimeter of a circle made with an opposing hand, a motion that depicts a cooperatively worked out intersection of bodies. But the finger in giving the finger, while it may be accompanied by a sadistic smile, demonstrates no desire to please. The thrust of the message is a thrust, a movement that is passionate in its meaning but does not suggest eros so much as an unfeeling, even indifferent desire to force the other into unwanted feelings. The surreal intention is to get the finger into the other without subjecting the feelings of the finger's owner to the personal world he or she enters. So, the finger doesn't get one or the other "off" in the erotic sense of merged and mutually ambiguated identities. Instead, with a connotation of casual cruelty, the finger flips or flicks the other off. The suggestion is that the owner of the finger preserves his or her integrity even as he or she violates the integrity of the other.

The aesthetic features of giving the finger make a neat fit with the narrative tasks and communicative challenges faced by the gesturer. Consider direction. "Down yours" could be given an offensive meaning, but it does not signal as well. Pointed upward, the middle finger makes the highest profile that one finger can achieve, maximizing the possibilities that the message will be received effectively at a great distance. Note also that the finger does not achieve the intended meaning when it is pointed horizontally forward toward the target, much less back toward the gesturing party. The finger must be pointed upward anywhere from about a thirty-degree to somewhat more than a ninety-degree angle in order that its message reliably be thrust outward. Gestured in this manner, the finger shares a central feature with the shouted curse, which in another manner reaches deep into the body to pull out something ugly to be thrown at the offender.

"Up yours" is a phrase commonly used to capture the meaning of the gesture. That there is often an anal metaphoric target is suggested by the aggressiveness of the motion, which indicates that the penetration will have to overcome substantial resistance, and by the irrelevance of either the gesturer's or the target's sexual identity. With this gesture, an offended driver takes the offense out of his or her experience, where it was implanted by an inconsiderate intervention, captures it in a finger, and "sticks it to" the culpable party. By symbolizing a brutal assault on an anal target, it implies: "I'm messing you up by attacking your most primordial source of self-control to show how you've messed with me."

Relying on a deeply institutionalized community of understanding, the gesturer takes for granted that the targeted party will, in a moment's observation, appreciate an entire narrative that is indexed at the tip of a finger. Seeing the finger pointed up, the recipient is supposed to understand that it is nevertheless pointed at him or her, and that it makes reference to prior actions on his or her part that intervened in the world of the finger flipper. The finger is an effort to sum up an emotionally elaborate history, and the recipient is presumed capable of instantly recognizing that the finger is insisting on a conclusive commentary.

These various hermeneutic dimensions of the finger are not post hoc academic inventions; they are themselves appreciated by pissed-off drivers. Consider the experience of Mars when she found a woman

shaking her head at her. Mars understood that the woman was accus-
ing her of having changed lanes improperly. Mars then flipped the
other party off and screamed at her within her own car's sealed interior. The finger was useful in focusing anger.

> I believe that I interpreted her shaking her head at me as her trying to
> instill some feeling of shame in me. . . . I guess I turned whatever shame
> I may have felt into anger so as to avoid placing blame on myself. I also
> focused my anger on her by yelling and giving her the finger.

For the finger-throwing party, the pointed nature of the gesture is
central. As a practical matter the victim often has a very small "window of opportunity" for sending a message to the offender. Traffic
may soon create insurmountable perceptual obstacles between the
two. For example, the other soon may not be facing in a direction that
makes reception of the message possible. Or if the offended party waits
too long, the target might exit the road before receiving the finger.
The communicative power of the finger as an instantly recognizable,
narratively rich folk gesture tempts the angry driver to try to isolate,
package, and send off to the other the disturbance that he or she has
him- or herself felt.

Drivers do not invent the culture of the finger; they find it well adapted
to their interaction setting. The device of the finger, although it long
predates the invention of the automobile, appears to have been shaped
culturally in order to exploit the distinctive possibilities of just such interactions as are found in the passing relations of motorists. Where
the possibilities for sustained and intimate interaction are much greater,
for example when mutually hostile parties are seated face-to-face,
many fond users of the finger find themselves severely constrained. The
angry driver does not want to start a conversation with the finger; he
or she wants to flip it "off," using the finger as a final comment about
an intersection of lives from which he or she is speedily departing.

Eloquent in its silence, the finger communicates simply by being
seen. If picked up by its target, the victim-gesturer can take satisfaction
in the aesthetics of his or her storytelling. With the simple, quiet flip
of a single finger, the gesturer can metamorphose from a state in which
he or she had been molested by someone who rudely invaded his or
her space to a state of relaxation, once again sealed in quiet comfort
and moving through public space in a mobile private living room. The
finger in this way has attractions superior to yelling out obscenities,
an act that ruffles the avenger's composure and interferes with the ability to listen to the radio or talk on the car phone.

The finger points backward and forward at once, not spatially but in the temporal dimension of its narrative reach. It stands for an offense received and it depicts what would be a just fate for the offender. Even if no one but the avenging victim and the offender-recipient is aware of the gesture, the offender invokes the presence of "the community" as a third party to their interaction when he or she sticks up a middle finger. The community is made present by the compact hermeneutic character of the gesture. That is, the gesturer presumes, usually correctly, that the recipient will unproblematically draw on what both take to be a shared, preexisting, universal culture as he or she instantly grasps a rich narrative meaning. With the community present, the avenging victim can put the recipient to shame. As the recipient takes in the humiliating gesture, the avenger is cleansed of the anger that was born of his or her own humiliation during the earlier asymmetrical interaction.

The magical efficacy of this slight gesture in transforming the avenger's emotions is no less curious than the effect that the gesture has on the recipient. Finger flickers are no fools. They know that people to whom they give the finger are typically not gracious recipients of the gift. Indeed it seems that most people find it impossible to see someone giving them the finger and not get mad themselves. In such cases, what the gesturer essentially accomplishes is a mutual acknowledgment that the emotional lives of the two are intertwined. The gesturer might not get away with it; the offender-recipient might get in a responsive finger that sticks in the victim as the offender exits the highway laughing. But they are now joined, emotional gut to emotional gut.

This joining, this intertwining of spirited emotions is essential to the transforming power of the gesture. In heavy traffic, Bill, who sells computer equipment through mail order, grinds gears on purpose as he shifts from second to first. Making the car bear audible witness to his suffering helps a bit, but, like shouting into a closed car, Bill's way of representing anger has clear limitations. The angry finger flipper, by contrast, works more strategically to get out of his or her insulated world in order to get back into it peacefully.

The magical efficacy of the finger is that when the recipient sees it he or she will feel it, and that when the sender sees the recipient seeing the gesture, this will excise the irritation that caused the gesturing party's anger. Angry drivers attest to their belief in this magic in various ways. An angry driver who has been cut off by a car that is now in front of him or her may hold up a middle finger in the confidence that it can shoot its magical energy successfully if the offender will just look up to the rearview mirror for a brief moment. The offender's glance to the rearview mirror is taken to mean that he or she is acknowledging guilt. Joyous that an offender has received their gesture, angry drivers sometimes proudly prolong the erection of their middle fingers, confident that so long as the offender sees it he or she will continue to feel it, and understanding that if the offender stops looking it is because he or she cannot take it. Finger flippers also know that they can geometrically increase the power of their message if they can arrange suitable eye contact. If the victim-gesturer not only sees the recipient seeing the finger but also perceives the victim seeing that he or she, the gesturing party, is watching as the target takes in the gesture, that will be much more forceful. One recipient in such a scenario complained that the other party was "mind fucking" him. After the finger transforms the visual into the tactile, the eye contact drives it in, not just as a figure of speech but as a figure that works actively to restructure the recipient's experience.

The gesturer assumes that even the recipient, though unwilling to receive the message, cannot resist its emotional impact. In effect, a form of consent that is mutual has opened a bidirectional communicative channel even though on one side it is grudging. Now the intertwining that the victim lost when he or she was cut off is reestablished in a new direction with the offender-recipient. The surreal dimensions of both extensions of self into the world—that of the lost dwelling-in-the-car and that of the new projection of a finger into another person's experience—are equally real.

The victim's objective is to drain off the electric reality of anger by grounding his or her moralistic understanding of their interaction in the offender's corporeal experience.[20] This is why Will, the college psychology professor, could not resolve his anger at a rude young driver simply by calmly articulating a rationale for his irritation and delivering a lesson that would improve his adversary's driving manners. The angry driver wants to stir up the enemy sensually, not really to change the other's mind but to change the other's bodily experience so that he or she can change his or her own corporeal experience. If the avenging driver wants to be a teacher, it is the pedagogic style of the desk-pounding or bible-thumping moralist that he or she exhibits, not the enlightened patience of a driving school instructor.

On Automobilized Mimicry and Domino Games

As disturbing as the event may be, the target of a finger also receives an implicit offer to end the interaction. Because the angered party's purpose is to flip one's anger off, the target can usually end the interaction by taking it in the sense of not visibly returning the officious present or otherwise resisting its accusation. Yet the compliant recipient, in not protesting the characterization of "punished offender," does not have to see nonresponse as making him or her a loser in the transaction. Shaking one's head slightly, one can assume a posture of martyred indulgence toward such pathetic and coarse people as are these finger flippers who make so much of the inevitable petty disturbances of life.

Beyond the finger, there is a variety of ways to transform anger by dramatizing the interaction. Anger-transforming devices share two characteristics: (1) implicating the community as an audience, and (2) a practical activity that physically dramatizes one's superior moral understanding.

One neat way of accomplishing a satisfying ending is by activating third parties who damn the offender for the victim and on behalf of the community as a whole. Drivers who are pissed off when they are delayed by a car that is waiting to make a prohibited left turn may keep their horns blasting in the hope of attracting the attentions of a fortuitously passing police officer. Even if no cop arrives, the angry horn blower has grounds to feel satisfaction in the awareness that he or she has publicly punished the offender with the fear of apprehension. If he or she sees that other drivers are present, the horn blowing calls them to witness the moral incompetence of the offender. Then, having become just another member of the audience, the aggrieved driver can move discreetly to the background. Thus Paul Ramirez honked his horn loud when a slow driver put Paul in danger by slowing even more in order to allow a truck to merge.

> I tried getting everyone else's attention—just to show them what a pitiful driver is on this freeway. To humiliate him and make him responsible for almost making me crash.

In some cases of invoking communal authority to redress one's identity as a victim, the metamorphosis out of anger does not require that one witness the final act in the drama. Max was driving a diesel back to the truck yard from the Downey area, trying to get onto the 60 north, when a young "Mexican male" in a paint-primed, older American car "would not speed up or slow down to let him in." Max explained why he did not brake but forced the offender either to accept being hit or to move over: it takes his diesel four times as long to stop as it takes a car. The offender then cut in front of Max and slowed down. Thinking of "a news special he had recently heard, which was about how Mexicans were purposely braking in front of cars on the freeway, to get rear-ended and get some money," Max devised his revenge.

He decided to get on channel 9 on his CB radio, which is the emergency channel, and report this driver as being a drunk driver who was disrupting traffic in many ways. . . . after he had radioed in his information, Max started honking and yelling at the other driver . . . [who] finally took off, speeding away and flipping off Max. Max said that this just made him laugh, because he was thinking about how the driver would feel when the police pulled him over.

The driver's anger is instantly transformed by the perception that the curtain has fallen on the drama just after a public definition of his or her superiority. The following incident is unusually instructive in this regard. Cutting off "a perfectly coiffed woman in a green Jaguar" who had just cut her off, Imelda recalls that she

> pressed hard on my accelerator to make a big cloud of smoke puff out at her. I gave a wicked giggle and smiled to myself as I hurriedly drove on to meet my friend.

A couple of weeks later, however, Imelda's understanding of the drama was transformed, and so were her emotions, when she received notification of a smog inspection that was triggered by a complaint against her car. Revisiting the incident, Imelda realized that the last critical narrative moment in the interaction was not the trail of smoke behind her but the display of her license plate as she sped off.

The angry driver's narrative project is to package his or her anger in a story of moral superiority that, if neatly sent off, demonstrably received, and not rejected and returned by its targeted recipient, will effectively carry his or her anger away. Perhaps the most convincing proof that the angry driver's story of righteous indignation has been well told is evidence that its target has become angry. Bruce, a respiratory therapist, is cut off by a black Jeep ("he came an inch away") as he drives with his girlfriend on the 101. Bruce then works hard to end up with the proverbial last laugh.

> Because it "really pissed" him off, Bruce maneuvered for several minutes until he could "cut that asshole off." The Jeep driver then "flipped" Bruce off and again cut him off. Ignoring his girlfriend's request to "knock it off," Bruce, who at this point was "on fire," cut the Jeep off and smiled as he was passing, "just to tick him off." As Bruce moved to exit to the 134, the Jeep driver, at this point unable to equal the score, "pulled up next to" Bruce "on the shoulder of the freeway [and] was screaming something" and "flipping" Bruce off. Now ignoring the fellow, Bruce "suddenly found the whole thing funny." Exiting at Victory,

Bruce thought "the guy was an idiot for risking a ticket or his life to catch up."

Like Bruce, Catherine, a housing inspector, takes cathartic satisfaction from seeing her own anger reappear in the experience of an offender.

> Driving home depressed after having given a "Mexican family of ten or twelve" a notice to vacate their home within five days because of their failure to remedy longstanding health violations, Catherine finds that it's stop-and-go on the freeway. She notices a car weaving around traffic behind her ("so stupid . . . they're not going to get anywhere that much quicker than everybody else"), "there was no way I was going to let him get in front of me. So I drove for awhile keeping him boxed in by speeding up or slowing down when I had to. I felt an almost sick sense of pleasure in watching him get mad!"

Emotions in everyday social interaction live and die in contextually situated metaphors. By changing the metaphor that describes the course of his or her relations with others, a person can transform the very body of his or her experience. The right metaphor, well enacted, will serve effectively as a bridge that allows anger to pass naturally from one driver to another. For a closer understanding of how this metamorphosis works, we need to trace the path of anger over this symbolic interpersonal bridge. Simply to say that the victim's anger is "displaced" is to leave confused the temporal and causal ordering of emotional change, and to obscure the practical story-creating work through which the victim endeavors so earnestly to undermine the offender's emotions.

It would indeed be magic if the "victim's" anger left his or her body before showing up in that of its target. Instead, anger stops controlling the driver's experience only after he or she sees it shaping the experience of his or her opposite number. If the victim can re-create the process through which he or she became angry in the offender's experience, the victim gains a spectacle to stand off from and admire. And if the angry driver's dramatization of revenge is sufficiently artful, he or she may take the appreciative perspective of a spectator on his or her own performance even without witnessing the transformation of the other's emotions.

As spectacle and as practical narrative project, the angered driver's dramatization of a revenge scenario provides a publicly recognizable place in cultural space from which to savor the transformation of a rudely fractured experience. If fingers are used, what they will often raise is an oblique awareness of sexual and violent themes. These bring a resonance and provide additional fascinations in which the avenging actor can delight. No longer an impotent victim, the once-pissed-off driver becomes a titillated observer of the autonomous life force that his or her symbolic creation has taken on.

Meanwhile, however, the other party is likely also to feel like a victim and to experience vengeful actions as cutting off his or her own ongoing involvement in driving. Adopting the same strategy of representing the sources of his or her anger in order to transcend it, the target of revenge often produces a specifically complementary response. Here is an everyday example. Carolina is cut off by a BMW as it exits a gas station. She then "laid on my horn and threw my hands up." At this point Carolina employs a new modality, the obnoxious sound of the horn, to cut objectively into the offender's experience, and with her hands she dramatizes how he had interrupted her hands-on involvement with driving. That performance would have been a satisfying one for Carolina, except that the BMW driver then blew *his* horn and threw *his* hands up, mocking the moralized story that she had been conveying. In effect, he undercut her story line by cunningly exploiting it as a narrative resource, effectively dramatizing his superiority, not only as a driver but also as a warrior in righteous road battles. At this point, Carolina attempted a coup de grâce by maneuvering successfully to cut him off with her car.

If Carolina is successful and meets with no reciprocating response, she will have restored herself to the relaxed embrace of a moralized social form, and the BMW driver will be left cut off both from his pre-Carolina involvement in driving *and* from the brief dramatic career that he had launched. Drivers who have been cut off love to get revenge but even more they love to leave the offender hanging on to an aborted effort to reciprocate their vengeful response. The spectacle of a rude driver writhing in frustration, unable to relax back into an unselfconscious engagement in driving, is one they can enjoy almost indefinitely.

As drivers insult each other, they use complementarity as a tactic, not as an end in itself. Pairs of drivers can create virtual sagas as each seeks to give a finishing touch to the public story of what has been going on. I will describe here two of the forms these sagas commonly take.[21]

The first is an extraordinary incident in this data set, although it illustrates the dynamics of a kind of news story for which L.A. became famous in the 1980s. B.G., a lab technician, was trying to move into the right lane on Rossmore in order to make a right turn where it ends at Wilshire, and he found that an old Arabian man driving a Nissan [in the right lane] wasn't advancing and wasn't slowing down, he was maintaining his speed . . . so that B.G. couldn't pull into the right-hand lane.

B.G. felt forced to cut the Nissan off in order to make his turn. The Nissan's driver then moved to the left lane and flicked off B.G. while passing him. B.G. responded in kind. His

finger forcefully jabbed up into the air and halted suddenly, then was lowered a bit and quickly jabbed up to the same level again for emphasis. The man in the Nissan, however, kept his finger calmly up the whole time B.G. was giving him the finger and then turned.

Two minutes later B.G. saw the same driver speeding by, while shaping his hand into the form of a gun pointed at him. Explaining that he "felt violated and invaded," B.G. sped to catch up with the Nissan, then reached under his seat to pull out and point a gun. B.G. "now felt powerful." Proud of his "counterattack," he said to himself, "This isn't a finger, is it buddy?" The Nissan driver slammed on his brakes, and so did B.G., who then watched his opponent leave the scene on a side street. As B.G. saw that his opponent "had become submissive," he commented to himself with sarcasm and relish, "I guess he doesn't want to play anymore."

B.G.'s use of the play metaphor suggests that a kind of game theory is necessary to understand the social-psychological dynamics of anger in evolving interactions. Pairs of angry drivers often produce sets of moves along the lines of a game of dominos. Dominos are played with rectangular tiles, each of which is divided in half, each half either showing a blank face or displaying a set of one to six dots. In placing a tile, a player matches an as-yet-unmatched half of an opponent's tile and leaves a new challenge for the opponent to match. The winner is the player who adds his or her last tile to the growing chain, leaving his opponent stuck with unplaced tiles. The basic procedure of such a game, which is at once to match and provide a new challenge, is what often binds together the gestures of two angry drivers.

Unlike dominos players, however, drivers are not bound by common norms or a shared affiliation to rules that frame the domain of play within bounds of civility. Each may be quite willing to violate norms of safety and criminal laws while seeking to meet and go beyond the opponent. The dominos motif is produced through a shared understanding that one may transcend anger by re-presenting its provocation. Frequently the re-presentation is not quite identical to the pre-

ceding move but captures it in a new modality or adds the flourish of
awareness that the re-creation is a re-creation. In the last incident, for
example, B.G. provides a hard touch of reality as he mocks a mock
gun with a real one.

As in dominos, a player-driver cannot just repeat his prior moves
if he or she is to transcend anger by re-presenting it. What each gesticulating driver strives for is a narrative ending that will recast the
meaning of the entire interaction as leading up to this, the moment of
a last laugh. In search of a story line that will leave him or her one up
just as the last scene ends, the angry driver changes genres, tropes,
modalities.

The following example of automobile dominos reveals just such a
desperate and inventive search. Cesar, fifty-one and "middle class,"
has taken the day off to help his daughter handle the problems with
bank and credit card accounts that followed the theft of her purse. As
he approaches a stretch of road where a right-side lane ends and
merges into another, he sees a woman in a Jeep coming up the right
lane rapidly from the rear. He sees her as trying to get ahead substantially in traffic by exploiting the empty space that had been created by
cars that, like Cesar's, had already moved left.

There now develop four complementary moves in at least four
stages. The first phase of a given stage is designated A and its complement "B."

> 1A and 1B: Cesar accelerates so that the Jeep would not be able to
> cut into his lane, and then he watches the Jeep run up onto the curb,
> pass on the right, and cut in ahead of him anyway.
>
> 2A and 2B: Cesar honks, tailgates, and flips her off. She returns the
> hand gesture.
>
> 3A and 3B, and 4A: She turns right and he follows, racing up to her,
> lowering his window and shouting obscenities including "you goddamn
> bitch!" She responds with "you motherfucking cocksucker!" and [4A]
> she swerves her car to the right, toward his.
>
> 4B: As both throw insults and fingers toward each other, Cesar takes
> a turn that follows his route but takes him out of the interaction, but
> not before instructing his daughter to write down the license plate of
> the Jeep.

In 1A and B, Cesar meets his opponent's speedy effort to better
her position against everyone in traffic by mimicking her strategy and
adding a personal note, which he does by speeding up specifically in
response to her. She speeds and adds a new element, the innovative

use of the curb as a passing lane, an egregiously illegal move that attests to the power of her will.

In 2A and B, Cesar introduces nonverbal, audible and visual means of cutting into her experience; she responds in kind, holding on to the advantage of being ahead of him.

In 3A and B, Cesar adds insulting language, bringing the sexual theme, previously suggested by finger flipping, into the manifest focus of interaction; she responds in kind.

In 4A, she adds an element of physical assault. In 4B, Cesar appears to abandon the conflict, leaving her as the victor. But he has her license number and through his work in the insuring of cars, he tells his daughter, he will use her license number to access personal information, implying that he can affect her license or insurance costs. Cesar leaves, his anger transformed into a private, as yet unspecified scenario of sweet revenge. The scene ends as a win-win situation, each driver imagining that he or she has been left in the lead.

Doing battle on the public streets of Los Angeles, driver-storytellers do not need advice of the sort that is common in the area's sales-driven culture: "Close, close, close, always be closing." Anger rises in search of its transformation, and the drivers' chase evolves as each proposes to the other a finishing touch of this, that, or another sort. In the way that each attacks the other, he or she invokes an idiom of discourse, illustrates a form of vulnerability, and becomes a receptive audience for a sarcasm-tinged return of the complement. Each driver's fate is locked to the other's in perversely created stages of reciprocated assaults.

In the Wake of Angry Encounters: Some Common Negative Cases

Earlier I reviewed some examples of the celebratory spirits that can emerge when road warriors triumph in their battles. Obviously such happy outcomes are not always the case. What happens then is especially instructive about the causal contingencies of anger in everyday life. Cut off from a tacit engagement of their bodies in driving, losers of auto conflicts sometimes find that the experience leaves persistent bodily traces. It is remarkable that when people are interviewed on their experiences of becoming pissed off while driving, they commonly reach back months, even years to produce highly detailed versions of the events, and in the process of recounting them, they sometimes begin to relive the anger, becoming visibly animated, uptight, and voluble in front of the interviewer. The asymmetry of the recounting ("Here

I am, stuck with this unpleasant memory, while the real villain, indifferent to my pain, has escaped!") begins to re-create the emotion itself.

In the immediate aftermath of frustrated efforts to make in situ sense of road conflicts, interviewees provide the following sorts of reports.

> Flordelina, a twenty-two-year-old bank employee, recalls being cut off by a car pulling out of a parking lot. She also recalls noting that "the driver was a young male, possibly of Filipino or Spanish descent, in his early twenties." After she honked at him, he tailgated her and she found she could not lose him until she drove to a police station. "When I saw that he was completely out of sight, I could no longer hold in my emotions. I began to cry hysterically. I could not control myself. The tears raced down my face and my hands started shaking." Calling the bank, she excused herself from the day's work by telling them that a "family member was in a car accident. I could not tell them the truth. How could I? They would have probably thought that was the stupidest reason to miss work. I felt ashamed making up such a terrible story and I felt that they knew I was lying. What a weak person I am that I can not admit the truth. I felt so little. I went straight home to bed. My head was throbbing."

More commonly, angry drivers who fail to obtain in situ narrative victories soon manage to segue out of emotional distress. Often after a marked interval they gravitate to more modest forms of pleasure as they reassume their tacit corporeal involvements. Craig shows how a sigh facilitates the change.

> A doctor of Chinese medicine, Craig, thirty-six, father of three, divorced, is driving to dinner with his hand on the thigh of Maria [the interviewer], his girlfriend of four years. When a truck cuts in front of him, Craig yells, " 'He didn't even look before he changed lanes!' " After cutting off the truck in return, the truck cuts Craig off again, and Craig "whines, 'Geeez! Why don't ya just run me over and get it over with? You asshole!' " Then Craig sighs, marking a closure, and after the truck exits the highway, "Craig returned his right hand to my thigh, glanced at me with a smile, and asked what I planned to order at the restaurant."

For systematic reasons, there is relatively weak evidence on precisely how people move beyond anger when the emotion trails on and only diminishes gradually. When anger ends with a neat narrative flourish, the driver usually relishes the opportunity to recount the triumph. When the failure to construct a transcending drama leads to a rash or to hives, that too is easily recalled. But when the self-conscious awareness of anger fades more subtly into a renewed involvement in the practices of everyday life, almost by definition it will be more difficult for interviewees to recall just how the vanishing operation was brought off. It appears that what most commonly happens to such drivers is that anger fades as they get back "in the flow" of projects other than driving. A conversation is picked up with a passenger or with a co-respondent on the car phone. The radio is turned on or the station is changed, providing a new focus of attention. Thoughts turn away from the here and now to projects in scenes remembered and anticipated.

The social logic of emotional transformation that such examples suggest is that anger fades as one contemplates enacting a socially recognizable role in some other time or place in which his or her competent performance can be taken for granted. Just as the experience of being cut off or thrown out of tacit engagement in social interaction is the catalyst to anger, so envisioning oneself being embraced by some version of community appears to be the typical process for anger's mundane transcendence.

Sometimes, however, angry drivers want a quick fix. Unable to win a battle and impatient to transform their spirits in service of more fruitful ends, they often adopt proverbial formulations.

> Clarence, an accountant, screams impotently at traffic, " 'Fuck!!! We have barely moved in over half an hour!' " as he "pounded his fists against the steering wheel." Seeing a car attempting to bypass the blockage by driving on the right shoulder, he yells: " 'I am not going to let this fucking bitch in front of me.' " For a long stretch they play "cat and mouse" as she tries to get onto the road and he blocks her, until finally he gives up and lets her. " 'It's not worth an accident,' he said softly. . . . Oh well, fuck it. Life's a bitch.' "

"Life's a bitch" is not unlike Craig's device for marking the closure of a losing episode, his sigh. Indeed the phrase seems to articulate the subtext of many sighs, and the two work along similar lines to segue oneself out of anger. A sigh releases one's bodily hold on a situation, allowing one to relax or collapse into a new seating for experience. As a means of shifting the sensual base of experience, a sigh is a cultural convention and a neat corporeal trick.[22]

"Life's a bitch" casts Clarence's experience as just another instance of something that many others have come to recognize as part of the unavoidable unpleasantness of everyday life. "Life's a bitch" could be a caricature of a blues song. Like blues music, the phrase as used by Clarence implies not the dubious proposition that misery loves company but a wise strategy of emotional self-help. The phrase reframes a particular situated problem as a kind of misery that "everyone" is familiar with. Phrased as such, an instant's aggravation can be allowed to fade out of anger and into the communal background of all individual action.

4. Angry Drivers in Southern California's Public Life

It may seem by now that driving the streets of Los Angeles is routinely the stuff of high drama. There are good reasons for that misrepresentation. The most obvious is that this inquiry is not about driving in general but about a certain type of dramatic moment that occurs in the everyday practice of driving. The primary challenge here is to specify the conditions for the rise and decline of anger when driving, not to characterize the experience of driving in general or in any particular place.

A less obvious bias toward colorful interaction in these writings is built in for methodological reasons. The logic used here to relate evidence to explanation is analytic induction. Unlike quantitative social research and its probabilistic findings, data are described here only if they show a novel wrinkle of the explanation being advanced. The reason that I provide information on ethnicity, age, occupation, and other background factors in data passages is the same reason that I present materials that indicate differences in philosophies of life, musical taste, personal tactics, and the like. The objective is to demonstrate that the same social-psychological processes hold true even when we look at cases in which these factors vary. Each qualitatively different case presents a rival hypothesis to the explanation as advanced to that point, for example that the argument holds only within certain ethnic groups or personality types. In qualitative research what one worries about is not how high the pile of confirming evidence can be mounted but that one will have missed a way of life, an interaction strategy, or a kind of event that the reader knows intimately, and that in consequence the reader will come up with a counterexample that demonstrates the inadequacy of the explanation. As a result, qualitative social research that is boring to read because it reports many similar cases is likely to be weak in its evidentiary logic.

A third way that these writings are biased toward the dramatic is their social-psychological focus. The overall objective of this volume is to demonstrate what can be revealed about emotions when they are studied just where the socially situated and the biographically (or psychologically) transcendent dimensions of personal life meet. Whatever the failings of the current exercise, this topic and these materials are methodologically wonderful because they are so well suited to that demonstration. From a social-situational angle, the reports of angry drivers show the respondents paying close attention to their perception by others and creatively working to alter others' perceptions and responses. As for a perspective on biographically transcendent significance, the interviews allow us to see, within a very compact segment of the respondents' lives, much that is typically unavailable to a driver's accidentally chosen opponents. Through self-reports and close observations by passengers we can see how a situated interaction became meaningful to a driver as a phase he or she segued into from a prior involvement, as an obstacle to reaching an anticipated destination, and as an interruption of other, contemporaneously maintained attentions.

It is exactly at the intersection of the situational and the transcendent that everyday life routinely takes on its emotional force. Playwrights know this well, and the three lines of inquiry I follow in this volume track a familiar structure in dramatic theater. Playwrights often focus on (1) situations of conflictual interaction that (2) carry transcendent significance and (3) are best conveyed when the audience is drawn to focus on how actors represent the conflict in idiosyncratic corporeal ways. Materials structured along these lines are likely to be frequently poignant, often histrionic, sometimes very funny, and a very good way to summarize everyday life at what William James called the joints of experience.

In combination, these methodological considerations mean that a qualitative study of emotions—a topic that ought to be sensually interesting—*should* feature materials that border on the sensational. This is important to appreciate in order to avoid a false impression about life in Los Angeles. Of the approximately 150 people who were contacted for the data in this research, virtually nobody had any difficulty recalling an experience of becoming pissed off while driving. Diversity of background and personal style is itself a good reason for locating the study of everyday emotions in Los Angeles (although on those grounds there are numerous, equally attractive sites in contemporary world cities). But the number who would say that these conflicts represent a constant quality of their driving experience is a good deal smaller.

Yet if these materials do not provide a representative picture of everyday life in Los Angeles, that does not mean they fail to say something significant about Los Angeles. Certainly they do not show that driving is more productive of conflicts in Los Angeles than elsewhere. Angelenos might be surprised to learn that many Europeans consider Southern California drivers to be relatively "good." American academ-

ics often swear that Boston drivers have discovered regions of driving
incompetence whose very existence remains beyond suspicion elsewhere in the civilized world. Residents of Mexico City warn, without
any touch of humor, that it is out of the question to respond with a
finger to someone who you think has cut you off, and not because
drivers there are unlikely to appreciate the meaning of the gesture.

And New Yorkers, whose streets are filled in far higher proportion
with commercial traffic, might well regard Angelenos' experiences of
becoming pissed off while driving as amateurish rather than amazing.
Vince, a former Manhattan delivery driver, recalled for me his coworkers' practice of collecting (metal) slugs in dishes in the company vans
so that they would be readily available to be thrown at "assholes."
Vince also described professional tactics for exploiting New York's
unparalleled traffic jams, including that of leaping over car roofs from
the conveniently elevated perch of the van in order to stamp an appropriate message onto the thinly covered heads of offending drivers.
Traffic is rarely bad enough to permit those tactics in L.A., despite
hyperbolic references in L.A. to "gridlock." The term itself is revealing
in its apocalyptic significance, in contrast to the unremarkable, everyday realities of "traffic jams" in New York and "embouteillage" in
Paris.

For the most part, there is no reason to suspect that the conditions
of the emotional metamorphosis of the pissed-off driver obtain
uniquely in L.A.[23] Virtually everywhere driving is likely to be a dumb
way of moving around in public. Encased in a relatively mute form
for movement, the driver senses an asymmetry in interaction: one suspects that one watches others more than those others are oriented to
pick up the meager expressions of one's inexpressive vehicle. This
asymmetry of perception is turned on its head occasionally, and then
to great effect, when drivers manage to be seen extensively without
appearing to care who is watching. Such inversions of driving's routine
perversion of complementary perceptions are accomplished when
"low riders" cruise Hollywood Boulevard on Saturday nights and
when Rolls Royces inch their way through the narrow streets of St.
Tropez during high season. But such practices of putting cars on parade are no more typical of everyday life in France than they are in
Los Angeles.

The current data set does not permit the testing of themes of national or regional cultural differences in what might be termed mobilized awareness contexts, or how drivers monitor the awareness that
other drivers may have of them. But it is not likely that a model of
awareness contexts on Southern California's public behavior can be

extended without severe qualification to other settings.[24] Images of cold New Yorkers aside, in many European and Latin American small towns as well as big cities, in uncrowded as well as in crowded circumstances, strangers routinely negotiate physically intimate pedestrian passings without acknowledging one another's existence. The custom in some U.S. settings of offering smiles and greetings to passing strangers, an act that presupposes that one will not only allow but encourage the other to see that one is looking at him or her, may be relatively odd. The intensity of road rage in the United States may well be related. Where people are unusually eager to have strangers acknowledge and respond to them with fleeting positive moral communications, they may be especially vulnerable to feeling offended when they are treated indifferently.[25] Being cut off is perhaps more likely in L.A. than on European streets, but partly because of a marginal difference in the embodiment of the driving experience, not because of differences in driving practices. The U.S. auto market is somewhat exceptional in encouraging drivers to feel that when their cars are cut off, they are cut off personally. The makes and models available in the United States far exceed the diversity available in most other affluent nations, which still maintain severe restrictions on auto imports in order to protect the domestic industries. The result is a kind of vehicular sumptuary code that limits the differentiated display of motorized personality. The diversity of makes and models available in the U.S. market elaborates and individualizes the vehicular expression of social stratification to an extent unparalleled elsewhere. When the symbols one displays are more matters of status than expressions of individual personality, attacks on those symbols may be less intimate matters.[26]

To the contribution made by America's capitalism and its free trade automobile policies Los Angeles adds a justly famous, dispersed economic geography and a limited system of public transportation. These factors flow together to outfit an especially high proportion of its citizens with exceptionally personalized car bodies that they will inhabit for unusually large parts of their everyday lives. Given the range of activities that Angelenos pursue as they drive, it is no exaggeration to say that their driving is a way of sustaining private involvements while moving around public space. The use of stickers to display political views, spiritual philosophies, and peculiar versions of humor on the rear ends of cars indicates that the drivers take for granted that their automobilized doings are intertwined directly with their personal beings.

With respect to the narrative expression of anger, Los Angeles is also at the extreme in the universality with which drivers comfortably dramatize their aggressive disdain for each other. It is not surprising to see an elegantly styled, middle-aged woman, perfectly coiffed and cosmetically sealed, who, while driving through Beverly Hills in a speck-free, gleaming new Mercedes SL 500, suddenly raises a three-karat-diamond-studded fist to project "the finger" to an unkempt driver of a shabby, ten-year-old Japanese economy car. What is striking about such scenes is that any sense of incongruity is apparent only to the sociological observer. Crude gestures lose no face where face depends exclusively on the display of such hard realities as diamonds and cars. No doubt it is true that in L.A., as in Latin America, in their private lives "los ricos tambien lloran" (the rich also cry), to borrow the title of a popular Mexican soap opera. What is extraordinary in L.A. is the motif in public life that "los ricos tambien se enojan" (the rich also get angry). It is, in a way, a triumph of Southern California's version of democracy that, substantially independent of their social status, people feel free to engage in behavior that elsewhere would be eschewed as shamefully common and rude.[27]

Even if becoming angry while driving is not more common in Los Angeles than in other cities, I would submit that the experience still has special significance within the context of Southern California life. For one thing, public culture here has relatively few resources for managing conflict among citizens. It is paradoxical that in Western European settings with enviable reputations for civility, it is not uncommon to see motorists standing outside their cars, gesticulating broadly and trading round after round of shouted insults at each other, with mere centimeters separating their noses. In a sense, the ability to trade insults in close interaction bespeaks faith in a cultural fabric strong enough to absorb pointed interpersonal thrusts while blocking actual physical contact. Meanwhile, drivers in Los Angeles, citing news stories of highway shootings, report a growing sense of anxiety about how other drivers might respond were they to meet face to face. Where avoiding sustained, intimate interaction with an offending driver is deemed essential, flipping off from a safe and speedy distance should be especially attractive.

Even within the United States, there appears to be a peculiar resistance in California's public culture against accepting the inevitability of conflict. In New York, as Calvin Trillin noted in a piece on residents' reactions when repairs of a subway station finally were completed, the removal of an everyday justification for expressing anger can lead to something like withdrawal symptoms on a massive scale.[28] In California, in contrast, anger in public is more likely to be treated as pathological, and this perspective has given rise to a distinctive remedial response, the effort to inoculate the driving public with Zen teachings.

Zen-inspired writings on driving call for an involvement in the sensual and aesthetic rhythms of the practice. Countering the familiar critique of highway driving as a major failure of modern civilization, Zen writers wax poetic on the possibilities "where the road and the sky collide."[29] This philosophy, by revealing the profundities potential in a total involvement of consciousness in driving, might seem geared to exacerbate anger by building up the value of what other drivers might cut off. But the claim is just the opposite. Unpredictable, even dangerous moves by other drivers are appreciated as just another source of provocation, like the irregular contour of the road, to which one should maintain a lively responsiveness.

Zen driving neatly avoids the rise of anger, or any emotion other than the metaphysical pleasure of remaining in the flow of responsive driving itself, by avoiding the possibility of being cut off from concerns that transcend driving. With regard to the explanation advanced here, this philosophy in effect calls for the negation of the asymmetrical state of social interpretation that sets the stage for the rise of anger. The Zen driver is no more able to make him- or herself heard or seen as a person by other drivers, but there no longer is any asymmetry because other cars are no longer seen as managed by personalized beings. Driving in this manner, one is perhaps even more with others in an objective sense, interacting smoothly as part of a collectively arranged pattern of cars on the highway, but one no longer is with particular others. Once the windshield has been converted into a kind of computer game screen, it makes no sense to get mad at enemy attackers; the point is just to stay alert and respond effectively to them. But if driving takes on novel forms of pleasure when other drivers are transformed into blips on the windshield screen, they no longer appear in one's experience as moral beings. If a driver does not read through the outward appearance of other cars into the personal awareness that other drivers have of him or her, those other drivers cannot be people whose gracious courtesy demands acknowledgment or whose dangerous narcissism requires that they be taught a lesson they will not soon forget.[30]

In effect, Zen teachings call for drivers to abandon their efforts to do folk sociology on the road. Focusing solely on the aesthetics of driving, one abandons the effort to learn through interacting with strangers the kinds of people who are out there and, by juxtaposition, to discover and test one's own nature and to learn whether one is more or less aggressive, courteous, alert, capable of simultaneous engagement in multiple activities, etc. That can be seen as a kind of loss. In the course of one's routine activities, at no extra monetary cost, conflicts in driving provide regular sessions for a personal working through of a central dilemma of urban life, the challenge to shift rapidly across encounters with indifferent others in diverse and unpredictable social situations while trying to keep aligned with the transcendent values of one's life.

Perhaps a mass conversion to Zen driving would substantially improve the physical, economic, and mental health of California drivers. That is not the issue here. The peculiar appeal of Zen in California culture indicates a discomfort with accepting conflict as part of public life. Other such indications include the lack of the biting political satire that is traditional in older urban centers throughout the Western world. For over twenty-five years, the prevailing image of the mayor of Los Angeles has been as a "nice" man, black or white, a man who neither issues nor receives much public ridicule, who shows no relish for humiliating opponents, makes and receives no nasty charges of personal incompetence, is innocent of ego-celebrating wit . . . in sum, a mayor who fails utterly to produce the cultural stuff that can make urban politics an involving show for the masses. Dramas with just those culturally innovative moral passions are going on every day in Los Angeles, but the site is the road, not the press. Played out not among figures on a communal stage but among individuals who meet as strangers in fleeting contacts on public roads, these moralized passions contribute significantly to a sense of chaos and lack of metropolitan community in Los Angeles.

Oddly enough, car travel puts people in Southern California in a relatively communistic social place.[31] Belying its name and socialist appeal, "public" transportation segregates commuters by social class and ethnicity in Los Angeles, as it does in other American cities. Public transportation groups and separates metropolitan residents, the extreme case being the suburban train commuter who parks in a pastoral bedroom community setting, travels above and under lower- and working-class neighborhoods, and then emerges from a city train station within walking distance of his or her office, where bus and subway commuters bring the night's accumulated faxes and the morning coffee. Adults in L.A. probably interact regularly in their commuting with a more diverse sample of the area's population than is the case in perhaps any other large city. However insulated and unrepresentative these contacts may in fact be, they encourage the construction of a personal image of the area as a whole. As population density and travel times grow, an image of conflictual diversity is displacing the area's prior image of homogeneity and tranquility.[32]

It would diverge too far from the social interaction data base of this chapter to examine at length the historical developments and the features of political and economic structure that have given Los Angeles its distinctive character. But one final point about the significance of these conflicts for the drivers in them may be brought out. Coming to terms with those everyday tensions is part of the larger struggle of the area to come to terms with being a massive urban center while still wearing suburban cultural clothing.[33] Drivers' conflicts in L.A. may not represent unusual levels of anger so much as an unusual inability to make communal sense of conflict. In turn, this inability makes the experience of conflict in public a challenge that is left to the creative devices of individuals who, in the afterglow of chaotic encounters, regularly look to dinner table conversations to get interpretive revenge against the assholes confronted that day.

Whether or not driving and its emotional upshots are any different in Los Angeles, people in L.A. think it is. The respondents who provided the data for these writings stressed one after the other how driving in L.A. is different from what it was in Nebraska, in Salinas, in New York, in New Jersey. Always there is more chaos in Los Angeles. (One charming myth about New Jersey, for example, is that there the truck drivers, acting like rough but lovable mafiosi, enforce a discipline on the road that ultimately works to everyone's benefit.) And from longtime residents of Los Angeles, one hears again and again, often as a preface to intimations that it is time to leave, how the incivility one now confronts on the road every day was unthinkable just fifteen years ago.

Having lost the ethnic homogeneity that underwrote a broadly publicized image of the area as America's last chance for a pacific (and white) community, experiencing on a personal level the impacts of massive population growth and diversification, served by a public culture that is ill equipped to recognize conflict, L.A. residents innocently enter their cars and drive with everlasting incredulity into daily encounters with impassioned chaos. It may well be that there is nothing about the area that goes far to explain why drivers so often get pissed off in Los Angeles. But residents' experience of getting pissed off when driving is one of the few resources that become routinely and democratically available in residents' everyday participation in public life for understanding what is happening in Los Angeles.

Appendix: Guide for Driving Interview

Your Written Product

Your initial objective is to record, as best you can, just what happens when people get mad driving around L.A. Your *report should not contain any analysis or any of your ideas to explain what happened,* unless you talked about that with your subject. The descriptive report should detail how the person you are studying experienced the events, not what you think they mean. The words, phrases, style should be those of the person you are studying: how did they act, how do they talk about the events, what do they think about the other people involved, what do they think these events mean.

Selecting a Subject

Find someone over thirty years old. Explain that you are in a class that is studying emotions in everyday life, and that there is a class assignment to get descriptions of what people experience when driving around L.A., in particular the scenes that make them mad. If you like, you might ask to take a ride with someone; that might get them to remember lots of events that they found irritating, even if they don't get mad at anything that time. And if the first person you meet tells you they never get mad when driving, find someone else. You should not have to look very far!

You may find that the person can describe one recent event in some detail. That's fine. Often, people asked about getting angry when driving have lots of stories. That's fine too.

How to Record

If you tape-record your discussion with your subject, you will find that you have to spend a lot of time transcribing the tape. That is not necessary. It's fine to have a natural discussion and then, as soon as you can after leaving the scene, write down as much as you can remember. If you want to take notes, just jot down a few phrases that will help you recall what was said. But don't start writing down everything your subject says. Your first commitment is to have a natural conversation with the person. Be yourself; don't let note taking make you artificial.

Anonymity

Don't identify the person by their real name; use just a first name or a pseudonym, even if they are related to you, even if they say you could use their name. Do identify the person by age, sex, occupation, how you know them, where they live (generally).

What to Look For

It's best to read these suggestions and absorb them, and then have a natural conversation, rather than holding up a list of these guides and following them mechanically.

Your description should include the five Ws: Who, what, when, where, and (in the view of the person you're studying) why or what they think the event means (about them, others, driving, life). You can check yourself, after you've written up a description, that those elements are present somewhere in the report.

But your organizing focus is *the big H:* How, as in, how did this happen? What's the process? How did it begin? What happened next? What happened after that? What did you do when he/she did that? What stages did the event go through? The report should describe how your interviewee is doing something with or to someone else, how the other is responding, and so on.

As background, you want to describe: How did your subject come to be at that place then? They were on their way where, for what? How had they been driving? What had been going on for them? What had they been doing? What happened afterward?

If You Get Stuck

If you get stuck in the discussion or interview, and you don't know what else to ask, and it doesn't seem you've got much, there are a few pretty reliable things you can do to get things moving. First, wait. Silence on your part will often lead the other person to think more and find more to relate. A little silence on your part is okay. You don't have to fill every moment with sound. The hardest part of interviewing is being a good listener. The less you say, the more you can be confident that what you record is their perspective and experience, not yours.

Second, after they've told you about something happening, you can ask them to set it in the Ws (where did it happen; when . . .), and you can ask them "just how" it happened. After they tell you about one event or action, you can say, "And then what?"

Third, you can play off of their experiences onto your own, with a "that reminds me of. . . ." A good way to interview people is to share your experiences; that shows them the sort of thing you're after, and that you're not judging them from some position of moral superiority. This approach would also tend to make the conversation a discussion rather than an "interview," and that's preferable. Then you can write up your own experiences with the interview, because your experiences will have been part of the interview.

What Are You Looking For?

If you look too closely for anything, you will turn the report into an analytic exercise, so the guides here have to be general and gentle. One focus is the practice of driving: Just how does this person drive? How do they get from here to there? What strategies, if any, do they use? What do they do when they drive? What do they look at and not look at as they drive? Another is how they "read" others: What do they see as signals from other drivers? What kinds of people do they think other drivers are? How do they understand what other drivers are doing? A third is: What are the especially emotional forms of behavior? If someone got mad, how do you or they know? What showed the anger?

TWO

FAMILIES AND FUNNY MIRRORS

Fun houses are sociologically provocative because they are not necessarily funny. Many visitors walk through halls of distorting mirrors at amusement parks without appearing to notice that their passage is shedding a series of weird reflections. Some treat the mirrors as opportunities for grooming, acting as if it is their appearance in everyday life that is distorted and not the hyper-elongated, fat and squat, or many-headed creature that the mirrors portray (figure 2.1).

Those who become pleasurably engaged with the concave and convex mirrors often develop interests that are other than humorous. Young couples strolling through the fun house arm in arm may silently catch a reflection of their bodies merging, and find the inviting outline of a kiss (figure 2.2). In the 1930s, André Kertész made alluring photographic studies of the nude female form by turning such mirrors on their sides (figure 2.3). In like aesthetic spirits, some visitors become intrigued to move their hands and torsos intently before the mirrors, seemingly indifferent to the fact that in their explorations it is their own identities that are strangely redesigned.

Halls of distorting mirrors are methodologically appealing sites for an inquiry into emotional process. Although the strip of laughing behavior that one finds there may be exceedingly narrow, it is massively recurrent. The contingent nature of laughter invites considerations of two sorts. What does it take to make the mirrors funny? And what meaning do people take from the experience?

On the one hand, the fact that humor, while "natural" to this setting, is far from inevitable in it points to the work that visitors must do in order to construct their emotions. In this vein, we will see that the participants exercise a highly refined attention to the details of interaction to show others that they experience the mirrors as funny and to create a collective warrant for the seemingly casual behavior of laughter. Finding these mirrors laughably funny is systematically

Figure 2.1 Grooming

Figure 2.2 Kiss

unimportant behavior but it is still elaborately skilled work. On the other hand, laughter here is not always just a matter of work. Although at times participants appear to "do" laughter instrumentally and strategically, at other times people seem genuinely, even overwhelmingly inspired by the free spirits they have conjured up.

We meet again the issue that introduced this volume. Emotions are at once subjective phenomena, experiences that are personally and idiosyncratically shaped, but also experiences of being pushed and pulled by the world, of being an object taken by forces beyond one's control. From Freud to the functionalist sociologists of the 1960s, study of the socially situated, interactive doings of emotions was neglected in favor of the motivational dynamics that compel emotional expressions. Such work would emphasize, for example, that laughter evokes and masks an aggressive wish or conflicted sexual desire,[1] resolves an apprehension of embarrassment,[2] or serves a purpose in sustaining hierarchical power.[3] But the authors paid little if any attention to the situational contingencies that govern the ripening of such ongoing and common motivational forces into particular and disparate moments of laughter. Our everyday lives would contain a very different mix of pleasures if embarrassment, hierarchical tensions, and sexual desires always produced laughter, but for better or worse, they surely do not.

Figure 2.3 Kertész © Estate of André Kertész

A generation of microanalytic studies, working first off of audio recordings and more recently from videotapes, have now made clear that motivating forces and purposes do not automatically, randomly, or simply manifest themselves in perceptible expression. The emergence of laughter, they show, is governed by a sensitive monitoring of gaze, pause, and sequential behavior, all conducted with an eye to the consequences for shaping interaction (usually conversations) with other people.[4] But microanalytic studies have overargued their case. Applied to humor and laughter, they make the mechanics of laughter appear to be so excruciatingly burdensome, one wonders how anyone could do so much onerous interaction work and still have fun.

The current study seeks to demonstrate that the machinations of "doing" laughter as well as the dynamics for being "done by" humor can be explained within a seamless analytical perspective. The data set consists of some eight hours of videotape recordings made with a Hi8 camera and standard microphone during eight visits to the Jardin d'Acclimatation, a Parisian public park located in the Bois de Boulogne, in 1991 and 1992. On pleasant summer days it draws thousands of French and international visitors. Close to the entrance is a triangular, Plexiglas-enclosed building with ten mirrors, several two-sided.

The camera was used openly in a variety of ways: held in a stationary position to catch groups passing before given mirrors; carried through the hall to document the sequence of stops made by a given group; held outside the hall and trained on passages through the exit and entrance portals. The videotapes contain 187 "episodes," an episode being defined as a workably clear audio and video segment in which, minimally, one or more individuals approaches, examines, "works," and then leaves a mirror that is the target of the camera's fixed focus. Most episodes fall toward the middle of a range that runs from fifteen seconds to two minutes in length. In addition, the videotaped record includes hundreds of people who are seen in more visually or audibly obscured ways, or who are clearly and completely traced when they are deeper in the hall but not at a mirror targeted by the camera, or who are picked up making fleeting contact with a targeted mirror.

Analysis proceeded in four stages. First, I logged each taping session, the entries consisting of identifying tags for each segment and notations about reactivity and audiovisual quality. Next, I developed narratives describing the visuals of each such episode and outlining the audio track. Then, for about two dozen segments in which reactivity was minimal, I worked with native speakers at the level of visual detail afforded by frame-by-frame playback, and we described audible and visual action for each person in relation to the ongoing behavior of the others in the segment. In drafting this chapter, I worked with these written descriptions and with the videotape itself, creating diagrams and providing further details for the interaction when required by the argument.

People treat fun house images as laughable through a three-phase process. In general, individuals who experience the mirrors in isolation from others do not find them laughably funny. It is necessary to construct a relationship that enables the would-be laugher to take for granted that he or she and another person will share the would-be laugher's appreciation of the distorted image. Section 1 describes the maneuvers by which visitors create a presumptively intersubjective experience of the mirrors.

In order to laugh at the mirror it is necessary to perceive a dynamic tension between a person as depicted by the mirror and that person's presumptively normal identity. Section 2 discusses this tension. Different sets of visitors use recurrent tactics and metaphors to build juxtapositions between contradictory realities. The initial force of the humor is developed out of a pressure to "get" the juxtaposition in order to demonstrate that one has not fallen out of relationship with another person. In effect, laughter initially emerges as a transformation into a positive expression of the potential for a shamelike recognition that one has awkwardly failed to maintain contact with a companion. Put colloquially, laughter here is a response to the question, "Got it?" where not to "get it" is to be "out of it."

Section 3 examines the socioaesthetic logic of the bodily practices of laughter. Laughter is not a thought nor is it simply a statement. In order to be recognized as laughing, the person must employ his or her body in specific ways. In effect, the laughing person fractures his or her body to represent corporeally the juxtapositions elicited by the mirrors. In laughing the person transcends the provocative juxtaposition, demonstrating that he or she "got it" by manifestly being in touch with two places at once. The process is best described as a metamorphosis, a transformation of embodied metaphor, along the lines of turning oneself inside out.

For adults, initial laughs in the fun house are often relatively artificial expressions to a companion that one finds the situation funny. At times, however, there is a marked shift from "doing laughter" to a phase of being "done by" humor. Section 4 examines this shift, which entails a second metamorphosis, a change in laughing that is corporeally distinguishable from the first, for example in a shift from exhale to inhale laughter or from an initial exclamatory bleat or chuckle to an ascending riff that takes off from a markedly higher octave. The grounds for the shift from doing laughter to being done by humor is usually the achievement of the first metamorphosis, in which laughing bodies are employed to celebrate the achievement of presumptively shared experience.

In the transition from "doing" to "being done by" the spirit of laughter, we see people bumping up against what we might call the laws of socio-physiques. Laughing is a way of expressing that one is in two places, or two frames of meaning, at once, and that one has the will or spirit to enjoy the challenge of appreciating the tension between them. People routinely laugh in neatly packaged forms when they are indicating that, while they "got" one frame of meaning, they remain firmly anchored in another that has remained essentially unshaken. The novel problem presented by fun house mirrors is that they can easily turn attentions to what had been the corporeal basis for laughter. As visitor-viewers try to use their bodies to laugh at given aspects of their appearance, they can easily find the mirrors irresistibly grabbing bodily machinations for laughing and throwing them onto the stage of mutual attentions. When the background bodily practices that are used to generate laughter themselves become socially visible, an existential limit on social interaction is reached.

As visitors watch the mirrors collapse *what* one is laughing about and *how* one is laughing, the corporeal basis of social expression breaks down and wild emotions break out. When funny mirrors get really funny, they reveal something quite serious. People can competently present themselves to others only when they can simultaneously guard the machinations for doing so in a hidden bodily domain.

It is not necessary for people to be family members to make fun house mirrors funny, but the fact that they usually are is not a matter of chance. Family relationships are active not only in bringing people to the amusement park and segregating the experiences of people as they pass through; people here work concertedly to create a humorous experience that will construct the family as a spiritually vivid entity (section 5 explores this phenomenon). Much is done, for example, to instruct small children on how to regard the images as funny in a specific, family-sharable way, and to alternate experiences as humorous target and responsive audience across generational divides. A powerful if tacit narrative about the family is constructed through these maneuvers. What is most commonly celebrated is the distinctive capacity of the family to make transcendent sense of the distorted images that the outside world makes of one's identity in everyday life. This microstudy of laughter in the fun house, then, is also an essay in the sociology of the family.

As the analysis follows this five-step sequence, the data presentation will narrow, moving from an ethnographic style to the examination of given families coordinating their movements and audible expressions. For various points, in particular in order to show people shifting from "doing" to "being done by" laughter, it is necessary to view specific gestures and utterances within the history of the interaction, and even though this history may be no more than a minute long, it takes substantial textual space to convey the relevant background—so much space, in fact, that the detailed description of more than a handful of cases would be impractical. For this reason the reader will become increasingly familiar with three key family interactions, known by the handles of *T'es bellle, Louis,* and *SupEr.*

1. Constructing a Presumption of Shared Viewing

The relationship between laughing and being with another is massive in the fun house. People usually do not laugh alone. But there are exceptions to this proposition and in these negative cases lie indications of the underlying rule. An individual not infrequently pauses before a mirror, works his or her reflection a bit, then lets out a clearly truncated laugh and quickly turns to summon others. Sometimes a person standing alone before a mirror will emit a brief laugh that itself effectively beckons a companion who is elsewhere in the hall. On some occasions a solo viewer's laugh appears to be spontaneous, but then the laugher will issue an explicit summons (here most commonly, "X, viens, viens voir!") or rush off to pull another to the scene, in either case providing a retrospective cover of community for the benefit of any observing strangers who might otherwise raise curious eyebrows. Such laughter-summons sequences are characteristically adult behaviors. Children occasionally laugh in so prolonged a fashion that the noise itself serves as an extended, nagging summons. Young children, in a pattern that belies the spontaneity of any one moment of their laughter, often repeat a laugh-summons sequence, returning again and again to the mirror to shriek and insistently call a distant parent.

In these cases, the laugher, although alone, pays tribute to the necessity of copresence by attempting to construct a social environment to sustain his or her laughter. But it is not simply physical proximity that is sought. In another common pattern, adolescents and younger children may tour the hall in tightly related sets, running after and pulling each other along, with each laughing briefly in unsuccessful attempts to draw the others' attentions to the laugher's mirrored image. A particular kind of attention from another is necessary if it is to sustain more than invitational bursts of laughter.

Seeing What the Other Sees

If one person observes another who is observing his or her own reflections in the mirror, neither may find the occasion humorous. Even when two people are "with" each other, moving as companions to stop before the same mirrors at the same times, laughter typically will not emerge unless both can assume that they are observing the same reflection. This may seem obvious, but it is a principle of laughter that adults must sometimes discover for themselves. In *Françoise, de toi*, for example, a woman of grandmotherly age [GM], acts rather stiffly with her young companion, a girl five years old,[5] Françoise, and only gradually comes to appreciate what we might term a first-order condition for making the mirrors laughable.

> As Françoise looks at the target mirror, GM points at a right angle toward the mirror *while turning* from the mirror *toward the girl*, and says, *"Françoise, de toi"* [Françoise, {there's a reflection} of you.] [figure 2.4.1]. Françoise, however, responds to the turn of GM's gaze, so that by the time GM's comment emerges, Françoise is no longer looking at the mirror but at GM.
>
> Françoise then shifts her gaze back to the mirror, but GM remains

Figure 2.4.1 GM and Françoise 1

Figure 2.4.2 GM and Françoise 2

looking at the girl, and Françoise, catching the direction of GM's gaze in the mirror, again turns away from the mirror toward GM. Françoise can see that when she is seeing herself in the mirror, GM is not, and the child responds to the direction of GM's gaze rather than to the target of her verbal urging [figure 2.4.2].

Neither laughs here. But moving to another mirror, GM alters her strategy. This time GM leads Françoise into a shared, squared-off, stationary position, *both oriented directly toward the mirror* with feet and gaze. GM further promotes Françoise's involvement with the mirror by taking a small step toward it, thus implying "look, I'm looking." On a recoil from this step, GM lifts her shoulders abruptly and issues a laugh, more or less a "WwHHhaay." The relationship necessary for eliciting laughter, this segment suggests and dozens of other initially "successful" episodes demonstrate, is not simply for one to gaze at another gazing at the mirror; *the two must appear to each other to see the same thing.*

Recognizing that Another Grasps One's Perspective

Even with two people attending to the reflections of one, humor also routinely fails to ripen into laughter when they remain strangers to one another. This hall of mirrors is often heavily populated, with many more sets of eager participants than "glaces bizarres" (or "miroirs déformants") to serve them. Little queues often form, with an emissary from one set waiting for a current set to move off so that he or she might step in front, personally test the mirror, and decide whether to summon others of his or her set. Even when a set of people in front of a mirror breaks into hysterical laughter, bystanders who look on from just behind or slightly to one side, often smile broadly but rarely laugh (figure 2.5). When the current laughing set vacates the reflecting space, members of a bystanding set will often immediately move in and quickly turn from a posture of pleasantry into emphatic laughter. The reflections that the new set projects onto the mirror will not be more bizarre than what they had seen from the sidelines, but what they now see *reflects back* onto their prior relationships to each other.

What does prior relationship provide that makes it a significant resource for finding fun house mirrors laughably funny? A stranger on the sideline can see a distorted image and can see the raw fact that a person is regarding his or her distorted image. The reflected party knows he or she is being seen in the mirror, and that his or her self-observing is also seen. The two may thus share a target of perception and awareness that the other shares the view. But those who wait on the side usually respect the fictive privacy of the reflected person's experience. And the person squared off in front of the mirror usually will not let on or demonstrate that he or she sees the stranger's seeing, at least not until he or she is ready to abandon the mirror. Thus, bystanders in the fun house routinely hang on the outskirts and unabashedly watch while a set of mutually acquainted people gaily laugh as they use their hips and chests to strike outrageously ribald poses, and the bystanders effortlessly maintain a demeanor of sober spectators. Companions, in contrast, can stand parallel to each other, conducting

Figure 2.5 Bystanders smile but don't laugh

a side-by-side looking into the mirror, and take for granted not only that each sees *what* is in the mirror but also that *each sees the other's seeing* of what is in the mirror.

It is, however, of fundamental significance that the reflected person in front of the mirror and the stranger observing from a near sideline may quickly move the interaction to shared laughter. A brief glance to the sideline observer by the reflected party can suffice, if the glance is caught or acknowledged by the sideline observer. Henceforth, the reflections can take on a retrospective aspect; they can become comments on the newly established social relationship.

Tactics for Intersubjective Seeing

Even for closely associated people, it often takes tricky work to create a common presumption that they share a perspective on the mirror. First there are serious physical obstacles. Much of the play with these mirrors consists of slight movements back and forth and from side to side to catch how the reflected image unexpectedly changes. People who are engaged in "working" the mirrors in these ways acquire evidence that a companion who is situated at a different angle or distance from the mirror may not be seeing the same thing. An adult who wishes to demonstrate the amusing qualities of a mirror will frequently lift a child clear off the ground, tucking the child's head right under the adult chin. Some mirrors in the hall are up on stilts that make it impossible for small children to catch any reflections of themselves without such assistance, but the lift that adults give to their minicompanions is also common at full-length mirrors, where it serves more specifically to position sets of eyes in a proximity that suggests that gazes overlap (figures 2.6.1 and 2.6.2).

A second major condition of the presumption of a common perception is resolving the aspect of the reflected image that is to be taken as distorted. The possibilities are infinite, although field observation quickly reveals that unrelated sets of visitors come up with several fairly standard solutions for each mirror. Thus, in front of the mirror that was the camera's target in the episodes examined in this paper, participants often referred to: the large head of a member of the set; contrasting distortions high and low on the mirror that could produce a "dwarf" with an enormous head; multiple images of a single person that could be produced at certain distances and angles; and areas of merging body masses. The hall resounds with such phrases as: "un p'tit nain avec une grosse tete" [a little dwarf with a big head]; "Maman, viens voir comment on est gros là" [come see how big we are here]; "Regarde le zig-zag"; "Il faudra que tes jambes grossIIISSEnt" [you must fatten up your legs, i.e., your legs are too skinny]; "grosse tête"; "I'ya deux têtes, eh" [there are two heads!]); "Shuis tout maig{re}" [I'm so thin].

One movement, an especially neat solution to the challenge of promoting shared awareness of a joint focus, was spontaneously popular with many visitors. The taller person in the set, in most cases an adult with a child, would slowly move his or her hand down toward the head of the smaller figure, creating a visual merger between the pointing-grabbing gesture of the taller and the center of perception of the smaller (figures 2.7.1 and 2.7.2). The adult would at once figuratively touch the child's subjectivity and put the child in touch with the adult's subjectivity by demonstrating where the adult's perception was trained.

Visitors would also promote a seeing of their seeing by invoking metaphors that, once grasped, could guide their companions through a sequence of references. In *SupEr,* for example, after initiating laughter, a father and son cooperatively create a series of comments around head and neck features. (In the process they establish a cadence that may have evoked the familiar series of comments by the wolf in the Red Riding Hood story.) In this segment, the son has ambled up to

Figure 2.6.1 Child raised to adult chin 1

Figure 2.6.2 Child raised to adult chin 2

the target mirror, has made a beckoning motion, and has called for and been joined by "PaPA." PaPA stands at well over six feet and peers into the mirror from a position directly behind his five-year-old, three-foot son, who has been squared off and peering in. When PaPA arrives and says "Oh," the boy starts laughing, and PaPA moves his hand toward the boy's ears (figure 2.8). PaPA then drops his hands back down and says, "Ah! les grosses oreilles" [Ah, huge ears!]. The boy tries to utter something, but is laughing, the trunk of his body

Figure 2.7.1 Adult touching child's head

Figure 2.7.2 Taller child touching smaller child's head

shaking, and what he emits is: "La d. . .{xxx} hhch {xxx} hhch." PaPA offers: "HAh!. . .{pause} les grosses dents" [Hah. Huge teeth!], and then, "Ah! le grand cou" [neck].[6]

Adults often provide more subtle and instructive introductory guidance by producing idiosyncratic and dramatic gestures that are geared to be seen by their companions before their companions land in a position to identify the matters designated. In *T'es bellle,* for example, a father arrives at the target mirror shortly after his four-year-old son, and then calls his wife and their seven-year-old daughter, who are tour-

Figure 2.8 Papa tickles his son's ears

ing mirrors further into the center of the hall. He must call several times before they begin to come, all the while trying to sustain the boy's interest.

What is of interest here is the somewhat strained posture with which he seeks to meet the interactional challenge of preparing wife and daughter to know, at the moment when they arrive at a position to see it, that they will immediately be seeing a particular image in the deforming mirror that they have never before imagined to exist. The father raises his arms and holds them out perpendicular to his body, like airplane wings; but it is not the substantive gesture alone that bespeaks his sense of interactional challenge. There is a peculiar, tortuous, inverse relation between his audible summonses and the alteration of his gaze from the mirror and toward the absent others. Three times he calls to his wife while facing directly the target mirror, turning to verify whether she is responding only after his call is finished. As he calls, he holds his gaze on the mirror's reflections of his airplanelike posture, pointing with his gaze to the target of his audible summons (figures 2.9.1 and 2.9.2).

A similar maneuver is used independently by a boy and his mother in *Louis*. In this episode, a five-year-old boy, Louis, finds the target mirror on his own, and repeatedly calls to his mother, fixing his gaze

Figure 2.9.1 Audibly calling without looking at person called

Figure 2.9.2 Looking without calling audibly

on the mirror as he calls. Louis then gives up and leaves the mirror to find his mother. She then emerges alone in front of the target mirror and repeatedly calls Louis to join her. As did Louis, so Maman holds her gaze on the mirror while audibly summoning and looks off to see if the summons has drawn a response only after she ends the call. We might expect a person who is calling another to come to look at the other to reinforce the summons and to see if it is directed and timed successfully. But in these three instances, the summoning party holds his or her gaze on what the summoned party is to come to see. Like someone absorbed in a difficult task who dare not look up and away, people before distorting mirrors issue summonses in ways that try to hold on to the image of interest while they call another to witness it.

In *Louis,* Maman's summoning strategy offers Louis additional assistance to find what she is attending to when he arrives. As she calls him to come, she gestures broadly and histrionically, doing something "funny" with her body that can be witnessed as such as her son approaches, before he gets into position to see its reflection in the mirror.

> While faced directly into the mirror, Maman beckons off to the side with her left hand and she moves her head as if it is extra-weighty or loosely attached to her body, in a silly, lolling manner. Then, while moving back a step and still staring into the mirror, she mocks laughter by rapidly lifting and dropping her shoulders several times, a motion that jiggles her dangling arms and hands up and down.
>
> Then she stops the head movement, looks off left, beckons with her fingers, and calls in a straightforward manner for her husband: "{Den}is. . . . Viens voir. Attends. Lâche-le. Lâche-le [Leave him be]. Viens voir."
>
> As Louis comes around the side and becomes visible to us (he had been visible to her), but before he can see her reflection in the mirror, she is again oriented to the mirror and in this orientation she restarts the mock laughter, holding her jaw out in a comical firmness that is opposed to her now more emphatic rollicking motions, even as she moves back from the mirror, making room for the boy, who is shorter than she, to get in front and see in [figure 2.10].

Note that Maman's device of doing a puppetlike mock laughing points out not simply what should be seen—which is a relatively flat reality—but also, and simultaneously, the more profoundly three-dimensional matter: how what is seen should be regarded. The call is not, strictly speaking, to see something out there in the world, this funny image displayed on the mirror; but to "see my seeing," to see "how I see it." The urgency in the calls and in the odd fixing of gaze on the mirror during the summons responds to a fragility not in the image itself but in the spirit of its sudden humorous appreciation. When children, in whatever language, excitedly issue calls to their parents—mira!, look!, regarde!—they are inviting attention not simply to what they see but also, and more importantly, to their experience in seeing it, a distinction captured perhaps most evocatively in French, which in practice becomes an abbreviated invitation to "regard my regard."

If laughter only required the viewing of images in a mirror, the condition of copresence would not be so strongly related to laughing in

Figure 2.10 Maman mocking laughter

the fun house.[7] The presence of others serves the process of making the mirrors laughably funny by stimulating self-conscious awareness of one's seeing. Merleau-Ponty (1968) has written of various ways that we need others to give us an awareness of our own bodies; in this case it is the sensual awareness of our seeing. Eyes may provide an individual with sight, but one's gaze is conferred by others. When one's seeing is seen, it comes magically alive, metamorphosing into an active force that can emerge through self-reflective implications as laughter. With the presence of others or, strictly speaking, on a presumption of another's awareness, one's seeing instantly can be transformed into a self-probing, self-tickling gaze.

2. "Got It?" . . . "Get It!": Building the Momentum to Laugh

Koestler (1964) has elegantly argued that humor is in its essence a simultaneous orientation to two or more inconsistent perspectives. But if a sense of logically untenable juxtaposition is a necessary condition for laughter, it does not suffice. As is so often the case with intellectual works on humor, reading Koestler's text is not likely to provoke laughter. A good pun read in a text rarely will provoke laughter, but bad puns in ordinary conversation routinely do. The difference is the ongoing pressure to make sense with the punster, a pressure that authors rarely can sustain through their inert medium. Scholars kill the comic impulse when writing on humor, not because their analysis is too heavy but because their relationship to readers is too light.

In the fun house, bystanders can see that the person who, in one perspective, looks like a midget with an enormous head also looks relatively normal standing there before the mirror. But unless some nicety is first negotiated between the two, the stranger is under no compulsion to enact an integrated sense of the two conflicting images. If it is to provoke laughter, a formal inconsistency of perspectives must become practically untenable.

Shaping the Juxtaposition That Is the "It" to "Get"

Visitors to the fun house elaborately demonstrate a tacit folk understanding that humor is structured on principles of perspectives in tension. They know that the mirrors by themselves do not automatically or necessarily "distort," that to characterize the mirrors as "distorting" is already to take a major leap, a leap that constructs a tension between a flat image on the surface of the mirrors and an independently existing, three-dimensional personal reality. Thus parents work hard to guide small children to grasp that the image in the mirror in one sense certainly is them, through noting that it is not quite them. "See how skinny your arm is [there]?!," the adult says to a child who is initially soberly absorbed. The adult takes on as a task the noticing that a reflected arm somehow belongs to the child, even though, because the child's arm is not nearly that skinny, the child often will not immediately take for granted that the proper way to regard the mirror's image is as a reflection of him- or herself.

Among adults, the running commentary differs. On the assumption that competent members of society will appreciate that they somehow naturally "own" the images that their bodies cast onto mirrors, adults draw attention not so much to the mirrors as to an alternate perspective that can complete the juxtaposition. Adults draw the attentions of adults to normative expectations about body image in everyday social life. One "helps" an adult companion see that "that's what you'll look like with a few more desserts" (figure 2.11). Anticipating that such a comment may soon be forthcoming, one hastens to offer: "I should go on a diet." Or, conjuring up the contrast without any commentary at all, adults at once draw out a shameful view of themselves and take distance from it. Thus, by shaking one's extra-large bottom

Figure 2.11 With a few more desserts

as depicted on the mirror, one can silently but very effectively say,
"And what if I looked like that?" taking for granted that companions
will take for granted that one really already does not.

In order to be appreciated as funny, the mirrors must be taken to
effect a double and contrasting depiction, between, for example, the
huge head on the mirror's surface and the smaller head that one presumably has in everyday interaction. Companions who laugh at one's
image before the mirror do not typically cast ridicule, they support
the assumption that the person reflected does not appear that way in
everyday social life. This is one reason that strangers hesitate to watch
others' reflections. For to be seen seeing a stranger's fat head or bottom
and not to laugh is potentially to convey that one fails to see a distortion. In effect, these mirrors are artful social devices for producing
confirmation from associates that, however much one may be dangling
out at the end of the bell curve of body images in "normal" life, one
is still relatively normal. Indeed one wry way of building humor in this
setting is to cast a glance at a mirror that depicts a grossly overweight
companion and remark brightly: "Let's find a mirror that makes you
look fat!"

No particular normative theme is required to define the mirror's
image as a distortion. One of the most innocent devices is to perform

Figure 2.12.1 Aping   Figure 2.12.2 Muscular monkey

a routine activity with a slight gloss, say walking in place with knee lifts that evoke hiking, to see what the mirror makes of it. The norm at issue here is not a matter of morality; it is "das Man," the typical way of appearing when you do typical things.

Other ways of working humor into encounters with the mirrors do not rely on the mirror to originate a distortion but invite the mirrors to magnify gestures and movements that, independently of the mirror, create a juxtaposition between normal and bizarre bodies. Thus arms are draped straight down, hands are cupped, and chimpanzeelike sounds are emitted. And men, boys, and girls puff up their chest and flex their arms like musclemen (figures 2.12.1 and 2.12.2).

Small children also produce subtle reflections of the mirrors' distorting reflections by moving their bodies in the style of puppets, their arms lifting and falling as if controlled by invisible strings. In effect, they shrewdly reproduce the puppetlike character of the images on the mirrors. Images on the mirror reliably jump in response to tugs of invisible strings and in forms that, like the Pinocchio of Italian folktale, tease and caricature their masters.

Paradox, irony, contradiction, absurdity, and the like do not simply happen to be at the heart of humor, waiting to be discovered by the insightful analyst. They are put there, deliberately and ingeniously, by people making fun. Grasping the idea that the mirrors should be fun, and that fun requires juxtaposition, many visitors, young and old, do "monster" shapes and mock aggressive movements. Thus, after PaPA in *SupEr,* in order to guide his son to laughter, makes a sequence of comments marking the boy's "big" ears, teeth, and neck, the boy responds by making voracious predatory animal movements. So does the father in *T'es bellle,* when he invites his family to respond to his display of a growling large mouth.

In some of the most intriguing ways of working fun into the mirrors, visitors create a juxtaposition of opposites in their own movements, which they then allow the mirrors to play with. In *Louis,* Maman "calls" Louis to the target mirror by lifting and dropping her shoulders in a puppetlike way that mocks laughter. In part because the target mirror produces images of large heads, some native French viewers of this segment were reminded of Pierrot, a moon-faced, sad clown who, with his large shoulders, may move like a puppet, and who embodies juxtaposition in his bittersweet identity: he is beloved because he lives only for the love of his audience and therefore has no life of his own.

Sets of visitors who develop extensive humorous interaction in front of the mirrors commonly do so by in effect playing "catch" with the mirror. After they grasp how the mirror has reflected them, they take a pose or launch a gesture that reflects the mirror's image (e.g., moving one's body up and down like a worm, in response to the zigzag lines created by the mirror; figures 2.13.1 and 2.13.2). Then they turn the play over to the mirror, which makes a revised reflection (perhaps producing its own internal juxtaposition, of a huge head on a dwarfed body). Then they do a physical gloss on that reflection; and so on. In this way, the visitor incorporates the principle of the mirror, caricaturing it, then becomes a person caricatured by the mirror, in a series of emerging juxtapositions that seem to take on a life of their own.

Creating the Tension to "Get It!"

How do those spirits arise? If any of these portrayals of substantive juxtaposition are to provoke laughter, they need to acquire dynamic force; they must initiate or proceed from a tension built into social interaction. In professional comedy, a team, like Abbott and Costello or Martin and Lewis, can create a juxtaposition between separate, mutually uncomprehending, intractable, or inaccessible personal worlds, and throw onto the audience the task of resolving the tension through laughter. In recent (postmodern?) forms of professional comedy, a single comic, like Robin Williams, will inhabit a diverse social space, jumping from one to another character with lightning speed, compelling audience members, if they are to maintain coherence in their

Figure 2.13.1 Zigzag 1

Figure 2.13.2 Zigzag 2

watching, to build bridges with their laughing bodies. In the fun house, physical devices for conjuring up a provocative juxtaposition often entail the production of a corporeal tension. The person freezes part of his body while other parts move with a lively subjectivity. Postured in this manner, visitors call their companions to resolve their bodily tension by releasing them from it with laughter.

Young visitors commonly create a provocative juxtaposition between gaze and body mass. Usually we alter our gaze with an ease and flexibility that our body mass denies us. The eyes are used naturally as the agency of a lively subjectivity within the relatively objective frame for experience provided by our corporeal frame (cf. Kendon 1990). Jumping up and down, children reverse the everyday relationship between gaze and body mass. They peer steadily into reflections of their wildly mobilized bodies, stabilizing vision while giving an extraordinary mobility to their body as a whole.

Adults more often make an offering to the mirrors of a particular body part such as an arm or their buttocks, taking distance with the rest of their body to see what the mirrors do with "it." A split between a frozen and a lively body is unintentionally created by adults when they lift children to merge their lines of regard. When adults hook their arms under those of small children in order to raise them, they create an unanticipated split between the child's immobilized torso and the child's flapping legs, which then often become the focus of joint regards. The physical labors and contortions entailed in producing these juxtapositions create a tension, which laughter may readily resolve. After a laugh the buttocks may be withdrawn from display and returned to their usual background status, where they are discreetly employed to move the whole body on to the next mirror.

When one member of a set, in scouting for his or her group, comes upon a promising mirror, he or she will often call other members in the striking manner reviewed through the examinations of *Louis* and *T'es bellle* in the last section. The scout, looking squarely into the mirror and summoning a companion, either freezes a posture (e.g., the father standing with arms raised like airplane wings), or mechanically repeats a movement that creates a novel fragmentation of the body into stabilized and moving parts (e.g., Maman's puppetlike mock-laughing shoulders). In either case, the scout's bodily orientation toward the mirror in combination with his or her audible call to the side provides the interactional tension and motivational force that leads to laughter.

That the dynamic towards laughter is promoted by the summoning scout's embodied tension is most clearly visible in *T'es bellle*. (See figures 2.9.1 and 2.9.2.) The father here calls repeatedly for his wife to come, and it appears that she is within hearing range long before she responds. When she alters her gaze and sees him in the shape of a cross, her course to reach him becomes definitive. Glancing his way, she can immediately appreciate that she literally had been holding him up. The force of her laugh emerges as a transformation out of another force already in progress, a force in this instance that presses toward embarrassment or shame. It would be potentially discourteous, at the very least, to leave a companion suspended indefinitely in such an increasingly untenable posture.

Adults often create an embodied tension in children to make palpable the cognitive juxtaposition that laughter presupposes. We briefly reviewed *SupEr* above. The episode begins as a boy squares off before the target mirror, points in, and repeatedly calls his father, PaPA, through progressively insistent, whiney requests. When PaPA arrives, he signals his change of state with "Oh!" (cf. Heritage 1984a). In a motion that the boy can see in the mirror before he can feel it, PaPA extends his right hand towards the boy's right ear. The boy laughs on hearing his father's exclamation, "Oh!," and then bends forward and laughs in a riff as his father reaches towards and rubs the boy's ear between his thumb and index finger. The boy now collapses as he laughs, seemingly trying to escape the tickle-like provocation of his ear. Tickling isolates part of the body, inducing the person tickled to respond hysterically to the tickled area with the entire rest of his or her body. PaPA and the boy continue a similar strategy to sustain the laughter, as they isolate various parts of the boy's body (ears, teeth, neck), in effect freezing them as objectified parts of the boy to which he is encouraged to respond with laughter.[8]

In the fun house, the dynamic to laughter frequently arises initially out of a tension structured into the body composure of one of the members of an interacting set. When the summoning party adopts a pointedly frozen stance or displays a body part as an inert thing, he or she in effect asks for release. The summons and the indicated juxtaposition pose a question about collective experience: "Got it?" The construction of a hysterical or disabled body provides the imperative undertone, "Get it!" What transpires, when the interaction moves directly from this tension to laughter, is the metamorphosis of a potentially negative possibility, the danger of showing that one is awkwardly, even perhaps a bit cruelly, not "with" another who needs release, into positive gales of laughter.[9]

3. Turning Oneself Inside Out: Corporeal Resources and Transcendent Tasks of the Laughing Body

In order to explain a person's laughter in the fun house, we can point, first, to the construction of a presumption that another sees the same image that one sees and also sees one's seeing of it, and next, to an emerging pressure towards expressing that one gets a designated juxtaposition; but we still must ask, why laugh? Why would a person do the particular corporeal performances that are identifiable as laughter? Why not just say, "I got it," or "Ah, yes, that's quite funny"? What essential task is accomplished by the laughing body? And why do bodies laugh as they do? Actions like knee slapping and foot stomping often accompany laughter; why are they not sufficient? Why is laughing not done by a hand gesture, by tweaking one's ears, by sticking out one's tongue? Why is it especially fitting to do particular sounds and gestures, so peculiar that they are readily identifiable as laughter, to show that one is having fun in the fun house?

Ambiguous Denotations and Aesthetic Differentiations

When people laugh, they appreciate a rich variety of distinctive resources for interaction. Even minimal forms of laughter can be used to signal a differentiated responsiveness to a variety of collectively appreciated, emerging substantive themes. *Parrain*, a twenty-second segment that will be only briefly treated here, shows how laughter enables one to be in two places at once.

> GF, a bearded man of substantial girth, refers to himself in the third person as "parrain"—godfather. GD, his goddaughter, is about six years old. The two cooperate in an extended sequence of paired turns in which GF points out an aspect of either his or her image in the mirror, and GD follows with a responsive comment or a form of laughter.
>
> The segment begins as the couple approaches a mirror that stands to the left, facing the mirror targeted by the video camera. The first comment, uttered by godfather, is directed at this mirror: "Oh regarde, il est tout maigre, parrain. Regarde, parrain, il est tout maigre [Look, godfather is very thin.]." To this, GD responds with an utterance that mixes "ouais" [yeah] with a throat sound that suggests a laugh particle; what emerges is roughly "ohwhghey." GD overrides any ambiguity as to the spirit of her response by rocking her head and torso sharply in related but different arcs, creating an emphatic laughing movement that is visible in the mirror to both. They both then turn 180 degrees toward the target mirror.
>
> Here GF makes a series of comments about the girl's contrastingly large size in the target mirror, and then GF draws attention to his arms: "Hoh, regarde, {tiens} parrain, où-il-est. Regarde, parrain, les bras qu'il a [Hoh, look, godfather, where he is . . . the arms that he has]. *GD had become engaged in the reflection of her own image,* moving her arms and looking directly at her right arm and then back at the mirror, *but she now responds audibly in utterances that are linked not to her movements and body features but to GF's comments about his own body.* GD laughs in response to GF's reference to his arms even as she focuses not on the reflection of his arms but on hers [figure 2.14].

They end the episode as GF says, "Oh, dis donc!" [British: Well, I say!; 1980s American: Oh, wow], and GD, swinging her arms back and forth, responds, "On est fou, hein?" [Crazy, eh?]. GF then turns into the center of the hall. As GF is leaving, GD remains briefly alone

Figure 2.14 Looking at her arms, GD laughs

before the mirror, observing reflections of her arm swinging as part of her ongoing independent engagement with the scene.

Two aspects of *Parrain* document the resourcefulness of laughter as an interactional device for sustaining a "with" relationship. First, the girl is able to respond with precision to godfather's comments even while she pursues her own interests. Godfather's comments call her repeatedly to get it. She responds to the potential awkwardness of not getting it, and demonstrates that she is still "with" him, by repeatedly laughing, even while she develops interests that take her away from being exclusively with him.

Laughter is available to her as an expressive device that does not bother with the substantive content of language, which if used might draw her attention away from her independent interests. In fact, as her first, torso-rocking laugh shows, laughter, perhaps especially laughter before a mirror, does not even require sound. Godfather highlights the presence of features of the scene that provoke him, thereby establishing the challenge that if his companion does not show that she is also provoked by them, they might fall a bit apart in their experience. She uses laughter to transcend the potential separation.

It is not just the absence of substantive language content that provides this utility for laughter. Goddaughter varies the aesthetic aspects of her expression by laughing at different lengths and in musically contrasting phrases.

> In the course of their interaction, GD produces three different forms of laughter, all done mostly through the nose over a closed throat. She laughs in a musically downward phrase, more or less like "nnhh hhnnh hhn − −hnn− −hhnn−hhnnh." Then she laughs in a shorter phrase with a final lilt, on the order of "hhnh hn+ho," quickly followed by a briefer, nasally closing, slightly downward bleat, "nh−hhn."

This aesthetic utility enables her, without diverting her consciousness substantially from an engagement with themes of her own interest (e.g., the mirror's play on her arm rather than his), to demonstrate a continuously responsive attention to a variety of his comments.

One reason that laughter is so firmly associated with relaxation is that people can laugh at the right time and in a decorously fitting way even while they don't know what they are laughing about. Language presumably makes more demanding calls on consciousness.[10]

THE SOCIAL LOGIC OF LAUGHTER'S CORPOREAL METAMORPHOSIS

As a corporeal process, laughter invokes the body as a form that can be inhabited to different degrees. This metaphysical potential makes laughing a rich resource for quickly creating a complex narrative structure. Let us review the course of events that makes *Parrain* an episode.

Start: Laughter first emerges as an inadequacy of language. GD's initial "ohwhghey" appears to be "ouais" tainted by the undermining power of humorous spirits. And her body motion makes clear that more is going on than language may represent.

Middle: As the episode develops, GF offers a laugh token, "Hoh," to mark his experience of being provoked by a new item of interest. GD's laughter quickly emerges as an expansive riff ("nnhh hhnnh hhn − −hnn− −hhnn−hhnnh"), after which, through a two-step progression in subsequent riffs ("hhnh hn+ho," "nh−hhn") GD shortens her laughter in length and alters its musical course, opening up the sound just a bit and then ending on a relatively truncated note.

End: The device they use to end the interaction is to assert explicitly and clearly that the situation is humorously provocative, which GF does with "Dis donc!" and GD with "On est fou." Once language is used explicitly to define a scene as compellingly funny, it is a good bet that it no longer is!

The richly ambivalent relationship of laughter to language is exploited by the pair to understand more or less where they are at any given moment in an unfolding narrative path, even as they mutually construct an episode that has a beginning, a compelling and variegated middle, and a satisfying end.

Again and again in the fun house, one member of a set points out that a mirror has split a person into two images, creating an image on the glass that mocks the person's image in everyday life. This move risks splitting the set apart. Then laughter, which is in substance a practice of transcending routinely observed boundaries of the embodied self, is used to overcome the potential gap and keep the set together. As a corporeal practice, laughter often draws deeply from the chest, pulling with it guttural sounds or noises that suggest operations for clearing nasal passages (hence the frequency of "ch" and "gh" particles in attempts to render phonetically what is heard of laughter).

Laughter also splits and recombines the elements of respiration and of audible utterance, making exhales, which are usually employed as tacit vehicles for speech (at least in the language cultures treated here), suddenly part of the presented content (hence the "hh" particles that, perhaps more than any other, reappear in attempts to transcribe laughter). Whether in the form of a silently shaking chest or in laugh tokens full of "hh" sounds, people commonly laugh by reversing the relation of respiration to audible expression, truncating or even fully suppressing linguistic utterance to highlight the exhale itself.

Laughter thus routinely appears to emerge from an extraordinary depth of the self, and as such it is well tailored to express that one has stayed intimately in touch with another who has been touched by an "extraordinary" provocation. Reversing the relationship of respiration and audible sound, laughter is a distinctive metamorphosis, a process of turning the body of the self inside out. Thus the colloquial ways of relating that one had experienced a situation as funny: "I almost peed in my pants," "me cagaba de la risa." Whether by making respiration witnessable, by opening the mouth unusually wide, or by suddenly ejecting a sound that leaps out from deep within, laughter gives social visibility to aspects of the body that, in everyday social life, are routinely employed tacitly in the conduct of emotionally unremarkable behavior.

A folk understanding of the socioaesthetic properties of laughter appears to be a universal feature of socialized competence throughout contemporary Western cultures. In the fun house, as in everyday informal social life in work settings, members exploit the transcendent significance of laughter by putting it to paradoxical ends. It is common, for example, for work associates to search, at times a bit frantically, for something they both can treat as laughable in order to end an interaction that has become too long for both. In American university halls, where handshakes are too formal and kisses have become too dangerous, laughter provides an effective embodied demonstration that two people have been especially together, enabling them more safely to part.[11]

How Humor Tickles: On the Edge
between Doing and Being Done by Laughter

Laughter's metaphysical, three-dimensional formal properties lend it distinctive charms. As a vehicle for expression that can be inhabited to infinitely varied degrees, laughter can easily be mocked. Of course everyday language can be used to feign being all manner of things that the speaker is not, but mock laughter requires an emphatically corporeal dimension of simulation. Recall, from *Louis,* Maman's use of a puppetlike, silent mock laughing as a summons to her son. With such a profoundly embodied device, Maman walks close to the edge between doing laughter and being taken by humor. In the next section we will review her fall over this edge. Here the point to note is that, for the same reason one often "had to be there" to grasp much of humor, it may quickly become especially tricky *not* to be there when one "does" mock laughing as a device.

Language is a cultural product that is specifically suited for disembodied expression. The words on the page can work as effectively as the words seen and heard in their speaking. It takes relatively little art to lie with language. Laughs, on the other hand, don't work at all in the same ways when they are witnessed firsthand and when they are read, a truth demonstrated by the deadly adolescent epistolary practice of adding "ha ha" to postcard text. Laughs have to be perceived as produced three-dimensionally, through a person's body, to be effectively conveyed, and that requires some aesthetic finesse. (Mechanical laughter in an amusement park is more effective in the house of horror than in the fun house.) Lies with language can be left for reckonings much later with the devil. But, like a finger used for a demonstrative touch that surprises by returning a feeling, mock laughter can immediately raise spirits that overwhelm the pretender.

If laughter is essentially a corporeal phenomenon, it is the distinctive embodiment of transcendence that enables laughter to be socially recognized *as* laughter.[12] Laughter is never convincing when heard as a matter of a monotonic "ha ha." On the contrary, such regulated sound production is a common way to mock another because it indicates that, despite the production of sound against sound, the utterer is not caught between juxtaposed perspectives. If laughter is to be expressed through two syllables, they must vary in some qualitative manner, presenting different phonetic forms (ha hi), rising or falling in musical pitch, bursting outward, attacking the self as if caught in choking, etc. In the fun house, initial laughs are often audibly single syllables that are, nevertheless, singular outbursts.

Laughter as an Artful Device for Connoting Collective Experience

Finally, we may look again at *T'es bellle* to appreciate how formal properties make laughter distinctively attractive for accomplishing extraordinary moments of collective integration. Language becomes a barrier to communication in some situations by virtue of the same formal properties that make it so useful as a communicative tool. Just because words are so effective in conveying finely differentiated import, if too many people speak at the same time, no one knows what anyone is saying. With laughter, any number can play and all can be assured from moment to moment that they are nevertheless in the same game. In *T'es bellle,* the extraordinary achievement is the production of a four-part collective peaking that is built on the course of a stream of laughter.

The scene develops as father (F) faces the target mirror, standing behind his son (S), who is about four years old. F tries to engage S in the mirror with pointers such as "Et là, et là, et là" [And there . . .] and "il est grooah" [he's bi.ig] and by grabbing the boy and raising him from the floor F picks up S by hooking his arms under the boy's, a move that induces the boy to move his arms outward, horizontal and sideways from his body. F then puts the boy down and works on summoning mother (M) verbally and by holding up his own arms like an airplane, straight out from his shoulders. F finally succeeds in getting their attention.

While the female half of the family approaches, and while he is looking in the target mirror, S raises his arms rapidly, imitating F's arm posture.[13] Meanwhile, F looks to M as she is coming and then F looks back at the mirror, and he says to her as she approaches and sees him looking into mirror, in a low voice that presumes her proximity: "viens voir le gros . . ." [come see the big . . .]. His reference appears to be to a reflection of himself.

Within two seconds, the four coordinate a collective expression of a peak experience. The interrelations of the four responses are illustrated by the following representation, in which slanting lines indicate the approximate points of onset of one person's action relative to another's; audible expressions are in bold face; capital letters indicate loudness; + and − indicate directions in pitch (figure 2.15).

Figure 2.15 Four-person peaking

The four-part expression takes shape as M and D, holding hands and with broad smiles of anticipation, join F and S at the target mirrors. They quickly separate, M moving to the rear of the group, D coming up close to the mirror. The four are now composed as shown in figure 2.15.

1. M begins the audible response (a corruption of either "oh la la" or "oh l'aut[re]," the latter being a colloquialism for "look at him, how silly he is"). Melodically, M's response (the whole of line 1) is sung in a form like a script "u," with an initial slight upward tick, then a descent to a broad bottom, then a sharp rise, and which launches riffs of quickly quieter laughter that end markedly on an in-breath syllable.

2. D shapes her mouth into an "O" at about the same time that M starts her exclamation, and a moment later D starts emitting a sound, like a distorted "oo la la," that quickly gets louder and then turns into a very thin riff of laughter.

3. As M and D hit their initial peak, F begins raising his arms from their horizontal position. F does not laugh.

4. S is the last to join the collective act. He has been distracted from the mirror by the arrival of M and D, and by the rapid coordination of the others. While he is constantly trying to join the others, he takes a bit longer to catch up. When he reorients his gaze from the others

```
        Phase 1.          Phase 2.
                        [quickly diminishing in volume]          [in-breath]

                                    |                    |

 1  M:  O+h l--aa++ah eh! uu uua++AAA--Aa+a  +++++ah ha ha ha .ah
 2         \    \
 3          \    \          [high, very thin sounds]
 4           \    \              |              |
 5  D:        \   oo++WA AA    hihi hihi hh huh
 6            \        \
 7    D's "O" mouth    \
 8                      \
 9                       D moves right hand up to her wide-open mouth.
10                      \
11                       \
12  F:                   F silently moves arms up from initial perpendicular.
13                      \
14  S:               \ hh hha+ hi+hi+
15                        \
16                         S moves hands to mouth (see figure 2.15).
17                            \
18  F:    growls               aaaah aaaaaaaah aaa
```

to the mirror, he starts to laugh and then moves his hands to his mouth, paralleling a movement that D has just launched.

With striking speed, a unity of the four is represented. F provides the context by finding the mirror with S, then by striking an arms-out pose that imitates a form that F had accidentally sculpted in S when he lifted him up, and then by calling M and D to appreciate what he has found. If F provides a visual scaffold, M, by bursting out with a long exclamation that quickly segues into a laugh, complements F by providing an audible track on which the others can sequentially arrange their responses. Note that M's exclamation-laugh extends/embraces the others, continuing even until S tardily organizes himself to join the others' celebratory expressions.

Simultaneous with M's exclamation, D shapes her mouth into readiness for her own exclamation but her sound doesn't emerge until after M's laugh is audible. F does not laugh, but moves his arms upward, following the tonal course of the audible responses of M and D. S tags along, both laughing and moving his hands to his mouth well after the onset, and in apparent imitation of, the others' expressions.

As with *Parrain*, it appears on close inspection that the members of the set may not in fact be responding to the same stimuli. S, for one, is too short to have the same line of gaze as the others, and he comes into the collective act more precisely after having perceived that it is in progress than on suddenly grasping F's provocative image, which for some time has been available for him to grasp. D registers the image that F calls to the group's attention, but even before she has finished her first outburst, her gaze appears trained on the reflections of the motions she has produced in response to F's posturing. (F soon will acknowledge this with his comment, "T'es bellle," an utterance that dwells pointedly on the "l" sound.) M's line of gaze covers the reflections not just of F but also of D and herself. What is clear is that *none of the members has firm grounds to assert confidently that all share the same focus.* But the sensuality that is collectively produced goes beyond these differentiated perceptive parts, constructing a collective experience that is at once *a myth in its referential claims and a palpable reality in its aesthetic dimensions.*

With regard to the expressions by the females, exclamation sustained becomes laughter. Alternatively put, laughter is employed here as a polysyllabic device for reiterating exclamation long enough that all can join in. M and D begin their expressions with forms of exclamation that they effortlessly convert into riffs of laughter. M's exclamatory phrase is sung, and its musicality segues readily into riffs of laughter. D's initial phrase momentarily wavers between "oo la la" and a laugh; she gives to the familiar French exclamation so much throaty emphasis that its vowel sounds provide a short, slippery slope to laughter's core respiratory sounds.

F tracks his arm motions along the sharply upward arc of M and D's laughter. S has been struggling to stay with the others; he is most obviously responding, not to any common reflected image but to the audible and visible forms of the others' laughter. But despite these differences, in one way or another, each member of the set instantly uses the aesthetic features of laughter to fabricate *a common sensual body* for the group.

To what extent did the four lines of experience come together? Language is shaped to leave memorable traces that facilitate retrospective examination of mutual understanding. But laughter runs in the flow of interaction in ways that leave little space for one to turn and question the others. The very speed of the multiple-party, coordinated interaction that laughter facilitates ensures that, unless they videotape the moment, participants will be hard pressed to reexamine the experience and wonder to what extent their domains of experience actually coincided. And as it occurs, the performance of laughter as noisy outbursts with rapidly jolted head movements itself impairs the ability of the participants to monitor the others for indications that they are responding to the same provocation. *Laughter constructs the myth of collective experience by artfully masking the laughers' empirical abilities to research the question.*[14]

4. A Second Metamorphosis

After companions respond with laughter, the participants sometimes move on to a more complex stage of laughing interaction. *Louis, SupEr,* and *T'es bellle* all display this more elaborated structure. In each episode, one or more of the participants goes through a second metamorphosis, clearly moving from "doing laughter" to being "done by" the humor of the situation.

The same three dimensions are useful for explaining both the first and the second metamorphosis. Being "done by humor" can be distinguished from "doing laughter" by examining its corporeal forms, or the way that humor is embodied; by analyzing the way that the laughing person is monitoring the perception of his or her behavior by others; and by specifying the narrative challenges that inspire laughing transformations of self.

The theoretical implications of documenting a double metamorphosis may be far-reaching. If "tension" or other background dynamics cause an onset of laughing, as classical psychology would have it, it is not clear how the same factors could explain the immediately subsequent emergence of a second transformation. Likewise, the strategic objective of being seen laughing may explain some initial doings of laughter, but that cannot also be a sufficient explanation of an emergent phase in which, as it were, the laughing body takes over its subject. A new order of social psychological comprehension of corporeal aesthetics (perhaps the closest antecedent is Plessner 1970) is required to understand the second metamorphosis.

A Difference in Corporeal Form

I first came across documentation of contrasting, sequentially ordered, corporeal forms of laughter in an examination of transcripts of audiotapes created some twenty years ago by Gail Jefferson.[15] One episode, "orchid/organ," was critical. The recorded occasion was one of a series of group therapy sessions attended by several young people and a therapist. The speaker, Ken, is talking about his family and at one point refers to his grandfather playing with his orchids. Roger, who has a long-standing antagonistic relation to Ken, is kibitzing, scoffing, and otherwise trying to draw the other members, Al and Louise, into laughing at Ken. Gradually Roger picks up other members to join his attack. With minor exceptions, Jefferson transcribes all the laughs in this phase as occurring on the exhale.

The attack mounts, Ken becomes a bit flustered, and a turning point is achieved when Roger treats Ken's enunciation of "orchid" as if he misspoke and said "organ," i.e., as having unintentionally said that his grandfather was masturbating. In effect, Roger claims a transcendent moment, that Ken finally capitulated by unwittingly joining the effort to ridicule his family. Roger wins the support of others for this reading, and even gets a somewhat ambivalent, wooden agreement from Ken, even though the hearing of "orchid" as "organ" seems to have been imposed. Roger identifies the turning point by erupting with laughter as he inhales. Others, in particular Louise, are so taken by the turn of events that their breath is taken away and their talking, even their audible laughing, is "impaired" by the moment's spirit.

In sum, Roger first pointedly uses laughter as a strategic weapon, and then constructs the interaction as if a spirit of humor got loose and took over even Ken, the long-resisting butt of the joking, the upshot being a "fantastic" turn of events that undermines Roger and Louise as well. The two narrative phases are marked by changes of laughter's place in the respiratory cycle.

Something similar occurs in our three key episodes. In *SupEr,* PaPA begins his laughter in a very regularized and edited manner, exhaling isolated spurts of "heh heh" and "Hha!" to mark funny features. Then, as the references to big teeth, ears, and neck work to tickle his son into riffs of laughter, PaPA's laughter is elaborated. It emerges in a crescendo form and then turns into a silent chest rocking followed by long, audible braking inhalations that retrospectively indicate efforts to hold laughter back.

In the other two episodes, the footing of participants becomes increasingly problematic as laughter intensifies. In *T'es bellle* it is the little boy who most obviously laughs strategically in order to join the others, and then most completely collapses as he steps rapidly backward from the mirror and stumbles. Only his father's legs and arms keep him from falling completely. In *Louis,* Maman specifically "does" laughter, by lifting and dropping her shoulders and mouthing the form of exhale laughs, as a means of beckoning Louis to a laughing regard of her reflection. When Louis responds by producing a long riff of laughter, Maman responds to his response. As with the father in the *PaPA* episode, she show signs of a struggle to sustain breathing against the force of muted laughter. The struggle mounts to the point of endangering her footing.

Because people laugh so idiosyncratically, it seems unwise to attempt a list of universal corporeal features that will identify one stage or the other. The point is more precisely documented by standardizing for each individual on his or her initial phase of laughter and watching for a second change. In these cases, the second change comes via a loss of firm footing, a marked alteration of the relation of audible laughter and respiration, in the shift of laughing to a sharply higher octave, or as a quickly accelerated pace of laughter syllables. The mother in *T'es bellle*, for example, shifts from an exclamatory, U-shaped tone at the start of her laughter to a birdlike upward flight of sound that seems to disappear in the stratosphere. Her daughter's laugh makes a parallel jump in register.

Respiration appears to be the single most revealing continuum of transformation. In "doing" laughter, laugh elements are disciplined to mark a controlled flow of respiration. An extreme example would be the mechanically punctuated exhale laughter of the department store Santa Claus. When being "done by" humor, audible laughter gets "hysterical" in the sense of impairing willful control of the body. With PaPA and Maman, laughter bubbles up in the chest and risks imploding. The sense of humor, not allowed to flow out freely, becomes a force one fights to suppress or mute. Often the struggle surfaces as interruptions of the essential inhale phase that, in Western culture at least, is normally held as a private reserve generally kept off limits from the projections of spoken language.[16]

The two transformations of the laughing body indicate the use of a folk corporeal aesthetic to closely monitor and dramatically exploit the symbolic dimensions of the respiratory cycle. Exhale laughs are common means of projecting oneself outward to join "with" another after the maintenance of intimacy has been threatened by a challenge to "get" a tricky juxtaposition. Following the giving out of such exhale laughs, a person whose laughter then demonstrably interrupts and impairs his or her respiration, especially the inhale phase, indicates that "I can't take it (in)" anymore. From laughter being shaped to accommodate respiration, the demands of respiration are overwhelmed by a sense of humor.[17]

Fun house visitors make analogous changes in their posture when laughing. Initially, as noted above, an unusual relationship between a *fixed* posture and gaze toward the mirror is commonly used by a summoner to aid the party summoned to identify the target of collective regard. Then postures used to set up initial laughs frequently become shaky. To understand why people struggle to contain humor to the point that their footing breaks down, we need to reexamine the interactional challenges they face when laughing.

Altered Relations to Others

A shift to a second metamorphosis of laughter also occurs in the laugher's relations with others. Initial laughs are typically timed and shaped for others to witness so that they might aid the achievement of a collective experience. In *T'es bellle,* we reviewed a relatively elaborate arrangement of a multimedia peak that marks a four-party shared provocation. Father moves upward with his arms, to be followed a bit later by son, while mother and daughter coordinate exclamations and then produce rising riffs of laughter that disappear into the ether. Subsequent riffs of laughter often develop on the floor, as it were, of such a collectively manifested unity. But then, members of the set develop laughter along individual paths for exploring the mirror.

The title of the episode, *T'es bellle,* is taken from a comment made by the father in the second stage of the family's collective appreciations of the mirror. His phrase is directed at the idiosyncratic focus that his daughter has quickly developed. After recognizing the father's funny image, the daughter, while continuing to laugh, shifts her focus onto reflections of her own body motions. By saying, "T'es bellle," the father attempts to maintain a shared experience with her.

Similarly in *SupEr* an initial joint response is followed by idiosyncratic explorations. The title of the episode refers to a phrase that PaPA uses to call his wife while he literally puts out a "thumbs up": "Ah! (Il) est supEr..là" (figure 2.16). The immediate catalyst to his declaration-summons is the emergence of his independent appreciation, over his son's head and after commenting on his son's ears, teeth, and neck, of his own reflection and of the generally fantastic potential of this mirror.

When a person in the fun house laughs to summons a companion to an initial joining in an appreciation of humor, the solo laugh is rapidly truncated if it does not bring a supporting response. But once the set has constructed the appearance of a collective experience of humor, its members have earned a bit more of a right to laugh on their own. There appears to be a kind of afterglow that facilitates some solo dancing in the moonlight. In *Louis,* the boy responds to his mother's summons by coming to the mirror, his father trailing close behind. Louis quickly bursts into riffs of laughter, soon lunging at the mirror. Father, behind Louis, reaches out to pull him back at the waist. The phases of explosive, self-sustained, and self-absorbed humorous exploration of one's own reflections by daughter in *T'es bellle,* by PaPA in *SupEr,* and by the son in *Louis* would be, if not inconceivable, very unlikely before first reaching a moment of collective celebration. The

Figure 2.16 "Ah! (Il) est supER..là"

first metamorphosis is typically a precondition for the second because it establishes a collective flooring from which humor can take idiosyncratically fanciful flights.

As the sense of the humor of the mirrors develops, the interactional challenges change. When one party is laughing to call a sober companion to join his or her experience, the challenge is relatively simple. But once both are laughing, a laugh can be a pointing out of something a companion should recognize or a response to something funny that the companion has designated or unwittingly created on the mirror. When the adults in these episodes attempt to hold back their laughter, and lose their footing in the attempt, it is because a tension has developed between the prosocial, or "joining," implications of their laughter and the danger that their laughter will indicate a focus of attentions that a companion will be unable to follow. Laughter shifts from "doing" to "being done" corporeal forms for quite practical interactional reasons.

Generational Differences in Interaction Narratives

For a brief period of their lives, many children come to know a form of collective hysterical laughter that entails laughing about the interactional process of laughing. In such experiences, they are discovering what adults know, that laughter is a two-edged interactional resource. Laughter can easily change aspect from a response that emerges from the background to acknowledge what another has indicated is a candidate for collective attentions, and become histrionic conduct that leaps out of the darkness of audience responsiveness onto the stage of attentions itself. Adults and children both recognize the two metamorphoses of laughter, but they act differently when they "do" and when they are "done by" laughter.

Each stage of laughter is driven by a distinctive theme of transcendence. Initial laughs that demonstrate that one "gets" another's seeing of a funny reflection often suggest an objective of covering up or bypassing shame.[18] In the fun house, there is a common gesture of moving one or both hands to a mouth that has opened to begin recognition laughter. In *T'es bellle,* daughter and son both enact this ritual shame- or modesty-related behavior, as does Louis when he begins laughing in his segment. The hand-to-mouth gesture is dropped in their subsequent, second phase laughter.

In using this gesture, the children in these episodes, and adults in many others, indicate an awareness that they are covering over a morally vulnerable opening. It is not the mouth alone that is potentially too open, it is the opening created by the summons to recognize the humor. The hand-to-laughing-mouth gesture at once portrays and transcends a gaping interactional pit. Young children rush to join the laughter of other members of their family with an urgency that suggests their understanding of the following proposition. If everyone else in your group is responding with wild enthusiasm to something designated as funny, if you do not, and if that nonresponse will be visible to others, you risk showing you are alienated from the spirit of the collectivity.

Nevertheless, "doing laughter" is done similarly by adults and children. They use identical devices: (1) to summon one another (e.g., "X, come see"); (2) to embody the tension that will unfold as humor (e.g., freezing a posture and pointing their gaze into the mirror while calling); (3) and to exclaim through laughter that they "got" the designated juxtaposition. But the second transformation follows sharply divergent generational lines that reflect a different awareness of the interactional stakes.

Like Icarus, the young child frequently soars in passionate response to his or her experience of the newly manifested family bond, jumping up, falling back, or lunging forward, putting limb and bystanders at risk. At the same time, adults quickly find themselves in a compromised position, their loyalties and attentions divided. Caught between

fascination with the emergent specular possibilities and a sense of responsibility to keep the members of the set united in a presumptively
shared experience, adults, like Daedalus, anticipate a fragmentation
of collective experience. The adult's comprehension of interactional
risk breeds a different kind of transcending humor, one with a dialectical, occasionally bittersweet motif.

The appreciation that now becomes possible for the adult takes several forms. One is that of a moment frozen in time: the adult turns
from the mirror's reflection to register, in lightning-fast retrospection,
the achievement of a collective laughing that has transcended a vast
generational gap. Alterations of gaze by adults are pronounced in these
moments. In one episode, *Bottom Shaking,* a woman who is accompanied by three young children and is standing at a right angle to a mirror
first laughs as she sees the reflection of her shaking of her buttocks in
the mirror. Then she turns to appreciate the laughing response of one
of the young targets of her performance. Seeing his laughing response,
she throws her head sharply back and dramatically escalates her laughter. The initial shakings and laughings bring the group together. The
second phase of laughter takes off from the adult's appreciation of the
child's achievement in joining the collective action, an appreciation
that at once celebrates a shared social competence and ironically may
well go beyond what the child can share (figure 2.17).

In another frequent occurrence in the fun house, adults lose composure while laughing in and through their efforts to sustain progressively
effective humor with children. Preadolescent children commonly get
recognizably "carried away," laughingly pursuing self-reflections
without working continuously to enable others to keep seeing what it
is that they are seeing. With an adult looming behind, perhaps holding
them back from the waist or lifting them up by the armpits, children
generally take for granted that adults share their perspective, and they
laugh freely without otherwise marking provocative reflections for
their companions. Adults, in contrast, typically try to sustain a process
of denotative gesturing and facilitating commentary that will enable
all to keep laughing at the same thing (or, more precisely, to keep
believing that they are laughing at the same thing).

Adults make both prospective and retrospective indications that are
designed to promote joint laughter. Prospectively, they point out aspects of the reflections that may be regarded as funny, waiting to laugh
until a companion is ready to laugh as well. Retrospectively, they point
to explain why they and others have just been laughing. The mirrors
make it difficult to keep the temporal directions of indication clearly
separate. When one points at the mirror to show something that one

Figure 2.17 Bottom shaking

has found funny, the pointing itself may be reflected in a bizarre manner. Is, then, the gesture a "pointing" to something that was there, or is it a creation of a new, funny image? If a companion responds with laughter, it can quickly become unclear whether the two streams of laughter are aligned or pursuing separate interests. And this dilemma itself may spontaneously be appreciated as humorous. Like mirrors reflecting mirrors, the possibilities for confusion become infinite.

Put another way, the more successful one is in marking humorous features, successful in the sense of eliciting quick and emphatic laughing responses, the more quickly and sharply one must abbreviate the markings in order to stay "with" one's partners. One's own laughter interactionally turns on itself; it points out and becomes what is pointed out as warranting laughter. It is the effort to master these difficult interactional dialectics that leads to collapsed postures, choked-down laughs, and occasionally to the absurdity of finding the situation so extraordinarily pleasant that it must be abruptly abandoned. In *Louis,* Maman's pointing out of what she and the others are responding to becomes a sputtering effort as her pointings are themselves reflected. Finding that her fun threatens to distract rather than inspire the others, she rushes away from her group in such hysteria that she nearly smashes into the father-son pair (figure 2.18).

Paradoxically, the more effective the laughing appreciation of humorous possibilities, the more challenging are the interactional demands to indicate to all that they are continuously engaging the same perspective and sharing the same reality. This is why the arrangement of a stage with performers segregated from an audience is so helpful for organizing ongoing mass laughing. The formalities of the stage-audience relationship make clear to audience members not always what all those other audience members are laughing about but at least where to look to find out. In the theater, you take a fixed place because the construction of mass collective experiences requires limiting bodily

001314

Figure 2.18 Laughing Maman almost crashes into son

orientations. So much has been made of "life as theater" that we may miss the insights behind taking theater seriously as a strategic social structure. As a social form, theater is artfully devised to solve problems in manifesting presumptions of intersubjectivity, problems that severely limit the ongoing, everyday dramatization of emotions.

If staying together while laughing at deforming mirrors is a problem for each set of participants, by the same token the interaction challenge is a neat solution to the problem of organizing mass experiences in the fun house. Just because tricky interactional dynamics routinely emerge before each mirror, sets of visitors rush from one mirror to the next, making room for successor sets. The more a set enjoys a mirror, the more they are constrained to abandon it. Fun houses thus need not use price, barriers that make movement unidirectional, or time-limited tickets to regulate usage of the mirrors. The sociological magic of the mirrors is that, while inanimate and passive, they generate interactional power that keeps the crowd moving.

Visitors commonly take it for granted that, after the second phase of being "done by" laughter has been reached at a particular mirror, the set cannot return to "do laughter" at that mirror. Within moments after reaching a collective peak of laughter that celebrates collective experience before a given mirror, the group routinely scurries off to a new mirror, where the process cycles back to the start of the first phase. In some groups, hysterically laughing parents will abruptly pull the arms of children who are hysterically laughing at a given mirror, in order to get everyone in the set to rush together to another mirror, where they all momentarily stop cold and take up from scratch the challenge of locating a common perspective for regarding the new reflections as funny.

5. Families and Funny Mirrors

Fun house mirrors crystallize a challenge that haunts all social interaction. The mirrors take the appearance a person presents to the world and they throw back a distorted version of his or her identity, and with it the challenge to make sense of the distortion. In a way, a similar deformation occurs in all social relations, as the others with whom we interact always have an understanding of ourselves that is, with respect to the identities we project, somewhat off the mark, perhaps overly flattering, perhaps maliciously uncomplimentary, perhaps just a bit uncomprehending and weird. An individual's identity in society is, in a formulation first introduced by Kai Erikson (1957) and later elaborated by Erving Goffman (1971, 340–41), composed of who he or she is, as enacted in his or her conduct towards others (the "self"), and who he or she is as implied by the conduct that others take with respect to him or her (the "person" one is for others). Because the biographical histories and trajectories of individuals and their "others" never quite mesh, there is always a bit of a disjuncture between the two versions of one's identity.

Of course, fun house mirrors need not be seen as presenting any challenge at all, and when visitors tour the fun house alone they easily manage to "normalize" the distortions that the mirrors throw off left and right. And so it goes in much of everyday social life. Each of us routinely knows that the dozens of other people we may encounter in any given day have views of the kind of person we are and assumptions about our intentions that are based on a limited knowledge of our past and of our future. Relative to what we know about ourselves, their views of us distort our identities. Routinely we normalize the discrepancies, ignoring, making adjustments, even apologizing for them.

It is the raw principle of being confronted with a distorted image of oneself that is grasped in the humorous appreciation of fun house mirrors. The ways the mirrors are worked differ for different visitors: some adopt frozen poses and see a static caricature; some walk back and forth, varying their distance from the mirror to animate a bizarre character; some merge their image with that of another in their group. The metaphors elicited from the mirrors also differ: some visitors play on fat-thin variations from "normal" body forms, some develop their possibilities as waddling ducks, some become strongmen or puppets or squiggly worms. Certain humorous provocations are hit upon recurrently, but the inventive possibilities are endless. And the possibility of not noticing anything bizarre is also always present; indeed, even for groups that respond actively to some mirrors in the hall, there will be other mirrors that they pass by and peer into without giving the experience any special notice. The essence of the humorous appreciation of these mirrors, the principle that cuts across the substantive variation in ways of making them funny, is the recognition that they provide a distorted image of oneself. Grasping the principle of confronting a distorted image of oneself, laughing visitors draw on their personal and social resources to make some particular form of meaning that will at once acknowledge the challenging encounter and soar in spirit beyond it.

That fun house mirrors derive their humor from the social-psychological structure of personal identity is indicated by the fact that their challenge comes alive only when their deformations can be perceived in the eyes of at least one other person. And then the challenge expands to geometric proportions, because what another person sees of oneself in a deforming mirror is doubly distorted. The additional distortion is due not simply to the curvature of the reflecting surface but to the difference between two embodied perspectives, a difference that is existential. Another person can never see my reflection from the same spot that I see it. While this is true of normal looking glasses, fun house mirrors emphasize the philosophical point. Raise up on your toes a bit or step a bit to the left and the image changes radically. This variability too is a challenge one confronts in everyday life. When two people approach a setting or a task, they inevitably see it from within two different ongoing biographical projects. The natural histories of their current attentions are always at least slightly different. And what each focuses upon, what each literally sees, hears, and feels, is always unique. So when images in fun house mirrors are worked by a visitor in ways that pose the challenge, "get it?" to a companion, the operation epitomizes a dilemma that underlies, and is routinely kept asleep beneath, everyday social life.[19]

That it is primarily families that awaken to the challenge and set off excitedly to make joyous sense of it says something important about the distinctive resources that families bring into the fun house and something significant about the tacit message that their laughing appreciations take out. Families are distinctively attracted to the fun house; they are uniquely driven to acknowledge the challenge it offers; and they are uniquely successful in reconstructing their identities through the encounter. The fun house is a casual place where we may learn something quite telling about families just because families do not treat the place as holding profound implications about themselves.

Family as Laughter's Resource and Product

People in the fun house gather up aspects of the social reality of the family into a collective celebratory focus, aspects that have been operating all along in less dramatic ways. Episodes like *Louis, SupEr,* and *T'es bellle* do not occur when families randomly happen collectively to bump into a given mirror's reflections. Someone takes on the job of scouting, a job done for his or her family and only for that family. The process of assembling the group before the mirror already mobilizes and heightens a sensitivity to family relations. In *T'es bellle,* for example, when the father approaches the target mirror he is already in the process of trying to convince his son to appreciate its distortions ("tout petIIt" [you're so small], he says), and when mother responds to his summons, she is already holding hands with daughter and so "naturally" brings daughter along. Indeed, mother and daughter only drop hands, breaking their physical relationship, in order to leap into a collective appreciation of the reflection of father's arms-out posture. Ongoing intrafamily relations are used to whipsaw family members onto a shared stage.

Positioned before the mirror, family members are differentiated as an isolated unit by those who are not family members. Strangers commonly wait off to the side until a family is finished working a mirror. And families abandon mirrors collectively, at times pulling along a stray child somewhat abruptly if he or she dallies while a stranger indicates readiness to take over the site.

Rights to participate in laughing at the mirrors' reflections are rigorously maintained within family lines. With little or no hesitation, strangers can look on and look into the mirrors from the sidelines, but they usually don't laugh along with family members. As discussed above, in order to laugh, one must presume to see not just the person before the mirror, and not just that person's image in the mirror, but that person's seeing of his or her image, or what it means to that person. Strangers on the sidelines may smile, often quite broadly, but they rarely risk the presumption of a laugh.

For their part, family members treat strangers on the sidelines in a manner that emphasizes the emotionally delicate nature of their collective experience. Family members don't ignore strangers on the sidelines who are queuing up to occupy a reflecting space, but only rarely do they directly address them either. People before the mirror typically respect the presence of waiting strangers by abbreviating their doings before the mirror and hurrying off, but without ever making eye contact with the strangers. When these routines for accomplishing civility by indirection are done on behalf of the family or by family members acting in unity, they construct a vivid sense of a morally powerful, invisible boundary separating the spiritual life of the family from outside life forces. Consider the themes tapped for its members by a family like that in *T'es bellle,* which constructed an intense four-party "peak experience" while in the knowing midst of strangers who stood passively and quietly by, waiting to occupy the provocative space. This is a set of people that not only takes its family relations along on vacations, it also drags along its home, in the sense of a collective emotionality that is usually lived behind private walls.

Drawing on family relations to construct their experience of the mirrors, visitors find that the mirrors throw back to them not simply caricatures of their individual idiosyncrasies but caricatured characteristics that all of them share. Standing before the mirror, all of the family members appear to be of the same Don Quixote–like elongated clan, to come from the same tribe of dwarfs, to share the same genetic tendency to bulbous bottoms. The mirrors metamorphose blood- and law-related family members into a race of people physiologically distinguished from all others not then standing with them.[20] The laughter of family members emerges in a unity isolated from outsiders, at once lightly throwing off the mirror's image and firmly embracing its implication of a unique collective ontology.

And race itself, as commonly understood, doesn't matter. Of all the demographic principles supposedly so powerful in determining people's identities in society, in the fun house family structure reigns supreme. The Jardin d'Acclimatation is an eminently multicultural site, drawing working-class visitors and visitors from neighboring wealthy "quartiers." Parisians come, as do residents from all regions of mainland, overseas, and formerly colonial France. One hears American, British, Canadian, and South Asian varieties of English, and diverse languages of Europe, of Asia, and of Africa. Family ties organize relations without respect to any of these differences, and independently as well of sex. Family operates as an effective resource for producing laughter through the processes examined in earlier sections of this paper, seemingly in any language and ethnic style. Ethnicity, language, and gender may well play a role in how summonses are done, who scouts for whom, how the vowel sounds in certain exclamations slip into the respiratory tracks of laughter; but only family relations are routinely and directly implicated in the key causal contingencies, in particular that of presumptive intersubjectivity, or seeing another's seeing.

If gender and ethnicity do not shape distinctive emotional experiences in the fun house, neither do they segregate people there. Race, national origin, culture: none of these bases of difference have a chance to separate people because family relations already do that effectively. There is little chance that the Pakistani will join in the laughter of the French family, because there is little chance that any stranger-Frenchman will join in.

It is, thus, essentially only families, and virtually any ethnic kind of family, that appreciates as humorous the split that the mirrors create between one's portrayal on the glass (actually, reflecting metal) and one's identity in everyday life. And it is only the family that rises to the challenge of transcending different perspectives on fun house reflections by challenging its members all to "get it" at once. All types of families, but generally only the social unit of the family, grasp the images that the mirrors create, throw them out to the group in a way that potentially creates splits between its members—if you don't "get it" you're "out of it"; and then laughingly celebrates the transcendence of the challenge it has constructed.

Personal and Collective Competence in the Family

The family in this setting is mostly an intergenerational entity. Adult couples, and sets of children on their own, may become engaged in fun with the mirrors but they do not commonly construct the narrative sequences we have been reviewing. When lovers move through the fun house, they often do so in a stroll, arms linked, paces coordinated. In order to laugh at the mirrors, a challenge of transcendence must be engaged, and that requires an initial separation of perspectives that is often anathema to the embracing aura of a romantic mood.

Conversely when children, from toddlers through adolescents, move through the fun house without accompanying adults, their separation is commonly too great to be overcome through constructing the narrative laughing sequences we have been examining. *"This one is cool"* indicates the narcissism that so often makes adult participation necessary to bring experiences in the fun house together (figure 2.19).

Four American children, a boy of perhaps sixteen, another of eleven, and girls six and four years old, explore the hall extensively, and despite

Figure 2.19 "This one is cool": parallel independent exclamations

numerous attempts by all to do so, they fail to meet in an extended collective expression of humor. Several times, one or the other of the boys uses laughter and phrases like "This one is cool" to call his companion to share an experience of the funny character of his, the summoner's own, reflections. On each occasion the latter responds, not by laughing at the former's image so much as by using laughter to reverse the relationship and get a laughing confirmation for reflections of his own body, and with as little success. The girls trail them, using even louder laughs and more explicit pleas to draw one of the boys to be a witness. They get no response at all.

The family that most commonly perceives the challenge and rises to it in laughter does so through the medium of relations between adults and children, especially preadolescents. The notion of family that is constructed most commonly in the fun house is an intergenerational kinship unit for socialization. There is a widespread appreciation among adults who come to this fun house of the value of the mirrors for testing and improving the social competence of very small children. It appears to be unproblematically understood that it is proper and important family business to induce young children to appreciate and to celebrate overcoming the mirror's distortions. It is as common a sight here to find parents and children laughing together as it is to see parents maneuvering young children, even wheeling baby carriages to face a mirror while adding encouragement to humor, and failing to get any visible or audible response (figure 2.20).

Parents repeatedly face a double challenge in shaping the orientation of young (three- to seven-year-old) children so that they can competently join the drama of family laughter. On the one hand, small children are often having too much fun to be specifically taken by the mirrors into laughter. On the other hand, they often become too engaged by the mirrors to react to them with laughter. In both cases the problem is a lack of self-consciousness, a failure to build a sense of juxtaposition through composing a semihysterical, partly frozen and partly free, body.

Small children often skip or bounce around the fun house, emitting various sounds of excitement. They may address particular mirrors by jumping up and down before them, by doing monkeyshines, by moving their arms like puppets, by sticking their tongues out at a mirror, and so on, and by issuing accompanying shrieks and shouts of joy. In order to bring a child into laughing interaction with the family, a parent will often have to lay hands on him, grab a darting boy at the shoulders, hold a lunging child at the waist (perhaps after issuing an order like "touche-pas!" [don't touch!]), or pick a jumping girl up off the ground. By these actions, parents stabilize children so that they can subsequently fall into expressions more clearly recognizable as laughter.

The problem for the parents with the joyously bouncing child is that the child in effect already knows the principle for making fun that the mirror represents. By jumping, skipping, and dancing about, small children create successively framed environments that delight them, in part by creating an emerging series of juxtaposed images. Put another way, fun house mirrors take a principle of playful childhood physicality, the creation of perspectives that distort or radically alter the embodied experience of the world that is produced by conventional posture, and package the experience as a situationally confined, narratively discrete, narrowly perceptual experience.

By laying hands on children, adults encourage the search for juxtaposition to turn more exclusively to the mirrors. But then they often encounter a second problem. Young children often find the mirrors' images fascinating but not funny. It is common for adults to hold children up off the ground, undercutting the ability of the youngsters to produce changing perceptual environments by themselves, only to find the kids staring soberly, even transfixed into the mirror. No longer

Figure 2.20 Testing baby

bouncing about and having the mirrors slip in and out of their attentions, young children often become intensely absorbed monoliths in front of the mirrors.

For adults the problem with children's sober interest in the mirrors' images is that it is essentially aesthetic. Small children often take an interest in exploring variations of the images as extensions not reflections of themselves. It is the rare parent who will assist a child in such explorations through an extended tour of the hall, for example by drawing the child's attention to the zigzag lines or to the "worms" that are created by up and down motions. Most adults limit a child's sustained aesthetic appreciation of the mirrors in order to elicit the collective experience of laughter.

Parents often must laugh to show small children how to split experience into subjective and objective domains. Such laughter readily conveys to the child a potential split between parent and child: "laugh if you want to stay with me." And if the parent has picked the child up so that their heads come close, the construction of intimate proximity makes the potential of a split all the more vivid. Even among parent-child pairs that have soberly explored several mirrors, adults often find it irresistible to laugh in response to a child's pointing out something interesting. Yet laughter immediately risks suppressing aesthetic spirit. It offers a neat completion of the interaction, and it turns attention from involvement with the fascinating image to a comment on the admirable ego of the child.

Through stemming both the child's spontaneous joy in bouncing around the hall and the child's inclinations to become transfixed at the mirrors, the parental pursuit of a laughing appreciation of the environment pushes the child to break from an unreflective, intertwined relation between body movement and perceived environment. In order to make the mirrors laughable, the adults must induce the child to set the environment off from him- or herself, to appreciate a fun house mirror not as a screen on which extensions of his or her body magically appear but as something that can create alien reflections of him- or herself. Small children often come into the fun house and find its images bizarre, but then their unconventional, playful body movements routinely create bizarre perceptual environments, both in and out of the fun house. The parents' contribution more specifically is to make the bizarre strange. By making the experience a laughable event, parents cut the environment's independent power and tuck the child gaily back into the family fold.

Held to a stable posture and then encouraged to laugh by adults, children are urged to appreciate that the mirrors' images are distortions of their identities as known by their family members. Text and subtext combine to make a juxtaposition that warrants a laughing response: "Look at your ear there. (That's a silly ear, not your ear as we know it, feel it, love it.)" The mirrors become alienated, "other" to the children. And the intergenerational family, a necessary resource for recognizing the juxtaposition, emerges as the sole agency that can joyously overcome the deformed image of the child's identity. The thrust of parental efforts is to awaken in children an appreciation of how a strange environment effortlessly misrepresents them, and that it is the family and only the family that works to enable the child nevertheless to embrace his or her "normal" appearance.

Family Experience, Fused and Divided

The socialization lessons of laughter in the fun house are collective family products in both intergenerational directions. If small children generally need adults to make the right sense for laughing at the mirrors, adults also generally need children to make sense of entering the fun house in the first place and then of acting in "silly" ways before the mirrors. And once the spark of humor is struck with either child or adult, the interaction often becomes intergenerationally democratic: a member of first one and then the other generation becomes taken as the butt of the humor. In *Louis,* Maman offers herself as a ridiculous image, then encourages all to find the father's image funny, and then aids the father's work to get Louis laughing at himself. In *T'es bellle,* the father first urges his son to see how absurdly little the mirror makes him, then offers his own body as a collective focus for humor, then encourages the daughter to focus on herself. In *SupEr,* the father guides the son to laugh at features of his face, then calls his wife to appreciate the generally "super" quality of the mirror as illustrated with his own reflection.

The narrative structure of the experiences we have been examining has three overlapping acts. In the first phase, there is an effort to assemble the family as a whole before the mirror. In the second phase, there is a coordinated expressive outburst that identifies and celebrates the collective experience. In the third phase, the collective formation is quickly dismantled. The rapid dismantling of collective family interaction is due not only to the fact that it is very difficult to sustain the presumption of shared seeing for more than a few moments. It is also unnecessary. Once there has been a coordinated expression of transcendent spirit, a satisfyingly coherent collective episode has been fashioned.

Figure 2.21 The camera is used as a substitute for laughter

The neat narrative ending that laughter provides can be created with other devices. Here a North American family experience is instructive. When a girl joins her father and sister, the three share a moment of coordinated exclamation, and then mother arrives and takes up the camera. She will take a photograph to memorialize the interaction, using her camera rather than her laughing body to mark its transcendent significance (figure 2.21). The process of taking the photo introduces a break in and designs an end to the episode of interaction, and as soon as the shutter is snapped, all can leave without further ado.

Commonly begun with an awareness of the challenge to a young child's competence, the sequences before the mirrors quickly become a challenge to the family's collective competence. The excitement expressed by the collective laughter is over what appears, in the details of a sequential empirical inspection, to be a virtual miracle, the creation of a manifestly (if often deceptively) shared seeing that transcends differences in lateral and vertical spatial position, in age competence for socialization, and between the body image of one or more members of the family as known in everyday life and as depicted in fun house mirrors.

The narrative meaning of the fun house experience is writ small in the details of given family interactions and it is writ large for observers who see the repetition of these short-lived narratives for an endless stream of visitors. Venture into the world beyond the family and, as happens to characters in picaresque novels, all manner of strangers will approach with unexpected, myopic views of your identity. In the fun house, at least, the family can, through emotionally intense and lightning-fast coordination, produce the transcending smoke of a collective sensuality. Laughing together, family members can hold fast to the conviction that they share a common experience, seeing the same things despite the world's tricky powers of distortion, knowing who each really is despite the monsters each may seem to be in the eyes of others, even as each must wander about, for long stretches isolated from the others, in a world of cold, bizarrely reflecting surfaces.

THREE

SHAMEFUL MOMENTS

Early in this century, the "looking glass" became a leading trope for understanding the self. At midcentury, Erving Goffman perfected this appreciation of personal identity with elaborately detailed analyses of people designing versions of themselves to shape how others would respond. We now need a more three-dimensional version of the self, one that will allow us to grasp something that is true in general about the self but that should be impossible to ignore in the emotional moments of social life: reflections of self that are cast off for others to see are at the same time refracted elaborately within. Perhaps we should replace the looking glass with the prism as our guiding image.[1]

In keeping with the two-dimensional perspective, sociology students are encouraged to describe conduct in the active voice, as someone doing something with or to someone else.[2] Such advice is unproblematic so long as one holds on to a Cartesian conception that sees personal identity as the outgrowth of a process of turning on the self from the standpoint of another, a process of self-reflection like thinking or like the anticipatory reading of others' readings of one's behavior that U.S. sociologists after Herbert Blumer have called "symbolic interaction."[3] An alternate view, presented in midcentury philosophy by Martin Heidegger and Maurice Merleau-Ponty and still struggling to work its way into empirical social science, holds that a person exists in the first place as a being thrown into the world, doing things, including the self-reflection of thinking and social interaction, while already and more fundamentally being corporeally engaged with other people and other things.

As the last phrase suggests, the active voice is awkward for capturing the reality of a prereflective intertwining of self and world. In order to get the point across that drivers embody their cars and dwell at a moving point up in the road ahead, we can talk about how they "construct" an understanding that their body has extended itself to include the steering wheel and tires, but we risk saying something misleading in the process. For all but novice drivers, that understanding is not sensed as constructed; it is already and naturally there. If our language does not allow us to see people dwelling naturally in the world, we will not be able to set up problems for explaining how different forms of tacit involvement develop. And if we do not take on that explanatory task, what we are left to explain is, if not exactly epiphenomenal, still relatively superficial with regard to behavioral process and a small part of the variation with regard to causal determination.

To say that we "do" or "create" our relationship with the world is in a way true, in that what we do is always the result of a personally contingent process; we always *might* do something else. But such language risks implying that we are located somehow outside of our landscape, existing as floating mental entities that from time to time make commitments to become grounded in "external" realities. Since there is no time out from involvement in the world, no pause in which one can begin constructing relations to others, it can be misleading to write about behavior or experience as a project. The project (or "act") implies a discrete starting and ending point. The active voice risks what, following Whitehead, we might term a fallacy of misplaced temporal boundaries.[4] Even the perception of another is accomplished by a stance and line of gaze that are unselfconsciously corporeal, that exclude and include what can be perceived without deciding, choosing, or reflecting on how one is defining one's horizons of awareness. One is always in society in an active manner, anticipating how one's action will be seen by another; but one is also always already in society in a tacitly embodied manner, in one respect or another unreflectively assuming the external stance from which one will view one's own conduct.[5]

What one finds in the self-reflection of emotional experience is, then, a truth about personal identity that has escaped traditions of analyzing interaction processes. The self in emotions is not only seen as an object from the standpoint of another, it is also experienced as being objectified: the self is sensed as taken by and as part of forces that are beyond one's subjective control. This the active voice fails to capture.[6] We can use a tortuous formulation to write about drivers who "construct the perception" that they are cut off and "construct their anger." The idiosyncrasies of drivers' ways of interacting with each other make some such language about personal construction necessary. But if that is the limit of our analysis, we will miss what is distinctive about the experience, which is the sense that "I am cut off," that I am passive, a victim, an object used indifferently or cruelly by the other. What it is to be a victim is to know in the first instance that "*I* don't victimize *myself, they* victimize *me!*"[7]

Shame is an essential topic in the study of emotions because, unlike emotions that prominently take behavioral forms such as laughter, anger, and crying, shame is especially resistant to the effort to perform an exhaustive analysis in the active voice. There is no close analogue applicable to shame for "he cries about" or "she laughs with" or "he rages against." A person is "in" shame when he experiences shame. The most common way of referring to shame is not as a doing but as a qualification of one's state of being: "I am ashamed." If "I shame" someone, I take an aggressive action against another and for me the experience may be joyful, not at all shameful. When others see me actively "putting myself to shame," it may well be because they see me as experientially shameless. The effort to capture shame in the active voice runs an unacceptably high risk of missing the phenomenon.

Embarrassment and the blush are the closest forms of shame that allow us to write descriptively in the active voice: "he shamefacedly withdraws," "she blushes," etc. But embarrassment, as Goffman noted, is itself a triumph over shame in that it demonstrates that one naturally recognizes one's indiscretions.[8] As we will see, part of what distinguishes shame is a sense of incapacity for action and a confession to self of moral incompetence in some regard. To the extent that one manifests embarrassment, one caps shame by showing that one's ineptness is a situational rather than an essential feature of one's identity.

We are used to thinking that tickles provoke laughter, pains provoke crying, irritations provoke anger. The converse is also true and it is more interesting: laughter, crying, and anger are behavioral forms of emotion that define a provocation by responding to it. Thus laughter acknowledges that one has been tickled; crying tries to dissolve pain that others otherwise may not be able to see; anger, by attacking the irritant, tries to show the offense that has been received. With these three emotions, the relationship between feeling and expressive behavior is so continuous that the behavior can elicit, or perhaps better, perfect the provocation. Indeed, expressions of laughter, crying, and anger not uncommonly precede and construct their provocation. Laughing, I encourage you to realize that you have started to say something funny. Acting mean, I provoke you to give me an excuse to attack you. By contorting my face into the outlines of crying I elicit from you a hug that enables me to break down completely. Such understandings of the relationship between feelings and expressive behaviors are part of the universally shared but private social psychology on which people shape the idiosyncrasies of their personal identities.

Shame, in contrast, recognizes its provocation by a vividly sensed inability to respond. There are many experiences of shame that leave the person at a prolonged loss for socially expressive conduct, experiences in which the feeling runs far beyond any situated interaction gesture that would capture and convey it. Indeed, it is by displaying my inability to respond, or my ability to respond only with a blush, that I may bring a sense of shame to everyone in the situation. My shame then gets behaviorally materialized, not in my own conduct but by provoking others' face-saving attempts to create a distraction that takes the sting out of my passivity. If there is any single common behavior of shame, it is a nonresponse, a being nonplussed.

The behavioral forms of laughter, crying, and anger are more closely intertwined with the feelings that provoke them than is the case with shame. Insofar as shame has behavioral forms of expression, such as rituals of modesty and gestures of embarrassment, they can be engaged without provoking any three-dimensional resonance at all. It is not clear, however, that prolonged laughter, intense expressions of anger, or tearful crying can be produced without a profoundly three-dimensional substratum. It is instructive to try to shout at someone without allowing any strong emotion to flow into the expression. The active and the passive dimensions of laughter, crying, and anger are more of a piece than is the case with shame. Indeed, ritual and habitual mannerisms of shame, or modesty, are useful for avoiding feelings of shame.

Accordingly, the study of shame requires a tone and methodological design that are less appropriate for the study of the other emotions treated in this volume. In the studies of anger, laughter, and crying, we start from an observer's perspective on the emotional conduct of the person whose emotions we are trying to explain; we work, as it were, from the outside in. From the outside, we initially wondered why people do the seemingly senseless things they do when they get angry as they drive along. Later, we followed the machinations of people in the fun house as they call others to respond to a provocative juxtaposition of images with laughter. In chapters 5 and 6, we again initially take the standpoint of the "other" as we trace how a teacher works on ending a child's whining and how police interrogators work to provoke crying by a murder suspect. But the investigation of the structure of the experience of shame must begin with materials describing the experiences and understandings of people in shame, not data taken from the standpoint of the other people who are interacting with them. In this chapter, in fact, I pay little attention to what the ashamed person does to shape others' perception of him- or herself, much less to what others do to provoke the subject's shame. Indeed, quite often, others are not present at all.

Another way of describing the relatively passive character of shame is to note that the experience highlights one's being more than one's doing. With respect to other emotions, a person's attention to his or her expressive forms often overwhelms any three-dimensional reality of being taken by them. Laughter often does not have more than the briefest three-dimensional character, as when a person exhausts whatever humor he or she senses with a single bleat of deep-chested laughter. With respect to crying, when the crying person turns to contemplate the sensations and technical production of the emotion, the emotional expression risks appearing to be false. Whining children are characteristically self-reflective and, as we will see, they may turn the behavior of crying into a bodily instrumentation that, far from engulfing the self, is subject to strategic, even playful manipulation. As for anger, the more one focuses on its provoking irritations, the more one is tempted to "act out" and shift focus away from the self and onto a troublesome other. That shift is, in a way, just what angry behavior is about. But with shame, the more self-reflection, the deeper the shame.

And conversely, the deeper the shame, the more self-reflection. Profound laughter, collective and ritualized crying, and anger mobilized into an attack are all useful for avoiding painful self-reflections. Collectively victimized peoples develop exquisite senses of humor and rich joking cultures as an alternative to mass depression. When intimates are arguing about deeply probing conflicts, crying offers a frequently effective device to stop or at least fundamentally shift the discussion. And in the twentieth century, anger, made into authoritarian regimes and then war, has been an appealing way to put off the day that privileged groups must face up to losses of status in the process of inexorable historical changes. Shame is a distinctively prismatic experience in the phenomenological sense that the more one is in shame, the more one abandons oneself to follow the meanings bouncing around or refracting within oneself. Indeed, obsessional thinking about one's inadequacies makes for a powerful form of shame.

In this chapter I will consider shame as a prismatic experience in several senses. One is that each experience of shame is likely to highlight a given aspect of the emotion, but all of the other elements of shame will be present and traceable at some recess of the experience. I find ten, but the number and the separation of elements for purposes of discussion is admittedly somewhat arbitrary. The experience of shame refracts in so many shades of feeling and takes such diverse metaphoric shapes that the literature is filled with contrasting definitions of the phenomena, each definition stressing elements that assist the author's objectives for shaping therapy, developing sociological or psychological theory, or making a philosophical argument. My theoretical objectives are to show the utility of the tripartite inquiry in this volume as a whole, and to understand the connections of shame with laughter, crying, and anger.

Thus a second use I will make of the figure of the prism is to arrange the elements of shame by considering the emotional experience as a phenomenon with three sides. The first set of elements clarify how shame is an interpretive process, or a way of seeing oneself from the standpoint of others. The second set shows shame to be a form of impotent praxis, a sensed inability to take control of one's identity and organize a response. The third set describes shame as a feeling in metamorphosis, an unstable sensuality that desperately seeks metamorphosis into the expressive corporeality of some other emotion. The overall argument is that shameful moments distinctively have in common the following features. As a form of self-reflection, shame is an (1) eerie revelation to self that (2) isolates one (3) in the face of a sacred community. What is revealed is a (4) moral inferiority that makes one (5) vulnerable to (6) irresistible forces. As a state of feeling, shame is (7) fearful, (8) chaotic, (9) holistic, and (10) humbling.

The original data that I analyze come from solicited autobiographical statements, videotapes of eight-year-olds playing Little League baseball, interviews with prosecutors and intimates of targets of white-collar crime investigations, and university students who, over several years, were asked to provide anonymous descriptions and to challenge a changing version of an explicit statement of this theory. In addition, I draw on the well-developed literature on shame, a corpus that frequently draws on works of fiction. The prior analyses of the nature of shame by Helen Merrill Lynd,[9] Helen Lewis,[10] Carl Schneider,[11] and Francis Broucek[12] have been particularly helpful, as has a series of recent studies of self-conscious emotions (Tangney and Fischer 1995).

For this volume as a whole, what we obtain from the following inquiry is a standpoint for understanding something that is otherwise difficult to grasp about emotions in social life in general. We will find that there are two constellations in which these ten conditions come to dominate experience, and that these two constellations are complementary forms of shame. The person in social interaction is constantly moving between shaming him- or herself as less than competent—

what Max Scheler called "body shame"—and shaming him- or herself
by pretending to be beyond tests of competence—to Scheler, "spiritual
shame." [13]

Emotions are dialectical tensions between doing and being done by
interaction with others; but they are also dualistic. Each type of emotion has a predominantly spiritual and a predominantly bodily form.
The study of the nature of shameful moments will set up a particularly
useful way of summarizing the social-psychological theory of this
volume.

1. The Interpretive Dimension: How One Sees Oneself in Shame

An Eerie Revelation to Self

Perhaps the most frequently noted element of shame is that of revelation. Powerful images of shame, from Adam and Eve's effort to mask
a newly unbearable nakedness to a child's periodic bouts with psoriasis,[14] emphasize revelation in the form of exposure. Early in the life
cycle, sphincter control becomes a challenge that provides a universal
socialization into the phenomenology of shame, and later in the life
cycle incontinence often provides a reminder that early concerns about
involuntary exposure are not simply childish.

It is part of the unique complexity of shame that the exposure it
implies is to an audience but that that audience is in the first instance
oneself. Others' discoveries about oneself are not shameful unless one
learns of their discovery. It is necessary to register the occurrence of
a revelation about self from the perspective that others take on oneself.
But concrete, face-to-face encounters with others need not be involved.

University student reports are full of instances of shame at events
like shoplifting in which the student successfully "got away with it"
in a practical sense. Such accounts might suggest that revelation is not
essential to shame, except that the construction of a scenario of exposure is part of the characteristic halo of these experiences. In a dreamlike manner, one imagines circumstances of revelation to others. As in
a dream it is not necessary to flesh out the faces or identities of those
who are observing; they are often present as phantoms. Even when
they are identifiable in imagined exposures, the observing others remain phantomlike. One account, for example, was of shame experienced when looking at photographs in the Los Angeles room of a
friend who had authorized use of her room but had specifically forbid-
den inspection of the photos. When looking through the photos, this
young man recalled the strange sense that "she would walk in the door

and see me at any moment, even though I knew she was in San Francisco and that this was impossible."

The eerie quality of shame's revelation points to the emergence of a problem in bounding one's identity from that of others. When there is a moment of revelation to others, the ashamed person often cannot or will not lift his or her head to perceive the others' regard. As a practical matter, he or she maintains a phantomlike sense of the "others" whose knowledge brings shame. In these cases, it is not actually seeing others seeing oneself that brings shame, since one may never quite catch their gaze. What brings shame is taking toward oneself what one presumes is the view that others would have, were they to look. As with Adam and Eve, in shame one anticipates revelation to another whose presence is ubiquitous and yet not necessarily materialized. Shame gets its transcendent power from a failure to focus on the situationally specific character of the other's gaze.

Its eerie quality is fundamentally due to the dialectical character of shame, which is at once an experience of revelation and a mystification. The experience hovers between exposure and cover-up. What is revealed is something that one does not yet and perhaps cannot fully confront.

Full revelation promises to overcome shame. When one truly cannot resist persistent exposure, for example after one is caught shoplifting and is subject to public denigration, shame seems unbearably intense but just for that reason, typically it eventually fades.[15] Where criminality leads to shame, punishment may be welcome for making public and for defining what is necessary for restoring the miscreant to the moral community.[16] A student who was caught burglarizing neighbors' homes recalls:

> Being angry as my parents were, they punished me severely; I felt as if I deserved it. This punishment felt like the only outlet from such a wrong feeling.

A star university athlete who was caught "illegally" partying on a road trip expressed regret at a lost opportunity for catharsis. Drinking, drugs, and sex were involved; but what the coach actually knew about and objected to was never revealed, due to the discreet way the matter was handled. The administrator in charge

> explained that this incident should never be spoken of because it would look bad for the program itself and to the whole UCLA athletic department. . . . I would have felt more at ease by suffering from a solid or noticeable punishment given by someone else. Instead, I suffered from my own shame, embarrassment, and humiliation.

As long as it persists, shame carries the sense that there is revealed an undeniable truth about the self. The matters that one is ashamed about are acknowledged as fundamental to one's character. But what that truth is remains mysterious. What is implied about a man's nature in the discovery that he regards his foot as shamefully ugly?[17] Shame is that paradoxical experience, the revelation of a personally powerful symbol. What is revealed in shame is not an answer, a solution or the key to self-understanding. *What is revealed is the existence of an abiding mystery, a personally resonant something-that-had-been-and-must-be-kept-hidden.*

Thus there is an ambiguity in the self-revelation in shame. Sartre wrote, "Shame is by nature recognition. I recognize that I am as the Other sees me."[18] But the fact that it is the Other who sees me means that the revelation is never complete, for I can never see myself quite from the perspective of another. Paradoxically, the other can know much about myself than I cannot. Logistically speaking, the other can see behind me, underneath me, the way I turn my torso and head to regulate my gaze. What is revealed to oneself in shame, as Adam and Eve discovered, is a kind of omniscience about oneself that only the Other can possess.

On the one hand, since shame is a recognition of the essentially social foundations of personal identity, it is surprising how warmly contemporary psychology has taken up the topic. On the other hand, the phenomena of shame describe the classic data of depth psychology. Experienced as an attack on what is sensed as one's personally indispensable symbolic clothing, shame highlights rather than destroys a personally salient mystery. Shame proves the necessity of repression.

Isolation from Community

Shame carries a sense of isolation from community. Any particular individual in relationship to whom one feels shame is regarded as representative ("symbolic") of a diffuse group from which one feels isolated. "Soiling oneself" may provoke embarrassment by creating a problem in managing one's identity in a given social situation, but when it provokes shame it is through the implication that one lacks the measure of self-control that would be required when interacting with any set of others.

Guilt is often specific to given relationships, but shame inherently generalizes. For example, guilt at not having cared sufficiently for mother during her final illness has a haunting power even as the sentiment emphasizes the uniqueness of that relationship. But in families where a working father is the primary bridge between the domestic household and participation in the public institutions of society, father's "discovery" of one's "weakness" often implies not only one's failure to meet family expectations but a devastating segregation from the community of responsible participants in society.

Isolation from community, if sufficiently extreme, will for many people provoke shame without any element of specifiable fault and independent of any relationship with a particular other. Imagine being given the assignment of walking across the football field during halftime at the Rose Bowl, there to be observed by the tens of thousands of spectators who are present in the stadium as well as by the millions who are viewing through TV screens. Would-be actors and actresses delight in such a prospect, as they can anticipate roles they might adopt as vehicles for their performance, but most others would anticipate nakedness and horror. The problem is not one of a moral failing in any indictable sense, but one of being *before the community without being part of the community* in any recognizably competent way.

The contingency of isolation helps explain how shame is experienced by elite suspects in the course of white-collar criminal prosecutions. During a study I conducted in the U.S. attorney's office in Brooklyn, several prosecution and defense lawyers described the following pattern.[19] While the common criminal defendant develops relationships with his or her defense lawyer and the prosecutor from the isolation of jail, white-collar defendants often manage to stay in a position of control in their business and political worlds, right up until the moment they are sent to prison. Defense lawyers report dramatic swings, from refusals to provide necessary documents and personal information, to efforts by the client to participate in the case as a colleague. It appears that members of elites often appear shameless in the face of scandal because they have distinctive resources for putting off their isolation from their prior community. They become part of a spirited team during long periods of investigation and then trial. Even after conviction, isolation is avoided while the defendant appeals to friends and professional colleagues to write letters to the judge in praise of the defendant's character. Prosecutors report that they can easily dispose of character witnesses who assert that the crime is radically inconsistent with what they know about the defendant, simply by asking, "So if you had known that he was guilty of committing crime, you would have had to revise your view of the defendant?" But defense lawyers understand that the ritual solicitation of support is in part therapeutic work that they do for their clients. The process elicits an emphatic, diverse community embrace of the defendant, one in which strangers often volunteer to participate. It is not until the defendant is sentenced to confinement that he or she must, for the first time, abandon control and anticipate the practical experience of isolation. Defense lawyers report that this stage in the process is rich in shame and, along with the initial need to break down the client's resistance to disclosing secrets, emotionally it is the most difficult transition for them and for the client to negotiate.

Despite the commonplace journalistic and political wisdom about the matter, when plant closings and economic downturns lead to mass unemployment, the collective dimensions of the problem mean that unemployed individuals are not isolated from the community, hence we should not expect shame. In their classic study of a whole community of the unemployed in a southern Austrian village in the early 1930s, Jahoda, Lazarsfeld, and Zeisel found apathy rather than shame to be the dominant emotional problem. The village had been dependent on a textile firm; when the industry failed, everyone suffered unemployment. Apathy itself was by no means an inevitable response. When they would congregate, "whenever we had a chance to observe such gatherings" they "would strengthen optimism and cheerful sentiments."[20]

Isolation from a Sacred Community

Standing out "like a sore thumb" is a common reference to shame. It is not enough that one stand out like a thumb, the thumb must be sore. That depends on the person's discomfort at being an outsider to the group. A student who moved from Boston to the San Fernando Valley when he was seven years old recalled vividly, some fifteen years later, how the class laughed as he read out loud a story about "bahn yahd" animals. He quickly learned to lose the accent. It was irrelevant to his feelings that his classmates, delighted in his innocent idiosyncrasy, might have shaped for him a unique place of affection in the group. The issue at seven years of age was not one of being seen positively but one of folding oneself into the cultural fabric of the group so as not to be subject to its devastating gaze.

In primordial understanding, the sacred is a power that, however beneficent, cannot be withstood when regarded directly by a person.[21] Thus a mortal's encounter with the gaze of a Greek god who had become his or her lover would be devastating to the mortal, notwithstanding the immortal's desires. In shame one discovers the communities that one cannot but regard as sacred.

One may discover shame in self-reflections that find one's essential sensibilities existing outside of any group. This is a neglected dimension of the shame of masturbation, a shame that has persisted long after moralistic cultural prohibitions have weakened. Masturbation shame is not simply a result of "internalized" collective disapprobation. On the contrary, the shamefulness of masturbation can develop in the realization that one has in effect asserted, as a form of hubris, that one can be in touch with one's fundamental feelings independent of contact with others. Part of the justification for the moral condemnation of masturbation is an understanding that human identity is essentially social, an understanding that one cannot complete oneself except through connecting to others. Shame's understanding is not that masturbation is damnable because of religious doctrine or because of conventional morality, but because it implies narcissistic self-satisfaction.[22]

If shame can be created by acknowledging to oneself that one has pretended to have a kind of sacred core outside the group, simply being in conformity with others does not guarantee insulation from shame. Thus one may feel shame as a citizen of a society that has lost a war, but not because there is any other society that one views as more honorable. Sensing the disgrace of the fatherland as part of a defeated mass of people, one feels isolated not from others but from the group's rightful destiny and from the sacred version of community that collective mythology honors. The collectivity before which one feels isolated in shame is more clearly symbolic than historical; it may not exist other than as a framework for self-respect.

A wide range of shame experiences are triggered by the sense that one has primordial ties to another person whom one sees as shamefully exposed. It is common both for members of groups that are elite and for members of pariah groups to sense shame on the revelation of disgraceful doings by a group member. Such shame can be experienced when privately reading a scandalous news story about a stranger. Shame may emerge in these circumstances even though one does not feel personally exposed or at fault. What is critical is the realization that group membership does not provide a taken-for-granted basis of self-respect, and the realization, which may come for the first time only when public scandals unfold, that one had regarded a subgroup as a sacred community. Dual affiliations are revealed as the person recognizes that his or her self-respect depends on the respect that a larger community confers on a social circle to which he or she is inalienably tied. In a domestic variation on this pattern, one student reported shame about his father, who sported a ponytail and rode a motorcycle, and shame about feeling this shame. Here the surprising revelation was not the young man's spiritual affiliation with the smaller group (his family), but the conventionality of his dependence on the larger community's whims of fashion.

Paradoxically, shame about the activities of a group in which one had been a member often emerges only when one no longer is in the group. The paradox is resolved if we appreciate the sacred or charismatic aura that a group may sustain. One student worked in a telephone sales job during graduate school, and until he left the job he failed to question the "borderline oil and gas company" whose stocks he was promoting. As he put it:

> By believing your own performances, as well as that of others, you get caught up in the feeling of the group. You deceive yourself in order to avoid the shame of your actions.

While he was in the sales group, he was part of a vigorously expressive, ritualized collective effort to enhance self-esteem, in a spiritually animated social world not unlike that of charismatic Christian groups.[23]

Shame is thus common when one has abandoned as well as when one feels that one has been abandoned by the group. It is a common subject for high drama, but the fate of relatively few people, to find that both dilemmas are present in a given moment when loyalty to the group is pitted against loyalty to the values that make the group an honorable collectivity. One such experience was provided by a student who attended the last show of the comedian Dick Shawn. Shawn had made a moderately successful career as an unusually eccentric or "mad" character. He often played on the ambiguity of whether he was in or out of role, posing the unstated question, "Was he really that nutty or was he just 'doing being nutty'?" During his last performance, he collapsed on the stage without notice. Joking comments began to emerge from the audience: "Is there a doctor in the house?" "Take his wallet!" "I want my money back!" A bit later some ladies were heard to complain in disgust, "This isn't funny anymore!" As the actor remained on the floor, the audience continued to laugh sporadically but in an increasingly nervous tone.

The student reported his mounting shame in three stages. First he debated the shameful possibility that he "didn't get it," that if he intervened he would stand out from the crowd as the only square who was insufficiently hip to understand the comedian's humor. But then, as the houselights were turned on, paramedics ran in from the wings to administer CPR, and the audience was asked to leave, the student became ashamed that he had been part of a mass of individuals who had been so reluctant to risk standing out from the group that each would let a man die before his or her eyes. A group that had been laughingly celebrating its shared, unconventional sensibility as the audience-complement for Shawn's oddball presentations of self was suddenly revealed to be a collection of individuals clinging in mortal fear to a superficial appearance of conventional form. In retrospect the student was additionally ashamed that he had participated in a group that had, however unwittingly, made fun of a dying man. He was, thus, triply ashamed: first, that he might not fit this hip audience; second, that he was a member of a group so insensitive and timid that it deserved no respect; and third, that through collective self-deception and cowardice he had participated in a sacrilege.

Ivan Morris, in his review of patterns of honorable suicide in Japanese history, points to further subtleties in the way that shame is related to isolation from a sacred community.[24] When military and political leaders commit ritual suicide after losing a war, and when Wall Street leaders jump out of skyscrapers when stock markets crash and financial frauds are revealed, commentators often assume that unbearable shame motivated the suicide. Morris makes clear that while these are shame-related suicides, they do not necessarily follow experiences of unbearable shame. Rather they may be ways of maintaining one's honor and thus of avoiding shame. Matters of fault are, again, not fundamentally relevant. Mistakes may have been made in military strategy, frauds may have been committed with the investors' money, but that is not necessarily the motivating concern. People who hold elite positions often know that mistakes and frauds are common in their fields and that their peers will not presume that a revealed mistake or a fraud was causally responsible for a disaster. There is no disgrace in failure itself; indeed, there is a "nobility of failure" if the disaster is taken as an opportunity to demonstrate, through the self-sacrifice of suicide, that one is committed to the group.[25]

Those who presume that guilt feelings lie behind such suicides fail to appreciate something rarer that is emotionally decisive. Members of elites know that they cannot escape the privileges of their status. When wars fail and markets crash, leaders know that they will not suffer as much as will the lesser participants they have long called upon to sacrifice and maintain the faith. For those who were in elite positions, there may be no way to avoid living in the disgrace of relative comfort if they continue to live, and that comfort would now belie their long-professed commitments to the collective enterprise. In their suicides they honor their elite status as having always been based on a communal spirit. Through suicide the self is taken out of society in order that a noble spirit may remain in support of the community. In the eyes of the honorable suicides, their self-sacrifice is altruistic, helping those who remain sustain the faith that their sufferings are rooted in honorable commitments.

2. The Dimension of Praxis: Shame's Impotence

Shame is not just a unique way of seeing oneself from the standpoint of encountered or imagined others; it is also distinguished by a sense of negative practical possibilities. The coherent behavioral practices that follow shame are metamorphoses of shame into some other emotionally charged conduct, such as crying or anger, which cover shame with their own expressive logics. These ways of transforming, "bypassing," disguising, or repressing shame we will review in section 3. Until the person in shame finds such a path, which is already an escape from shame, he or she confronts irresistible forces and an overriding sense of moral inferiority and personal vulnerability.

Moral Inferiority

Whether or not shame is preceded by an act that one treats as one's fault, there is a sense in shame of an inability to do the right thing. Student athletes commonly report shame upon failing to win a competition, without any finding of guilt about a lack of effort or a breach in training routines. Women who have been raped often report a combination of anger at the rapist, anger at anyone who would suggest they were at fault for "inviting" the violation, and shame that they were unable to prevent the crime. Something similar often occurs in the wake of nonsexual crimes. Con men rely on their victims' sense of shame to help "cool out the mark" and facilitate their getaway.[26] The rape victim, like the person whose digestive system is suddenly and unexpectedly overwhelmed by an amoeba that he or she can't resist, may feel shame that her body has betrayed her by being vulnerable to alien forces that transcend her will.[27] The rape victim's suffering is dialectical and absurd in that it protests in vain against an event that is not the victim's fault yet promises to leave an ineradicable stain.

This existential sense of a shameful inability to shape one's identity along morally desirable lines despite one's will and best efforts appears in various forms of vicarious shame. A black student reported his sense of shame on seeing black employees working at a club to which he was refused entry on the grounds, he believed, of his race. In countless ways, this young man's identity in contemporary U.S. society will be shaped by others' perceptions of his race; he is linked, willy-nilly, to the social identities shaped by others of his race. He is here triply impotent: unable to keep other blacks from working at such clubs, unable to resist sensing that he shares a responsibility for the decisions of others of his race to work in such places, and unable coolly to brush aside the suggestion that he would want to participate in a club that would not want him as a member.

Instances of vicarious shame include watching painfully awful performances in a theater. Having paid to attend a bad performance, one might more sensibly be outraged. But the performers' shameful incompetence may be experienced as one's own.

Social situations are replete with undesired implications that one's character complements the proceedings at hand. An audience member may be uncomfortable with a sensed responsibility for calling out a performance liked too little, especially if he or she has brought friends to the event. And a therapist may sense shame in the implication that, through voyeuristic pleasure, he or she likes work too much; seating positions that avoid face-to-face relations help to repress this implication.[28]

Vulnerability

In guilt a person imagines how he or she might have acted to avoid a faulty act; in shame, the person feels that his or her fate is determined independent of his or her will. Poverty's shameful character is ancient because of the close connection between indigence and vulnerability. If poverty in its public display as homelessness seems surprisingly shameless today, still public welfare opportunities in the United States remain grossly underexploited, in part because of the persistence of the shameful implications of dependency.[29]

Rituals of begging are to be understood not only in light of what must be done to put the would-be donor in a willing state of mind but also as a kind of occupational self-therapy. For centuries, at market sites located on European bridges, beggars would offer bits of street performance or recite formulas of praise for the moral character of their passing would-be patrons.[30] These rituals, which persist today in the form of short speeches, brief puppet acts, and fragments of musical performances delivered between stops on Parisian subways, fight shame by overcoming implications of vulnerability in three ways. They initially address the donor as a member of an audience, avoiding the sense of assault that a direct individual request can engender. Correspondingly, they clothe the beggar as a performer on a stage, providing a role of moral respectability. And the performance, however labored, cynical, or conventionalized, requires an effort at artfulness that has the potential of showing the supplicant to be of a more refined sensibility than his or her begging, dress, and odor might otherwise indicate.

The element of vulnerability is highlighted when shame is triggered by false accusation. Many students reported that being caught shoplifting was an intensely shameful experience, but a few students noted that their most shameful experience was being falsely accused. Recalling incidents that remained vivid after a period of ten years, they explained that in their culture, Asian-American in these cases, the very suspicion of such an act was sufficient to occasion shame. The aspect of frustration here—that one can unarguably win the battle of reason but still find that victory to be of no avail in resisting the emotion—is characteristic of the practical dimension of shame.

When sexual conduct is the shameful matter in student reports, what is shameful usually is not the violation of religious principles or conventional morality, but a loss of control, that is, the vulnerability of reason either to sexual urges or social pressures. The problem is that:

- "I could have been such a fool" as to have maintained an intimate relationship with a man, a coworker whom she'd been warned was a con man, and who, she progressively discovered, had a live-in girl-friend, owed her and many others a lot of money, and had given her a venereal disease;
- he acceded to the other's urging and to his own desires when he slept in the same bed with another Mormon fellow from his mountain state hometown, even though they promised they "wouldn't do it";
- her cover story disintegrated when she indiscreetly stayed out until 3 A.M. with a married man, after which she was upbraided both by her mother and his wife (for some time, she had cultivated a friendship with the couple by bringing them food and clothes, cleaning and cooking for them, and frequently conversing with him in the front room for hours after the wife, who was pregnant, had retired to sleep in the back room).

Each of these three reports has indications that the young adult in question was coyly playing with the ability to control his or her own conduct. In these cases, the potential for shame is so clearly signaled in advance that the circumstances seem exploited for titillation. Titillation consists of cyclical turns between subjectivity and objectivity, between an artful guidance of one's body and a letting go of control. What made these histories titillating was that their subjects wittingly structured a similar drama into unmanageably delicate relationships.

The relationship between shame and sex was not simply that sexual activity provoked shame. Sex became shameful only after shame had been exploited to make interaction sexy.[31]

Sex occasions shame not simply because of moral precepts but because shame and sex, as experiences of forces that transcend one's control, easily evoke each other. That sex and shame share a powerful dimension of vulnerability is also indicated by shameful experiences of trying to reestablish family order after sexual conduct has shattered presumptions of stability. The family problem may arise because of one's own conduct.

- She attempted suicide when her parents decided to send her back to Korea for a while, when a scandal broke out after she woke up naked in the apartment of a fellow whose family was socially related to her own.

- At twenty-two, within a three-year relationship, she finds she's pregnant. The problem wasn't the revelation of sexual activity; that had not been covered up. The problem was confronting a devout Catholic mother about abortion, and that "I knew that if anyone were to talk to me about my situation, somehow they'd humiliate me and make me feel like an incompetent, inferior, unintelligent human being" because she was someone "who was not supposed to get pregnant, so anyone who found out or knew about it was compelled to ask why and how."

The sense of vulnerability implicated by sex is not always directly a matter of one's own frailties; it may emerge when a parent's secret sexual life is discovered. In one case, a young woman discovered her father's mistress through her boyfriend's socializing with her father.

While my mom was working her tail off from 9:00 A.M. to 2:00 A.M., he was parading around with his bimbo on a cruise ship in company of my boyfriend. . . . To top it all off, it appeared that everyone, family members, friends, business clients, even [her boyfriend] knew about my father's affair. [Twice she confronted her father's mistress.] I came face to face with the woman who had stolen everything I valued in life. But rather than "her" feeling beneath everything human, it was I who experienced shame. Here was this woman with no morality, snubbing her nose at us. Her friends stood there calling us names one even called me a whore, and even though I am a virgin, I was ashamed, and I can't explain why.

In another case, a student reported her struggles with a long-term situation that still puts her identity unpredictably at risk. Her father lives with her mother and with another woman, simultaneously; he alternates sleeping at the two houses; she has "stepbrothers."

> I have gotten used to the idea that all my relatives know about this, but I still feel ashamed. . . . When I would find out from another relative that my father had been there to visit them with his other family, I would turn red all over and that feeling of shame would come to me again. When I was in the public schools, I would dread one of my friends finding out about this, so I never discussed it with no one. When there was an event in school and my parents were able to attend, I would be very happy but at the same time I would be tense to have anyone recognize my father as to be living with another family and now they find out he has another family and another wife. I feel shame for something I cannot control but that at the same time it is painful to me.

Note that it is not just the sense that the young woman's identity is out of her control that sustains her shame, but the absurdity in the situation. Despite the awareness that their fate is beyond her control, the young women in the last two examples cannot resist trying to escape their fate. As symbolized by Adam and Eve's hopeless effort to hide from God, shame is an experience of doomed efforts to escape.

Irresistibility

Closely related to the sense of vulnerability is the sense that the matter provoking shame is irresistible. Both features are highlighted in the experience of unrequited love and that of being abandoned by a lover. One can in these circumstances struggle for expressions of affection, but the effort risks humiliation since what is desired is an unconditional acceptance. Here is the classic setting, both fictional and factual, where attempts to resist shame fail and turn into irresistible rage.

The difficulty of limiting the investment of self to a situational identity is what separates shame from embarrassment. As Goffman put it:

> Whatever else, embarrassment has to do with the figure the individual cuts before others felt to be there at the time. The crucial concern is the impression one makes on others in the present—whatever the long-range or unconscious basis of this concern may be.[32]

Shame is a disturbance that transcends the machinations of situational self-definition. Thus one may privately sense shame when losing a game even though, or just because, one's opponent graciously attempts to save one's face by brushing off the outcome as "only a game." It is also common that games end in a mixture of embarrassment and shame. One middle-aged student reported shame on losing a game of Monopoly, after having humorously taunted his opponent with remarks like, "You don't have a chance. You can't beat me. What gives you the idea you could beat me?" When the game ended, he had an embarrassing problem of negotiating a transition from his arrogant posture as well as a sense of shame over feeling the loss.

A common feature of the experience of shame that is directly related to the sense of irresistibility is a desire to turn the clock back and take another course of action.[33] Fantasies of escape are common; one may think, for example, that "maybe it's not too late to change my name and move to Costa Rica." The anguish in this dynamic of hoping against reason is crystallized in those experiences when one realizes, on acquiring some new bit of knowledge, that long ago everyone present in a given scene had privately and collectively understood that one was pretentiously using language, invoking a reference, claiming a friendship, etc. Even if the original misuse was innocent, and even if no one else actually took notice of the fault, the immediate experience is an excruciating awareness that one cannot go back to the situation and correct oneself, and that it is improbable that one will ever have an opportunity to put a new, face-saving gloss on the long-past situation.

3. Metamorphosis: The Search to Escape from Shame

In addition to its features as a way of seeing oneself from the standpoint of another (as isolated from some community that one regards as sacred), and its features as a form of practice (an absurd struggle against an irresistible sense of vulnerability due to moral inferiority), shame is a corporeal experience, a dynamic feeling. Seized by fear, the person in shame searches desperately for a behavioral path of escape, but the only immediately effective resolution of shame is its metamorphosis into forms of emotional expression with their own coherent scripts, such as crying, anger, or a brief and contorted form of self-mocking laughter.

A Fearful State

Shame is a fearful state. In an illuminating study that asked people to describe what they were feeling in a recent shame experience, Janet Lindsay-Hartz turned up descriptions of cringing, of wanting to run away but being unable to do so, and of related fantasies of becoming invisible.[34] Like Adam and Eve, people in shame try not only to cover up, they also want to run away but know that the others from whom they would escape are omniscient. People cower in shame, looking down, Georg Simmel noted, so that others cannot as easily see how they are responding to the moment.[35]

The fear that animates shame finds its most perfect expression in a desire to return to the womb.[36] Several of Lindsay-Hartz's respondents describe their wish that the earth would open up and swallow them:

> Let me just cover myself up and nobody can see me. Shame is just total— and you want to disappear. . . . I can't put it a better way than to say, like of [sic] there could only be a hole in the ground, I could sink into and nobody would see me. . . . You want to hide yourself. You want to be where you cannot be seen. There is no way out. Just by your mere existence is causing you shame. . . . I kind of even sank into my chair. . . . You hope for yourself not to be there. . . . You feel like burying yourself. . . . It's like if you hide someplace, that's what I think of as sinking into the ground.[37]

The desire is not for death, not for a punishment of being buried alive. It is, instead, a desire to be alive but without so much as breathing because that might draw attention. The wish should be read as: "I wish I could get rid of the visible evidence that this damned body makes of my spirit"; i.e., for a secure refuge for the spirit, not for its destruction. The fantasy of being taken up by Mother Earth and to exist but in a nonbreathing and invisible state, protected by a power that one cannot see, imagines a form of prenatal life. Helen Lewis writes: "One could 'crawl through a hole,' or 'sink through the floor' or 'die' with shame. The self feels small, helpless and childish."[38]

Chaos

The phenomenology of shame begins in fear and moves immediately to a sense of chaos. Adam and Eve are frequently depicted as running helter-skelter in search of a hiding place.[39] In Greek tragedy, it is unspeakably shameful events that throw Thebes into chaos. Again, something similar is part of everyday experiences of shame. We have seen some of the indications of chaos already, in the dead-end maneuvers of imagining the clock turned back; in the realization that one's identity is linked to a dishonored group or historical event and so will be irremediably stained; in the effort to exist without breathing. Helen Lewis observed that "shame is a relatively wordless state."[40] Helen Merrill Lynd earlier had observed that chaos is one of the ancient meanings associated with shame; in her pioneering work on shame she saw the emotion as a "search for identity."[41]

Shameful dreams of having forgotten an obligation to attend an exam provoke the everyday anxiety of being late for social obligations. Being late carries for many people a fear that it will convey to others the characterological implication that if one cannot shape one's private affairs to the social calendar, one must be incompetent for virtually any social responsibility. In night and daydreamed anticipations of being late, a shameful sense of frantic frustration indicates that some form of emotional chaos is in motion.

Decades after Freud noted the phenomenon, it is still a common nightmare for college graduates, years after receiving their degree, to dream that they are shamefully unprepared for an exam the next day. It is specifically the sort of problem that one can do nothing about that is represented by this kind of dream, which transforms a more mysterious self-doubt into a practical problem that, were it true, one could solve. A psychoanalyst, Melvin Lansky, has found that when seriously disturbed patients have nightmares about long-past traumas, they are often using their troubling dreams to construct a false biography that only indirectly represents haunting matters of shame.[42] The chaotic presence of shame is indicated by the artificiality of the narratives that give coherence to the nightmares.

Led by developments in psychoanalytic thought, a large community of researchers have been pursuing the transformations of shame into other emotions.[43] Tracing these transformations is challenging because shame is, behaviorally, a kind of nondoing. Taking on this challenge in their studies of shame becoming anger, Thomas Scheff and Suzanne Retzinger have developed indicators, such as downcast eyes, tortured smiles, and gestures that cover the face, for coding the presence of shame independent of the rise of anger.[44] Shame can then be found to be "bypassed" in interaction, i.e., to occur even though the person in shame soon acts in a manner that draws the focus of the interaction to something other than shame, such as by creating an angry conflict.

In videotapes of eight-year-olds playing Little League baseball, I was able to document a recurrent multistage metamorphosis from shame. Baseball, as compared to youth games popular in other cultures such as soccer, is especially shame provoking.[45] As the batter awaits the pitch, time suspends and the entire audience, which includes members of both teams and, commonly in the United States these days, parents and siblings who accompany players to the field, is focused on an isolated player. A third strike occasions a decisive rejection; the batter is out. His disgrace and temporary exile from the field of play are especially abrupt if he did not swing and miss but was in effect ordered out of the batter's box by the umpire's audience-stirring shout of "strike three." Following a strikeout, the boys would frequently avert their eyes and sit in isolation on the bench with their face covered by their hands.

The chaotic presence of shame was indicated by the emergence of each of the other emotions treated in this volume. Laughter was a rare upshot. More often boys would move from being stunned on striking out into a tortured smile, which would then become a crying face giving signs of a struggle to suppress audible evidence of crying.[46] Anger was also a common upshot. Soon after striking out, a boy would often search for someone to blame, perhaps the umpire for erroneously calling the pitch a strike, the opposing team members for having made taunting remarks, or even a teammate for supplying the wrong bat.[47]

Most common was a combination of attempts to escape from shame into the corporeal forms of other emotions. In a sequence that appeared in three videotaped games and for three boys, crying was a common intervening behavior between shame and anger. The following metamorphosis occurred in four discernible stages. First the boy would strike out, be stunned for a moment, cast his gaze down and avert eye contact with anyone. Then he would begin to cry, as indicated by a contorted facial expression and sometimes tears. While crying, when done in relative privacy, may be a way of escaping shame by embracing the self or calling for an embrace by a parent, when a boy cries on the open field where he is the focus of collective attentions, he can anticipate that his crying will be taken as a further acknowledgment of vulnerability and inferiority. Here crying, like the blush in other settings, provokes further shame. Third, the boy would use a cry-broken voice to designate a reason for his anger or to invoke pathos, such as by claiming that his failure was due to the continuing effects of an earlier injury. Fourth, the boy would melt back into an emotionally indistinguishable member of the scene as the collective focus shifted to the fate of the next batter, or, if he had made the third out, as his team jogged off the bench to take the field. The insight in Genesis, that people in shame are in desperate search for any form of socially recognizable clothing that will cover their nakedness, is vividly and elaborately illustrated in these poignant moments.

Essential, Holistic

The fear in shame and in its nightmares is that the chaos cannot be limited to any specific act or fact. The experience of shame may start with the revelation of some minor stigma, like an ugly foot or a malapropism, but it quickly sweeps through the self. Helen Lewis again:

> Shame is about the whole self. It is possible in moments when one is not ashamed to regret or grieve over a specific disfigurement or personal failing. At the moment when one is ashamed of specific shortcomings,

shame affect involves the whole self. This global target of hostility makes it difficult to find a solution short of a sweeping replacement of self by another, better one.[48]

Shame may be about intimate matters, such as private parts or secret corruptions, or it may be about matters that are superficial in the general regard but that are uniquely meaningful to the person ashamed.[49]

For adults whose respectable status is secured by their positions in multiple social circles, shame becomes holistic through a progressive stripping process. In investigations of white-collar crime, a range of associates may be drawn by the chief suspect into the effort to resist charges. As they are themselves brought under investigation or withdraw in fear of stain, shame becomes generalized in the target's social relations.

In a Los Angeles case in which I interviewed friends of the target, an in-house lawyer for a major corporation was indicted for taking kickbacks to send work to outside law firms. But the target had another understanding of the events, one that showed that he was, despite everything, a man of honor. In his account, the CEO of the firm had urged him to take the kickbacks as an indirect form of compensation and as a way that the executive could keep him in a vulnerable position. Truth be known, there was, then, nothing shameful about the kickback scheme. Indeed, it only illustrated his loyalty to his employer, his oppressed status, and the integrity-challenging atmosphere of intrigue that was common in his line of work. Of course, when the scandal broke, it was inevitable that his employer, like the CIA when an undercover operation is revealed, would deny that he had authorized the kickbacks.

The fellow lost his job, but his intrigue scenario, which is not uncommon in the authority relations underlying bribery regimes,[50] initially had some value in insulating the target from shame, at least among the circle of friends with whom he could share it. It was also useful as an insider's explanation that his therapist could use when soliciting supporting letters at the penalty stage of the case. But as the scandal evolved, the fellow became increasingly isolated in his understanding of the events. His boss did not know that he had been holding private negotiations for a senior position in a major local law firm. The firm's representative happened to be a neighbor and regular social acquaintance (and the source of my information). The latter professed his astonishment at the revelations and withdrew the offer, fearing that his firm would be drawn into the disgrace. While the target still met socially with close friends and neighbors, they found themselves avoiding comment on the scandal and treating the target in an artificial manner, as if nothing unusual was going on. The face-saving value of the story of intrigue collapsed in a suicide attempt.

Humbling

Shameful feelings alternate among fear, chaos, and humility. When put to shame, one is cut down, forced to abandon a prior, arrogant posture. When one stumbles into shame, one shrinks down, trying to become small in order to escape notice.

Occupants of honored, elite positions confront a distinctive dilemma of shame precisely because of their difficulty in negotiating a posture of humility. It is a peculiar feature of recent U.S. politics that powerful forces in the public stubbornly insist on uncovering matters of personal biography that are inconsistent with the honor that large parts of the public insist on conferring on their leaders. The days have passed when such matters as presidential mistresses and habits of smoking would be kept off the record by opposition leaders and the press. Whether the matter is lascivious desire or a playful act, leaders are ridiculed when, with an informality that belies their status, they acknowledge their human frailties, as occurred with Jimmy Carter's report of "lust of the heart" and Bill Clinton's description of smoking but not inhaling marijuana. Leaders cannot as a practical matter avoid setting themselves up for shameful revelations because they cannot themselves control the forces of adoration that motivate their followers. Similarly, people who receive routine demonstrations of respect, such as the maître d's fawning "Doctor, your table is ready," live within walls of dignity that may be unwanted but that in any case will be undermined if a professional license is stripped away.

On the domestic front, fathers often must walk a tricky line between leading their children to unfounded adulation and attacking their children's need for faith in parental perfection. A son catching his father taking something cheap, like coins left in a phone booth, can put both to shame, even though the father had never assumed a character that would make such a discovery the revelation of hypocrisy.[51] Conversely, and perhaps empirically related to children's adulation, a form of shame frequently reported by my UCLA students is shame over disappointing parental expectations about grades, sexual behavior, drinking, and car driving. Whatever the reality may be on the parental side, these students indicate a sense that they lack any means of downscaling parental expectations to a level that they would regard as realistic. On the one hand, glorifying the other is, for many at least, an inextricable part of loving the other; while on the other hand, the child and the parent, each unable to have his or her own limitations accepted by the other, collaborate to institutionalize a vulnerability to shame on both sides of the generational divide.

Common folk practices for extricating the self from shame contain a telling socio-logic. After the onset of a shameful experience that appears to be interminable, people often report that they returned home and began to busy themselves with tasks of restoring their domestic environment. Lynd reminds us that

> Tolstoy makes clear both the shame of discrepancy arising from the sudden loss of all known landmarks in oneself and in the world, and the way in which one seizes upon familiar details of daily life in an effort to regain a sense of one's own identity and rootedness in the social situation.

Anna Karenina, recognizing her feelings for Vronsky, busies herself with details of everyday life at home to dispel shame, although no one else knows of her feelings and no shameful act has occurred.[52]

This may be understood as an effort to build up a private sense of self that is independent of and immune to the threats of participating in society; but that formulation is only partially accurate. The busyness of perfecting the domestic order, by cleaning and putting things in their place, by taking up neglected responsibilities, or just by polishing an order that is already well established, has no substantive relationship to the matters that provoked shame. These must be understood as ritual practices honoring the congruence of one's nature and an order—any order—that is clearly moral. In cleaning, putting things in their place, paying one's bills, and so on, one humbles the self, becoming a servant of a predefined, typically conventional notion of propriety. Symbolically, the logic of self-salvation here is to do a kind of penance to some version of collective morality, trusting that in the process the environment will once again take up and silently embrace the self. But symbolic logic is not enough. A metamorphosis, or change in the lived corporeal vehicle of action, is necessary, and as a practical matter, in taking on such tasks one changes the employment of one's body in thorough and precise detail.

4. Negotiating a Passage between the Dual Risks of Shame

Max Scheler distinguished between "body shame" and "spiritual shame."[53] Body shame is a matter of not staying covered by social clothing. It is occasioned by the faux pas that indicates a general lack of education; by "animal" releases and indiscretions that occur when social actions are not properly embodied; by incompetencies due to poverty, poor health, membership in stigmatized groups, new immigrant status, etc., that put one below the minimal level for leading a "normal" social life. If body shame is a matter of sensing that one fails to satisfy the definitions of minimal social competence prevailing in a given society, spiritual shame is occasioned by recognition that one has made claims to transcend conventional restraints because of extraordinary qualities. The fall of body shame is to a childish or animal nakedness; the fall of spiritual shame is that of Icarus, a fall from arrogant pretension. Body shame often emerges independent of imputations of personal fault; spiritual shame emerges when one needs shame to manifest a humility that will do penance for transgression.

Dick Gregory neatly illustrates both forms of shame in his autobiography. As a poor child, he was ashamed to wear the Mackinaws that were distributed by the local charity. Ashamed of his poverty, the signs of which he literally wore as a constant provocation of body shame, he risked spiritual shame when, during a campaign in school to raise money for the community chest, and in order to impress a female classmate, he offered to bring several times the average class contribution from his father. This is how he recalled the teacher's response:

> "We are collecting this money for you and your kind, Richard Gregory. If your Daddy can give fifteen dollars [it was Depression time] you have no business being on relief. And furthermore," she said, looking right at me, her nostrils getting big and her lips getting thin and her eyes opening wide, "we know you don't have a Daddy."[54]

Frequently the two forms of shame are merged in a given event, but they are still distinguishable, as in the multiple shocks in the sucker's realization of his or her fallen status. Con schemes typically proceed from the sucker's willingness to believe that he or she is "wise," i.e., a partner in a scheme to con others.[55] In a pigeon drop, for example (the following is from an experience in Mexico City's Chapultepec Park that was related to me some twenty-five years after it occurred), one stumbles across a bag of money at the same time as does a stranger. The stranger offers to leave the bag with you while he or she searches around to find someone who would claim title to it. In the meantime, the stranger must trust that you would split it honestly when he or she returns. To show your reciprocal good faith, the stranger suggests that you make a loan of your watch. Before the stranger returns, you run off with the bag. When you have time to look more closely, you find that only the top bills are real. Now you must confront (1) the hubris in your assumption that you would fall upon an abandoned

treasure, (2) the pretentiousness in your effort to trick both the ficti-
tious person you never met and the real stranger you did meet, and
(3) your fundamental incompetence to recognize an ancient con trick.
The shame of the experience rings in two keys: it was just by pretending that you were especially smart that you came out a fool.

One may err painfully in being overdressed for an occasion or in
being underdressed; when arriving at an appointment much too early
or much too late; by failing to bring a gift of value sufficient to honor
the recipient, by bringing a gift that is so valuable that it seems to be
an insulting attempt to lord one's status over the recipient, and by
bringing a gift either too soon or too late, since errors of timing in
either direction can indicate the lack of an appropriate sense of the
social relationship.[56]

Each of the ten features of shame that we have reviewed characterizes spiritual as well as body shame. In the presence of what one regards as genius, stunning beauty, or unsullied innocence, one cringes
or *humbles oneself*. There is evidence here of *chaos* and *vulnerability*:
"For many there is a reticence, awkwardness, speechlessness, diffi-
dence and fumbling before great people."[57] There is *fear* in meeting
the great scholar or artist at the cocktail party, fear that one may undermine the other's comfortable display of his or her marvelous sensibilities and talents. One cringes at the risk that something *sacred* may
be defiled because he or she is too mediocre or conventional.

At children's first music recitals, it is not uncommon for parents to
find an *irresistible* catch in their throats as they watch precious performances in awestruck silence. Shame unwillingly begins to metamorphose into a silent form of crying. Such experiences are often surprising
revelations to self of one's dependence on another's fate. One may
experience shame even as one is being praised by a community regarded as *sacred*. In shame one feels *isolated* within the community's
honorific embrace.

For some, a creative sensibility depends not on overcoming the fear
of shame but on sustaining shame and *a fear of shamelessness*. Henri
Matisse was horrified when reviewing a slow-motion film that revealed
the motions he made before his pencil touched the paper. "I never
realized before that I did this. I suddenly felt as if I were shown naked—that everyone could see this—it made me deeply ashamed."[58]
As the blush is a form of shame about shame, so modesty, when it is
not merely a pose but a sensually lived experience of humility, is a
kind of self-inoculating experience of spiritual shame that guards
against the naked feelings of body shame.

The transcendence of body shame is not necessarily to shamelessness but commonly to a new embrace of the spiritual power of shame. John Updike recalls that after the sun would cure his periodic bouts of psoriasis, he could walk with his family on the beach in a bathing suit, with a pride that was at once a form of humility.

> It was, for me, a matter of pride, a willed achievement, to be among these nearly naked strollers, to be an inconspicuous part of this herd, to be in this humble sense human.[59]

In some discussions, what I am here calling spiritual shame is distinguished as modesty or the practice of protecting oneself against shame by living it constantly in a mild form. What is crucial for theory is not a specific vocabulary but an appreciation of the existential dilemma that animated Scheler's discussion, as it points to the challenge of personal identity in society as one of constantly negotiating a path between the Scylla of body shame and the Charybdis of spiritual shame. A dualistic perspective on shame is inconsistent with the prevailing thrust in American culture and in much social-psychological commentary that sees shame as inherently negative and something to be transcended.

The empirical reality of spiritual shame is distinctively tricky to see in data, just because it is a matter of the style, spirit or manner of conduct. As Erving Goffman wrote, the obligation to present a self in society is not simply one of giving an impression that one is a particular kind of person (father, professor, market shopper, car driver . . .), but also of "giving off" that same impression, that is, of acting one's roles and features of identity "naturally" or with a grace that makes them appear to be effortless emanations of one's character.

> The expressiveness of the individual . . . appears to involve two radically different kinds of sign activity: the expression that he gives, and the expression that he gives off.[60]

If we know, through cross-cultural research, that much about styles of masculinity and femininity, character features that change with age, and personality dispositions associated with high and low statuses in work institutions vary enormously among societies, we also know that, in any given society, gender, age, and status characteristics are usually enacted as already there. Personal identity everywhere is an achieved performance of ascriptive characteristics. One learns how to enact fundamental features of personal identity in ways that suggest that the features are inherent, natural, matters of grace, and not products of years of culturally guided practice. It is difficult to see how members of society give off their personal characteristics just because members work constantly from early in life to obscure the machinations of producing their identities.

The posture that risks spiritual shame by implying a natural guarantee for the accomplishment of social life has its rationale in the faith that it produces, a faith that is necessary to ordinary social interaction. Were Matisse to watch his hands as he attempted to draw he would lose his genius.[61] Any line of social action, from a casual conversation to an artistic performance to a sexual interaction, is vulnerable to breakdown from too-close attention to its necessary machinations.[62] Awkwardness, not just practical ignorance, threatens to provoke a destructive shame. But the alternative is not the transcendence of shame. A constant running on the surface of shame is a necessary foundation of social action.

The implications of a dualistic conception of shame are decisive for the study of emotions in general. Just as there are two forms of shame, so there are two forms of humor, slapstick and inspired wit; two forms of anger, hot and cold;[63] and, as we will review in the next chapter, a crying that proceeds from loss and a crying that recognizes what is awe inspiring. Just as it has been especially difficult for scholarship to grasp spiritual shame, so there has been a parallel failure to appreciate uplifting as well as tendentious forms of humor, the pleasures of meanness and cruelty as well as the dynamics of rage, the tears that issue in joyful celebration of innocence and creativity as well as the tears that mourn destructions of the self.

5. Master Narratives and First Causes

As the twentieth century ends, shame has reappeared as an attractive explanation for a range of problems in a way that is oddly reminiscent of an episode in the history of psychological thought near the start of the century, Freud's early (acknowledged) mistake of attributing his patients' neuroses to childhood sexual manipulation by adults. In Hollywood dramas over the last fifteen or so years, in countless TV and cinema products, flashbacks revealed toward the end of an anguishing story show that childhood sexual abuse was the cause of the otherwise incomprehensible destructiveness. Also at this time in American history, local prosecutions in various parts of the country have promulgated elaborate stories of devil worship and sexual abuse of preschool children by their teachers.[64] The recent widespread popularity of shameful sexuality as an explanation for imagined problems[65] (and in the Hollywood case, problems of the imagination) should give us pause before using shame to explain social-psychological problems. The combination of shame and sex makes for an intoxicating interpretive brew in our time.

Academic social-psychological thought has been less sexy, but here shame on its own has had a strong run as a source of ideas for remedying social problems big and small. Shame is said to lurk behind everything from poor school performance (in the form of "low self-esteem"),[66] to crime,[67] to troubled marriages and the causes of world war.[68] But if shame becomes too widely used in explaining the "how" of behavior, it will not be very useful for addressing questions about the "why."

The investigator will not fail to find shame behind problematic behavior, because shame is at the edges of all human conduct. Once found, earlier scenes of shame can easily be read to imply that something had been repressed from which the person desperately sought escape. That, after all, is close to a phenomenological description of the situational experience of shame: the individual in shame fearfully and chaotically recognizes a mysteriously rooted, usually hidden feature of his or her nature that he or she cannot and, in the case of body shame, feels he or she must transcend. Shame is specifically unspeakable. When we are searching for a repressed cause, shame is a fitting candidate.

But if we are to accept that shame in robbers' childhoods explains the high rates of U.S. street crime, does shame also explain the highly punitive response to street crime that Americans have taken in recent years? (Imprisonment rates, in California and nationally, have quadrupled since 1980.) And if national shame in European history after the First World War explains the embrace by a generation of Germans of Nazi anger, why should we not look to shame to explain anger toward Nazi war criminals? For the explanation of problems that are personally and historically contingent, shame is more reliable when used as a constant filter for conducting inquiry, one that brings inarticulate resonances of conduct into focus, than as a telescope for reaching back in time, isolating first causes, and magnifying them for a clear view.

It is one thing to claim that shame is a lynchpin in the metamorphoses of other emotions, another to say that shame should be the primary metaphor in the understanding of one or the other, much less all emotions. In other cultural times and places, any of the other three of the emotions studied in this volume might make for more convincing master tropes. How is it that we do not regard each other, with Rabelaisian humor, as walking, talking bags of piss and shit?[69] To put the point in a more contemporarily acceptable guise, instead of looking for shame we might do better by following these leads for keeping an eye out for the absurd in everyday life: the emperor is naked and the so-prano bald; social life is always a conflictual, interactionally precise, and highly perceptive process of collectively agreeing on what will not be seen and what will remain unarticulated, or of sustaining a consen-sus to pretend there is an underlying, guiding normative consensus; people are always covering up unremitting doubts that they under-stand each other, not so much by taking the other's perspective on oneself as by sharing ritual procedures for convincing each other that they are taking the other's perspective; we are always hiding the sleights of hand by which we raise the spirits of what seem to us to be the external provocations of our conduct.

And if the humor of the absurd is not compelling, why not make anger the central metaphor for social psychology? We might soon come to the point in the development of sociobiological thought of locating angry sex as central. Anger aids fighting and thus gives an advantage in the competition for mates. The linkage of anger and sex is enshrined in a unique wisdom of the bodies. Only through sex can human beings focus all of their energies in using a small part of them-selves to physically attack each other with unparalleled intimacy and unrestrained force, with the miraculous result not of injuring, much less killing, each other but just the opposite, of exchanging pleasure and creating new life. As we look back into the foggy, formative eras of human history, is it not clear that the species thrived as anger and sex were fused, such that those more capable of physically mobilizing anger tended to reproduce themselves?

And if that image isn't sufficiently depressing, we can also easily work crying into a myth of the origins of our emotional life. Is not the leading emotional narrative that we should take out of sexual gene-sis an interactive relationship between an angry male and a weeping female member?

The trope of shame fits the sensibilities of our times (sensibilities that are suspiciously similar in both academic and pop-cultural do-mains) better than would any of these alternative perspectives, which currently appear to be disgusting, ridiculous, and gratuitously insulting of the human condition. But I would suggest that, instead of taking any given emotion as protean, our guiding focus should be on some-thing that exists outside of any one emotional form: the personal expe-rience of falling out of a taken-for-granted incorporation into social form. Falls lead to shame no more regularly than they lead children to crying, burlesque audiences to laughter, and injured parties to anger. The fall, I would suggest, is present for us as a challenge even before Adam and Eve introduce shame onto the scene.[70]

What we can confidently take from the analysis of shameful moments is more modest than psychological or sociological notions of first causes. We can, however, still emerge with essential theoretical leads. We see in the experience of shame a taken-for-granted, ubiquitous, even ontological demand that the individual make sense of his or her conduct in society, which means shaping his or her behavior in some coherent relationship to collectively recognized forms; and, further, that the process of making sense be itself disguised aesthetically, i.e., by becoming a seemingly natural, idiosyncratically tailored way of being with others. An appreciation of the dual forms of shame as posing an ongoing existential challenge for social action gives us a fruitful standpoint for closely examining the empirical dynamics of emotions, including, at least, the range of emotions examined in this volume.

More generally, the study of shame argues for a social-psychological form of analysis. So long as the emphasis in the study of shame remains psychological, analysis is likely to highlight the destructive, inhibiting, and negative aspects of the emotion. The valuable features of shame are more visible when we ask, what is necessary *so that people may act together?* Then we can appreciate that manner, style, grace, and other ways of acting so that one's role appears to emanate naturally, as if through some kind of transcendent guidance, are always difficult, always contingent, but always necessary elements in the process of sustaining the identities of the others with whom we interact. Psychologists may find this perspective useful on the understanding that it is, after all, through the process of sustaining others' identities that each person elicits the responses that sustain his or her own.

The dimension of grace that is necessary for competent personal action need not be morally admirable or appealing in light of any conventional aesthetic canons. Its typical vehicle may be a combination of national or regional cultural style, an ethnic or racial or gendered way of doing things, a professional demeanor, a personally distinctive, even eccentric manner . . . some mixture of collective forms that are invoked as inherent, ensured, already there, confidently guiding the production of particular acts. Through the matter of manner, one provides a basis for others to take for granted that there exists a collective ground, independent of the participants' machinations, for the conduct on which they collaborate. The social order appears to demand, not only that naked self-interests be covered by the substance of conventionally recognizable social roles, but also that each put the self aesthetically at risk of spiritual pretentiousness in order to sustain the identity of others.

FOUR

WHAT IS CRYING?

What should we make of the relative absence of crying as a topic in social and psychological research? If research is to be responsive to the concerns of its subjects, certainly crying must stand among the more compelling signposts for directing efforts in the human sciences. What people are saying when they cry is, we will see, systematically indirect, but it is difficult to review crying as it occurs in a wide variety of situations without getting the message that something important to the people involved is usually at stake. Whether it is authentic or dramatized, a rare or an everyday event in a person's life, crying says something along the lines of: "I'm touched with a special force. I am moved to an unusual depth. What's going on now hits me just where I live. Something has struck at one of the primordial homes of my identity."

No one decides not to study crying; everyone just decides to study something else. But it is enigmatic that in some major subfields in the human sciences where the phenomena of crying would seem obviously to be of central relevance, the topic is barely on the horizon of research. Students of child development have developed a strong field of studies of the child's process of "acquiring language" through subtle forms of social interaction,[1] but crying still gets virtually no notice. Yet from the start crying is the newborn's way of using voice responsively in social interaction. Isn't it a reasonable bet that the study of how crying changes as the child's social experience develops would offer clues of major importance for the understanding of what is entailed in language competence? For the young child, speech is often an option among various vocal and nonvocal means of using the body's expressive possibilities in order to elicit responses from others.[2] From the child's perspective, one of the first things that speech is is audibly not crying.

There are hundreds of social-science studies that, in an ad hoc way, take up crying as a variable, but virtually never is their purpose to understand how crying is a way that people relate to others and to themselves. Thus there are studies that address debates over gender differences by investigating whether women cry more often than men do. (Yes, a lot more, but what does that mean?)[3] For adults, if not for children, crying (at least crying about losses, pains, and absences) appears to be much more common in private than in face-to-face social interaction,[4] but what does this finding mean for the understanding of crying when it occurs in the company of others? There are studies that measure infant crying as an indicator of how mothers' drug-taking practices during pregnancy may affect their children, indicators that are of potentially great diagnostic value for practitioners who need to know quickly what may be wrong with newborns. This is certainly important to know, but such work is not very helpful in understanding what crying is.

Studies of crying as a kind of social interaction are concentrated on such practical questions as whether solicitous mothers encourage their babies to cry more. In a happy inconsistency that can support a wide range of mothering strategies, some research provides comfort to solicitous mothers by finding "no"; other research provides comfort to less responsive mothers by finding "yes."[5] Another hot practical issue is whether colic explains differences in infants' crying.[6] Yet despite the prescriptive and counseling focus of much of the research, patterns of infant crying, for example the part of the day in which crying is concentrated, may well differ by society,[7] indicating that the mother-infant interaction system is shaped sensitively in response to cultural fabric.

In all these studies, the operationalization of crying would seem to require some notion of what crying is. But contemporary research virtually always glosses the descriptive question.[8] In academic psychological research, a tape of someone crying can be played to see what determines different responses (e.g., by gender); because the tape does not change for different subjects, it is not necessary to describe closely what the crying stimulus is.[9] Survey and interview researchers often ask subjects whether or not they cried and then take for granted the meaning of the responses, without clarifying what if anything is in common in the experience or behavior of the crying that the subjects are referring to. Crying is an old theme in anthropological studies, but the tradition has been to describe when and where in social rituals and kinship relationships crying occurs, leaving the description of the behavior of crying itself to such glosses as " 'The wailing begins. The women get on their feet and shout loudly, throwing themselves on the ground. The wife of the deceased cries more than anyone else.' "[10]

Recently, the descriptive question has been transformed into a study of how people, after the fact, *talk about* their emotions or interpret the emotions of others. If studying the representation rather than the experience of emotions is the favorite dodge in current anthropological and sociological research, psychological research misses the phenomenon in the opposite direction. There, crying commonly is *reduced* to dimensions such as duration, sound frequencies, and the distance between peak and final moments.[11] Such dimensions are measurable by precise and reliable instruments but they cannot speak to what is understood by the others who witness someone crying, much less what may be strategic and artful in using the body in this expressive manner.

Almost always, crying is treated as the dependent variable in a study that tests for the effects of gender, maternal interaction, prenatal conditions, environmental stimuli, and so on. Very rarely is crying treated as an independent variable. Research generally neglects that crying is a distinctive way of eliciting responses from self and other.[12]

For establishing a broad research agenda to study crying, the literature provides two sources that, not coincidentally, are both inspiring and oddball. One is a fifty-year-old semiphilosophical essay in psychological anthropology by Helmuth Plessner[13] that compares what people are doing and how they are relating to others when they laugh and when they cry. The other is a ten-year-old book by a biochemist, William Frey, who was led to study crying on the suspicion that emotional tears were organically different from tears provoked by physical irritation. On the way to (positively) resolving the relatively unimportant question that launched his investigations,[14] Frey developed several productive research instruments: a large-scale questionnaire survey, a systematic diary operation for recording fresh descriptions of the settings and minicareers of crying episodes, and a personal correspondence with people who wrote to him at length in order better to understand their own experiences in crying. His book provides a wealth of useful information on such matters as who cries when and where in contemporary American adult life, on the reactions that people anticipate from others when they cry, and on the strategies that frequent criers develop to manage the interaction problems they repeatedly confront. But neither Plessner nor Frey offers a research agenda that could lead to a comprehensive understanding of crying as a distinctive form of socially sensitive behavior.

I will not attempt to explain why the history of social-scientific research on crying is in its current sorry state, but two critical points are unavoidable. One of the central problems is the great enthusiasm with which sociologists and psychologists study all manner of issues without looking closely at what they are studying in its natural habitat and in its own terms. Ironically, the general scientific objective of discovering just what stuff is like, the enlightened curiosity to get as close as possible to distinctive things and learn their natural histories without imposing extraneous concerns on them, is forgotten when sociologists and psychologists launch rhetoric about the scientific status of their work. Thus crying, like anger, shame, and laughter, is easily made a variable in research without providing descriptions that allow the reader to hear, see, and feel variations and changes in the emotion being discussed. The perspective of the ambitious naturalist, whose greatest passion is to see something that no one has seen before and to bring it back alive, or at least on videotape, or at least in the form of reliable representations of how it functions in the full context of its own everyday life, needs a lot more support in the American social scientist's understanding of what science is about.

A second problem in intellectual history has been especially troublesome for progress in language-related research. This is the belief, increasingly powerful at least since Wittgenstein, that language is primary and sui generis. Consistent with this belief, studies of language have found speech to be a transformation of gestural forms of conversationlike social interaction. The relevance of the child's prespeech behavior is appreciated essentially only to the extent that it contains primitive forms of the rational discursive world of language. The wide range of the child's exploitations of the audible possibilities of his or her body, a range within which crying figures prominently but certainly not exhaustively, is accordingly neglected. Without contesting the sui generis qualities of language, we can recognize the utility of an alternative focus on the various prelinguistic things that children do with their bodies in interaction. This perspective would see language as a particular kind of corporeal activity, one among a range of prior, protean orchestrations of the body's expressive capabilities. Speech might then be seen as a particular application of a broader aesthetic knowledge, an application of a more general technology of the communicative, socially interacting body that lies behind both talking and nontalking audible conduct.

For an initial effort to suggest a research agenda on crying, coverage of the following topics seems essential. We want to *appreciate as full a range of crying narratives as possible.* This means that we must ask what sense people are constructing when they cry joyfully as well as in sad times, at least to the extent of considering the relationship between these two contextual uses, or meanings, of crying. In order to appreciate that there are various relationships that crying may have with speech-articulated forms of expressing meaning, we should also at least sketch some of the differences in the way that people cry over the life cycle.

We should further note that, behaviorally, *crying varies with the type of social situation in which it occurs,* both with respect to the interpretive issues it creates for the people immediately involved and with respect to the ways that people structure situations in order to induce, deter, or diminish their own and others' crying. And throughout our inquiry we should keep uppermost in our minds the fact not only that crying is an emotional "expression" in the sense of a meaning conveyed, and not only an interaction strategy in the sense of a way to elicit desired responses from others, but that there is great artfulness in the behavior. We must be ready to see crying as a panoply of *distinctive, aesthetically guided ways of mobilizing the expressive body.*

In order to make a manageable beginning on the general social-psychological study of crying, I propose the following three chapters. First, in this chapter, drawing on various forms of data, I will examine several dimensions on which a wide range of crying varies. Then, in chapters 5 and 6, I will examine particular segments of videotape in order to focus primarily on an individual as he or she cries in a given type of social situation. The first subject is a two-year-eleven-month-old girl who whines almost continuously over a seven-minute stretch as she sits at her desk in a preschool. The second subject is a thirty-eight-year-old man who, for a few seconds in the course of a four-hour interrogation by two police officers in Texas, cries sporadically as he develops his confession to, among other crimes, the murder of a middle-aged woman in Ventura County, California, and the murder of an elderly man in Las Vegas, Nevada. It is hard to think of two instances of crying that would be more likely to have less in common. That is precisely the reason for focusing on them in tandem. They offer detailed tests of the utility of the three lines of inquiry that, in this chapter, are applied to a more methodologically diverse array of materials.

1. What Sense Does Crying Make?

Two Crying Narratives

Can we find any general patterns describing what people are trying to express when they cry? Is there some coherent and recurrent commentary that people are making about themselves or their situation when they are crying?

Among the risks facing an attempt to specify the narrative meanings of crying, especially troublesome is that of misrepresenting crying by transforming the effort it entails into a linguistic statement. Crying is not talking, or if it is, it is a distinctive way of talking, and part of what it "says" may be inherently mysterious. Whether by default or design, crying is a form of expression that creates a special challenge for interpretation.

People often cry as they talk coherently, but crying is not just a gloss on talking. People often cry without talking at all, and at such times they may achieve expressive coherence without any assistance from words. So there is sense to crying, and the sense that crying expresses is not wholly separable from its form of expression. We are thus haunted by a methodological problem. In the kind of relationship that writing allows, author and reader only have silent words as aids to capture a meaning that, like speech, exists in the first instance audibly, but that unlike speech, exists in a kind of opposition to language.

But if crying is inherently mysterious, at least in the sense of resisting linguistic expression, still we have good reason to attempt to specify the meanings of crying. Even newborns do not begin and stop crying randomly. It is possible to sort out the meanings of a wide variety of crying by examining their social contexts and testing hypotheses about what people through crying are then trying to do. If there is a great risk in trying to capture the meaning of crying as if it were a linguistic utterance, we risk less when we attribute intentionality. Crying provides rich evidence that it is an effortful doing that a person knowingly alters (which is not to say "freely" alters) in response to variations in his or her context. I have gathered a mass of bizarrely diverse instances of socially situated descriptions of crying. This data set is used here as a base for testing generalizations about the narrative meanings of crying.

It is the strategy of this volume in general to analyze emotions in their most accessible and narrative form, that is, when they take a form most like commentaries that people make in the presence of others and in response to independently observable changes in a social setting. It may be that the bulk of crying, for adults at least, arises and diminishes outside of observable social situations. There is no assumption here that the meanings of crying that emerge from the following analysis will apply simply and quickly to the many lonely experiences of crying in grief, depression, sustained physical pain, etc. The only assumption is that, after a century of using depth psychology to understand crying-rich emotions in their least accessible state, knowledge can be gained by looking at crying when and where it is most accessible for investigation.

The Dualism of Sad and Joyful Crying

Following a lead from Max Scheler's work on shame, one that was reinforced by Helmuth Plessner's inquiry into laughing and crying, it is useful initially to recognize that in many instances, a theme of *loss or pain,* often bodily loss, is prominent in crying, while in other instances a theme of spiritual *glory or triumph* is notable. Some examples of the former type of crying occur:

- when experiencing pains of injury and of hunger;
- as people part, whether because of death or in a situational ritual that temporarily ends ongoing relationships;
- after falls, whether physical or symbolic, such as falls in social status and losses of face that result from rejections, criticism, and betrayals;
- empathetically, when reflecting upon one's guilt in harming others or through identifying with others' losses and crying.

Most adults also have intimate if infrequent experiences with crying of a spiritually very different sort, crying that emerges:

- as one stands with friends on a boat's deck to view an eclipse, when one hears an especially pure or beautiful performance of a favored piece of music, upon directly viewing a painting that one has admired in reproductions for many years, or in the wake of sexual ecstasy;
- on witnessing the unparalleled achievements of a nation's representatives or the heroic achievements of the handicapped;
- on personally receiving awards for distinguished accomplishments, or just when entering a room to find that "Surprise!" friends have assembled to honor your birthday;
- when receiving a profession of love, making vows at one's own wedding, watching the birth of one's child, or when witnessing a child's first music recital.

Of such cryings Plessner writes:

Before the sublimity of a work of art or a landscape, before the quiet power of the powerless simplicity of their being, before the fragile beauty, the touching candor and familiarity of children, we sink inwardly to our knees as before a grandeur that transcends every relation to ourselves.[15]

In several respects, these two forms of crying are inversely related. One is about sadness and loss, the other about a gift of grace and a joyful advance in life. The former emphasizes the negative, the latter the positive. The sad, negative, loss form of crying focuses on being cut off from others; while the positive, spiritually inspiring form is an experience of being joined with something transcendent, something larger than oneself. One is about nonbeing: absence, lack, loss; the other is about an excess of being: being overwhelmed with thankfulness, being overcome with pleasure, being overawed with beauty.

Three dimensions that have been useful in examining other emotions in this volume will also be useful in grasping the contrasting narrative dimensions of the two forms of crying. In *temporal perspective,* sad crying looks to the past with regret and anticipates the future with dread. Joyful crying, in contrast, responds to a moment as if it is eternal; the person whose eyes are tearful with joy is frozen in a blissful, sanctified, immortalized present.

In *spatial perspective,* sad crying recalls a lost home for the self and reaches out to be "there," in some other place, such as in the space of another's embrace. Joyful crying, in contrast, senses an extraordinary presence, the magic or beauty of being precisely "here." The awe-filled moment seems to summarize the meaning of one's life. Other pursuits, the sorts of things one does in other places, seem trivial.

The two types of crying may also be contrasted by considering what each implies about the *self as known privately,* from within, and one's identity as known *publicly,* from without. Loss crying is a cry to the outside that pleads for help to cope with internal sufferings. Or, as Schopenhauer suggested, sad crying is a kind of self-pitying self-regard, a way that one comforts oneself as if from the standpoint of another.[16] Joyful crying, in contrast, is a humble acknowledgment of an evident glory, a recognition of something wonderful that others see, feel, or know. In tears, one accepts a universal truth of beauty, joins in a communal celebration of national pride, and recognizes the existential insistence of emergent new life.

For empirical research, the idea that crying comes in two dualistic forms, each the inverse of the other, means that observations made about one form should be reliable guides to the location of opposite features in instances of the other. Let us test this use of the theory. We find that joyful forms of crying emerge as a person witnesses the transcendence of a contradiction. An example would be the tearful appreciation of how Vermeer's painting, a laboriously produced, rare, and elaborately framed artifact, timelessly and tranquilly grasps an eminently everyday, specifically natural, and transient reality, such as a young woman in a kitchen pouring milk from a pitcher.[17] If in joyful crying, what would seem to be existentially in *tension,* the artificial and the real, miraculously *dissolves,* then sad cryings should reflect an awareness of an insurmountable contradiction. They should emerge when what had been whole becomes *irremediably split apart.*

Thus Phyllis cries when coworkers Dol and Ada leave Stich Company, not because her work will change in a technical sense but from a sense that being at work will no longer mean being with friends: "They were like sisters to me, I don't want to work here anymore if they're not going to be here."[18] Using temporal, spatial and public-private dimensions to capture the contrast, we can see that the Vermeer painting magically, effortlessly brings *"here,"* to the time and place in which it is observed, a public museum wall in 1990, *what was "there,"* a fleeting moment in the life of an utter stranger, a moment lifted from the interior of a private house in the seventeenth century. And with respect to narrative meaning, Phyllis's crying registers the understanding that every foreseeable day on the job will bring her *a sense of* absence, of *what was and no longer is,* a yearning awareness of loved ones being out of reach, hopelessly elsewhere.[19]

Continuing the investigation of whether we can locate dimensions of sad crying by isolating dimensions of joyful crying, consider the experience of shame when becoming tearfully overcome upon witnessing a moment of pure innocence. Parents often have such experiences when silently watching their children perform at a first school play or music recital. The production of such precious moments is a mainstay of business in mid–Los Angeles at a Yamaha music school.[20]

At a church a few blocks away, sad crying is evoked with even greater regularity from a largely black, homosexual, and AIDS-plagued congregation. At the Unity Church, participants sequentially take hold of a mobile microphone and rise to describe the sufferings of their corrupted bodies. Only as they talk do they cry, in part because only as they talk do other church members move and murmur their support, demonstrating that the purified spiritual embrace of the community stands ready to catch the sufferer should he or she fall. Paradoxically, it is the *parents* at the music recital who, in witnessing the innocent beauty of the child's performance, *become ashamed at their crying,* fearing that it will corrupt the scene by diverting collective attentions from center stage to themselves. Meanwhile *crying at Unity Church works to overcome* any *shame* that the isolated speaker may feel as he or she rises in public confession. The congregation embraces the speaker in an extraordinarily vocal and visually noticeable manner, demonstrating, in the spirit of the ushers who literally hug each person as he or she enters the church, that there are no pariahs here.[21]

Again, if we find singularity as a subtheme in joyful forms of crying, we should expect to find some version of its opposite in remorseful forms. If the *singularity of joyful* tears takes the form of *"firsts"*—of unprecedented events, unrepeatable moments, history making, record breaking, beginnings of life and of relationships—we should expect to find a theme of *banal repetition* in remorseful crying about losses. Of course death is no less unique a life event than birth, and any birth is just another instance of an endless series, but our reference here is not to independent philosophical perspectives but to what is appreciated by the crying person. Thus we expect to find, in such cryings as those over getting fired, being rejected by a lover, and suffering another's death, that part of the experience of loss is a sense of permanent departure from something unique. The person cries through realizing that he or she has been transformed forever into an ex-, into *just another* person thrown into the bulging ranks of the unemployed, just another foolish romantic who has been scorned, just another bereaved mate who must deal with the common practicalities of separating from a shared life. Pain is most painful when it seems endlessly repetitive. Medical personnel know this intuitively, so they may help patients to manage an uncomfortable treatment by announcing where they are in the series of steps that must be taken. Such commentary allows patients to locate their pain in a trajectory with an end. Acting on this folk-sociological understanding of the phenomenology of pain and suffering, patients appreciate timetables that will enable them to identify their progress in the sequential execution of brief (e.g., a series of injections) and extended (e.g., tuberculosis cures) treatment programs.[22]

If sad crying is provoked by the futility of personal struggle against loss, tears of joy are provoked by personal responsibility in the metamorphosis to an elevated state. At weddings and awards ceremonies, ritual (standard phrases said, familiar music played) gives a gloss of the eternal to a particular relationship. An official's words or garland-bestowing action draw group attentions to the honored individual. Then he or she must add the idiosyncratic sounds of a personal voice to the classic arrangements that have been set on the stage. The first moments of that movement, when the focal person moves out of a respectfully observing stance as a formally decorated ritual landscape feature, into the role of speaking participant, can take on the shattering burden of representing a biographically unique metamorphosis.

For a final theme of contrast in this initial review of the narrative content of the two forms of crying experience, we can focus on the relationship to community. *Joyful crying* is not inevitable, not universal, not necessarily even admirable when seen from the outside, but when it does occur, from the inside it *celebrates a joining.* People cry in joy as they respond to orgasmic mergers with another person and as they recognize their bliss at divine acceptance. Eyes well up when people are joined to each other in marriage ceremonies and when the birth of a child fuses the parents into a family. People are tearfully overcome as they sense nature's glories humbling them to an egalitarian status with all of life. And in moving from observer to participant at an honor ceremony, people may find that, against their better judgment and hypocritically with respect to their previously expressed political views, their eyes drip with patriotism, ethnic group pride, or institutional allegiance. Conversely, we should expect sad crying to feature themes of loss of community. At all points in the life cycle, people may be provoked to sad crying when experiencing not so much a threat to life as evidence of *existential isolation* on the model of an infant's protest against separation from mother.

Dialectics of Crying

A key issue for the analysis of emotions is whether their meanings are unidirectional or dialectical. Does the meaning of emotional behavior have a coherently uniform, unambiguous, and straightforward thrust, or are people, in their emotional moments, always in conflict, always experiencing a form of tension, at once both going forward and cutting back on themselves? Are we, in our emotional experience, like objects blown by winds that come strongly from one direction and then die down to be replaced later by winds of a different provenance? Or are we more like objects taken one way by surf and simultaneously drawn in an opposite direction by undertow? With respect to crying, should we consider given instances to be simply sad or joyful, unidirectionally about loss or about gain, wholly negative or positive? Or should we consider crying always to be an internally tense phenomenon, an expression that constructs the self in some respects while it undermines the self in others?

The more fully we examine the narrative meanings of cryings as actions taken in social and biographical contexts, the more their meanings appear to be dialectical. The dualistic contrast of sad and joyful crying holds up, but as a contrast of independently dialectical phenomena. Within each form of crying, the theme that is uppermost in experience exists in contrast to an opposite theme that underlies the experience. The overall relationship of sad to joyful crying can be described in a configuration in which an entity with a $-/+$ structure is related to one with a $+/-$ makeup.

Consider the following *Los Angeles Times* news report from September 30, 1991. The dismantling of Soviet authority enabled masses of people to reestablish ties with cultural identities that had been long suppressed. One woman had survived a Nazi massacre at Bergen-Belsen by fainting and falling one hundred feet onto a mass of corpses that included her husband and children. She had remained silent about her experience, even through two subsequent marriages to Russian men who never learned of her Jewish identity. She reports that after she went to a newly opened Jewish cultural center, she cried "constantly" for six months. Only then could she speak about what she had witnessed and what had happened to her family. She had not been able to talk about the experience for fifty years.[23]

Crying is here not simply a part of the loss itself but a part of a process of transcending loss through representing it in the dramatics of a crying body. Such crying is overwhelmingly sad, considering its manifest cognitive frame. At the same time, considering the act within a whole biography, by depicting a process of breaking up and dissolving, the crying is more subtly a positive step beyond hysterical shock and a step toward the recovery of a buried segment of life. Similarly for many readers of this newspaper story: the biographical squib provokes tears, not simply because of the horrors it brings to mind but because it invites a quiet celebration of a narrative of transcendence from unspeakable despair.

The positive side of sad or loss crying is present from the start. What adults call the infant's "cry" is a series of sounds and motions that adults see as manifesting distress in the form of a broken composure and that they honor and empower as a strategy for acquiring a variety of, for the infant, self-constructive results.[24] However much infants may owe their care to the charms that their objective features have for their parents, it is primarily through mobilizing their abilities to convince adults that they are suffering and to affect adult experience negatively that infants themselves play an active role in mobilizing the specific situated actions that promote their survival.[25] As an ongoing practical matter, it is essential for the positive development of the self that we master the production of negative indications about the self.

Many sad cryings, however, cannot be understood as strategies for obtaining succor or embraces from others. In Frey's studies, several women reported learning to manage their response to criticism so that they would not be seen as either helpless or manipulative by crying at work; they worked up the ability to put off crying until they were in the privacy of their homes. Even so, they provide extensive testimony that crying offers positive rewards in the form of a relief that may be found in dissolving and washing away a spoiled self-image.[26]

Notions of psychodynamic release do not adequately capture what is going on in such private moments. A social-psychological dramatization is involved. The bodily transformations produced through crying appear to offer a kind of embrace by a virtual other. If children open up their bodies audibly and through extensions of their limbs as they cry, adults more typically close down on themselves, enacting an embrace of themselves as they seek to hold back distress and muffle audible dimensions of their cries. The ability to comfort oneself through crying, to construct an embrace that at times will be more accessible than any that can be obtained from another person, may be mastered at a young age. Such self-comforting and self-reassuring aspects of crying were epitomized in a field note on a three-and-a-half-year-old boy in a preschool playground who protested angrily in a crying voice against an adult's intervention: "Don't take my tears away!" It was this part of the range of crying experiences that Schopenhauer appears to have had in mind when he theorized that crying is a kind of self-pity, a crying by oneself for oneself.

"Self-pity" is a harsh term for crying over lost loved ones. A more sympathetic understanding would see crying as a struggle to sustain a positive view of the person lost, and to confer a derivative mantle of honor on the suffering of those who grieve the loss. This in any case appears to be the logic by which funerals become occasions for crying. As rituals, funerals collectively honor individuals' losses, providing a setting in which personal disorientation and existential protest is socially elicited, witnessed, embraced, and shaped. In turn, crying by the aggrieved parties, who presumably have especially intimate knowledge of the deceased, promotes faith in the value of life among all the observers. Public grieving, which by protesting against death sustains the myth that life is worth commitment, is thus a public service that elicits complementary expressions of sympathy for the aggrieved. The minimal work that funerals must do is to honor grieving by constructing the value of the loss suffered.[27]

If we are to take seriously the claim that crying that on the surface manifests a theme of sadness has a positive theme on its inverse and more implicit side, there are difficult cases we must confront. What often makes the positive themes in crying elusive is the fact that other people cry over matters that provoke no tears in us. Unable to see the tragedy, we find it difficult to see what the value is in what the person crying is holding onto. In Jennifer Friedman's research on struggles between mothers and adolescent daughters over matters of social and sexual independence, she reports the following excerpt from one of her interviews:

> Like if I want to go to this party or whatever, my mother doesn't really like me going to parties. . . . She'll be like, "You know how I feel about the party things, you know you can't go." . . . [crying] I know that I can't change her because I'm only one person. . . . I just have to live with it. I can't do anything about it.[28]

Presumably this crying honors the self that is denied by the mother. Characterized pejoratively, the adolescent's crying might seem to be self-martyring. Less judgmentally we might say that through crying the girl sustains a claim that she is worthier, more of a whole person than her mother allows her to be. Tears, even if they are common, are still precious, and their production appears to be inevitably linked to claims about what is precious in life or in one's own nature.[29]

Turning to the dialectics of joyful crying, a transcendence of loss or pathos is sometimes obvious. Often there is a delicate balance between the negative and the positive themes. An example would be retirement celebrations that anticipate a community's loss even as they manifest, not so much the value that the retiring person has had for the community but the value of membership in a community that so honors its members.[30]

Triumphs over handicaps provide the dialectics for many forms of tear-jerking dramatizations. A Los Angeles primary school reliably produces joyful crying at its winter holiday assembly, most predictably during a uniquely orchestrated performance of a Christmas song. After musical and dramatic numbers have been performed by different subgroups of the student population, the assembly reaches an emotional high point as students stage a mass performance of a sign language version of "Silent Night." A professional, adult-sung version is played simultaneously on a tape cassette running in the background. Immediately as the children begin to gesture the lyrics of "Silent Night," the audience snaps into a complementary silence. Parents begin realizing that, in order to surprise them, their very young children have been practicing secretly at school for months to become competent in sign language. As the audience moves to overwhelming applause, parents throughout the auditorium can be seen brushing tears from their eyes. The fact that the school has virtually no other relationship to the deaf than this annual musical number does not limit the power of the performance simultaneously to invoke and transcend the theme of pathos.

Many joyful crying experiences have a bittersweet character because they celebrate a sense of relief at overcoming something terrible. Relief looms large in the background of the crying by the student who opens the letter informing her that she has been admitted to the college of her choice. Relief also bubbles near the surface for the man who cries as a doctor tells him that all has gone well in his wife's cancer surgery. Audiences moved to tears by replays of Dr. Martin Luther King's "I Have a Dream" speech respond with the knowledge that it took a century of struggle before the Lincoln Memorial event could mark an irreversible turning point from slave and Jim Crow oppression. Indeed, as the years pass and viewers are increasingly removed from personal awareness of the suffering transcended, the extraordinary dramatic qualities of King's speech become increasingly valuable for attesting to the magnitude of the turning point being celebrated.

But if negative themes are at work underneath instances of joyful crying, it is not always clear where they lie. One can impute anxiety behind the new father's tears as he watches the birth of his child, but if this birth is the third in the family, and all have been the outcome of normal and unproblematic pregnancies, the only evidence of anxiety may be the crying itself. Similarly, behind the tears of audience members at weddings one can impute a sense of the bride's lost innocence or a realization that one's own youthful possibilities are now past, but such theoretical imagination seems too risky, too convenient, too self-satisfied. And where is the relief or the negativity overcome when tearfully witnessing a sunset or an eclipse; when crying in the wake of sexual ecstasy within a relationship that has not known sexual frustration; or when witnessing an athlete receive a gold medal when all along he or she was the one who was expected to win?

Something negative is appreciated in joyful crying, but it is not necessarily a prior negative experience or anxiety. Indeed, the overwhelmingly positive character of a moment may evoke crying. In some cases we must look at the corporeal metamorphosis of crying itself in order to find the negative theme. By undermining posture, deconstructing face, and dissolving the self, crying enacts a humility that recognizes, acknowledges, attests, and defers to what is worthy of pride, respect, honor, etc. Crying is a means of responding to beauty, the sacred, inspirational music, etc., because in the face of such positive forces, crying is an appropriate figurative negation of self.

Does this analysis impute too much self-design to emotional conduct? A particularly enigmatic kind of crying is especially useful for showing how subtly and unselfconsciously people simultaneously monitor the definition of the situation that their emotional composure constructs and shape a responsive message embodied in the behavior of crying. In these events, crying emerges directly out of a holistic bodily engagement in some other emotion. One example, described in Frey's and other materials on crying, is crying after sexual orgasm.

Here are three other examples, one from "loss," one from "gain," and a third with ambivalent features.

- A professionally trained dancer reported that after dance classes in North Hollywood many students would regularly cry. The classes were exhausting workouts in which instructors pushed students to physical extremes. Crying would occur whether the class was led by the "mean" instructor, who would criticize students incessantly, or by the "nice" instructor who would urge them on with supportive comments. The crying appeared to emerge from being "carried away" by the music and by the instructor-guided exercise. Somehow the accomplishment of an extraordinary workout became the launching pad for crying. [from an interview]
- A four-year-old child, who had come to spend his first sleep-over night at a friend's house, was laughing wildly with his friend at the dinner table. Without an apparent break or hitch, he began to cry. When the host mother asked if he wanted his mother to come pick him up, he said "yes" through his tears. [from field notes]
- A young, slight, petite Asian woman collapses in tears in a martial arts class. She had just concluded a practice session in which she had worked herself into a frenzied counterattack on a six-foot-plus black male who was playing the role of her sexual assailant. [videotape][31]

The thoroughness of the physical involvement in sex, exercise, laughter, or aggression can put one at an edge from which, without any intervening external provocation, one may slip out of a prior socially shaped identity and into crying. It is as if, like the cartoon character, one realizes that one has moved off of the firm ground of the cliff and for some time has been walking on thin air. Suddenly realizing that he or she has moved beyond the ability to deploy the body instrumentally, but now under the irresistible power of self-consciousness, the person suddenly collapses in tears. For the adult and for the small child as well, the development of too much pleasure or too much power can occasion a sense of being carried away from familiar and reliable grounds. Whether the departure from the mundane was desired or not, crying dramatizes a fallen self, thus simultaneously bearing witness that the ground for constructing a self has given way and beginning a rescue effort.

Sad crying expresses a dialectical narrative in that it *re*-presents loss. Joyful crying is the upshot of a *consciousness about the dialectics of metamorphosis itself.* Weddings, births, a child's first music recital, sunsets and eclipses, sexual orgasm, the ritual induction of a winner into the ranks of immortalized heroes, the rise of a denigrated people into the ranks of respected citizens, a physical involvement so total that it carries one to unprecedented success or ecstasy . . . : all of these entail transformations in which an individual, a group or some element of nature is understood to become transformed in the most fundamental bases of identity.[32] Events *of* metamorphosis are recognized *in* the corporeal metamorphosis of joyful crying.

The basis for asserting that joyful crying is a dialectical narrative expression is the *bittersweet* sensibility of joyful crying itself.[33] People "feel like fools" and become ashamed when they cry for joy. Chills come up the spine; the throat chokes down; tears are wiped away almost in a shameful fear. The fear is double edged. If one does not wipe away the tears, they may become too prominent and draw attention from the proper focus of the collectivity and onto oneself. But if one does wipe the tears away, or clear the throat as a prophylaxis against breaking out into a more audible sob, one's attempt to stay in the background itself risks being seen. Thus, watching her child at his first piano recital, a mother struggles to hold back her response so as not to interfere with or corrupt the innocent emergence of independent competence on the stage. The dialectics of joyful crying are experienced as a challenge to show proper respect for something sacred without intervening in the scene in a way that would pollute it.

Often there will be real fear, suffering, loss, or pain in the background of joyful crying. But even when there is no memory of the negative in the background, the awareness of metamorphosis itself is bittersweet. Births, weddings, sexual ecstasies must be gone through, passed, let go of, in order to be lived. Sunsets and eclipses are evocative by capturing the idea precisely. It is not just philosophers or poets who agonize over the realization that every great step forward in life is a step closer to death.[34]

In sum, the variety of crying experiences appears to be not only dualistic but also dialectical. Crying may be validly distinguished as sad and joyful. And each type has its inverse, more tacit side in which what crying manifestly means within the context of its expression is juxtaposed against the embodied experience of mobilizing the message.

2. The Hermeneutic Mysteries of Crying

Whether manifestly responding to sad themes of loss or to joyful themes of transcendence, the person in crying is making an emphatically embodied statement. The unique corporeal movements of crying address a distinctive problem in communication. The crying person is trying to relate what he or she understands to be two worlds that do not have a common symbolic system. In effect, crying tries to relate two worlds that cannot share a language.[35] An interpretive ambiguity, expressed audibly as a nonverbal cry, a defect in speech, or visibly and tangibly as a liquid opaqueness in the eyes, is an essential feature of crying. In addition to being a kind of narrative statement, crying is also a distinctive kind of interpretive and expressive struggle.

After searching for as wide a range of adult crying experiences as he and his hundreds of cooperative subjects could note, William Frey observed that "adult tears can appear in response to almost any imaginable emotional situation."[36] An implication is that, for any given instance of adult crying, although people may tacitly agree to assume that they know what they are crying about, if pressed a bit, the matter will not be so clear. In contrast to language, crying distinctively obfuscates the definition of the situation to which the person is responding. A memorable illustration comes from field notes on a wedding in which the mother of the groom was crying. When I naïvely suggested to the groom's sister that the mother might be comforted with the adage that she is gaining a daughter, not losing a son, I was quickly corrected: "That's why [she is crying]."

When tearfully crying, one does not necessarily glaze vision to the extent that the ability to see out gets impaired, but the ability of others to see in is more effectively disrupted. What one is specifically looking at gets ambiguous when gaze gets fixed, thickened with tears, covered with hands, or turned to the ground. Diminished in their ability to track the crying person's gaze as it may respond to specific alterations in the situation, observers become less capable of fixing the aspects of the situation that are provoking the crying response.

Quite often, when people cry they have reason to anticipate that if they don't cry, their perspectives will be misconstrued, or at least construed to their disadvantage. Thus, for an award winner, crying may be employed as a disambiguating device, showing more clearly than any spoken declaration how "really overwhelmed" he or she is by the honor. And this may work with the audience. But the audience may not correctly appreciate the situation that the crying person is imagining, especially if he or she is a professional actor, trained to remember tear-provoking scenes when the current script fails to provide them. The behavior of crying is at once effectively iconic and enigmatic as to the god that is being honored. A nice example from recent television news coverage was provided by a night club patron who had filed suit against the boxer and convicted rapist, Mike Tyson, for "talking to her in an inappropriate way and then assaulting her by sucking on her face" (i.e., kissing her on the cheek). She briefly brushed away a tear as she sat silently in the background while her attorneys explained her suit to the press.[37] One has to take a position on the proper outcome of the trial in order to identify the concerns crystallized in that tear.

Of course language, no matter how articulated, is also open to multiple interpretations on the same dimensions of authenticity, motivation, and transcendent implications that make the meaning of crying problematic. The point is that crying commonly emerges when people recognize limitations on the expressive possibilities of language. For one thing, crying often occurs when one is alone, and in that circumstance people typically will presume that talking makes little sense.

For another, adult crying is specifically valuable for creating a fog about one's language-expressible understandings of a situation. An editor at an academic publishing house explained to me that she often cries in arguments with her spouse when he cuts so deeply and persistently in arguments that he gives her the sense that anything she says will provoke a deeper cut. Left speechless by his discourse strategy, hers is to cry. Whether one views such crying uncharitably as "passive aggressive" or, following the commercially successful folk wisdom of love guru Leo Buscaglia, as indicating a private preserve that one should respect by not attempting to interpret,[38] in either case crying achieves its interactive power as a negation of speech.[39]

Indeed, quite often the only way in which we, both as social actors and as sociological analysts, can perceive that an adult *is* crying is by noting odd defects in speech. But it may be misleading to characterize crying as an incapacity for speech. On the contrary, crying often does not emerge until an occasion for speech arises to evoke it. Here are three initial appreciations of the dialectical relationship of crying and speech.

1. *Speech as a necessary condition for crying.* At a Section Eight office, an applicant for a housing subsidy may begin to cry as she explains that her housing problems arose after the death of a man she had been living with.[40] Without suggesting that such crying is in any way inauthentic, we can note that the applicant's loneliness existed without the power to undermine her composure while she waited silently for her interview. Speech here is not inconsistent with crying, it is its necessary condition.

2. *Speech that prepares for crying by setting a context of ambiguity for its emergence.* In a set of field notes and videotapes that I created on one seasons' Little League baseball games, I found that the full blossoming of crying would almost always require the development

of a particular kind of speech occasion. The players would silently move into markedly precrying stages—eyes watering, faces compressed tightly, gaze following lines that avoid eye contact—just at those times when the game's narrative provided a warrant for a damaged self-image: when striking out, making the last out for the losing side, getting tagged out, or after a batted ball had run under one's mitt. But audible crying and a full stream of tears typically would be contingent on an opportunity to articulate, usually to a coach or to a parent, some other reason for being disturbed: a member of the opposing team made a rude or ridiculing remark, the umpire made a bad call, an arm was hurt in making a vigorous swing, or a leg muscle was strained in practice. The boys fight hard to ensure that crying will emerge only behind a screen of some secondary explanation, one that explains upset while making the cause of tears ambiguous.

3. *Awaiting a turn to express what cannot be said.* Examined more closely, it is not talk alone but specific openings to talk interactively that elicit crying. A fitting example comes during a mediation session in a child custody case that I reviewed on videotape.[41] There were women on both sides of the case, the mother on one side, the father and his mother on the other. The mediator asked each party in turn to step outside so that he might talk with each adversary alone. Every time a woman remained alone with the mediator, she would quickly begin to cry as she began to talk. Clearly it is not just what one knows about one's dilemmas that is the necessary condition for crying here. What is necessary is the constellation of a specific challenge to express oneself to another in a particular kind of speech situation. Notably, so long as the women were together with the mediator, neither would cry when her turns for talk arose. Each woman cried only when, with the other woman absent, she had an open field to express what she could not say.

For much of adult life, what crying is is a finely embodied way of being in tension with speech. As members of society, we commonly perceive that an adult is crying, or is on the verge of crying, not by seeing tears or hearing audible cries but by observing formal compromises of speech. Here is an initial list of indicators of how crying is practically shaped as a negation of speech.

Balking at Speech

Arthur Ashe, famous as the first internationally successful African American tennis player as well as for his even-tempered demeanor under stress, called a press conference to reveal his affliction with AIDS.[42] For four minutes and thirty seconds he delivered a prepared text in his customary polished style, speaking of his diagnosis, medical history, and the cause of his infection. Explaining that his illness was widely known among friends and in the medical community, Ashe expressed thanks for "a silent and generous conspiracy to assist me in maintaining my privacy," which "has meant a great deal to" himself, his wife, and his daughter. After pronouncing his daughter's name, he fell silent for fifty seconds, during which he adjusted his glasses, put his hands to his forehead, and moved his lips as if to speak. After his wife came to his side, he returned to his text, managing to say his daughter's name and that she "already knows," at which point he again fell silent. Sub voce and pointing to the text, he asked his wife to "just read that part there for me," which she did, reading "that perfect strangers come up to daddy on the street and say 'hi' . . ." Having completed her delimited assignment, Mrs. Ashe stopped and Mr. Ashe finished reading his prepared text and took questions for twenty minutes, all with full composure.

Several contextual features contributed to the powerful impression that Arthur Ashe was overwhelmed by emotion and on the verge of "breaking down" in tears. These include our assumptions that his health problem must be terribly difficult to bear and that it would be especially painful for him to focus on the meaning of his dilemma for his family. Who wouldn't cry in such a situation? But if this kind of experience is to be included in the phenomena of crying, then crying exists in the methodologically inconvenient status of a nonexpression, or more precisely, as a particularly expressive silence.

Taking Turns with Self When Speaking a Monologue

Here are three examples of how crying is made perceptible by what happens in pauses between uttered phrases. One is based on field notes that describe how a woman, talking on a telephone in a hospital, cries as she explains to a friend that her initial test results indicate that another series of tests will be required. In the hospital phone conversation, the patient speaks a series of phrases ("And now this!"; "It's just too much"; "Everything is weighing down on me"). All words are spoken clearly and smoothly, but between each phrase she audibly sighs-shudders on the exhale, and as she inhales she audibly gasps.

The second example is a videotape showing a preschool director sitting in the middle of a large classroom and informing the children that one of the teachers is moving to another state. The director sporadically cries while the teacher in question, who sits on a bench behind her, cries more continuously and mostly silently as she receives a parade of hugs from parents and children. The school director speaks in a series of phrases of unequal length that are separated by pauses of regular length, during which she frequently smiles and looks around the room in silence. The director's smile emerges repeatedly but unaccompanied by any talk that would warrant a happy response. Her smile appears to be a discrete device, a way of literally putting a good face on an effort to hold back tears.

The third comes from the 1996 Academy Awards. In one televised segment, Gerta Weisman Klein delivers her acceptance speech for an award honoring a documentary of her experience as a Holocaust survivor. Early on in her speech we perceive that she is moved. Her phrases have a clipped nature; they are uttered in short bursts after pauses in which she appears to gather resources for the phrase to be uttered next. (Klein's moving speech, which becomes audibly disturbed most prominently at the end, will be revisited shortly).

In each of these examples, a person is engaged in a monologue, a stretch of talk that requires no turn taking with the talk's recipients. But the speaker creates a conversationlike interaction in her respiratory and speech cycle, riding on exhales, fearing inhales, competently carrying a phrase to conclusion, risking danger in the pause before a new phrase is begun. Gerta Weisman Klein clips a phrase to a stop, takes a breath, and launches another phrase. The school director utters a sentence, stops, freezes her face in a smile, and surveys part of the room before beginning again. The hospital patient gasps and shudders as she comes out of and goes back into a line of talk. The manifest problem is not a private misery or pressure but specifically the struggle to keep one's body actively and articulately within a provocative situation for social expression. Independent of evidence of tears or audible cries, we see crying here because we see that the speaker is *perceptibly taking turns with her own speech.*

Strangling the Self in Speech

The presence of crying commonly becomes perceptible in speaking through two opposite ways in which speech becomes problematic as a shell for the self. On the one hand, the speaker's voice may get thin and high, as if the speaker's body has turned back on him or her. No longer a transparent, facile source for expression, the speaker's chest and throat become heavy and press down and inward, strangling speech.

Flight of the Self from Speech

Alternatively, the speaker's body may appear to fall away on vowels, leaving a voice soaring upward on its own. Notably, the pressure to cry does not create a stuttering on consonants; it distorts vowels, emerging between consonants as a fluctuation of pitch that is not called for to convey linguistic meaning. Especially in syllables in which the speaker must move to or from "h" sounds through vowels, multiple steps appear where a single step is appropriate: home as "ho-ome," mother as "mu-hhh-ther." Or "h" sounds are inserted as a kind of desperate grasping for firm ground within vowel stretches: loves comes out as "luhhuvs." It is as if the speaker has suddenly become culturally naked, having lost the skin of language that normally allows him or her to cover up the vibrations of his or her vocal cords. Or as if the soul, searching for a point to escape the cultural prison of language, tries to leap through the brief windows of opportunity that vowels provide.

Of course, we can say that these phenomena are not "really" crying, reserving that category for more methodologically convenient products of the body like tears and noises that are emitted apart from talk. But then we give up the raison d'être of our inquiry, which is an effort to capture what crying is in a large part of human experience so that we might try to explain it. What crying is is a phenomenon dialectically related to speech, a phenomenon that often speech calls into existence in order to make problems for speaking. Crying is not just a "feeling" nor just a series of effects; it is a subtle range of corporeal doings, such as a balking at speaking, resonant markings of pauses between utterances, and a manner of depicting the body as too light or too heavy a vehicle to bear or to hold on to language. If we want to understand what crying is, we must address, as directly as possible, its distinctive ways of doing battle with speech.

The dynamic tension between language and crying gives us an important clue to a necessary condition of crying, whether or not talking is involved. In order to make crying a compellingly sensible thing to do, adults must in effect explain why they can't express themselves in language. This necessity for warranting crying holds whether or not anyone else will observe the person crying. For people who can use language, part of the phenomenon of crying is an artful and emphatic not-speaking. One cries on the understanding that *the situation requires a personally embodied form of expression that transcends what speech can do.*

Perhaps adult crying has been so well and so easily ignored in university social and psychological studies because it attests so extensively to the expressive tasks that cannot be achieved in lives lived within the disciplined forms of language and discursive reasoning alone. Every instance of crying makes a statement of the ontological limits of language in bridging parts of life that can "speak" to each other only through crying. The following paragraphs begin a list of the ways that crying acknowledges what speech cannot grasp.

How Crying Acknowledges What Speech Cannot Grasp

1. *Wordless provocations.* People cry in response to music, to pictorial art, to sunsets, and to eclipses. These cryings honor experiences that in their nature go beyond words. When words are present, they risk detracting from the provocative experience. It is not what the tour guide says about the cathedral, not what is written on the placard under the painting, not the phrases that appear on the screen over the opera stage that bring tears; it is something unspeakable, something responsive to the "different keys"[43] in which art communicates. Attending too much to words that purport to describe what one is to understand of an experience can stand in the way of a resonant experience.[44]

Crying emerges when culture forces people to embody a response that they cannot say. Music is often part of the situations that provoke crying. Music surrounds one with a continuous pressure to become a vehicle for a perspective that goes beyond language. Unless one diverts one's attention, there are no physical barriers and the music will enter one's experience and compel a response. Where social customs demand a respectfully silent and stationary watching, tears often emerge as the only outlet for an irresistibly responsive grasping of the happenings. Crying is a predictable response by respectfully frozen guests at funerals, children's school recitals, awards shows, weddings, movies, and patriotic ceremonies.

2. *Words that say too much.* Events that mark status passages, like weddings, or that mark status elevations, like awards ceremonies, are common places for crying by the adults who are at the center of collective attentions. A speech act that otherwise is so simple and unproblematic as to pass execution without any serious attention (uttering the little words "I do," recalling the names of people one works with every day) for once carries transcendent implications.[45] The crying body represents an understanding for which the commonplace words seem inadequate.[46]

3. *Words that deny feelings.* Less familiar in folk culture but in fact far more frequent as a part of everyday adult life are occasions in which crying emerges when a person senses a situation as having transcendent meaning but gets a response from another who speaks of it as mundane. The following example is from a mother's autobiographical essay:

When I was seven months pregnant with my first child, Zach, I called my obstetrician with an urgent question. I was having irregular mild contractions, and it worried me; I wanted to know if this was normal or not. I'll never forget her infuriating response: "My dear, you are worrying entirely too much for your own good. There's no need to be concerned." With that, our conversation was ended, and I began to cry.[47]

In circumstances of such unprecedented and infinite significance to a patient, words that seem to a doctor to be a perfectly reasonable recognition of a patient's emotional as well as technical concerns can become, paradoxically, emotionally provocative.

4. *Postconversation depression.* Even when all parties treat a turning point in the life of a person as exceptionally significant, crying can emerge when he or she must reenter mundane life. Joan, a Hollywood executive, volunteered a description of crying suddenly emerging to bridge a shock of "coming down" from a recent and great high.[48] Joan is the main breadwinner for her family. She had left a well-paid job under a difficult boss at a successful production company, living through several months of anxiety as she searched and then negotiated extensively over the conditions for a next job. Her new employer, a "name" star with a long record of producing commercially successful, high-quality feminist movies, seemed ideal. In the interview that had concluded the negotiations successfully, the new employer's unmitigated optimism and dazzling superlatives about her qualifications complemented Joan's own extraordinary enthusiasm. As she left the scene, Joan was imagining the spirited conversations with spouse and friends in which she would share her good news. Then, without warning, as she went through the routine of getting into her car and starting toward home, she suddenly began to cry. Her thoughts had turned to her terminally ill grandmother, whom she had just visited on the East Coast, and to the "plug pulling" question the family was facing. The practical task of starting the car into motion was the catalyst to a fall from a glittering conversational haven back to dismal responsibilities. Crying made an appropriately shaky bridge between the high and low grounds of her life.[49]

5. *Adam, Moses, and God: Existential language gaps between generations.* Adult crying commonly emerges out of an appreciation of a gap in expressive relations between generations. The next field note requires some background. Marcos is forty-one years old and a technical specialist in a Hollywood video equipment store who for several years has guided me reliably along the low-cost edge of state-of-the-

art recording equipment. My two adult sons sometimes come to see him for their own needs. On this day I am alone.

> Marcos mentions that I look a lot like my son. As I comment on number-one son I realize he may be talking about number two, and while I am still lost in confusion Marcos turns the conversation to his relations with his children. He tells me that one of his sons is a problem, always bringing home Fs and lying about absences from school. His other sons and daughter do well in school. He brings his problem son to work with him, giving him tough jobs when he cuts school, but he can't reach him effectively. Then his voice begins to waver, his gaze goes off to the side and his eyes glaze as he tells me that he was brought up severely in El Salvador by his mother. He explains that he was without a father from the age of nine because his father "killed himself." I react to this with a start and ask, "Killed himself?" He adds, offhandedly and somewhat obscurely, "drinking and going around."

The theme of an ontological gap that blocks communication between fathers and sons is a common one in tear-jerking songs in popular culture. Country music radio channels often keep at least one in circulation. Harry Chapin's song, "Cat's Cradle," is a standard oldie on American pop music charts. Using the format of a phone conversation, it tells of a father who is too busy to speak to his son and then as an old man finds his son too busy to speak to him. From high culture, Michelangelo's Sistine chapel image of God reaching to touch Adam is a classier and more optimistic turn on the theme. A similar gap is represented in the speech defect with which Moses must act as God's agent for relating to mankind. Currently, "men's groups" hold retreats in which one man role-plays a distant, silent, macho-styled father, and tells his "son" that he loves him. As the "father" overcomes the mythical silence of his role, the message of love is received through teary eyes.[50]

On a more everyday basis, mothers are moved to tears as they silently regard their precious children. In an impromptu interview, Loretta described her awkwardness recently at finding herself crying as she walked along with her four-year-old son. Just looking at him she was moved to tears of joy. But she fought against the tears because from prior experience she knew that if she did not, her son would become disturbed.

I am suggesting that a sense of an ontological divide between worlds of understanding, in this case a generation gap that words cannot bridge, is not only part of the phenomena that crying produces, it is a causal condition of crying. In contemporary Western culture, among all the varieties of interpersonal love, parental love lacks a language. Parents often begin to recount iconic scenes that are intended to show others the lovable qualities of their children, only to find, in signs of their correspondents' labored listening, that the storytelling is impossibly inadequate. The touch of frustration in such narrative efforts is parallel to the existential shock that Loretta recalled as she explicitly recognized that her tearful appreciation of her child's precious nature had a bittersweet quality. The parent's appreciation of the child's preciousness also acknowledges the child's existential distance from the adult.

6. *Existential language gaps with one's younger self.* There is also a bittersweet quality to sensing one's own age when seeing a child's promise. This theme was highlighted in Janie's account of her difficulty in coming to her child's preschool graduation. Crying at home as the family prepared for the trip to the school, she thought she "would not be able to make it." Her second and last child was graduating, and the event to Janie had a significance she could not convey to her children: "They can't know that this is the best time of their lives."

Romanticized memories of childhood suggest another form in which a generation gap provokes crying by blocking language. In this instance the gap is between the generative periods of one's own life. Nostalgic cryings, such as hearing at middle age a song that brings recollections of one's youth, are examples.[51] That younger person, the one who was moved by those tunes thirty-five years ago, must still be around somewhere in one's experience, but the distance is now so great that that younger person cannot be addressed directly. One realizes that one must have had that past, but now it has moved out of reach.

Another and more mysterious variety of nostalgic cryings is of the type that evokes ties with a past that one never had. An example would be finding oneself moved to tears by an ethnic song in a language whose accents one recognizes but whose words one cannot understand. The provocation of crying when making contact with a firmly inaccessible part of one's past is captured by Alice Kaplan as she describes what it has meant to her to become a French teacher. In one passage, Kaplan reflects on her experience of crying from happiness after hearing a student doing an "explication de texte." In her crying response, she discerned the provocation of an autobiographical mystery blocking speech between the stages of her own life.

> I thought back on that moment from class and had time to savor it. I cried, not sorrowful tears but tears of happiness from discovering something I hadn't known about before. Why was I so moved by what she

said? . . . I was thinking about being a child myself and seeing and hearing but not being able to say yet, not having the words for what I saw.
Or having them, but no one asked.[52]

By implication, her own book is itself an effort to speak to the past.
When she was a young child, the father whom she dearly loved suddenly died, leaving behind much that was felt long before she would
have language to say it.[53]

7. *Language gaps with other species.* Stories in which animals or,
now, extraterrestrial creatures, develop protolinguistic means of
"communicating" their care for people are effective movie conventions
for touching viewers. Such events highlight ontological gaps even as
they show extraordinary achievements in transcending them. The
movie *E.T.* was famous for bringing grown men to tears. Two powerful moments come when the creature articulates the phrase "E.T.
phone home" to explain his desire to build an interplanetary communication device, and when a glow appears at the end of E.T.'s finger
as he seeks to heal the cut finger of his ailing earth friend, the child
Elliott. Both moments subtly exploit many traditional representations
of heroic attempts to transcend ontological language gaps (such as
"Lassie come home" and God's E.T.-like, elongated and relaxed finger
as He reaches toward Adam's hand as they float over the Sistine
chapel).

8. *Language gaps between metaphysically separate fields of experience.* Hindi movies regularly jerk tears from the audience by dramatizing existential struggles to overcome gaps in communication. A recurrent provocation is that of putting the audience in the position of trying
to be a silent bridge between two personal worlds that cannot speak
directly to each other. The moviegoer watches in a position of transcendent understanding, wanting to shout out clues as two brothers,
separated at birth, move through situations in which they are repeatedly about to but never quite succeed in recognizing their common
origin. Or star-crossed would-be lovers follow life trajectories that
reach toward but do not (until the end) quite meet each other.

Dreamlike sequences are often used to set up the most emotionally
powerful moments. The metaphysics of dreams make it understand-
ably difficult for the characters to speak directly to each other. Instead,
would-be lovers drift-dance toward a meeting that is yearned for but
congeals in the viewer's tears long before it appears on the screen.

In her fieldwork on the Hindi cinema experience, Lakshmi Srinivas
analyzes these structural strategies for evoking audience response. And
she describes how young male moviegoers in Bangalore fight against

emotional manipulation by giving sarcastic voice to the movies' characters. Shouting out wisecracks that complete the thrust of plot themes, they ground dreamlike characters in flesh-and-blood bodies, thus blocking the possibility for a weeping response.[54] The theater becomes a ground for battle over the emotional experience of the movie. Other audience members shout back comments intended to silence the young men who frustrate their desire to leave the characters floating on the screen so that they can have a good cry about their frustrations at speech.

9. *Words that must not be said.* Some situations provoke crying by stimulating understandings that, if transformed into spoken words, would be intolerably counterproductive. "As my great-grandmother said grace" at a large family Thanksgiving dinner, a young woman recalls from an experience when she was a child, "I remember tears coming to my eyes and not being sure why." She recalls her mother's elaborate preparations, the huge family guest list, and, years later, she could articulate what she gathered everyone around the table had assumed. As her great-grandmother's health was very quickly fading, "we were afraid that it would be her last Thanksgiving with the family." Of course, no one could speak that understanding, and there was a collective silence at the end of the prayer. The embarrassing moment was broken when it was noted by the ancient lady herself, who remarked to the effect, "Cat got everyone's tongue?" Crying here emerges to carry the imagination of what must not be said.

10. *Audience segregation problems: Messages that must be at once received by some but not heard by others.* In some instances, a person by crying effectively conveys to one part of an audience what cannot be expressed directly to another part. My field notes describe an instance in which the principal of a public school and several members of her audience shook with emotion and became teary eyed when she addressed a meeting of parents, teachers, and staff about an upcoming strike called by the L.A. teachers' union. The local administration, the teachers, and many parents who had been active in the school's planning all wanted to keep the school open and to encourage children to attend so that the school would receive state reimbursement. But in order not to undermine the teachers' union, they did not wish to create a substitute curriculum, even if it was introduced as a temporary measure. Without anyone announcing this plan directly, the meeting, which was not visibly led by either the principal or the teachers, appeared to be drifting toward this outcome.

Then a father stood up and began talking in the thinking-out-loud spirit that the meeting's crisis atmosphere seemed to invite. He stressed how precious the children were, how this meant that all in the community must be committed to providing children with uninterrupted education, and how everyone had to be imaginative in the current situation. Perhaps parents should come in and develop curriculum, call on lawyer-parents to sue the state to provide an alternate staff, pool resources to hire temporary teachers, set up satellite minischools in parents' houses, or—he mentioned as if a light bulb had just lit up within—maybe they needed to find "a Ross Perot type" to lead them to some new thinking.

At this point the principal rose, taking the microphone for the first time. Jaw rigid with emotion, voice wavering, gaze steady but thick with tears, her torso shook as she announced, "There will be no scabs here!," and delivered a stirring defense of the union principle. Several parents next to me were moved to tears.

The principal's speech was strikingly dramatic in style and content. No one had previously spoken in the terms of the union movement; the principal's emotions and substantive comments made a striking contrast with the relaxed and rambling comments of the parent who had just spoken. When I questioned some members of the audience about what had so moved them, they indicated an understanding that the principal was responding to "this dumb man" who himself did not understand the subtext of the meeting. What they sensed at stake was the survival of a twenty-year-old set of collective arrangements among parents, teachers, and the principal, a woman of almost mythic reputation who had founded the school. The strike had been discussed elaborately for months. Now the "bright ideas" of a casual participant threatened the collective understanding. The moved parents also saw reflections in the director's rhetorical dilemma of their own struggles, in their own work worlds, to remain polite when dealing with destructively insensitive troublemakers.

What was specifically moving about the director's speech was what it did not say directly. In content her speech was directed toward the community of solidarity, but in the sequence of speaking roles her talk was implicitly directed at the "dumb man." The response of crying carried an appreciation of just how what was explicitly said reverberated with heavy meanings of what could not at the moment be stated.

11. *Socially stratified unsayables.* Crying sometimes emerges on an understanding that a situation calls for the expression of something unsayable. Unsayables do not occur randomly in social life. Social stratification shapes their distribution. As with the school principal in the last example, people at elite levels in organizations are often limited in what they can say because, in a kind of bureaucratic noblesse oblige,

as part of their work they must be diplomatically indulgent in their public relations work with ignorant outsiders.

For converse stratification reasons, pariah people often cannot speak things they understand because their status in society entails an everyday suffering of indignities in silence. Elias Canetti provided the unforgettably bitter (fictional) example of tears filling the eyes of a "blind" beggar who had to suffer the humiliation of publicly thanking people who had thrown buttons instead of money into his hat.[55]

In the vividly real setting of Unity Church in Los Angeles, pariah people are regularly moved to tears as they rise to take the microphone to tell the church of their problems. Many members of the congregation come to services in drag. Bishop Bean encourages his flock toward greater self-respect by attacking the masks they wear: "I'm watching you, I know what you're denying . . . like how some homosexuals hate femme types . . . that is self-hatred . . . and how some just want the other to be 'more butch' and that they'll suffer anything for such a person." As services start, church leaders parade to the stage, carried forward by a rhythmic hymn that the entire assemblage creates through song and movement. Then the microphone is given to members of the audience, who rise and are immediately moved to the brink of an inability to continue speaking. One parishioner struggles against tears and, through a whispered voice, asks communal prayers for her upcoming lung operation. A young man shakes with emotion as he delivers a political speech criticizing homosexuals for failing to support their public action organizations more vigorously. A woman cry-talks the story of her recent and still tentative recovery from years of disgraceful neglect of her children while she supported a cocaine habit through prostitution. In effect church members pay for the regular opportunity to cry in public. As speakers rise to cry-talk, their emotions are inspired by the understanding that the church community pushes them, as multiply pariah people, to dare to say publicly what they are elsewhere encouraged to deny.

12. *Words that break when stretched to bridge worlds of intimacy and mass community.* Next we may consider the familiar scenes of crying by people receiving awards, being honored at retirement parties, or being interviewed because of their celebrity or notoriety. Technological developments have given unprecedented force to the challenges that are faced by people who are placed at the center of collective attentions and are then asked to make personal responses in public recognition of their glorious or inglorious achievements. Even in a two-person, face-to-face interview situation, a rolling camera encourages an interviewee to anticipate an infinitely large and eternally observing

audience. Whether rising before the academy to accept an award that recognizes one's superlative contributions to a professional community, or responding to questions on one's bloody criminal career, the person who breaks down in tears is likely to break down at much the same narrative points. Crying emerges where he or she attempts to utter words that bridge relationships between an infinitely large communal audience and intimate regions of private life.

Here, from a stock of such events that I have collected on videotape, is a range of instances.

- In a documentary made by the visual anthropologist, Dan Marks, "Joker," an ethnic Samoan gang member from Long Beach, California, is being interviewed by a former gang member who has become a social worker. Joker begins to shed tears as he recounts a scene in which his mother cried when she visited him in jail.[56]
- Gerta Weisman Klein, accepting an Academy Award as the subject of a documentary on her experience as a Holocaust survivor, quivers with emotion as she calls the audience to recall the sufferings she survived as "you go home and have the luxury of another boring evening with your family."
- In a documentary aired on commercial TV, Leonard Callace, who was freed from prison when DNA evidence indicated that he was not guilty of the rape for which he had served six years in prison, cries, first in an interview with a journalist and again before the judge who will release him, as he recounts that the most difficult part of his experience was not being at his mother's side when she died. Outside the courthouse, his adolescent son is asked, "Are you proud of your father for not taking the plea?" (of guilty in order to minimize his incarceration). When he replies, "Yeah. I'm very proud of him and I'm glad he's home", his voice trembles with tears specifically on the word "home."[57]
- At a party held in a public park to honor a school director at her retirement, a succession of past presidents of the school board take the mike to reminisce. A college student, standing in for his mother, breaks down as he describes how the director was a second mother to him. Later the director's office assistant of many years holds her composure well until she comes to a passage in which she recalls the director bringing a "teddy bear" to her, a reference to the director's now-adult son.
- In the following press conference, award ceremonies, or TV interview situations, the speaker breaks down specifically when he or she addresses mother, father, or family: Mayor Richard M. Daley, apologiz-

ing for his son's irresponsible behavior at a racist-tinged party at which a young man was injured; Richard Kuklinski, a convicted contract killer, when he is asked if he regrets the damage his career has done to his wife and daughters, who before his arrest had been ignorant of his occupation; Mira Sorvino, as she thanks her father, actor Paul Sorvino, who is sitting in the audience as she receives a Best Supporting Actress award.

Movies and then television have enormously increased the frequency of events in which people struggle to make themselves a live, immediately observable, visible bridge between the largest and the smallest social worlds that they inhabit. The juxtaposition of the solitary figure addressing an infinite audience—a classic and early example of which was the isolation of Lou Gehrig as a tiny figure addressing a packed Yankee Stadium at a day honoring him on the occasion of his disease-occasioned retirement—once required extraordinary organizing efforts to create. Now an analogous interaction environment can be created for a speaker by the introduction of a video camera at the most casual retirement party.

First made familiar on newsreel and then on TV screens, professionally produced and glamorous versions of cryings have become folk-cultural resources for structuring the narrative high points of a wide range of amateur-produced situations. Everyone in attendance anticipates the way that the person who is the honored focal point of the event will handle the crucial moment. As a speaker tries simultaneously to address usually segregated audiences, often those from work and those from family life, crying allows him or her to capture in embodied reverberations the unspeakable ramifications that each social circle has for the other.

It is, however, rare to catch a glimpse of the inverse crying situation: occasions in which people privately cry as they sense the public ramifications of something that is quietly transpiring. A creative arrangement of one such moment was described by Christopher Buckley, as he recounted the mechanics of dedicating a book he had authored:

> I was finishing "The White House Mess" just as I was about to be married. I asked Lucy to put a sheet of paper in the typewriter, and I said, "Now type, 'For my wife, with love.' And she cried."[58]

Presumably the immediate emotional force would have been somewhat blunted had Buckley asked, "What do you think of this as a dedication for my book?" providing Lucy with an occasion to speak her sense of relating their private and public identities in this manner.

Instead Buckley invokes a multilayered, interaction-triggered, and deeply implicit irony to give the moment explosive force. He uses an ending, of the book writing, to mark a beginning, of their public identity as a couple. She is honored, by being asked to perform a menial clerical task. He makes her a partner in his professional life. And he instantly summons a larger audience to their wedding than any caterer could conceivably handle. As Lucy performs the task, the two become married before either gets to say "I do," at least in the sense that the dedication commits them to an eternal public revelation of their commitment to each other, making a record that, compared to the legal force of the papers they will soon sign, is eternally irreversible.

13. *Talking for and to the dead.* We cannot complete an investigation of how limitations on speech occasion crying without considering the many silences created by death.[59] In response to the special communicative challenges for maintaining conversations with the dead, cultures have responded by creating traditions of loud, histrionically elaborate, and collective funereal or mournful crying.[60] But the mystical strategies involved are not limited to traditional or exotic cultures. In contemporary Alabama, the spirit of the dead is routinely invoked to bear witness in legal pleadings.

The proceedings in question consider releasing a convicted murderer from prison. Adversaries at Alabama parole hearings speak in emphatically different emotional forms. In controlled and steady tones that bespeak their reliability and firm character, relatives of the convict consistently advocate release. Relatives of the convict's victims then as regularly move to the verge of tears as they recall how the murder has changed their lives. They implicitly make their critical point by demonstrating the still-vivid presence of the deceased's absence from their everyday routines. More than the substance of their pleading, their crying makes this absence present, in visible, audible, even tangible forms.

Cry-talk by the victim's relatives conveys not only the burden of speaking their own feelings but also the burden of being possessed by ghosts. Appearing as vehicles for the sensibilities of the silenced victim, if the relatives do not cry they deny the deceased his only remaining channel for expression. They are saddened by their loss, but the victim is angry about the injustice that he will surely remain dead long after the offender's possible release, whenever it comes. Their pleading must be an on-cue yet stirringly authentic delivery of a complex mix of powerful emotions.[61]

Crying provides a conversational voice that death would deny. Members of a Walt Whitman club were audibly moved to tears as they listen to a previously undiscovered recording of the poet reading one of his texts.[62] When Whitman speaks, devotees who have only known him through his writings and through others' voices suddenly are being addressed in the poet's own rhythms and tones. The occasion for discourse is surprising in more than one respect. The prior communicative asymmetry of the relationship is turned on its head. Now that the long-imagined speech of the dead immortal can finally and truly be heard, the spoken response of his living followers is muffled by tears.

The shock of hearing Whitman speak was attenuated by the fact that the speech was not directed specifically at his little adoration society. When the dead do address one in a personal manner the effect is likely to block crying. It is difficult to get good sociological data on what happens in such circumstances, but the American military cemetery at Colleville seems as useful a field research site as we are likely to find. Colleville is a burial ground and memorial for the thousands of soldiers and sailors who died in the D day landing at Normandy. The cemetery displays the following text on a walkway leading from the parking lot to the entrance.

The Longest Night
Visitor:

Look how many of them there were.
Look how young they were.
They died for your freedom.
Hold back your tears and keep silent.

Many people visibly move to the brink of tears even before they leave the parking lot to enter the cemetery grounds. Crying, the poem implies, is self-indulgent. It masks, withdraws, and insulates by commenting to the self in a way that the dead cannot hear. One can observe a virtual shock of emotional reorientation, an abrupt sobering up among visitors when they read to the end of this unexpected command for silent respect. The message speaks to them in an authoritative voice that comes, if not directly from, at least officially on behalf of the dead. The message seems to be that if the dead are to be truly acknowledged, one must attend with full powers. In trying to hear what the dead have to say, crying, a futile attempt at speech, will only get in the way.[63]

14. *Being alone.* We are searching for the various ways that adults satisfy the precondition for crying that they must in effect explain to themselves why they can't express themselves in language. Being alone is nicely suited to crying, at least among people who presume that speech requires someone else to talk to. Of course, being alone,

like any of the other factors in this list, is not a sufficient condition for crying. But in any case the being alone that often is a basis for crying is loneliness as a phenomenological and not merely as a physical fact. The key sense is an existential aloneness, a matter of having no one to speak with about a particular problem, or no longer having the possibility of speaking with a particular other about anything.

15. *Multiple sources of silence.* To this point, in order to explore the range of limitations to language that make crying compelling to adults, I have been considering single features of given social situations. But often multiple sources of silence are present at once, and crying emerges as a person senses compound barriers to speech. Brent Staples provided a poignant example as he recounted his reactions to the death of his younger brother, Blake, at the age of twenty-two. Shortly before his brother's murder, Brent had seen Blake laughing about having made fools of the police while bearing a line of stitches on his hand that he, Blake, attributed to a recoil from a shotgun. "I lacked the language simply to say: Thousands have lived this for you and died." They arranged to meet the following night, but before Brent could try another strategy to change Blake's life, he got a call informing him that Blake was dead.

> As I stood in Chicago holding the receiver . . . I felt as though part of my soul had been cut away. I questioned myself then, and I still do. . . .
>
> For weeks I awoke crying from a recurrent dream in which I chased him, urgently trying to get him to read a document I had, as though reading it would protect him from what had happened in waking life.
>
> His eyes shining like black diamonds, he smiled and danced just beyond my grasp. When I reached for him, I caught only the space where he had been.[64]

There is here the silence of language that tries to reach another's soul but becomes stalled and minimized in conversational maneuverings. There is the silence sensed in the wish to continue a conversation with the dead. And there is the silence of a conversation held in dreams, and in this dream, the additionally silent language of a document's unread text. Indeed we may suspect that the sleeper's sense of the mute nature of his dreaming body itself played a role. Staples, his body too heavy with sleep to speak, dreams up a frustrated communication that captures his impossible wish to speak with a correspondent who has become too insubstantial to respond to language.

3. The Corporeal Aesthetics of Crying

I offer three conditions to explain crying. Crying will arise to express one of two, inversely related, dialectical narratives. Crying arises to embody what speech cannot contain. And crying entails distinctive aesthetic transformations of the embodied foundations of the self. The argument is that crying will display the joint operation of these three processes.[65] But each condition exists independently of the others. Thus an inquiry into the embodiment of crying will not lead to any simple relationship to the two narratives of crying that we reviewed earlier.

If one turns off the sound and watches videotapes of people delivering and receiving praise at a retirement party, one might well imagine that something terrifying is happening. Here is a professional example of the same ambiguity. Watching in the audience at the 1996 Academy Awards, actor Paul Sorvino appeared to break down and cry like a baby, gasping, doubling over, and sobbing profoundly, when his daughter, in accepting a Best Supporting Actress award, thanked him personally from the stage. A viewer who saw only his crying might think that he had just learned that his child had died. One of the questions we must address is why similar corporeal aesthetics seem to fit both sad and joyful crying. My answer will be that the fabric of culture provides an essential skin for the self and, regardless of the moral or narrative thrust of the pressure on it, this fabric is vulnerable to tearing in patterned ways.

It does not seem particularly odd to investigate the corporeal aesthetics of crying when the person crying is a child. Adults perceive and make interactive use of the formal properties of children's crying. In a field note written in Copenhagen's airport, I described a mother comforting an infant by what might be characterized as "aestheticizing" the child's expression. Described crudely, the child's cry moved up in pitch to a peak, covering the complete exhale phase of respiration, sometimes hitting a rough passage at the end. Picking the infant up, the mother worked to mold the child's crying, smoothing it out, by molding herself to it. She mimicked the audible progression the child had suggested, but in a more melodic form, without roughness in the transition from audible exhale to silent inhale. And she underlined her transforming efforts by accompanying her song with the complementary movements of an arm-cradled swing, carrying the child up to a high point on the exhale, then down to the starting point of the swing on the inhale. Such commonplace events are now familiar in the data of child development studies as ways mothers spontaneously know how to be with infants. (The next chapter takes up an example in the context of a teacher responding to a whining child in preschool.) But whatever their consequences for the child's development, for our purposes they indicate the facility with which adults can recognize, grasp, and elaborate on the corporeal aesthetics of crying.

It is also common to observe children experimenting with their crying as if it were the product of a kind of musical instrument. Parents will recall hearing toddlers who, left to cry alone in their rooms, may be heard playing with such possibilities as that of making muted trumpetlike sounds. At preschools and in private homes, one can often observe children of two and three years of age engaged in prolonged periods of whining in which their crying, produced with a closed mouth, becomes a sort of hum, but a hum that emphasizes an "n" more than an "m" sound. In the reverberations it produces, such an elaboration of the tactile corporeal possibilities of crying appears to offer the child a kind of embracing, comforting skin.

I wish to suggest that adult crying is no less sophisticated in its aesthetic exploitation of the body even if, in contemporary Western culture at least, that artful knowledge is much more obscured. Young adolescent girls at rock concerts can collectively scream and produce tears in large flows, but this is perhaps the last time in the life cycle that Westerners can freely go all out in crying seemingly without limitation and in large orchestrated groups. We may urge people to "have a good cry" but we don't review how well or poorly they do it. That is not the case in all cultures.[66]

We have already seen that for language-competent adults, crying exists in a complex tension with language. Occasions for speech are often the critical conditions for provoking a form of crying that emerges, not as a sensual and aesthetic production in its own right but as a defect in language. In effect, for an adult, part of the project of crying is to cry in a way that explains why one cannot say what is meant, intended, or felt. But if adult crying often seems less elegant than the child's production of flowing tears, tortuous body configurations, and extended sounds, its aesthetic competency is no less refined.

Anything approaching a definitive statement of the aesthetic creativity entailed in crying will have to await far more research than I will present here. My objective is only to indicate that the effort is quite promising. I will suggest what should be a generally productive angle for inquiry, and, in the following two chapters, offer demonstrations of what a sustained examination of specific instances can pin down. In the rest of this chapter, I examine the aesthetic technology that people unselfconsciously exercise in crying. Crying exhibits a poetic logic by which people bring to the surface and mark things that are routinely effaced in ordinary, nonemotional conduct. They hit upon, transform, and present dimensions of the routinely invisible, natural three-dimensionality of their conduct.

As they begin to cry, people find that various parts of their usually invisible speaking system are becoming intrusive. Their throat may begin to choke down. Or the nasal passage, which one might think sits aside in wait of an opportunity to inhale and plays no role in the exhales that convey talk, suddenly shows up to reveal its role in keeping language sounds open. In a TV interview conducted outside a theater showing *Schindler's List,* a woman responds to a journalist's question about her reaction to the movie (about a Christian German's efforts to save Jews from Nazis). A nasal sound appears and she is quickly moved to tears as she says, "It just reinforces what th, that the world should never forget what happened there [pause] because it could happen again if you turn your back on it." Her nose is suddenly very much there in the word "there." She then takes a pause that allows her to assess the resources she has at hand for continuing speech. And her next phrase barely achieves enunciation as an overwhelming spirit of horror and sadness appears to sweep through her.

It may seem odd to imply that people "do" these little turns into their bodies, seizing on resources that they do not in any cognitive sense seem aware that they have, in order to produce the corporeal practices of crying. But if the person involved does not make a tacit turn on his or her body to find the material stuff of crying, who or what does? It is inadequate to dismiss the question with the view that the behavior of crying is somehow "wired in" to people as an inherited response pattern. Cultural and situational variations in the practices of crying are sufficient to keep the issue vigorously alive. Biological explanations just beg the question of how they work their influence into human behavior in nonrandom, socially situated patterns.

On the other hand, if we cannot find how people search and find bodily resources for crying, it matters little, from a pragmatic or social-science perspective, that we insist on an active understanding of the subject. But the idea of the embodied self being brought from the background to the foreground in emotional behavior is neither an abstract proposition nor simply a license for lines of speculation that can remain happily indifferent to data. We make headway into describing the self-explorations of crying when we examine its embodiment closely.

A common initial step of self-exploration in crying is to alter the landscape of perception. Consider gaze. When people cry, they often scrunch down their faces, press hard to their eyes with a bare hand or cloth, or, doubling over into a balled-up figure, they throw their gaze to the ground. Eyes may be raised to the heavens in search of hope or held on another person but clouded by tears. Averted from a close correspondent, the crying face may be made into a rigid mask that holds gaze in a steadied state, no longer quickly responsive to movements in what had just been the field of vision. The crying head may be buried in another's embrace. Like the instant effects of shutting one's eyes, each of these actions will promote a tacit turn of consciousness toward the bodily inner lining of behavior.

Certain features of culture direct people into crying by recurrently suggesting to them a heightened sensitivity to the natural three-dimensionality of their conduct. In several strips of cry-talking in my videotaped data set, people who are in extraordinarily different positions in life find the word "heart" especially fitting for capturing what they are feeling, and they find that enunciating this word has especially powerful effects in provoking them to cry. Here are three examples.

Gerta Weisman Klein finished her speech at the 1996 Academy Awards, where she was honored as the subject of a documentary, *One Survivor Remembers,* on her six years in a German concentration camp, with the phrase, "I thank you on their behalf with all my heart." "Heart" is the most troubled word in her emotional speech. It comes out in a broken form, with an internal micropause, as if, perhaps, the experience has left a silence at the core of her heart. The challenge of uttering the word strangles her voice toward silence and occasions a pronounced dry swallow in which she seems to scoop with her chin to obtain lubrication for her voice.

Her acceptance speech is stunningly moving for the audience, and one might easily think that "heart," as the last word she utters, is so powerful simply because it has to do the work of summing up the enormity of her life story. But the same word proves troublesome to Joker, an ethnic Samoan member of a Long Beach street gang. Crying emerges as Joker speaks about the effects of his injuries and incarcerations on his mother. After he recounts his mother's tear-filled, unwavering support for him when he was knifed and jailed, Joker is asked about his overall relationship with her. He says that they often argue, shout at each other, but "deep down in my heart I would die for her." "Heart" he enunciates with a pronounced waver; and saying the word appears to cut him deeply, an observation whose double entendre appears to be grounded in his own three-dimensional hearing of his narrative. Joker's consciousness appears to follow the direction of the metaphor. His eyes cloud up, and a bit later when his voice has steadied, he takes his recovered composure as an opportunity to brush away a tear.

Leonard Callace uses "heart" to great emotional effect in an interview with a TV journalist that was conducted in jail while he was awaiting release after DNA evidence contradicted his conviction for rape. Perhaps unselfconsciously recalling the effect he achieved in the in-jail interview, Callace again employs the word to great emotional effect in the court proceeding that finally set him free. In the in-jail interview, he is recounting how, during his prison confinement, he was rushed from prison to his mother's hospital bed when she was dying (he notes that she was ill with cancer before his legal problems began), but arrived too late.

> I was tore up, you know. I figured she'd hold on until I'd get there. She couldn't. She tried, but she couldn't. [He is crying.] That's what gets me. [pause] That was my heart.

"That was my heart" reaches back to sum up the emotional reaction that his narration of the story has already provoked. A short time later, at the final court hearing, he repeats the gist of the story to the judge as he details how the injustice he suffered was aggravated by this personal tragedy.

> And while I was up there, my moh, my muhther passed away. [long pause, lips and jaw repeatedly moving slightly without sound] And that was my heart. You people just [short pause] took my heart away.

This time "heart" has come alive. "Muhther" has just been a problem, precisely at the "h" sound, where he pauses, restarts, and then utters the full word (which he gives a normal pronunciation), but with a hesitation within the word as if it contained a punctuation mark. Then, in a reflexively provocative utterance, as he sends the word "heart" out, the act of utterance appears to flash back on him, bringing out tears, squeezing his voice down in a pronounced fashion, giving him such emphatic warning of its power that he pauses before uttering it again.

That "heart" has unusual powers to evoke crying is a lesson that we can take from the improbably coincident reappearance of this word as used by three people in four different social interaction contexts. Callace appears to have innocently stumbled onto an awareness of this knowledge. This lesson appears to be learned professionally by people who, as a matter of their work, regularly must manage crying in social interaction. In a documentary about dying, a priest sits at the bedside of a woman in the last moments of her life and encourages her son to reconcile himself to her death. Asked to articulate his greatly disturbed feelings, the young man explains through a crying voice, "I don't want her to be just a statistic." The priest responds, "She'll never be just a statistic, she'll always be in our hearts." The son's crying then escalates noticeably. Just the hearing of the word seems effective.[67]

Why should "heart" be so provocative of crying? Notice that it combines an inward-pointing metaphoric denotation, directing attention to the center of the body's cavity, and a literal, physical marking of the three-dimensionality of the body in its spoken utterance. The long syllable begins with an "h" sound that marks the respiratory process audibly, proprioceptively, and with a tactile resonance. The speaker takes the utterance of "heart" as a provocation to crying by grasping the double entendre that is created as the thrust of its utterance joins forces with its content. A normally tacit truth comes to the surface, that using culture (language, symbols, metaphors) practically requires a three-dimensional bodily commitment.[68]

An essential part of what crying is is a person's sensual appreciation of the three-dimensional implications of conducting social action. As a person progresses into crying, from the person's stance looking inward, words and word particles whose utterance implicates inner regions of the body become troubled and begin to trigger or drag out perceptible expressions of the functioning of speech. And from the person's stance looking outward at the pressures of social interaction, crying is a balking at the demands for effacing the corporeal investment that ordinarily competent behavior demands. The person finds that he or she cannot "just" talk; he or she finds that talk, if it is to emerge at all, will announce the troubled workings of its corporeal processes.

Thus the person, in moving into crying, not only searches his or her body for resources to outfit the emotion materially, he or she also exercises a hypersensitivity to the demands that ordinarily unproblematic social action make on bodily commitments. Consider some of the common ways in which crying becomes socially apparent when people are talking.

A major pattern is the breaking of what routinely flows in normal speech.

- People break off speaking *after a sentence,* taking an unusually long pause or, as in the case of Arthur Ashe at his press conference, noted earlier, stopping completely.
- People put in breaks *between words.* At her 1996 parole hearing, Patricia Krenwinkel, one of the people convicted with Charles Manson

for the Tate-LaBianca murders and imprisoned for almost thirty years, pleaded (unsuccessfully) with the board through teary and constricted eyes, "I am paying for this [pause] as. best. as. I. can."

- People cry-talk by *breaking between word syllables* in the sense of not finishing a word or by finding their voice taking a sudden upward jump in pitch. Leonard Callace, as quoted earlier, has trouble with "mother": "And while I was up there, my moh, my muhther passed away."

- People also cry by *breaking between the letters within words*. A young mother who lost her two-year-old child to foster care after she had broken the girl's leg in a fit of rage tells an interviewer, "It's hard. It's hard when your baby's being taken away." She pronounces the word "hard" as a series of separate letters, as "h.a.r.d," with noticeable space between the sound of each.

- And people *break the audible dimension of speech from the motility of speaking*. They may move their lips and jaws silently between phrases, as if miming talk. Or they may begin a phrase with full sound only to find that by its end they are doing a kind of strained whispering, shaping a virtually silent flow of exhaled air with their mouths.

Experiencing such cry-implicated breaks in their speech, people move at a distance from language, treating it as a dangerous culture, which, if entered too thoroughly, might somehow whisk them away entirely. At times they speak gingerly, as if putting verbal toes in waters that are terrifyingly dangerous. What they are grasping is the usually unnoticed depth of personally embodied commitment that language, and more broadly social action, requires. Their speech may remain perfectly intelligible, but everyone knows that something is terribly wrong with their current ability to invest themselves in social forms.

What is wrong is that the person cannot maintain the necessary commitment to obscuring the inner linings of the embodied self. What is lost from speech in these examples is flow. The flow, the *processual* vehicle of action, *the smooth intertwining between self and society* that is routinely maintained in normally competent natural social action, is suddenly outside of reach. In emotionally unproblematic social action, culture provides a skin that is put on without anyone noticing the dressing operation. But in cry-talking, the skin of language breaks away and tentative efforts to flesh out the self in standard forms are revealed.

Cry-talking is a phenomenon formally situated at the negative in expression. When listening to audiotapes, we hear that crying appears in those places at which culture does not firmly impose a shell on the self, such as in the pauses between sentences, between words, between syllables. It shows up as extra steps in pitch and as extra syllables that get placed in vowels. Notably, crying does not show up as the action of adding gratuitous consonants, as occurs in stuttering. As one listens to a person whose talk displays crying, one finds evidence of crying in the speaker's vowel sounds, which appear to be encountered as dangerous gaps between the safe havens of consonants, which in turn are enunciated with relatively little trouble. Consonants appear to offer secure islands for the self, while the vowel sounds between suggest shallowness in the cultural waters in which speech must swim. Again and again, the crying person's voice loses a firm bottom as, speaking within vowels sounds, the crying person's voice wavers audibly. The vehicle that language normally provides the body is suddenly stripped away even to the point of indicating the vibrations of the vocal cords that produce speech.

Crying more generally reveals how, in and through their conduct of routine social life, *people create the body that makes normally competent action possible.* We might imagine that emotional disturbances first undermine the body's ability to speak in a normally competent manner, and that this impairment then shows up as faults in speaking. But that conventional view is clearly wrong. For one thing, cry-talking is not necessarily inferior in intelligibility. Frequently, everyone knows a person is crying as he or she talks and everyone has no problem in knowing what he or she is manifestly saying. Indeed, crying while talking often enhances the correspondent's attentions and clarifies the surface meaning of a speaker's utterances. Cry-talking is not necessarily a more faulty means of communication than is talking that suggests no emotional disturbance.[69]

Furthermore, if emotional disturbance came first we might expect to see signs of crying randomly distributed in speech acts, not concentrated in negative or unshielded spaces. And we would not expect to see the speaker so often show no sign of disturbance while listening and only begin crying when he or she starts a turn in speaking. Speakers appear to be vividly, sensually aware that as they speak they expose themselves, not simply by what it is that they say but precisely by how they say it. For the speaker, the act of speaking occasions a self-reflective awareness of how *the speaking body is naturally and alternatively taken up and abandoned by different formal parts of speech.*

Cry-talking reveals how, in speech that is not apparently disturbed by emotions, the speaker effectively hides his or her body by keeping it just behind and just out of the reach of the correspondents' focal awareness. Consider that people who are cry-talking sometimes seem to be doing an odd kind of singing. They add syllables to words (instead of pronouncing "I," for example, one might produce "Ayeee"), almost as if they had suddenly entered into an operatic performance. But what is distinctive about what they are doing is not that they are invoking a musicality that is unknown in routine, nonemotional speech; they are, in a way, just not keeping the natural musicality of competent speech hidden. In ordinary nonemotional talk, people do not appear to themselves or to their correspondents to be singing, but in a way they are. Speakers use musiclike phrases to join letter to letter, syllable to syllable, and word to word, so that gaps do not become audible. Because of this familiar musicality, we don't usually hear the spaces that, in a written text, are there to be seen between letters and words. Thus we can say that the aesthetic flow of ordinarily competent language usage is hidden in its usually disattended musicality. When people cry-talk, odd pitch changes enter their voice. The distinctive failure they demonstrate is not necessarily one of intelligibility nor in the first instance is it one of keeping rational control of their speech. It is a matter of not keeping the aesthetic spirits of routinely competent conduct in the relatively disattended background of interaction.

We can push this analysis of the proper understanding of the relationship between body, emotion, and language one further step. Speech that appears to be emotionally undisturbed not only hides the speaker's body, it *lends the speaker a normally competent body for speech.* The lack of flow in cry-talk points up one of the subtle ways that routinely competent speech provides bodily resources to speakers.

Ordinary speech provides lubrication to the throat that evaporates when people start to cry. As they confront unusual problems in the form of breaks between phrases, between words, between audible letters, etc., the elements of speech not only become clipped, sensually they become brittle. The metaphor of flow that is tacitly lived in the ordinary use of language is often turned upon as a person's eyes tear up. Becoming aware of a slow flow from the eyes, the person experiences dryness in the throat. This is confronted, not as a feature of imagination but as a practical problem in the corporeal mobilization of talk. Speech becomes unusually difficult because somehow the usual lubrication isn't there. Seeking to solve the problem, people often do dry swallows when they cry-talk, and they also sometimes do a scooping motion down, forward and up with their chins, as if they are trying to catch some lubrication.

This metamorphosis, this process in which the metaphor that had been tacitly employed to guide behavior is transformed to reveal the familiar signs of crying, is not specifically related to speech. Something similar happens to silent observers of awards ceremonies and other emotionally moving spectacles. The flow of respiration that usually passes through the throat unnoticed may start to show up elsewhere. Flow may turn up in the form of teary eyes that deteriorate vision, noses filled with mucus that require sniffling, or overstuffed nasal passages that threaten to shut down any speech that might be attempted.

The Socio-Poetic Logic of Crying

Georg Simmel once offered what at first glance may seem a uselessly tautological definition of "life as more life." The patterns that crying demonstrates in social interaction offer an informative reading of Simmel's processual idea. People routinely take for granted an invisible flow back and forth between personal body and cultural form. They tacitly rely on washings of liquid across the eyes to facilitate vision. They unproblematically manipulate the in-out flows of breath to carry speech. And they unselfconsciously position the body in a manner that brings given audible and visible landscapes into focus. When situations provoke a sense that routine perception and response is no longer possible, the sensual bases of ongoing life do not disappear; they become marked, transformed, and presented in forms of emotional expression. The flow of the individual's participation in social life neither ends nor begins in emotional conduct. Instead, the flow that intertwines person and world metamorphoses as it moves from the background to the foreground of experience. The person who is moved to tears while silently observing a ceremony becomes aware that his or her gaze is constructing the perception of what is overwhelming. Watery eyes simultaneously take refuge from current events and humbly acknowledge responsibility in constituting their force.

Here we come upon a central paradox that crying shares with all emotions. What distinguishes emotional experience is a distinctive combination of subjectivity with objective factors. The sense in emotional experience of being taken by outside forces independent of one's will or actions is created through a noncognitive, tacitly embodied turn to the self. People feel they are objects moved by the world in their emotional experiences, not by ceasing to determine their own experience and somehow relinquishing their will or capacities as subjects, but by exercising an especially deep searching of the embodied self. At no time is a person moved by "subjective" or "objective" forces alone. Conduct always emerges in and from a flow of experience in which the person is naturally intertwined with the world. In forming emotional behavior, the individual does not create manifestations of subjective state from whole cloth; he or she turns on and seizes expressive resources from the ongoing interpenetration of self and world.

Thus a person exploits the normal tearing process as a resource for producing the welled-up eyes of crying. But in what sense, and how? Most people are unaware that normal visual perception routinely makes use of a kind of tearing, that eyes are bathed frequently in a manner that promotes vision.[70] People cry by increasing their tearing to the point that it threatens to stand out as a phenomenon in its own right, becoming a layer of wetness that now stands in front of the person as a self-indicating reaction to the scene being perceived.

Within the experience of the crying person, emotional tears stand out in two directions. On the one side they juxtapose themselves to the self. Often a crying person will take distance from his or her tears while observing their surprising emergence from his or her body. William Frey provides an example from his own experience.

> [O]ne night I was sitting alone recalling pleasant moments with my grandparents, who are now quite old. An unexpected wave of sadness passed through me when I realized that my own young children would never really know my grandparents and would never experience their warmth, love, and wisdom that had added so much to my childhood. Suddenly, tears began trickling down my face. At that time I had seldom cried and was quite surprised by what was happening. I even ran to a mirror to assure myself that the wet drops running down my face were tears.[71]

Another example comes from my field notes. A mother of a six-year-old boy was describing a recent event. While taking a bath he told her that the night before, when he was in bed and thinking of his brother's departure to another state for college, "water was coming out of my eyes."

With regard to the world outside, emotional tears become a film separating the person from distressing pressures. This occurs similarly in sad and joyful crying. Tears at times are part of a self-embracing, self-protecting, self-isolating, and self-enclosing act that withdraws one from pain or indignity. And at other times tears emerge in a kind of self-humbling act that creates a respectful distance from something sacred, exquisitely precious, overwhelmingly inspiring, or awesomely beautiful, something that often gives chills as it penetrates what seems to be one's soul.[72]

In tearful crying, a person takes what is usually a functional, transparent film of liquid and converts it into a boundary between self and world. Tearing changes from a routine prophylaxis that, in battling infection, keeps the body in a background where it may be relied upon without being attended to directly, to a way of bringing the body to consciousness. And tearing changes from an aid to vision's ability to keep one in the situations of action so responsively that one's perception and response flow without any sharp division, to a product that partly clouds vision as it breaks the flow of a routine response.

If these transformations of the metaphoric structuring of experience proceed independently of the actor's ability to state the aesthetic principles involved, that does not mean that they must be left outside the possibilities of explanation. It does mean that we still face the challenge of understanding how these aesthetic operations, which, when written about, often seem very elaborate and finely discriminating, can occur so quickly and, from the subject's standpoint, so effortlessly.

There is vast sophistication and variety in the artful ways that people play their bodies into the instruments of emotional expression. Crying may consist of little more than breaks in talking at a press conference, a catch of breath in an intimate conversation, welled-up eyes in a darkened movie theater, or crying may become a drama of wailing to the point of prostrating oneself in a public square. The upshot of this analysis is a call to examine the socially disciplined patterns in which people, in crying, aesthetically probe the routinely hidden corporeal resources of conduct. For further progress, we now need to look in depth at given instances of socially situated crying.

AN INTRODUCTION TO
TWO CRYINGS

Rachel, the subject of the next chapter, is just shy of three years old. When the recording was made, Rachel had been coming to the school for about three months. While her whining behavior persisted longer than was typical for newcomers to the school, Rachel's experience at school was not deemed especially problematic by school personnel. The materials on Rachel's whining that are examined here are offered as exhibiting patterns that commonly occur when small children use whining to interact with others. In this instance, there are both tears and signs of the strategic use of crying, a paradoxical combination that many parents would appreciate as both enigmatic and familiar.

James Martin, the subject of chapter 6, was too common a criminal to become very newsworthy, even as a killer. Like most career criminals, Martin was almost consistently bad at crime, never having made a "big score" and having spent much of his life in jail or prison, primarily for relatively inconsequential thefts and petty credit and check frauds. From age eighteen to age thirty-seven, when he committed the first of the murders on which the interrogation examined here was focused, he spent the great majority of his time in confinement. At several points in his interrogation, Martin "breaks down" and cries. His crying is strategically related to the breakdown of his story, but it is also distinguishable by wavering and other features of his voice and by his subsequent use of tissues to clear his face of tears. Like Rachel's crying, Martin's crying presents a mixture of "real" and "artificial" aspects that is common in cryings that express pathos.

If Rachel and Martin's cryings make for a bizarre juxtaposition because of the contexts in which they occur—the one being a place to bring out what is conventionally regarded as the greatest evil in our society, the other being a place to cultivate what is conventionally regarded as the most precious good—they have in common one feature that makes them especially well suited for the current inquiry. In both settings, people in more powerful positions are frequently engaged in managing, as a matter of their professional work, the crying of people in less powerful positions. It tends to serve the interests of police interrogators when suspects cry,[1] and it almost always serves the interests of teachers when preschoolers do not.[2] As her teacher is trying to build Rachel up to stop her whining, so, conversely, Martin's interrogators are attempting to break him down. In both settings the authority figures succeed, and in both situations the professionals follow their successes with modest celebrations.[3]

It is, however, too facile to see the police and the preschool teacher as having inverse forms of expertise with respect to the interactional production and elimination of crying. Occasionally, preschool teachers adopt an interrogating role, pressing a child to admit to a cruelty imposed on another member of the school community, and to this end the child's crying may be unflinchingly provoked. Conversely, police interrogators are often disserved by crying on the part of a person they are questioning. This is commonly the case when the person under questioning is a witness rather than a suspect, but it is also in the police interest to restore composure soon after a suspect cries.[4] What interrogators are institutionally rewarded for is a bureaucratic achievement in case processing, not sadistic delight in the emotional punishment of the suspect. They seek the most quickly formed and most clearly expressed record of self-incrimination that they can obtain, and within an interrogation, just after the police have broken a man down, they are often providing scaffolding that will help him build up another line of deceit, one that they confidently expect to break down in due course. Separation anxiety, in the sense of a person's emotional difficulties in shedding an identity into which he or she had comfortably settled, is as routine a problem for professionals in the interrogation room as it is in the preschool.

These two instances of crying allow us to focus on generally occurring dimensions of crying by offering contrasts that are multiple and emphatic.

1. Rachel and Martin's cryings differ in narrative meaning. Our two subjects differ vastly in age and in what the moment's tear-provoking challenges imply for their futures. Martin's cryings are brief pauses in the police business of nailing down his culpability. Rachel's whining, in contrast, is an almost unbroken commentary on what is overtly treated as the proper objective of attention, the orderly assembly and disassembly of a series of wooden blocks. At another level, matters of the soul are uppermost in both settings, the point of the inquiry with Martin being to damn him, the point of the preschool work with Ra-

chel being to free her to discover that the world is ordered in accordance with a natural logic.

2. The cryings by the child and the felon also differ in interactional significance, in part because the professionals in these two institutional settings have radically different interests in shaping the biographies of their "clients." Rachel's teacher addresses the girl's crying directly only in an exceptional and late moment in the interaction, when virtually all indirect means to dissuade her from crying appear to have failed. On and on Rachel whines; again and again her teacher ignores the whining and explicitly directs Rachel's attentions to technical operations with the blocks. Martin's cryings, in contrast, are understood as comments on what is officially going on. When they flare up, Martin's cryings are welcomed by the police, as they immediately discredit long lines of his prior defensive posturing.

3. Rachel and Martin's cryings also differ aesthetically. The forms of Rachel and Martin's cryings vary from, respectively, obnoxiously elaborated and seemingly endless to heavily muted and barely detectable.

With these radical differences in mind, the idea is that if we can find common contingencies in the processes that lead Rachel and Martin into and out of crying, we should have provided useful touchstones for the development of the close empirical study of crying as a social phenomenon. If we had chosen instead to look comparatively at two children's crying experiences in preschool, or at two suspects breaking down in interrogation, we might not appreciate how varied crying can be in all three of these respects: as a bodily doing, as an interactionally managed event, and as a resource for commentary on the social business at hand. Of course, it would be preferable to do both, but as a practical matter only a very few instances can be examined at this point in the study of crying as it occurs in social interaction. We must pursue minute detail in order to document the distinctive phenomena and the precise turning points in the natural history of crying. As a secondary product of this inquiry, we may gain a new appreciation of what is entailed in the actual work of police interrogators and preschool teachers, especially the skills in "emotion work" that they must develop.

The chapters on Rachel and Martin also provide a useful test of the theory of this volume. In many uses, "theory" is a set of logically related propositions that summarize and generalize from what has been documented in the form of empirical generalizations. Without contesting that version of the term, I am using "theory" here with a different emphasis. Theory is sometimes useful in the meaning of a set of guides when exploring the unknown. Where and how should we start the investigation of crying? As I have tried to demonstrate in earlier chapters in application to anger, laughter, and shame, here I bet that there will be substantial payoff if we pursue three questions about the situation-specific doings of crying, and a fourth question that addresses the transcendent implications of those situated doings.

First we look to *the narrative work that crying does*. We expect to find that the formal details with which crying is expressed—the specifics of the "how" of crying—are not spontaneously, idly, or randomly related to the meaning of the interaction that is going on. We expect to find that, although Rachel and Martin do their cryings in radically different ways, the aesthetic details of the way that each cries is essentially, through and through preoccupied with making a commentary on the identity that is emerging for him- or herself in the interaction. Through her crying, Rachel is trying to tell an otherwise unnoticed story about how her life, her very being, is implicated in this situated version of herself as making or failing to make a certain degree of progress in a task with geometrically related blocks. And Martin, in the remarkably different sensual way he does his crying, is also trying to capture and express the meaning for his life of the kind of criminal he is confessing to have been. Through their cryings, both the girl and the con comment on the implications for their transcendent life stories of their situated actions.

Second I bet we will be well-advised to look at *how the crying person adjusts his or her crying with regard to how others present are understanding and responding*. We expect to find that the natural history of crying in both of these settings shows that the crying is collaboratively produced and collaboratively dismantled. Rachel's teacher and Martin's interrogators do not cry with them, but as they respond the professionals seek to shape the emotional responses of their subjects. The interaction of note here takes place tacitly and on a corporeal basis, not primarily through the content of what is said but through how it is said and through motions that accompany and form the ground for what is said. Her teacher works indirectly and cumulatively on Rachel's body movements, drawing the child, step by delicate step, into coordinated action with herself, building up a jointly mobilized pair of bodies and thereby preparing the ground for Rachel to abandon her whining. Martin, for his part, constantly seeks to authenticate one false version of his past after another by attempting to underwrite his statements with body motions that lend them verisimilitude. His interrogators are not unaware of the importance of his body motions in sustaining his story, and at crucial points in his interrogation, Martin's struggle with the police turns on dramatic changes in the ongoing struggle over control of his body.

The *third* inquiry that should produce distinctive results is the search for *the metamorphosis in which the crying body emerges or disappears*. In a metamorphosis there is a moment of transformation that seems somehow inspired and not simply guided by strategic interaction. For Rachel, the transition out of whining and into talk occurs through the deus ex machina of a brief fit of coughing. Coughing comes to Rachel as if sent by a force beyond her control, and it takes over the exhale phase of her respiration that had been haunted persistently by whining. Just after coughing, she speaks with bell-like clarity. Martin's crying emerges as a kind of fog that he produces when the police reveal that they have evidence that is inconsistent with key aspects of his defensive story, and as he finds himself slipping into what I characterize as a whirlpool. The metaphor of the fog and the whirlpool fits many cryings in which the metaphoric foundations that are routinely used to construct the self are themselves in a process of radical transformation.

And there is something more. None of us lives solely or wholly within any given social situation in which we are currently active, and we know it. For each of us, this knowledge of the transcendent meanings of our situated conduct becomes a matter of personal style, of accent, of sway or gloss, a texture or atmosphere that we produce in our actions as a kind of metacommentary on the situated selves that we produce. My final theoretical bet is that if we make soundings for the stuff of this transcendent project, we will find something distinctive that responds to our inquiry.

With James Martin, what I find is a characteristic fog. His crying is an attempt to blur his presentation of self, to create something to hide behind, and to obtain a moment in which he might plan his emergence out of the fog in some new deceptive guise. Many cryings are like that: they dissolve a destroyed self in tears at a moment when, not knowing how to build a new, strong, and shiny version of self, one finds at least the courage to go on to re-present the self. For some, a step into the fog of tears is a heroic move beyond a stunning trauma. For people in Martin's position, it is an alternative to a more brutal form of self-destruction, a confession that would be virtually suicidal.

Rachel's crying is more like a fugue. While it persists it seems endlessly sustainable and it has a basic melodic motif that skips up about a musical fifth as it recycles. In its distinctive timbre, Rachel's whine creates a homey version of an "other" who can accompany and be relied upon to provoke her in the intimate familiarity of her own respiratory cycle. Produced through the natural cycle respiration, audible on the exhale, silent on the inhale, the child's whining keeps her in touch with a dialectic that is sure to transcend any gaps one must enter while traveling between the disparate social situations and social worlds of one's daily life.

The treatment here is social-psychological, not psychological. Some aspects of James Martin's biography are noted to indicate how the fog he produces through his crying continues the foglike character of his identity in society generally. The fog is his habitus, the ongoing disposition from which he innovates responses to the precarious situations he regularly puts himself in. But my focus throughout is on the distinctive ways he does things in interaction with others, not on his psyche. For Rachel, I draw on no material beyond the short strip of whining that appears on videotape. When I address her whining as a transcendent strategy I am addressing nothing unique about this child's personality but possibilities known by all children when they orchestrate their bodily instruments for social interaction in the ways that we recognize as whining.

FIVE

AN EPISODE OF WHINING

A five-minute strip of videotape shows Rachel, a two-year-eleven-month-old child, seated at her desk at a preschool.[1] Rachel whines almost constantly. At one point she stops, only to start again after a moment. Rachel whines before her teacher joins her, while she works with her teacher, and after the teacher leaves her side.

The overall episode develops as a drama in three acts. Rachel is sitting at her assigned desk, hovering over a set of wooden blocks on a mat that she has brought to her desk. The blocks have a "self-correcting" logic: they can be combined into a cube and stored in their box only if assembled in an order of progressively larger or smaller volumes. Meanwhile her teacher, Tamara (below, sometimes "T"), is standing beside Rachel (below, sometimes "R"). Tamara asks another teacher to attend to another child so that she may focus on Rachel. Rachel is already whining when the camera turns to her and we see a wireless mike being clipped to the mat on her desk.

As the teacher illustrates the principle for assembling the blocks, the child's whining continues but it changes significantly in its relationship to the teacher's speech and movements. After the two make initial progress in coordinating their conduct, the teacher asks the child if she can move a particular block into position, and Rachel, who to this point has never stopped whining, shakes her head "no." The teacher now rises to leave Rachel's desk, telling her that she is competent to do the work on her own. This first phase of the episode ends at 2 minutes, 25 seconds.

In the second act, Rachel works alone. She moves her hands to the blocks for the first time and proceeds to work attentively, gazing in various directions away from her desktop but making adjustments in the arrangement of the blocks until she completes the cube. Her progress and success do not, however, end her whining. With the cube completed, Rachel puts her hands to the side of her face, becomes relatively immobile, and cries on. Act 2 runs only 35 seconds.

The last act runs another 2 minutes. It begins on a note of celebration, as Tamara returns to congratulate the child. She then instructs Rachel on disassembling the blocks and placing them back in their storage box. The child continues whining for 13 seconds; then coughs for 4 seconds; and then stops whining and begins to talk clearly with her teacher for the first time in the episode. The child and the teacher talk and work together through five units of interaction unblemished by crying.

At 45 seconds into this phase, and in response to comments by Alan, a boy seated at a desk facing her, Rachel begins to whine again. As the teacher addresses the boy, suggesting that he likes to make Rachel cry, Rachel completes placing the blocks in the storage box, crying continually. Finally, the teacher turns back to Rachel, asks why she is crying, unsuccessfully tries to talk her out of crying, and then leaves, telling the softly whining child to get a tissue to wipe her eyes.

Why is Rachel whining? We will discuss below the factors that the staff mention (e.g., separation anxiety, provocation by Alan), but their explanations will not be wholly satisfying. Such factors remain constant while the child's whining varies greatly in its character over the various phases of the episode and while it clearly stops. Psychological and extensive biographical data lie beyond the current inquiry, and without these data we can at most understand the situational attractions and social dynamics of whining. That may seem to be a limited payoff, but on the other hand, whining is not an unusual pattern among children new to preschool settings. What we can seek to understand here is the nature of whining as a form of personal experience and as a way of shaping social interaction. It is the fate of the whining, in combination with the progression of the puzzle work, that structures the episode as a classic drama.

The analysis is in four parts. First I examine how the child's interaction with her teacher takes on a narrative character specifically through their *joint* appreciation and collaborative *response to the aesthetics of whining*. The child frequently makes one whine-phrase different from another in both rough and fine ways, using her body constantly as a flexible expressive instrument. The aesthetic dimensions of the child's whining are used by the child and the teacher to coordinate their conduct with each other. Through their attentive responsiveness to the form of the child's crying, the two give their interaction a dualistic narrative character. At one level, the structure of their interaction takes the form of an episode with regard to the stages of the cube building and disassembly process. At another level, the episode takes shape as a drama about the child's distance from and immersion in her interaction with her teacher. This second level of narrative meaning is created and read by the participants through the career of the whining itself.

The second inquiry is into *the interpretive dilemma* created by the child's whining. As with the many forms of crying reviewed in the last chapter, Rachel's whining is hermeneutically dense. There is something strategically elusive about whining. Rachel's whining makes no simple statement; it is not a substitute for words or action but a way of acting that takes a stance toward another, ongoing stream of the child's expressions. Whining is in general a negative expression; here it is a means by which the child indicates that she does not fully embrace the self that her actions might otherwise express. At times, Rachel's whining creates a kind of double bind for her teacher: even as her whines express a protest, Rachel may promote cooperation with her teacher and accept her teacher's efforts to romance her into cooperation. Part of the answer to the question "Why is Rachel whining?" is that whining is a resourceful way for *expressing two contradictory messages at once.*

A third inquiry examines the natural history of Rachel's whining as a series of *metamorphoses* in which the child dramatically alters the embodiment of her conduct. As Rachel's whining disappears, so does the prominence of her body in the interaction. At the start of the episode she uses her whining as a noisy way of calling attention to herself as a protesting body. And when her whining stops and she begins to speak and work cooperatively with her teacher, her body becomes, in Merleau-Ponty's wonderful phrase, "effaced."[2]

That the child's body becomes invisible as she enters conversational interaction will be the most difficult point to get across. Perception of the child's body is equally available to us, as viewers of the videotape, throughout the episode, but for the participants, the child's body is on the foreground of the interaction as she whines, then moves to the background as she talks and works with her teacher, and then moves back out to the foreground as her whining begins again. This movement of corporeal regions between the background and the foreground of awareness is characteristic of emotional behavior in general.

In this case the metamorphosis is especially dramatic because of the strategic role that Rachel's cough plays in moving her from crying into speech. As she coughs, Rachel in effect tucks into the background of the scene the respiratory process that had been a sign of her insistent distance from involvement in interaction. With her respiratory cycle no longer signifying willful resistance, Rachel can move into the cooperative processes of speech clearly and cleanly. An analysis of the changing three-dimensionality of the child's presentation of self in the episode is an essential step toward appreciating the meaning and attractions of whining to her. It enables us to see that whining is a way of holding on to a sensually vivid awareness of dimensions of one's life that, like one's body in general, transcend the demands of any particular social situation that one may enter and move through.

A fourth inquiry brings us as close to understanding the causes of Rachel's whining as our limited data will permit. Here we examine how the emergence of a collaborative body, a body created through blurring and fusing the actions of child and teacher, becomes a substitute for the isolated individual body that Rachel had insisted upon through her whining. In the end we should be able to appreciate that for the child to give up whining, a leap is required. The child must risk giving up the surety of a sensual awareness of her own body to participate in the personally disembodied processes of conversational interaction. There is no step-by-step routine, no mundane bridge to that transition; it requires an act of faith. In this instance, it is facilitated by the deus ex machina of a brief spate of coughing.

As this episode highlights the critical role of the child's coughing in her transition from crying to speech, it may be particularly useful for challenging the frequent assumption that the concerns and the methodologies of interactionist sociology and of depth psychology are somehow intrinsically inconsistent. Although this chapter does not attempt to offer insight into the distinctive psyches of the people described, it shows just where subjectivity and objectivity, or doing conduct and being done by extrinsic forces, cross in experience. At this crossroads we can locate a port of entry into depth psychology that is as methodologically grounded as is any focus in interactionist sociology.

1. The Aesthetic and Narrative Resourcefulness of Whining

Like other emotions in social interaction, crying is a thoroughly narrative construction. We might say that emotions arise in a person's socially situated experience as a way of making a comment on the identity that the person is being conferred by others or is constructing through his or her conduct. But "comment," although helpful, can be misleading. Emotions are closer to mythical imagery and to music than to the discursive forms that language takes when language is used to explain, persuade, or tell stories. Rachel's crying is a whining, a kind of fuguelike song that she provides to accompany her practical activity, to respond to the talk that is directed at her, and sometimes as a vehicle that carries her own talk.

But what do we mean by saying that people when crying are using nondiscursive forms of expression to tell stories? Some leads are provided by those who have wondered how other nonlinguistic forms, like music, can tell a story. Treitler provides the example of a piece by Béla Bartók, "Mese a kis légyrö," or "A Tale about a Little Fly." At one point in the score, Bartók wrote the Hungarian equivalent of "Yikes! a cobweb!" above the notes. The composer took for granted that his suggestion of a story line would have some helpful relationship to the playing of the music. Treitler asks, "It is the piece itself that is a story, given *in music,* but. . . . How can that be?" He answers:

> In speaking of music's narrativity, I have reference both to its continuity and directedness and to the fluxes in its pacing, contour, tessitura, density, harmonic color, the consonance-dissonance dimension, rhythmic pattern, and yet other properties, that musicians and critics, especially since the nineteenth century, have felt as resonant with the flow of conscious awareness; for example, Robert Schumann's talk of music's successions as processions of ideas or of conditions of the soul.[3]

Whether listeners, to appreciate music, must know or detect the story behind the music is another matter. The musicians, in order to play, must mobilize their bodies holistically and in more or less continuous stretches, and for guiding that process in a uniform manner, a collectively appreciated story line can be very helpful. The story that the composer suggests bridges two mutually beckoning but foreign languages, the logic of the written music and the silent logic of corporeal movements that must be mobilized to make the music audible.[4]

The Narrative Resources in Whining

Rachel's crying has many properties that are similar to music's narrative resources. These properties become apparent when one struggles to transcribe Rachel's part of the interaction with her teacher. To begin with, the elements of her crying-whining do not sound exactly like letters from any language she knows. The most common sound in her

whine has as its most proximate phoneme an "n" sound, but because
the sound is sustained in a whine, because it is usually produced without the tongue motion of an "n," and because it is usually produced
within a closed mouth, a whine is not really made up by repetitions
of the letter "n." Children explore the uses of their bodies as musical
instruments even as they acquire language. Rachel in effect plays an
accompaniment to the gestural interaction as an alternative to talk.
Her whine should not be understood as a defective form of speech.
As Rachel shows late in this episode, she is fully capable of talking,
and in a touching, effective fashion.

The risk in transcribing her whine is not simply that the reader will
not be able to re-create the sound that one hears in reviewing the audio
track of the videotape; indeed, I quickly abandoned that goal as hopeless. The greater risk is that, if the transcription *could* successfully convey the whining as well as it does speech, it would fail in what is,
analytically, an even more important way. R and T know that the
whine is not speech; that it is a willful alternative to speech; that its
proximity to an "n" sound, which conveys a posture of negativity, is
not wholly arbitrary; and that, although they never address the matter
explicitly, their interaction is part of a constant effort to negotiate Rachel into clear speech.

If readers could pick up small children and play them, it might make
more sense to "score" whining-cryings than to transcribe them in a
clumsy analogy to speech. But even if children were willing to be manipulated like musical instruments, they would not be able reliably to
comply. So we must use transcription conventions, and as none have
as yet been established for describing whining, the best I can do is
to describe such phrases as 𝄞hnn+n+N+N−n−−nhn𝄟, provide some
commentary (+ means going up in pitch, − means coming down; capital letters mean an increase in volume; the musical notations indicate
the frames of a melodic passage), and invite readers to reacquaint
themselves with a whining use of their own bodies.

The narrative work that Rachel is doing with her whine is to comment on the fate of her consciousness within the social interaction at
hand. To follow her storytelling, we must examine three aspects of
the structure of her whine. One is the series of distinctive expressive
resources that she draws on in whining. The second is the meaning
that each whine-phrase takes on in relation to the series of whine-
phrases that she produces. (Whine-phrase are typically bounded by the
limits of given exhales.) And the third is the meaning of each section
of a given whine-phrase in relation to the other subsections of that
same whine-phrase.

As to the distinctive expressive resources that Rachel draws on in whining, I note eight subsets.[5] First there are elements that can be rendered on a dimension that conveys magnitude or scale. Rachel's whines vary, within and among whine-phrases, in volume (loud/soft), in length (short/long),[6] in pitch (high/low), and in numbers of steps (monotone/a few steps/many jumps up and down). The contour of her modal whine shows a peak.[7]

Second, there are differences in letter-like sounds. The most common is "n," but there are also "m" sounds that turn the utterance more into a hum and make it less nasal and negative. There are also respiratory "h," harsh "g," and mucusy "sh" and "ch" sounds.

In a third pattern, Rachel differentiates her whines by indicating that the currently audible moment is at a more or less tenuous place in the career of a particular phrase, which may be struggling to its end or which may be facing difficulty in getting launched. At times Rachel emits a creaking door, crunching, or muffled explosion sound, which I transcribe (with little onomatopoeic validity) as x, to indicate a breaking-up of the emission. Sometimes I write ʃx to indicate the combination of an emphatic wavering and a creaking door, crunching, or muffled explosion sound. At times Rachel sputters toward an ending, her whining becoming interspersed by milliseconds of silence before she takes a full pause for an in-breath. At times she indicates that she is going "all out" with her whine, extending an exhale until it is so thin that it can carry only "h" sounds. After such all-out efforts Rachel often ends the whine-phrase by emitting a brief "braking" sound at the start of the subsequent inhale.

Fourth, Rachel's whine sometimes indicates a variation in the extent to which she has control over its constituent elements. I use the tilde ~ to indicate modest wavering within a vowel sound, and I use a vertical waving line ʃ to indicate emphatic or polysyllabic wavering. This wavering, a common sign of crying in adult speech, suggests that emotions are getting too strong to sustain an accomplished and controlled whine. At the other extreme are segments of whines bracketed by ♫ signs. These indicate a recognizable melody. Rachel's whine has a repeated motif, which may be compact or stretched out. I transcribe Rachel's song as hnʃ♫+n+N N N n−nnn−n−n−n−n−n−n−n−nʃ. It starts at one level of pitch, jumps up quickly to a level about a fifth higher, becomes louder, and then, from one rendition to another, varies in volume and in the length at which it remains up and then comes down to or below the original level. In contrast to whines with many wavering (~) moments, melodic passages show a will in strong command of the musical instrumentality of the body.[8]

Fifth, whines may be produced on the exhale, the inhale, or in both phases of the respiratory cycle. When they are done on the inhale, they are rougher and express a greater intensity of emotion. Almost always, Rachel's whines are on the exhale. Inhales are, as we will see, key sites of interactional opportunity in Rachel's turn toward talk. But inhales are often not completely silent. Although they can often be observed on the videotape in movements of the chest, they are also often audible as "h" or somewhat liquid "sh" and "ch" sounds. Inhales are transcribed here with periods and in brackets: [.h.h.h.] or [.sh.sh.sh.]. These aspiratory and mucusy inhales are to be distinguished from sobbings, which are inhaled audible cryings with much higher and harder consonant sounds.

Sixth, the audible dimensions of Rachel's whine vary elaborately in relationship to facial expressions and other gestures or body motions. On first review, Rachel's videotaped whining episode is striking for the long passages in which, were the audio turned off, one would not suspect that anything is disturbing the child. She looks about with her mouth closed or slightly open, works effectively in assembling the geometrically related blocks on her desk, coordinates her gaze and hand motions with her teacher's gaze and motions, and so on, all without any visually apparent distress. With the audio on, one hears that virtually every exhale carries a whine. At other times Rachel's face takes on a classic cry formation, compressed at the eyes and mouth, tense, seemingly holding back a flood that is pressing to be released: ☹. If at times Rachel composes an almost absurd juxtaposition between a complacent face and the protesting negativity of a whine, during other passages her "cry face" portrays an equally striking dialectic. At such moments she may silently project crying through a dramatic repression of the face, bringing tears out by squeezing down powerfully on regions deep within.

Seventh, whining varies in relationship to other expressions of involvement in or distance from interaction, such as gaze. The meaning of Rachel's whining differs when it is done while looking at her teacher and when done while looking straight ahead or while looking at the teacher's movements of blocks in the task in front of them.

Eighth, whining, as a recognizable strip of conduct, has structural properties that the child exploits to create various relationships to the teacher's conduct. Two features of the teacher's dynamic conduct are at times targeted by the child's whining, the phases of the teacher's hand movements in demonstrating the puzzle work and the turns the teacher takes in speaking. At times, Rachel's whines begin and end simultaneous with the teacher's hand movements and talk. Occasionally, the child whines in a sequential response, or after a pause following a segment of the teacher's behavior. And at times the phases of the child's whining run courses that appear to be independent of any disciplined relationship to the teacher's conduct. In order to show the temporal relationship of segments within strips of simultaneous expression by T and R, I use arrows and blank space in a line to indicate where in one's conduct a segment of another's begins or ends. When the utterances or gestures of one are in the nature of a subsequent turn, or a strip of conduct that begins and ends after a strip of expression by the other, the space of one or more empty lines appears above or below descriptions of the actions of each.

Further analysis would probably discover additional dimensions of interaction resources that children exploit when whining. What these eight dimensions allow us already to see is that whining is not necessarily a problem in social interaction. The problematic character of this form of crying varies greatly. It is as arbitrary to suggest that whining indicates that the child is troubled as it is to suggest that a child who is functioning in a group is handicapped. Rachel's whine is at times a protest and at times a kind of song she sings to herself. For long stretches of time it functions in interaction as do many other "handicaps" and "problems" among preschool children, as a constant feature of identity that is not functionally problematic so long as everyone disattends it, and that may be gratuitously labeled as a problem by people too ready to impute pathos. In some stretches, Rachel whines easily and without impairing her practical actions, just as another child may accompany five minutes of work by rubbing her genitals in a masturbatory fashion. At other times, Rachel's tightly compressed "cry face" conveys a deeply internal disturbance and a desperate effort to hold back incapacitating emotions. And in addition to the cry face, other gestures and body motions that accompany her whining, such as a rocking of her torso in her chair, suggest the lightness or the depth of the struggle in which she is engaged.

The Narrative Structure of the Episode as the Course of a Mixed Tug-of-War and Seduction

In one sense, Rachel's whining has narrative meaning in that it emerges, changes form, declines, and reemerges over the course of the overall episode. But it is something more to claim that crying has a narrative meaning, not only in retrospective examination from the outside, but for the person crying even as he or she cries. After all, neither

Figure 5.1 Height of block environment and whine

Rachel nor her teacher knows for sure where their interaction is going when it starts. Even so, each of Rachel's whine-phrases quickly takes on a narrative meaning, because Rachel whines in highly differentiated ways, making use of the various resources I enumerated above, and because both Rachel and her teacher are closely attuned to alterations in her whining as a sign of the progress that is being made in relating their actions more closely to one other, and in negotiating Rachel's passage toward talk.

The teacher and the child directly address the whining only toward the end of the episode, after Rachel, having stopped whining, begins again. During the first act of the episode, they address the whining indirectly, mutually using various sensual dimensions of their interaction to become bound to each other. A key mutual focus for their bonding is the coordination of the teacher's hand movements and comments in demonstrating how to do the puzzle work, and the shaping of the child's whine. Repeatedly, the child's whine begins, arcs up and descends in pitch, and ends in parallel to the teacher's manual lifting, moving and putting down one of the puzzle's blocks (figures 5.1 and 5.2).

Here is how the child's whine and teacher's demonstrative action mesh in the middle of Act 1; another child, Gina (G), appears here.

Figure 5.2 Descending end of block movement and whine

```
 1  T:  [grabs   onto,        picks    up,     carries,   and    places        block down]
 2          ↑      ↑            ↑        ↑         ↑                ↑              ↑
 3  R:      hnhnhnhnhn♫+n+N+N+N+n+nnnnnnnnnnn−n−n−n−n−n−n−n−n♫; [silent]
 4
 5
 6
 7          A bit later, as a third child intervenes by calling for the teacher's attention, the
 8  pattern is repeated.
 9
10  T:  [grabs   onto,            picks   up,     carries, and    places   block   down]
11          ↑      ↑                ↑       ↑         ↑              ↑       ↑
12  R:      hnhnhnhnhn♫+n+n+N+N+N+nnnnnnnnnnn−n−n−n−n−n−n♫; [silent]
13                    ↑
14          ↑                                                                         ↑
15  G:  Tamara                                                                    Tamara
16
17
18                                                     [T marks finish with hand flourish]
19                                                                                      ↓
20  T:  [grabs,   lifts,                carries block,               completes cube]
21          ↑      ↑        ↑            ↑       ↑         ↑
22  R:      hnhnhnhnhn♫+n+n+N+N+N+nnnnnnnnnnn−n−n−n−n−n−n−n−n♫; [silent]
23
24                                                                                      ↑
25  G:                                                                            Tamara
```

This isomorphism occurs at least seven times in phase 1; in one instance, R's whine parallels in shape and length a statement rather than a movement that T makes. In all instances in which R's whine parallels T's movements, R's gaze follows T's movements. Note that *the coordination of R's and T's conduct is visible even to locally situated observers of their interaction.* G times her calls for the teacher's attention so that they fall just before the beginning and then at the ends of the whine-movement phases. G in effect validates that the bond being woven between T and R is a socially recognized reality.

The coordination of behavior here is more sensually profound than a flat transcription may indicate. Rachel's corporeal dedication to the interaction is a matter of *palpable dimensions* that she *adds to the mutuality of action.* First R's gaze becomes disciplined to the interaction with T. Her *vision,* with its proprioceptive resonance, more or less tracks onto T's silent hand movements. In the movement of R's eyelids, we can see that the course of R's gaze roughly pauses, follows T's movement of the block up and down, and then pauses again at the end of R's completion of a phase of puzzle work.

Second, as the bracketing and contours of the whines come to parallel T's movements, the length and shape of R's *exhales* become audibly *disciplined* to T's demonstrative *movements.* The child begins and ends exhaling as the teacher begins and ends a movement of a block. Their coordination quickly becomes very intimately developed. And the whine-phrase goes up and down as T moves a block.

Third, the whining creates a markedly *three-dimensional* channel for indicating their bond. It is useful to attempt a whine to appreciate how palpably profound an utterance is when it is whined. In effect, the teacher's hand movements reach deeply into the child's chest, or, alternatively put, the child provides a profoundly resonant tracing of the teacher's silent movements of her hand through the air.

Fourth, the exchange of inhale and exhale in R's *respiratory cycle* becomes *tracked* onto T's *movements.* The child not only exhales whines as the teacher moves a block, the child inhales silently between successive movements of blocks by the teacher. The effect is much more powerful than would be the case were the child to whine in an arc parallel to the teacher's hand movements and also whine in the pauses between the teacher's hand movements. By shaping both inhale and exhales to the teacher's movements, the child more completely and precisely portrays how much of herself she is offering to the involvement.

Fifth, Rachel's whining more perfectly tracks the teacher's hand movements when the teacher is attending solely to Rachel. At various points when T is demonstrating the puzzle work in Act 1, her gaze and talk shift to other children, even as her hand continues to show Rachel how to do the puzzle. At such times, the shaping of Rachel's whine does not fit well with the teacher's demonstrative hand movements.

Because of the intimate, palpable nature of the mutual effort to create a bond, the interaction takes on the sense of a drama that mixes a seductive dance and a tug-of-war. The teacher attempts to draw Rachel out of whining and into even-tempered work in the preschool. Rachel attempts to draw the teacher's attentions from other children and to herself. Neither speaks of their purpose. Each uses nonlinguistic corporeal dimensions to cultivate a mutual involvement. Indeed, near the start of the episode, as the teacher sits down with Rachel, she puts an arm around the child's shoulder, pulls her in tightly, and pauses silently to give the whining child a hug. As the arrows in figure 5.3 indicate, the teacher's right shoulder comes up and the child's left shoulder, pressed by the teacher's left hand, inclines in toward the adult. The child's attentions are being pulled into a frame defined by the adult, whose torso becomes a wall the child cuddles into. And the teacher, with her gaze cast down (thus we can see only her hair), likewise indicates that her attentions are limited to the child's world.

The beginning of the interaction sequence is marked, then, by a hug that creates relatively static, corporeal dimensions of intersubjectivity by emphasizing that limits have been placed on the bodily abilities of each to attend elsewhere. Note also that hugs also can make ambiguous where one ends and the other begins, overcoming some visual signs of separation and creating a sensual continuity. This is especially so in hugs like this one that are sustained in a motionless state for several seconds. The two appear to understand that before the relatively abstract channel of speech will be used for their interaction, they must first create a more intimate, multidimensional, corporeal basis of mutual involvement.

After the hug, as the two coordinate the arcs of the whine and the teaching gestures, they discover and exploit three dimensions that they share existentially but that are expressed by the adult through speech and teaching gestures and by the child through whining. Cutting across the differences in the modalities of their conduct, they mutually coordinate *temporal length*, startings and endings; *spatial verticality*, up and down; and *three-dimensional intertwining*, the expression of each finding an echo in the action of the other, an echo that for the child is palpable in her respiration. Ironically, although it is a sign of a "failure" to speak, the interactional accomplishments of this form of whining are in a way superior to that required for speech, which may be monologic, and perhaps even superior to the interactional requirements of conversational speech. In conversational interaction, one typ-

000068

Figure 5.3 The hug

ically waits in silence as the other talks. Here the two manage to stay together even as they produce expressions simultaneously. The teacher and the child have to coordinate the structuring of their modes of expression even as both hear and tacitly agree to ignore the noise and the protest in the child's whine. This is tricky and artful business.

Having worked out such a richly embodied way to coordinate their conduct, subsequent actions by the teacher and the child become narratively meaningful with regard to what has already transpired. The two have quickly shown each other, in what I call Act 1 of the dramatic episode, that they can be close and mutually cooperative. On the basis of this accomplishment, the teacher then asks Rachel to participate more overtly in the puzzle work. Tamara makes the task especially easy by asking the child only to move a designated block to a designated location, not to choose the next block to be moved nor to figure out where to put it. It seems that the child cannot *not* know what to do. All pretense that the child is not participating because she does not understand the work has vanished. Here is what happens.

```
1      [mild question-styled, upturning intonation]
2           ↓           [T gazes to block and points to block]
3           ↓        ↓        ↓   [T shifts gaze to R]
4           ↓        ↓        ↓        ↓
5   T:   Rachel.      Can you put this on top?
6   R:            gnnn+n+n+nnnnnnn~n~n~nnnn;
7                                         ↑
8                             [abrupt stop of whine]
```

R whines as T repeats the question, "Can you put this on top?" Then the child audibly inhales, shrugs her shoulders, and silently moves her head in a horizontal no. Now her teacher quickly begins to disengage from R, announcing, "I'm going to leave you alone" and "You are going to do this. . . . Because you know how to do this job." R whines throughout the disengagement process, but not in synch with T's talk.

The prior coordination of the child's whine and the teacher's movement made R's refusal especially forceful. Both had immediate evidence that they were attending to the same matters. R's lack of participation could not be attributed either to her incompetence to understand the puzzle nor to her distraction. The nod was made an especially negative act because Rachel notably did not then whine. She appears to hold onto an inhale as she gestures "no" in silence. She shows that she need not whine and that she clearly recognizes and understands conversational sequence (i.e., that it is her turn to provide a responsive expression), but still she will not either talk or overtly participate in the work.

A second example of the narrative meaning generated by the course of whining in interaction was alluded to above. At several points in Act 1, T is drawn to attend to other children who approach to ask her for help. During these moments, R continues to whine on each exhale but her whine-phrases become louder and they lose the melodic character they had when T was attending to her with gaze and speech. Through manipulating the aesthetics of her whine, R is negotiating for T's attention and protesting against her attentions to other children. As a gambit in her efforts to win over T, the child will make her whining more aesthetically attractive when the teacher is more fully attending to her and more in the form of rough noise when T devotes herself elsewhere.

Third, the natural history of R's whining becomes a narrative resource for the indications she makes about her involvement in the scene as she works alone in Act 2 (figure 5.4). Just after Tamara leaves, Rachel's whines take forms unlike any of her whines when she was (or later will be) present. Here is an example of what emerges.

[soft and muffled]

                    [continuous sad face, tears forming]

R: **they da** . . . ☹~~n𝅘𝅥𝅮~~n𝅘𝅥𝅮~~n𝅘𝅥𝅮nnn~~n𝅘𝅥𝅮nnnn~~n𝅘𝅥𝅮☹

       [lips   slightly   apart,   soprano tone]

       ↑   ↑   ↑   ↑   ↑

Figure 5.4 Beginning to work alone

There is no apparent coordination of the contours of this whine-phrase to the actions of any others on the scene. Nor is R's whine shaped in any apparent way in parallel to her own motions. Were that the case, she might be perceived to be humming as she worked, and thus as content and comfortable in the role she is performing. Instead her whine follows a rough structure of its own. Given the patterning of her whine earlier in the episode, her whining in Act 2 manifests her engagement in some perspective independent of that of the puzzle work, work that she neatly and quickly accomplishes. Once R is finished with the task of assembling the blocks, her whine goes on in various rough forms as she puts her hands up to her cheeks in a waiting mode, holding her gaze straight and immobile.

2. The Hermeneutics of Whining in Social Interaction

If we wish to understand why a child whines, it should be useful to describe what the whining means. This, however, is no simple matter. Since there is no standard linguistic content to whining, the search for meaning must go directly to the uses the child makes of this form of expression. We have seen that whining is used by Rachel to express her involvement in the scene, in her activities and her relationships with others there, and that the meaning of any given whine-phrase depends on its relationship to whine-phrases in other segments of the episode.

But is there anything we can say about the meaning of whining overall? After all, whining is distinguishable from any number of other nonlinguistic forms, both audible and visible, of childish expression. There is some coherence to whining, something that makes whining recognizable as such, over and apart from its internal variations.

Whining is specifically dense hermeneutically. It is, in a way, the presentation of a mystery. We recognize children as whining only if we believe they can talk clearly but will not. This is not to suggest that whining is mysterious to all who hear it. At times the meaning of a child's whining may seem to adults to be a simple matter of insisting on something that has been denied, or a sign that the child is "just tired." But from the child's perspective, every whine is a choice not to express oneself in a more socially accessible, definitive form, or to express that there is more to oneself than what language will convey.

Evidence of Mystery in Rachel's Whining

In the episode before us, there is ample evidence that the meaning of Rachel's whining is ambiguous, elusive, and hotly contested for all parties concerned. A sense of mystery as to why Rachel is whining becomes explicit when, in Act 3, Rachel suddenly begins to cry again after having spoken in a clear manner. For at that point, Tamara asks directly, "Rachel, what, why are you crying?"

Three different explanations are immediately provided. Tamara understands that the immediate provocation to Rachel's renewed crying is a remark by Alan, a boy who sits at a desk directly in front of her. For present purposes, it will be useful to say that in effect, Alan asked whether Rachel would have a sandwich or a pack of vegetables for lunch. According to Tamara (who explained this to me months later when I reviewed this videotape), Alan knows that Rachel often cries when she discovers a package of raw vegetables in her lunchbox. Tamara understands that Alan was observing the ongoing drama, saw Rachel finally stop crying, and sought to renew her crying by artificially raising the powerful symbol of her lunch. Tamara understands that children are often fascinated with other children's crying and that in this and other instances Alan wished to see if he could push the button that would trip Rachel's crying.

Alan, however, provides a different explanation. When Rachel begins to cry, Tamara for the first time directly asks her why she is crying. Alan overhears the question and volunteers a version of separation anxiety: "Because [pause] she wants her mommy."

The third explanation is provided by Rachel. When Tamara first asks Rachel why she is crying, Rachel says, "Because ve-eg," but is interrupted by Alan's simultaneous "Because [pause] she wants her mommy." Tamara asks again,

> T: Listen to me. Why are *you* crying?
> R: Because I want a sandwich.
> T: And what do you have today?
> R: A sandwich.
> T: So, why are you crying?
> R: Because *san*wich . . .
> T: And don't you love your sandwiches?
> R: Yeah, I don't love ve-eg. [gaze up and ahead; her whine-crying continues throughout]

Note that Alan's explanation transcends the scene in that it refers to causes that are not under the school's control. Tamara's explanation points to a situational stimulant, Alan's conduct, that is potentially under the school's control. (Tamara now briefly tries to get Alan to acknowledge that he likes to see Rachel cry.) And Rachel's explanation, which acknowledges that today she has brought a preferred lunch, is on the surface self-contradictory.

The absurdity of the colloquy indicates that the child's whining can be addressed successfully only if it is addressed indirectly. This has been the teacher's understanding all along. What is packed for her lunch apparently is a powerful symbol for Rachel; Alan had made a reference to a vegetable package before this videotaped strip of interaction began. As an interactional matter, the teacher has been taking for granted that the symbolic power of vegetables and the meaning of Rachel's whining are hermeneutically elusive and should be addressed only indirectly. As discussed in the last chapter, crying is always an expression that something cannot be put into words. Adults as well as children often cannot explain, after the fact much less at the time, why they were crying. Here I submit that it is not the child's age but a contradiction built into the interaction that blocks the possibilities of logical explanation by the child.

Whining as a Dialectical Interaction

As was discussed in chapter 4, crying in general is a double and dialectical form of expression. Crying either seeks to go beyond loss by re-presenting it or it humbles the self as a means of recognizing something sacred. When crying takes the form of whining, the dialectic takes the form of self-contradiction. Whining is an effort to bind by rejecting.

On the one hand, whining is a richly negative form of expression. It is full of "n" sounds. As a nonverbal utterance that is made by a child who can talk clearly, it is socially defined as regressive. And it is accompanied by actions refusing invitations or orders from others.

On the other hand, whining is a sophisticated way to construct relations with and obtain power over others. We have seen how Rachel draws on various aesthetic dimensions of her whine to mesh her conduct with her teacher's conduct. The two do a little song and dance with each other, the teacher largely remaining silent to enhance joint attentions on her hand movements, the child expressing her distance from the interaction by whining even as she stays sensitively with her teacher by shaping her whine to the teacher's movements. Multiply sensual, the child's whine and the teacher's demonstrative statements and movements corporeally lace them together.

Seen from the teacher's angle, the whining child presents a strategic dilemma. If the adult "babies" the child by excusing her from the effort to engage independently in the scene, the adult not only loses her own freedom, she honors a claim of incompetence that is denied by the very machinations of the whining expression of the claim. On the other hand, if the adult ignores the whining, she must bear several risks: that other children will become upset; that the whine will eventually force the teacher to pull her attentions from other children who also require attention; and that outsiders (visitors, potential viewers of the videotape) will judge that the school is not addressing the child's needs.

Seen from the other side, the child's whining responds to a complementary double bind. There are many indications that Rachel is trying to get close attention from her teacher. Here are just three.

1. As previously noted in Act 1, Rachel patterns the start, arc, melody, and close of her whine-phrases to the teacher's movements when the teacher is addressing her directly, and Rachel roughens her whine and overlaps the teacher's gestures and speech when the teacher addresses other children.

2. In Act 2, Rachel is left alone and she whines, but she quickly completes the cube, occasioning a return of her teacher for a celebration and further instruction. Soon after her teacher's return, Rachel stops whining and starts talking and actively participating in the work of disassembling the puzzle.

3. In Act 3, as she talks and works with her teacher, Rachel appears to be shaping a little space for herself and her teacher with her gaze and head inclination. And after Alan provocatively utters "vegetable pack," Rachel continues to work and keeps her gaze on the blocks

even while her teacher addresses Alan. Rachel breaks down most emphatically only when her teacher breaks from her, looks at Alan, and accuses him of purposively provoking her crying.

In various ways, then, Rachel's conduct indicates that her whining varies inversely to her teacher's attentions to her. The double bind for the child comes from the fact that if she does cooperate competently with the teacher and stops whining, she will more quickly be left on her own. In effect, the closer the child comes to the teacher in interactional focus, the sooner she will be abandoned by the teacher. But if she does not attempt to gear into the conduct designed by the teacher, she also risks being left alone.

Whining is a negotiating strategy of pushing away to come close, used here by a child whose embrace of the teacher's version of her role will lead the teacher to "abandon" the child in the sense of leaving the child to work on her own. Whether Rachel "misses her mommy" or is doing separation anxiety as a manipulative power strategy, the child faces an immediate dilemma that is the obverse of the one faced by her teacher. The self-contradictory dynamics of the child's whining respond to this dilemma, and they account for the hermeneutic density of her crying behavior.

3. Rachel's Cough and the Effacement of the Body in Speech: A Deus ex Machina in the Metamorphosis from Crying to Talk

Most of the materials that we have been examining in this volume have described people becoming aware of the three-dimensionality of their conduct as their experience becomes emotional, for example as they get angry, become ashamed, or set off a riff of laughter. Rachel's episode of whining is especially useful for studying the transition *out* of emotional behavior, in this case a metamorphosis out of crying. For a few seconds in phase 3 of the episode, she stops whining and starts talking with her teacher. Here we can see how the vivid awareness of the three-dimensionality of self that emerges as the child cries is itself transformed as the crying ends. In crying, the child brings routinely tacit, background regions of her embodied self to personal and to social awareness. In ending crying, she displaces a personal corporeal self-awareness with a focus on a collaborative body that she and her teacher devise.

The Three-Dimensional Experience of Whining

It will be helpful at this point if the reader would try to whine. Try to imitate the way that Rachel whines in this episode before she speaks.

Keep your mouth closed, and create your take on any of the phrases that I have tried to transcribe earlier. What results is reminiscent of humming in that it creates a deep resonance within. Whining brings cavities of the self to one's awareness. One then senses the three-dimensional spaces that are always employed when one makes audible utterances that are commonly disattended in speech.

It is as if whining were a means of making perceptible the powerful corporeal disturbances, echoes, and vibrations within that usually go unnoticed when people are talking to each other. Whining is naturally irritating to others because it highlights the explosive inner workings of all audible utterances. Rough whine-phrases give further emphasis to the three-dimensionality of the uttering body, as compared to smooth, melodic phrases. When Rachel whines in fits and starts, when she punctuates whine-phrases with "sh" and "ch" sounds, and when she ends whine-phrases with creaking-door sounds, the walls of the cavity she is employing are additionally marked.

That the child is aware of the three-dimensionality of the embodied self in whining is indicated not only by technical variations among whine-phrases but also by the natural regularity with which whine-phrases are produced. Unlike sobbing, which disturbs inhaling, whining is produced largely on the exhale. When Rachel is whining, she fills almost every exhale with a whine. Each exhale appears to raise the question in a fresh manner, will the whining continue? At times, the child appears almost burdened with the obligation to fill each exhale with a whine. This occurs when Rachel takes deep, slow, silent in-breaths, and her whines emerge almost as audible sighs.

Talking affects the length of phases of the respiratory cycle. When speaking, people do not simply lay words along preset lengths of uniform exhales, they truncate and extend their inhales and exhales to fit the requirements of what they want to say.[9] In speaking, respiration is literally subordinated to the production of coherent utterances. In Rachel's whining, this relationship is often reversed. Again and again, as the exhale phase of her respiration approaches, the child must make her exhale audible or be seen as no longer whining. The respiratory process precedes and structures the onset of her utterances, which in turn make perceptible the termination of the exhalation phase of the respiratory cycle.

In a sense, whining reverses the relation of the body and self in speech by putting the production of socially audible utterances in service of the body's autonomous life. Consider now what this means to the child as a matter of self-awareness. The child is reawakened to the social meaning of his or her body on each exhale. To whine or not to whine, that is for the child a naturally provided, endlessly renewed question of social being.

By whining, one marks his or her body as somehow outside the demands of the social situation. One resists in a simple fashion by projecting that one will not leave one's body in the background of collective awareness. Whining makes the crude statement, "I am here as an obdurate, sentient being, outside the reach of your demands." That is, in a way, what the body always insists. Our bodies transcend the demands of any given social situation that we may be in. Some part of the body that one uses for expression is always outside of the other's perception. Temporally, the body is the vehicle and the natural symbol that one has an identity that is not fully subject to any immediate demand that others may make, at least so long as the demands are short of fatal. Spatially, even as one manifests a thoroughgoing attentiveness and responsiveness to each situation that one enters, one's body in many respects stays constant as one moves here and there. The situational flexibility of the self is always countered by one's corporeal continuities. As one moves from social place to place, presenting different versions of self to sets of others who themselves remain isolated from each other, the continuity of one's identity is always available just behind focal awareness, in the form of the corporeal touchstones, resonances, and residues of behavior.

If this discussion seems abstract and philosophical, young children easily grasp and exploit its implications. Usually, whether we are engaged in speech or in silent activity, we live our respiration in a personally and socially unremarkable way. Routinely disattended, our breathing goes on in the background as we project aspects of ourselves for social attentions. The whining child simply notes and accepts his or her respiratory cycle's invitation to mark that he or she exists outside of the social demands of the scene. Obstinate to others, the whining child is snaillike to him- or herself. Breath-by-breath pulling out a resonant home around him- or herself, step-by-step persistently going nowhere in social interaction.

To use another idiom, we might say that by whining the child keeps aware of a habitus for the self that transcends socially situated demands. By whining, the child not only acts negatively, holding him- or herself off from whatever others may demand in the here and now, but also positively constructs a palpable, proprioceptive awareness that he or she always has a corporeal habitus to rely upon. The adult may focus on the negative in the whine, its indications of resistance and rejection; but for the child there is not only the protective security of a reverberant shell to retreat into, there is also the repeated discovery of a kind of an almost magical guarantee of a homelike ground for the self. Whining is, in its irritating aspect to adults, willful; just as, in its comforting aspect to the child, it accepts the reassuringly involuntary invitation that the respiratory cycle naturally provides.

That whining carries positive implications for the child is sometimes indicated by the experimental, even playful ways that whining children discover and work with the expressive instrumentalities of their bodies. The ease with which children sometimes whine on and on may be read by adults as a sign that the child is "manipulative." That view suggests that whining is other-directed and it neglects the internal fascinations of the practice. Consider the magic of discovering that the exhale phase of respiration eternally reappears without being called for. The need to exhale is like a gift from home, a seemingly endless reliving of the primordial gift of life from mother.[10] Whining is an audible act of acknowledgment, reception, and acceptance of this gift. It is also an appreciation of the power that inheres in the gift of respiration. When another turns to one for a response, one's next exhale becomes accountable because it conveys the potential to speak; whining, which is an audible not-speaking, then becomes the manifestation of an infinitely repeatable decision. At times Rachel's whine appears as a sigh, as a giving in to the burden of not letting a silent exhale indicate that she is moving more thoroughly into interaction.

Whining is a three-dimensional form of conduct in the sense that it brings into awareness a corporeal region that is typically left in the background in mundane, nonemotional behavior. This awareness is social as well as personal and internal to the child's experience. For the child and for others, whining expresses an orientation other than the one the child is called to in the immediate situation.

How the Teacher Maintains Secondary Orientations in the Tacit Background

Rachel's whining is distinctive, not because it is a secondary orientation in her interaction with her teacher but because of the way it *expresses* or *makes a social fact* of that secondary orientation. In all situations of face-to-face social interaction, the participants have secondary orientations. Part of the routine work that people do to sustain the socially situated character of interactions is to keep their transcendent interests in the tacit background, away from direct competition with a primary collective focus. Even as Rachel makes her body give audible testimony that she has some concern independent of the work she and her teacher attend to, her teacher herself invisibly stays in contact with

several other extrinsic matters. Put another way, just as Rachel emphatically indicates through her whine that she holds back from complete involvement with her teacher, so her teacher studiously minimizes indications of the numerous extrinsic concerns, people, and
situations that she is simultaneously occupied with.

What are Tamara's hidden, transcendent orientations as she interacts with Rachel? These may include such matters as:

- her anticipation of how this scene will reflect upon her to those who
  may subsequently view the videotape;
- her recollection of prior experiences with Rachel and Alan, and her
  appreciation of how the current scene fits into the careers of her relationships with them;
- her appreciation of the meaning of her interaction as a model for other
  children who may be observing and for other teachers who may take
  her conduct as instructive;
- the opportunity cost of not attending to her other work responsibilities;
- her sense of the kind of work day this is turning out to be.

Several of the teacher's tacit background concerns become evident
in the episode itself. Within Act 1, the teacher momentarily averts several times to other children. As she shifts her attention from Rachel
to these third parties, she reveals that she had been interacting with
them but in ways that were not visible either to Rachel or to viewers
of the videotape. An examination of one of these diversions, part of
which we have seen earlier, will demonstrate numerous ways in which
Tamara handles extrinsic concerns while defining her orientation to
Rachel as her primary involvement.

At 14 seconds into the episode, as the teacher is moving a block
into position and Rachel is whining homologously to the teacher's
movement, another child, Gina, calls the teacher by her name. Gina
repeats her call at 17 seconds and again at 23 seconds. On the transcription of this interaction at page 239 above, Gina's calls are at lines
15 and 25. Gina appears to respect the structure of the interaction
between the teacher and Rachel, issuing her call near the beginning
and then at the end of joint teacher movement/child whine-phrases.
The teacher responds to Gina at 31 seconds, turning to her and saying,
"Go get a paper so that we can trace the duck. Go get a white paper.
Okay?" a statement that runs until 37s (figure 5.5).

1. Note that the teacher waits about eight seconds before responding. During this period, there was no visible or audible indication that
the teacher had heard the call and would respond. This delay is the

Figure 5.5 Managing two engagements at once

first aspect of her behavior that shows how she keeps her body from representing a secondary concern, that of responding to Gina, from becoming apparent in her interaction with Rachel. She restrains herself from giving any noticeable sign of her background orientation to Gina until she is ready to address Gina directly.

2. Note that the teacher's talk emerges as an imperative. Tamara does not speak harshly but she uses a conclusive form: "Go get a paper so that we can trace the duck." The teacher does not ask Gina to specify what she wants. That would invite a more open-ended side interaction and give Rachel more reason for sensing that she had been abandoned. Instead, the teacher, in her response, takes for granted what it is that Gina wants by intuiting the child's question from the child's calling of her name, her interactions with the child prior to this episode of interaction with Rachel, and the child's posture before her. As she speaks, the teacher makes her talk a response to a question that was never audibly put, and *the form of her utterance as a command indicates that she is concluding her interaction with the intervening child even as she is beginning it.* Tamara *makes her turn to Gina into the start of a concluding phase* of speech.

3. Another notable feature of Tamara's turn of attention to Gina is that *she never stops her step-by-step demonstration of the puzzle's structure to Rachel.* Even as Tamara orients directly to this intervening child, she does so with a dexterity that manifests her continued foreground attentions to Rachel. The first call from Gina, at 17 seconds,

came when the teacher was illustrating the assembly of the blocks. Before responding to Gina in any recognizable way, she finishes demonstrating the assembly of all the blocks into a complete cube, and then begins disassembling the cube. Tamara has removed three blocks before she turns to Gina, and *her turn toward Gina occurs as she is in the process of removing the fourth block.* Then, as she speaks to Gina, she disassembles two more blocks. Thus, *even as she separates from Rachel to speak with Gina, Tamara continues her relationship with Rachel in a visible, practical manner.* The teacher's dual attentions are visibly linked through simultaneous, divergent deployments of her body: she looks up to her left and speaks to Gina as she continues disassembling the cube with her right hand. Rachel's gaze remains down on the table. This complex maneuver enables the teacher to be at the foreground of two social interactions at once. She remains at the foreground of her interaction with Rachel with her right hand, while from Rachel's perspective she orients to Gina as a background matter. Meanwhile, the teacher talks and looks directly at Gina while, from Gina's perspective, she maintains a background orientation to Rachel.

4. Thus when the teacher makes manifest an additional orientation, she does so in a manner that enables Rachel to consider it a secondary, background orientation.[11] A fourth feature of the teacher's conduct also helps keep her orientation to Gina, from Rachel's perspective, in a secondary, background status. Two "Okays" are used to bridge the teacher's orientations to each child. Tamara says to Gina: "Go get a paper so that we can trace the duck. Go get a white paper. Okay?" Then, as Tamara returns her gaze to Rachel, she says "Okay. Can you do this for me?" The "Okay?" that Tamara used to end her interaction with Gina was taken by Gina as a basis for ending their interaction by walking off to get the white paper. The "Okay" that the teacher uses as she returns to Rachel makes for a smooth segue. Even as the teacher indicates, with her "Okay" to Rachel, that she had been distracted and needs to rebegin the interaction with her, she indicates that in orienting to Gina she had maintained a continuous commitment to Rachel. The "Okay?" that she pushes off from to leave Gina becomes reiterated as the "Okay" that calls her back to a seemingly sole focus on Rachel. *Retrospectively, her diversion to Gina is made part of a continuously curving coming back to Rachel.*

The teacher is doing a great deal of complex work to avoid using her body in a way that indicates that she has a second, transcendent concern that competes with and potentially will overwhelm her involvement with Rachel. *The child is doing precisely the opposite with her whine.* The child maintains a systematically recurring, respiration linked, audible stream that indicates her ever-present vulnerability to slip out of involvement with the teacher into the pull of some alternative, more powerful involvement.

5. Finally, and perhaps both most significantly as well as most subtly, the teacher constantly and quickly effaces her bodily expressions in a way that the child manifestly does not. Young children often use their bodies in manners that are disjunctive relative to their speech or to their engagement in other interactionally shaped lines of action. For example, while talking to an adult, a three-year-old child may move his or her arms, legs, head angle, etc., without a recognizably coherent relationship to what he or she is saying or otherwise doing. Rachel's whining often displays this disjunctive relationship to her other, simultaneously ongoing lines of action. In Act 2, she produces a stream of rough, varying whine-phrases, even as she systematically assembles the blocks into a cube, without any apparent relationship between the form or emission of her whine-phrases and the steps of puzzle work that she is executing. Rachel's whine is manifest as a secondary involvement in something other than her solo involvement in the work *because it is not expressed as a resource for or a commentary on* discrete steps in her work.

The teacher, in contrast, virtually always *follows through* on her body movements so that they *become manifest* as resources for the interactional expression of a continuous intention. As Gina is calling her, the teacher does not shoot glances at Gina, shake her head, wave her arm, or in any other way indicate some involvement other than her engagement with Rachel. Repeatedly when the teacher moves her right hand off of a stationary position, she follows through by lifting and putting a block in place. The movement of her hand from a stationary position becomes retrospectively understandable as an "initial" phase in a step of puzzle work. The teacher effaces her body, putting her body movements in the background of attentions, by *following through on manifest movements of her body to make them emergently visible as parts of a project of demonstrating puzzle work.* Motions done in a halting or nervous fashion would, in contrast, remain on the foreground of collective attentions as indicators of some secondary involvement.

Adults routinely and endlessly present and then erase the presentations of their bodies in social interaction by making their movements understandable as resources for a recognizable focal social project that is emerging. Each of the parties to social interaction dissolves or looks through the bodily manifestations of the other as he or she follows the emergent materialization of the other's project or social intention. In this scene, the teacher is faced from moment to moment with demands for attention from multiple children. The side interaction[12] with Gina shows how, in order not to become distracted and in order to remain at the foreground of interaction with children in this setting, Tamara at times delays manifesting her attentions to children until she is prepared to shift in a way that will be retrospectively meaningful as the beginning of a coherent course of action whose end is visible at its start.[13]

In sum, the emotionality of the child's crying behavior appears not simply as a psychological matter but as an observable and distinctive three-dimensionality in her conduct. Everyone is, of course, always acting three-dimensionally, through a body that is not flat but has depth, that has both front and back regions. All recognized expressions are generated by unattended, tacit corporeal movements that produce what is witnessed. Part of what competent social actors are doing virtually constantly in interaction is flattening out the appearance of themselves by curtailing the recognized presentation of background regions of their behavior. As the teacher's behavior here indicates, prodigious and finely detailed work may be required to keep one's transcendent involvements in an invisible, tacit or secondary status, and to sustain the appearance of one's attentions as primarily loyal to matters at the foreground of the interaction. The whining child, in contrast, turns to her respiration for a naturally available resource to express that she is not disposed to perform a similar self-effacing operation in deference to the demands for involvement in face-to-face interaction.

Rachel's Cough as a Deus ex Machina

[E]ven questions about gods saving us can be brought down to earth and must finally be settled . . . by looking to the extraordinarily subtle and varied way our everyday practices actually work to give us an understanding of what it means for us and everything else to be.
—Hubert Dreyfus and Harrison Hall, *Heidegger: A Critical Reader*

Shortly after Tamara returns to her side and celebrates her assembly of the blocks, Rachel stops whining. Something unexpected happens that puts the child's audible body in the background of the interaction. Just before she stops whining and starts speaking and working with her teacher without crying, the child coughs. I will argue that this cough was a critical final condition for the ending of Rachel's whining. The explanation of why a given individual action occurs is a different challenge than we faced in chapters 1, 2, and 3, where we sought to explain conduct in data sets describing positive and negative instances of a phenomenon in the lives of many different people. But the logic of proof is essentially the same matter of making explicit and ruling out rival hypotheses. When one has only an individual case, one must look especially closely at variations in it in order to find evidence for showing precisely how the profferred explanation works and for ruling out rival hypotheses. The issue is never a mystical matter of reading the mind of the subject, nor simply a matter of providing a plausible account.

How could Rachel's cough function as the final, determining condition that ends her crying? We have seen that her whining was a way of expressing her willful alienation from the interaction by emphasizing the three-dimensionality of her body. Coughing is a manifest taking of the body by forces beyond one's control. Such moments are common in interaction. Scratchings of places that itch, readjustments of legs to make oneself more comfortable, nose blowings, etc., are routinely seen but unnoticed in the sense that they are treated by participants as bodily manifestations that are to be left in the unproblematic background of interactions.[14] Although they are in a way as manifest as is any other aspect of a person's presence, they are typically left in the tacit background of mutual awareness on the enacted assumption that they are unwilled, unmotivated, or not purposively arranged to affect the other's behavior.

By coughing just before she stops crying and starts speaking, Rachel in effect tucks her respiratory tract into the tacit background of the interaction. Coughing implies that one has been taken by forces that do not manifest one's intentions to act or not to act with another. Thus in her coughing, Rachel neatly puts into the background of the scene just that part of her corporeal processes that she had been using to manifest her resistance to involvement in interaction with her teacher.

One rival explanation for the end of Rachel's crying is that, having successfully completed the puzzle, when her teacher returns and enthusiastically celebrates the accomplishment, the child no longer needs to whine because she now feels positive support and has the adult's symbolic embrace. But the facts of the episode do not fit this explanation. At the start of Act 3, Rachel continues to whine, passing over several

Figure 5.6 "This is beautiful, Rachel."

opportunities to stop as her teacher congratulates her and guides her
into cooperative work (figure 5.6).

```
 1      1. Rachel whines as her teacher expresses strong positive emotional
 2  support:
 3  R:  hnnnɴxxnɴxxhnnnnhnnnɴ [tapering off]
 4  T:  This is beautiful, Rachel.
 5
 6      2. Rachel utters a muffled refusal and whines after her teacher
 7  quickly puts another task before her:
 8      [teacher   is    disassembling cube]
 9       ↓    ↓    ↓    ↓    ↓    ↓    ↓
10  T:  Now, let's try to put it back, in the box.
11
12  R:  hh+nn−n can't
13      [R gazes forward; hands at sides of face, like blinders]
14      [whine is very low in volume; mouth open, creaking door sound]
15
16      3. And Rachel continues to whine as her teacher expressly invites
17  her manifest participation in the work.
18
19  T:           How do you think that it goes?
20  R:  hnmmnnnnnnknnnnnknnhnniinninn+n+n~n~n~n
21           ↑
22      [R's gaze shifts from straight ahead, turning down and right,
23      toward the storage box]
```

Figure 5.7 Coughing

It is at this point that Rachel coughs (figure 5.7). In the following, note that Rachel coughs before she ever speaks a whole turn clearly and while she is for the first time in the episode responding cooperatively to Tamara's invitation to collaborate on the puzzle work. Note also that even as she coughs and participates, the teacher encourages her verbally and assists her in placing a block in the storage box.

```
      [R's gaze continually follows her movement of a large block]
      [R moves her hand to a large block]
        ↓  ↓   [R lifts the block,]  [R moves the block over box]
        ↓ ↓        ↓↓            ↓
        ↓ ↓        ↓↓            ↓
  R:  cgh.cgh[.h.] cgh.cgh [.h.h]              cghgh.cgh
  T:            Yeeee-es              Here.
        ↑   ↑   ↑                   ↑
      [holding gaze to R's hand]    [as R's hand reaches space
                                     over box, T takes block and
                                     completes placement in box]
```

Now Tamara quickly asks another question (figure 5.8). Rachel again moves in response but this time she also speaks a response. Her whining disappeared in the coughing sequence. Now, for the first time in the episode, she clearly speaks, and she speaks in turn, after rather than simultaneous with her teacher's question.

Figure 5.8 Rachel: "This one?"

[Both hold their gaze on blocks and on R's hands on blocks]
T: Now, [pause] **which goes next, Rachel?**

R: [moves hand among blocks, choosing a small block]   **This one?**

Rachel's speech appears without any residue of whining or crying,
with bell-like clarity, on a tentative, even tender intonation.

Note that the coughing did not split her embodiment of conduct
into two streams. Two things had been going on in the child's behavior
for much of the episode. In Act 1, she produced crying sounds as she
mobilized her gaze to follow her teacher's demonstrative movements.
In Act 2, she cried as she assembled the puzzle. When she coughed,
Rachel continued doing two things at once; she moved a block as she
coughed. But now her audible line of action was no longer socially
noticeable. It is audibly there on the sound track of the videotape, but
as a cough the sound is not heard as a meaningful expression of her
intentions, concerns, or identity.

Was the coughing "motivated" or was its occurrence, coming just
before whining metamorphosed into speech, just a matter of coincidental timing?[15] We do not have physical evidence to rule out the possibility that some foreign substance irritated her throat. But we may note
that the timing of coughing in interaction is not generally random.
Even if a physical irritant intervened, the forces that provoke coughs
are not so intolerant as to deprive the subject of all control over the
moment in which a cough will emerge. Coughing is often a kind of

scratching of an itch in the respiratory tract. We do not have to challenge the independent existence of itches (that they come to a person) to appreciate that the itch does not dictate when it will be scratched. Some people will hold off scratching in a private proof of strong will; others will indulge in hedonistic scratching long after the itch has lost its peak level of provocation. Coughing similarly is flexibly timed in interaction. It does not occur in relationship to speaking with the same surprising randomness as does, for example, sneezing. In this instance, in any case, we are not faced with a person whose coughing shows up here and there, randomly in the episode. This spate of coughing is unique in the episode.[16] The "coincidence" explanation carries the burden not only of explaining why Rachel coughed then but also why she did not cough before or after this moment. Given the narrative course of this whining, it is less strained to consider the coughing as an especially attractive clearing of the throat in anticipation of speech.

Where did the itch that provoked the cough come from, if not from a physical or foreign irritant? Consider the intimate way that the child had been engaged in playing with the relationship between her subjectivity and her objective body. She had regularized her whining by accepting the objective, intimately sensed, autonomously reappearing invitation in her respiratory cycle to mark her exhales with expressions of willful negation. And she also at times become overwhelmed with crying in the sense of producing streams of tears through a compressed cry face.

The practice of whining sustains an unusual self-consciousness toward the respiratory tract. Crying in long audible phrases with her mouth closed, sometimes breaking up her whines in staccatos (or creaking-door) phrases, the child was using her capacity for audible expression in an especially self-provocative manner. Coughing often responds to a tickle in the throat, and tickling is itself a playing with the tenuous division between the inside and the outside of the experienced body. It was a very short step for the child to tickle herself into coughing.

And if the child had anticipated soon beginning speaking, that would cast the advance shadow of another form of employment onto her vocal tract. Anticipations of speaking often bring a tickling self-consciousness to the vocal tract. This occurs in a commonplace way when throat clearings arise in the foreshadowing of speech. Rachel has vivid evidence, both tactile and proprioceptive, that she is moving to an unprecedented (in this episode) proximity to speech. She coughs at the same time that, for the first time in the episode, she moves a block in response to her teacher's request. She is crossing a threshold of involvement in interaction just as she coughs. As she coughs she has an immediate, "hands on" basis to anticipate taking the next step of involvement in interaction, that of speaking.

Whether or not we find Rachel's coughing to have been motivated, it is another matter to note that, having coughed, the child had altered her relationship to her body and the way she presented her embodied identity to her teacher. Whether the cough was a private, self-designed gift, or whether it was a gift from the gods in the sense of an intervention occurring at a remarkably convenient place in the episode, in either case Rachel came out of the cough with her body in a tacit background status that would facilitate a full engagement in talk and in cooperative work with her teacher.

4. Effacing the Personal Body in Collective Action

Perhaps the most important lesson in this episode is how, in her transition from markedly emotional to relatively nonemotional interaction, the child's body becomes socially invisible. When Rachel stops crying, she ceases to represent her respiration. It becomes covered, obscured by talk. Her talking diverts attention from the process that produces it. She no longer turns back on her body to dramatize that she is holding back from involvement in interaction with her teacher. From an outsider's perspective, her behavior is no less three-dimensional than it was when she was whining, but its three-dimensionality is much harder for the participants to see. The body that she works her conduct off of is especially well-obscured, because it is a collective body that she produces with her teacher.

There are several ways to describe what happens to the social appearance of Rachel's body when she stops whining. We could say that her body becomes effaced, somewhat rubbed out or erased from awareness, blurred, disguised, displaced, or moved into the background of mutual awareness. We will need to have a clear picture of the body of collective action that the child and the teacher produce in order to show the various senses in which their individual bodies become invisible.

As Rachel coughs and before she starts whining again, she and Tamara create five paired units of mutually responsive action. The five units of action are defined by the responsive relationship between Rachel's handling of blocks and by guiding gestures and comments by her teacher. In the first unit, Rachel whines simultaneous with Tamara's question, and then, after a tiny pause, responds with cooperative action and her riff of coughing.[17] Over the next four units, Rachel listens to Tamara without simultaneously whining and, after a pause, moves

Figure 5.9 R: "This [one] goes like that?" T: "Okay, keep on trying."

a block or speaks. The easiest way to read the following transcript is first to read the material in bold, and later to read the descriptions of gestures, gaze, and manual manipulation of the puzzle pieces. As an aid for working through the annotations, read the narrative description in note 18 on pages 371–72 (see figure 5.9).

```
 1                        [1st Paired Unit]
 2          [T's hands and gaze are at the open storage box]
 3           ↓        ↓        ↓        ↓
 4   T:       How do you think that it goes?
 5   R:  hnmmnnnnnnknnnnnknnhnniinninn+n+n~n~n~n
 6                ↑
 7          [R's gaze shifts from straight ahead, to down and right, at the
 8          storage box]
 9
10              [R's gaze follows her movement of a large block]
11         [R moves her hand to a large block]
12          ↓ ↓     [R lifts the block,]     [R moves block over box]
13          ↓ ↓       ↓ ↓                      ↓
14          ↓ ↓       ↓ ↓                      ↓
15   R:   cgh.cgh[.h.] cgh.cgh [.h.h]              cghgh.cgh
16   T:              Yeeee-es              Here.
17           ↑    ↑    ↑                     ↑
18         [holding gaze to R's hand]    [as R's hand reaches space
19                                        over box, T takes the block,
20                                        turns it, and puts it in box]
```

```
21
22                              [2d Paired Unit]
23      [Both hold their gaze on blocks and on R's hands on blocks]
24   T:  Now, [pause] which goes next, Rachel?
25
26   R:  [moves hand among blocks, choosing a small block]     This one?
27
28                              [3d Paired Unit]
29           [T moves her hand to point to a large block]
30       ↓      [said enthusiastically]    ↓                ↓
31       ↓     ↓                           ↓                ↓
32   T:  How abowwwwwwwwwwwgggt
33
34   R:  [moves hand to big block T has designated and picks it up]
35       ↑         ↑              ↑            ↑    ↑
36   T:  Now we're going from the biggest to the smallest.
37   [T's statement runs its course in parallel to R's movement in selecting,
38   lifting, carrying, and placing the block in the box. Both gaze at the blocks
39   that R lifts and places.]
40
41                              [4th Paired Unit]
42   T:  Now which would be the next?
43
44   R:  [picks up a small block and places it in the box]
45   R:  This [one] goes like that?
46
47                              [5th Paired Unit]
48   T:  Okay, keep on trying.     What else?
49       [T does not correct R]
50
51   R:  This one? [picking up another small block]
```

At this point, Alan's comment provokes a renewal of Rachel's
whining.[18]

Talk and Gaze

One way that Rachel's body becomes invisible as talk and cooperative work begin is by a joint shift of gaze away from the body of
either participant and to the work in progress. In the five units of
paired actions, Rachel's audible utterances lose their earlier, whining presentation of a competing focus for joint attentions. Now when
the child is heard she will be heard just as her teacher is heard, as
saying something that refers to a movement in the puzzle work out
in front of the two. For the first time in the episode, the child makes
herself audibly present in a way that invites her correspondent to *hear*

through her utterances to something that the child regards *away from her body.*

Now that Rachel is talking as she works with the puzzle pieces, Tamara can clearly see, out in the world, what it is that Rachel refers to. Both use forms of language that promote sustained attention out to the puzzle work. Each of the child's three statements ("This one?" twice and "This [one] goes like that?") requires that the teacher look away from the child toward the puzzle blocks to grasp the child's meaning. Likewise, everything that the teacher says ("How abowwwwwwwwwwwwgggt," "Now, which goes next?" and even "Now we're going from the biggest to the smallest") encourages Rachel to maintain her gaze on the puzzle work on the table.

The teacher also promotes attentions out to the work and away from corporeal self-reflection by repeatedly glossing over the child's erroneous choices of blocks to move, just as she ignored Rachel's muffled "can't" a moment earlier (see the transcription on page 258). After first choosing the largest block to put in the storage box, Rachel has chosen one of the smallest blocks as the next to go in. Rather than define that as an error, a move that might put attentions back onto the child, the teacher emphatically and positively invites attention to another block with her "How abowwwwwwwwwwwwgggt." Tamara makes a broad gesture to the block with her hand, stretching out her utterance in an enthusiastic manner. (Tamara also glosses over Rachel's error in line 45 when she says, "Okay, keep on trying.") One can easily imagine any number of alternative responses to the child's error that would promote self-consciousness and shame: "Why did you pick that one?" "What is the pattern we are following?" "No, try again."

Lending and Borrowing Bodies

Not only are both using language that puts the collective focus out in front of their bodies, most of what they say *requires* the other to look to the work materials in order to complete the speaker's meaning. Tamara, with her "How abowwwwwwwwwwwwgggt," leaves her question/reference for the child to finish. Tamara does not finish the question with "this one" nor does she invite the child to speak an answer. Instead, by pointing to a particular block, the teacher invites Rachel to complete her thought with her own body, by grasping the designated block. In effect, the teacher invites the child to lend her body to manifest and perfect the teacher's thought.

The pattern of body lending is a second significant way that individual bodies become invisible as the interaction moves out of emotional

Figure 5.10 Teacher: "Here" (joint movement of block)

behavior into talk and practically collaborative work. Body lending is
a reciprocal pattern in the five units of nonwhining interaction. Body
lending is quickly and multiply introduced by the teacher at the key
transition phase out of crying, during the cough sequence. When Rachel moves a block in response to Tamara's urgings for the first time
in the episode, the teacher supports her movement of the block into
the storage box in at least three ways. The teacher says "Yeeee-es" as
the child lifts the block, the stretching of her voice in effect joining in
and supporting the carrying effort. The teacher says "Here" as Rachel's hand reaches the space over the box. And, as she says "Here,"
the teacher takes the block, turns it vertical, and places it in the storage
box (figure 5.10).

Colloquially, we might simply say that the teacher gives the child
a hand. As the teacher joins the child's action, the block work becomes
a collective act. The critical point is that collective action takes place
through a collective body. Just as the child in effect steps out onto the
foreground of the stage of action as a principal player in the task at
hand, the teacher subtly blurs the lines of contribution. As the attentions of the child and the teacher remain riveted on the progress of
the block work, it becomes unclear whose understanding that work is
describing. Is the child responding to a cue from the teacher that indicated which block she should lift?; or was the child's choice of the
largest block a manifestation of her own understanding of the puzzle's
logic? Did the child intend to place the block in the position to which

the teacher guides it in the storage box? Is the teacher aiding the child's intention or imposing her own?

The metamorphosis out of emotional conduct is not simply a matter of the way Rachel uses her body to shape her conduct, it is a transition from *her use of her personal body* to *her use of a collective body* that she constructs with her teacher. Of course, the two bodies, seen as entities at rest, are wholly separate and equally prominent on the scene. But in the five transcribed units of mutually responsive interaction, individual responsibility for the puzzle work has become blurred in a new way in the episode. Recall that in Act 1, the teacher assembled and disassembled the puzzle by herself, and Rachel watched as a passive observer. In Act 2, Rachel assembled the puzzle alone. During both Acts 1 and 2, Rachel's whining manifested a second prominent stream of meaning that competed with attention to the puzzle work. Now, as the enactment of the storage work becomes a collaborative act, Rachel lends her body to the manifestation of her teacher's intention even as the teacher lends her body to the perfection/editorial alteration of the child's intentions.

There is a double sense in which these five units of relatively non-emotional interaction are produced through a process of body lending. In one sense, the teacher lends her body to demonstrate the puzzle's logic in order to induce the child reciprocally to lend her body to manifest the teacher's intentions and the puzzle's logic. In another sense, the teacher is lending her body to an interaction ritual in which she gives a responsive attention that satisfies the child's demands. Because the interaction is a negotiation over these two versions of the scene, it is especially ambiguous whose identity we are witnessing when we see or hear one of the two in action. Are we seeing and hearing the child imitating the adult? Or are we seeing and hearing the adult playing out an interactional role designed by the child? For purposes of transcription, we can easily attribute words and movements to one or the other of the two. But if we seek to attribute responsibility, to fix causal direction, or to clarify whose mind, intentions, motives, or identity is being manifested in what we see and hear, the picture becomes very much more blurred.

Transparent Speech: Talk's Call for Responsive Action Effaces the Speaker's Body

A third way that the child's body becomes invisible after her whining ends is that her talk becomes a transparent presentation of her body. Speakers routinely efface their bodies when their speech is interactionally significant. If I am speaking to you in a lecture hall, you may indulge yourself in fanciful considerations of my physique, my body motions, the idiosyncrasies of the designs that my gestures make as I speak, etc. But if we are talking with each other, you will be pressed to hear and see through my speech in order that you might respond to it. In face-to-face interaction, what one person says to another is almost constantly meaningful to the latter as a series of indications of when, how, and to what the latter should respond. As a result, the listening respondent in face-to-face talk is not free to focus on the speaker's body. The listening party is more or less constantly geared to the image of self that he or she anticipates creating for the other via various lines of potential response.

Perhaps the clearest way that each speaker in this episode rubs away awareness of her body as she speaks is by speaking questions that turn attention to the other. Their conversation of words and gestures has been long awaited, and when it finally comes it emerges as a kind of tennis game in which the contribution of each immediately deflects attention to the other. Each of the five units begins with a question (I am including "How abowwwwwwwwwwgggt" as a question), and each ends with a move in the puzzle work that responds to the question. In the ending of units 2, 4, and 5, Rachel poses a question that turns attention back to the teacher even as it addresses the child's own body motions ("This one?").

The collaborative body of action entails the constant production of what could be described as a transparency of individual bodies. In the five units of nonwhining interaction, the adult and the child are both constantly seeing/hearing *through* their perception of the other's actions. At lines 12–15, when Rachel first picks up a block to participate, the teacher does not sit back and observe the child's body or actions; she rushes in, making the beginning of the child's lifting motion a call for her action in following it through to a successful conclusion. At line 32, the teacher stretches her "How abowwwwwwwwwwwgggt" as she motions toward a large block, allowing Rachel's action in grasping the block to become a smooth continuation of the teacher's talk and gesture. Then at line 36, as Rachel is moving the designated block, the teacher articulates the logic that the child is manifesting: "Now we're going from the biggest to the smallest." The adult makes the child's action a provocation of the adult's response even though the child asked no question here, no pause occurred after the child's action ended and before the teacher's began, no explicit provocation was directed from the child to the adult. The teacher sees in the child's action the opportunity to respond with a teaching statement, one that, again, ambiguates who is doing the work ("we're going from . . .").

Transmogrification: The Decline of Emotion and the Rise of Spirited Interaction

A fourth way that the child's body becomes invisible as her whining ends can be appreciated only if we can sense the interpersonal implications of the spirit of what ensues. When Rachel is whining, it seems that something is bugging her. Some negative spirit is haunting her; something is possessing her body like an evil force, disabling her from joining the preschool society. All along the teacher has been trying in effect to exorcise this negative spirit. Early on in Act 1, the child's body began to move palpably away from subservience to the negative spirit of her crying. While Tamara does not directly challenge the spirit, for example by ordering the child to stop crying, she does not deny the reality of its presence, either. She has been constantly working around it, trying to lure the child to a bodily engagement with school work while leaving whatever is bothering her to its own fate. Now, when she returns in Act 3 to celebrate Rachel's accomplishment, she tries a strategy new to this episode. She in effect indicates that the child's spirit has jumped into her, the teacher's, body, where it can be seen as an eminently positive force.

The first thing that Tamara does when she sees that Rachel has completed the puzzle and returns the child's side is to announce, "This is be*au*tiful, Rachel." Note the juxtaposition of the inert child and the sailing enthusiasm of the adult. I want to suggest that the referent for this "this" is richly ambiguous. The phrase is said in a voice that is dramatically elated. The "this" cannot be the puzzle itself; that is an assemblage of blocks that look as static and commonplace as they always have. "This" refers to Rachel's accomplishment but also to the feeling that it has given the teacher. While the blocks are tangible and visibly present, the congratulatory phrase addresses something intangible and invisible, the child's process of assembling the blocks and what that means to the teacher. The elation in the phrase recognizes Rachel's transcendence of the negative forces behind her whining as she worked successfully to complete the puzzle, and it simultaneously manifests the spirit of Rachel's work moved into the teacher's body.

Several of the teacher's phrases have an enthusiastically animated, singsong, and elated character, not only : "This is be*au*tiful," but also "Yeeee-es," and "How abowwwwwwwwwwgggt." What such expressions suggest is that through interacting with the child, the teacher is picking up some kind of positive spirit that is behind and diffused through her own adult body, shaping her utterances in remarkably positive ways.

We could use other language to describe this process. We could say the teacher is trying to motivate the child. Or that she is trying to distract her from the concerns that have kept her whining. Certainly neither the child nor the teacher will describe what is going on as a metamorphosis of spirit as it moves from one body to another, or as a transmogrification. But such surreal or mystical language is natural to the experience of emotions. Laughter is "infectious." If someone "gives you the finger," you may well not register it in a flat display of "indicating their disapproval of me" but as a negative spirit that instantly pierces your body and messes up your feelings. When children delight adults, it is not simply because the adults have decided to dramatize the recommendations in a manual on how to socialize children. At least within families, fates are naturally intertwined.

The style and emotional quality of Tamara's encouragement of Rachel in Act 3 are reminiscent of a familiar form of mother-child interaction. If the child is bothered by separation anxiety, what she now receives is a mobilization of a motherlike role. Long before infants can recognize their own images in mirrors, mothers use forms similar to Tamara's here to encourage them to watch the positive power of their conduct as manifested in a sensually familiar, caring adult's body. We may describe such conduct as a kind of lightning hyperbole, a wildly exaggerated, hyperenthusiastic, instantly responsive taking up of a child's conduct long before the child can appreciate that she has done anything worth special notice. The description from inside the interaction, however, is likely to be less critical and questioning. Mothers' spirited responsive behaviors in face-to-face interaction provide children with a spectacle of transmogrification to observe: Look at what happens when the tentative actions hidden beyond the powers of the child's self-reflective ability become visible in the embodied actions of the big, confident adult body![19]

Tamara's spirited responses form a juxtaposition to the child's speech, which emerges with a quiet, tender character. Rachel's first spoken phrase, "This one?" is small and delicate. Tamara's "How abowwwwwwwwwwggggt" is big and strong. As Rachel tenders a movement in the puzzle work, Tamara greets the offer by transforming it into a more powerfully shaped and effective response.

In a sense, the teacher, by enthusiastically responding to the child's tender of a line of action, drains the negative spirit from the child and uses it to motivate her own response. The inverse relationship between negative and positive spirits in this interaction is not coincidental. The teacher's enthusiasm is, after all, directly related to the problem that the child's whining had represented for her. And the transformation of the child's spirit as it moves into the adult's body follows from something no less mystical, the teacher's ability to see and take over the child's mind. Once Rachel begins to participate in block work in Act 3, the teacher can grasp what the child is trying to do.

Through practices of body lending, through the transparency of self in the talk that ensues, through the shift of gaze out to the work on the table, and through the transformation of the child's negative spirit into the spectacle of the teacher's elated responsiveness, a collective project and a collaborative mind emerge as a graspable project in the world, and the child's personal body fades into the tacit background of the interaction. The episode started with the teacher embracing the child with a hug that went around the chest that was producing a whine. Now the teacher can see the child's mind as it acts in the world. It is striking that this seeming metaphysical absurdity, the visibility of mind, is so routinely achieved in mundane social interaction, and that its appearance depends on the production of invisibility for the tangible, holistic, and proprioceptive bodies working to constitute mind.[20]

5. Why Is Rachel Crying?

Why does Rachel whine? (figure 5.11). We might point to the fact that when this videotape was made, she had been in preschool for only a few weeks and, like many new children in preschool, her crying stopped completely as her tenure increased. Years later she "graduated" from the preschool with a reputation as an extraordinarily bright, strong-willed, and autonomous child.

We might also note that early in the preschool's year, many more children are crying than in springtime. Aging may play a role, and so may a cohort effect. Everyone gets more familiar with the school environment, which becomes a second home.[21] And as the incidence of crying in the group declines, each child's crying becomes more isolating as the year goes on.

We might also consider the impact of changes that might have occurred at home, such as the birth of a first sibling, parental separation, economic anxieties, etc.

Perhaps also the video camera recording operation was provocative. The camera operator, a familiar participant at the school, had been moving around the classrooms throughout the day, choosing scenes

Figure 5.11 "Rachel, why are you crying?"

to record seemingly at random. Rachel may have been stimulated to whine by his intervention into her world.

Then there is also the relationship between Alan and Rachel, and the symbolic meaning of what is packed for the child's lunch. Perhaps what I have referred to as "vegetable pack" has had some traumatic association. But Alan's apparent fascination with provoking Rachel's crying is reminiscent of teasing practices that have widespread cross-cultural appeal among young children.[22] Perhaps Rachel has no idiosyncratic symbolic sensitivity at all and is simply responding to the force of Alan's will.

If we look for the causes of Rachel's whining we might point to the mutually reinforcing dynamics of separation anxiety, idiosyncratic food symbolism, the influence of the collective ambience, peer pressure, the recording process, and so on. But without denying the possible value of any of these explanations, we are still faced with explaining the intrasituational variation of Rachel's crying. She cries a lot in this strip, but not constantly, and none of these background factors changes consistently with the many variations in her whining.

We may learn more about whining as a form of social experience and behavior by ignoring idiosyncratic individual factors. Setting aside psychological questions that require data from outside of this brief episode, we may still usefully ask, what are the attractions of whining? If we are not sure why it begins, we can seek its attractions by studying how it varies as it goes on, how it ends, and what then happens. In this narrow situational inquiry, we can see that what is at stake in the metamorphosis from whining to speech is a fundamental change in the embodied foundations of the self. The explanation of why Rachel whines is essentially because, if she starts speaking without whining, she will lose touch with her body. As put by Merleau-Ponty: "There can be speech (and in the end personality) only for an 'I' which contains the germ of depersonalization."[23]

Through whining, a child corporeally realizes his or her body as a situationally transcendent and thus secure home for the self. Adults implicitly grasp this logic of situational indifference or intransigence in the ways that they commonly respond. One common response is a hug that seeks to surround all of the child's experience. An opposite response, but one based on the same social-psychological understanding of whining, occurs when adults are tempted to shake or hit a whining child. Adults sometimes threaten to spank children whose crying they perceive as whining with the phrases: "You want something to cry about? I'll give you something to cry about." With a threatening sarcasm, the adult warns of a corporeal punishment that will create a situational reason for a form of crying that is irritating to the adult specifically because it demands attention to concerns that the adult would prefer to treat as extrasituational, secondary, and appropriately left in the tacit background of the current interaction.

The body is an endless emotional resource because it transcends all the situations a person moves through. Through her whine, Rachel brings her body out into the forefront of the scene to provide evidence that there is something that she wants honored independent of the self portrayed by her practical, school-defined actions. That desire is not just a manipulative expression presented for others, it is also kept sensually alive for herself. The evidence of bodily transcendence that her whine creates is both externally audible and unusually palpable internally. Her whine, in contrast to speech, is a closed-mouth procedure that, like a hum, creates an internal resonance. It produces a proprioceptive, even tangible definition of a cavern within, a habitus for the self that others hear but that also lives on independent of interaction with others.

CRYING IN THE WHIRLPOOL

A Murderer Breaks Down under Police Interrogation

In June 1991, a clerical error released James Martin from an Oklahoma jail. The charges against him, fraudulently obtaining hardware from a local merchant and associated parole violations, were relatively minor but his record was sufficient to have generated a hold that should have barred his release. In September, as local police were searching for him on a new charge of small theft and forgery, Martin left for California. For the trip, Martin took his wife's car, without her permission, and he stole a gun from the manager of a trailer park where he had briefly been employed as a mechanic. Arriving in Bakersfield, Martin looked up his relatives, several of whom had long records of criminal violence. He began a low-wage job repairing apartments with one of his brothers but quickly wore out his family's welcome.[1]

Martin then took public transportation to Ventura, where he tried small scams with local merchants before a well-outfitted recreational vehicle (RV) that was parked at a public beach near the pier caught his eye. On October 1, Martin commandeered the RV at gunpoint and killed its owner, a sixty-eight-year-old Canadian woman who had been traveling alone. Discarding her body off a secondary road in Santa Barbara County, Martin headed back to Bakersfield, stopping on the way to sell some of the RV's equipment to the family of an aunt and to seduce an underage cousin.

Martin's relatives in Bakersfield had a practice of listening to police radio broadcasts, and when Martin arrived he learned from them that a search was on for the RV he was driving. After returning to Ventura, Martin attempted to murder a homeless man in an unsuccessful attempt to steal his pickup truck. He then made his way to Las Vegas, where, in late November, after making use of homeless facilities for several days, he shot and killed a sixty-five-year-old blind man while burglarizing his residence.

In early December, while driving a car that he had fraudulently obtained from a used car lot, Martin was arrested at a checkpoint maintained by the U.S. Border Patrol between Alamogordo, New Mexico, and El Paso, Texas. As he was approaching the police stop, Martin tossed off the gun that he had used in the Ventura murder. The border police recovered it, and in his car they found a law enforcement badge, hollowed-out Teflon-coated bullets, and other men's identification materials. They soon made connections with California and Nevada police and tied Martin to both murders.

The interrogation examined below was conducted in an Otero County sheriff's facility while Martin was being held temporarily in New Mexico. His interrogators were Santa Barbara County sheriff's detectives familiar with the Ventura murder. They took Martin through a series of damaging admissions by inviting him to explain events and then challenging his version. Again and again, Martin abandoned a more self-protective version for an increasingly self-incriminating story. At two of these turning points, his voice wavered and his eyes filled sufficiently that he soon made use of tissues and cigarettes to restore his composure.

I will focus on the two moments in Martin's four-hour videotaped interrogation in which he can most clearly be seen to be crying. Even in these two moments, Martin's crying is subtle, never an isolated, distinct form of expression. It emerges as a subdued wavering in his speech and only in the thick of face-to-face interaction with his interrogators.

Here is the scene of the interrogation. Two detectives, Fred Ray (sometimes called "R" here) and Ed Skehan ("S"), are sitting across from Martin ("M") at either end of a table that runs about five feet in length. From Martin's perspective, Skehan is to the left, Ray to the right. The videotape constantly shows Martin's front, and from time to time Skehan comes into the frame in profile and Ray is visible in profile or from the rear.

I will analyze three contingencies of Martin's two episodes of crying. One of the preconditions of his cryings is his embodied representation of a crisis in his narration. When the police suddenly introduce new evidence, he realizes that the account he has been giving will not work. His crying is a re-presentation, in the form of a decomposing self, of the fall that he has just dramatically realized. Before and while he cries, he gestures in ways that conjure up vivid metaphors that describe him as experiencing a fall. But his crying is not just a cognitive realization of that misfortune, it is a transcending enactment, a way of starting a rescue operation on his damaged narrative.

In order to appreciate the narrative role played by his crying, we must examine how speech, gesture, and emotional comportment are interrelated in his conduct. Martin cries as he responds to a crisis in his story, but his crying is not the immediate and direct result of the crisis. Instead, Martin's *crying is the product of a spoken and gestural effort to alter the focus* of what he is revealing about himself in the interrogation. Distinctive forms of speech and gesture, each making its own narrative point, precede and shape the crying.

A second, temporally earlier precondition of Martin's crying is his loss of control over his body before he must confront evidence that undermines his story. His crying responds to *a crisis,* not just in the substance of his explanation but also *in the corporeal authentication of his narration.* The struggle between the suspect and the police operates simultaneously at two levels and in two scenes. At an explicit level, Martin and the police construct different histories of Martin's prior conduct in California. At a more tacit but still visible (on moment-to-moment videotape review) level, they struggle for control over Martin's speaking body in the New Mexican interrogation room.

I was first alerted to the two-channel struggle in interrogations when reviewing a police transcript of a kidnapping-rape-murder confession in which a young Pasadena man begins to cry and confess shortly after one of his interrogator's demands that the suspect "look me in the eye." Something similar happens in Martin's case. Throughout the interrogation, Martin had been giving positive and negative head movements that grounded his statements with gestures of verisimilitude, and it is this pattern of head gestures that the police undermine. Martin falls off of his prior narrative line only when the police first undermine his routine, tacit bodily practices for "giving off" his speech as an innocently motivated confession.

Martin is a career criminal who for all of his adult life has been in and out of institutions as a result of a series of frauds, most of them petty and nonviolent. Thus the struggle in the interrogation room is focused on the very way that Martin has lived from at least his adolescence to the time of this interrogation, when he is in his late thirties. Martin's type of criminality has been to deceive people in routine interactions, not to commit showy acts of violence in which he forces victims to show deference to his overwhelming power. Thus in effect the police are not only seeking damaging admissions, they are challenging Martin's general way of being.[2] If Martin cannot pull off his deceits casually, he cannot pull them off at all.

A third condition of Martin's crying is that it emerges only *within a distinctive sensual/aesthetic process.* The aesthetic properties of his crying are continuous with the sensual properties of his experience of fall. In their interactional significance, Martin's cryings are not so much concessions that continue his fall as they are processes of metamorphosis that seek to initiate a spiritual rebirth. In the two occasions of his crying that I will review, the police have revealed that they have evidence inconsistent in critical regards with his prior exculpating story. The bottom pulled out from under him, Martin begins to fall into a devastating whirlpool. By crying, he produces a kind of fog within which he scrambles to climb back onto solid self-defensive grounds. The foglike character of his crying, which warrantably ambiguates his speech and shields the intentionality of his gaze, is specifically useful in Martin's efforts at self-reconstruction.

1. Shifting the Show: Metaphoric Gesture, Impaired Speech, and the Re-presentation of a Fallen Self in Martin's Crying

In the Hot Seat

Martin first clearly cries when the police suddenly reveal that they have witnesses to his kidnapping of the RV driver. Early in the interrogation, Martin had taken the position that he stole the RV with no one in it. His long criminal record is made up of such crimes, and he relies on his record to indicate the improbability that he is a robber-murderer. The police allow him to solidify his story along these lines. Then they assert that two young boys saw him in a parking lot, pushing the RV's driver into the back of the vehicle and then driving it off.

A striking feature of Martin's first crying is that it emerges just after he enacts and also vocalizes the metaphor of "being in the hot seat." After the bombshell of the boy witnesses is dropped and the police

Figure 6.1 In the hot seat

wait for a response, Martin spends about a minute dodging the issue.
During this pause, the police suggest that perhaps the killing happened
accidentally. Skehan, softening the anticipated fall, offers: "There's a
big difference here between something happening intentional and
not." Martin is then asked squarely by the softer-spoken interrogator,
Officer Ray, "You did, you did take it [the RV] with the lady in it,
right?"

As Martin hears this question, he shifts his gaze to Ray and listens
with an open, noncommittal face. After Ray's question is out, he rocks
his torso in his chair toward the table and then back. In the process,
Martin *shifts his bottom in his chair;* his eyes briefly close and, rocking
forward and shifting his weight to his knees, he *raises his bottom
slightly from the chair, pulls the chair forward into the inner crevice
of his knee,* and says "Yeah" (figure 6.1). Treating his seat as somehow
no longer comfortable, Martin *does* the metaphor of "being in a hot
seat" as he positions himself to utter "Yeah," a single word with which
he makes a key admission that may effectively put him in the hot seat.
His immediately prior expressions of physical dis-ease anticipate a
one-syllable audible response that will fundamentally alter the rest of
his life.

```
1   S:  There's a big difference here between somethin' happening
2       intentional and not.
3   M:  [looking down, light affirmative headshaking, emitting a riff of soft,
4       sardonic laugh sounds]
5
6   R:  You did, you did take it with the lady in it, right?
7                           \
8   M:  [shifts gaze   directly to R]
9
10  M:  [lifting his bottom from the chair, his eyes briefly close and then he
11      looks down, below the gaze of R and S, as he rocks his torso toward
12      the table and back. At the peak of his forward rock, while his bottom
13      is lifted off of the chair, he shakes his head positively and softly says]
14      Yeah. [After rocking and sitting back down in the chair, and while
15      still shaking his head positively, he mouths "bu." Then, shaking his
16      head negatively, he utters a barely audible] but
17
18  R:  Okay, we knew that. Now, the gun, the gun, the gun that you used
19      to shoot her with is the same gun you stole in Oklahoma, isn't it?
```

A *verbalization* of the metaphor comes immediately after the next key admission. Without pausing to obtain reiteration that Martin had contact with the victim and without asking directly if he shot the woman, the police move directly to the murder weapon. Martin now learns that they have recovered a gun near the border patrol station. This revelation is explosive. One of the officers gesturally encourages a double (or triple) entendre by pointing a gunlike hand directly at Martin's forehead just as he tells him "We got the gun in there" (figure 6.2).

Martin has just learned that the police have two eyewitnesses. Suddenly he also knows that they found the gun that he tossed off as he approached the border control point. To Ray's question, "Same gun, isn't it?" Martin responds, "Yeah, basically, I guess." The police push for an unqualified admission, Skehan asking, "No, isn't it?" and Ray asking, "Same gun that you used to shoot her." Martin says "God," softly. His gaze still down, Martin then says, "Well, I know I'm getting, I'm getting the electric chair for this. You know." As he verbalizes this image, he wags his head "no" in a sighlike gesture of resignation.

After shifting in his seat and then verbalizing "I'm getting the electric chair," Martin displays the first suggestions of crying.

Skehan asks: "Let us, tell us in your own words. We're not trying to put words in your mouth." In Martin's next statements, his voice wavers as he produces evasive responses.

```
1   M:  I don't know. I'd been drinkin', and, um, [inaudible] know, crankin' it
2       up. I don't know exactly all what transpired in all this mess.
3   S:  Okay.
```

Figure 6.2 "We got the gun in there."

4 M: **It's been eatin' on me** [pause, hard swallow; speech impaired] **for—**
5 S: **I'll bet it has.**
6 M: **And, uh, the one point, border station I was gonna take the gun and stick**
7 **it in my mouth.**
8 ↑
9 [lifts gaze toward S but not fully up to S's gaze]

Note the theme of self-pity. Martin casts himself as a victim of alcohol, of "this mess," and of his own conscience. After being hit hard with the news of the evidence against him, he recovers the moral strength to begin lifting his gaze toward the police, albeit through imagery that first puts him in the electric chair and then frames a suicidal moment just before his capture.

Like all "loss" or "sad" cryings, Martin's crying will go beyond loss by re-presenting it. Martin is first shocked by the revelation that the police have eyewitnesses. He receives the news with a blank face and then with evasions. Searching for a new foundation for the self that he will project, *he enacts* something like "being in the hot seat," *then verbalizes* an image of himself in the electric chair, *then cries* as he tries to stir up sympathy by recounting how his life was filled with pathos. His crying, coming after his realization of loss (loss of a defensive line and of face), and coming after he has launched a line of self-pity, deconstructs and goes beyond the face that he had been presenting.

His crying is not a giving up or a giving in, but the third step in a quickly improvised strategy of self-preservation. Skehan treats Martin's crying as an admission of culpability, even though it is ambiguous in that regard. Martin's crying more clearly is a dramatization of a dissolving self enacted in the process of searching for a new overall understanding of the interrogation situation that he is in. His crying is of a piece with his nervously shifting in his seat and the capital punishment scene that he articulates.

Indeed it is only after he mobilizes his effort to find a new basis for himself, and after he depicts himself as the victim of the electric chair, that Martin's crying breaks out. And when it emerges, it is in and through speech with which he tries to construct a new self-serving self-portrait. Martin's crying does not emerge with the incriminating admission ("Yeah") that he took the RV with the lady in it, nor even when, a few moments later, he acknowledges ("Yeah, basically, I guess"), after the next stunning revelation, that the gun that the police have recovered is the same gun he used to shoot her. His crying emerges a bit later. *He is already on the road to reconstructing a new version of his story and of himself when he cries.*

Martin's sense that his story and self are in a quick process of dissolution temporally precedes and cognitively sets up the dramatization of self-dissolution in the behavior of his crying. Martin is in the truly rare position of realizing that he is caught in a whirlpool: the bottom has fallen out of his story; he is being sucked down. His crying is part of a desperate effort at self-rescue through grabbing onto whatever shreds of imagery he can catch as they may happen to float by.

Over the next minute, Martin introduces several new exculpatory elements, and as he does he produces elaborate if subtle signs of crying: his voice cracks, he struggles to grab breath, he shudders, his exhales become audibly nasal, he buries his head in a space that he creates with his arms between his torso and the table, his vowels shake noticeably.

Instead of describing his shooting of the victim, he indicates confusion and suggests that a third person was present, someone with whom he was in a big argument, someone who "took off with the van," making it necessary for him, Martin, to recapture it (and hence be seen by the boys as commandeering it).

1   M: [gaze down to table, in S's direction] **And I thought well, no, throw it**
2   **[the gun] away. 'Cause I don't know what transpired in, in, in the motor**
3   **home thing and, um, and another person in the motor home and, uh,**
4   **when it happened, and I don't know all what happened** [gaze up]

5   S: **Okay.**
6   M: **Hmmf.** [shudder, nasal exhale, soft]
7   R: **What happened then?**
8   M: [negative shaking of head] **I don't** [voice cracking, grabbing breath] **I**
9   **don't all know.** [voice cracking through last phrase] **Got a big-ass argu-**
10   **ment** [singsong] **and uh—**
11 R: **You and the lady?**
12 M: [negative shaking of head] **No, me and the other individual, the, tha**
13   **homeless guy.**
14 S: **Um-hmm.**
15 M: **Met with us,** [burying head a bit deeper in space defined by arms on
16   table] **and, uh, I don't know.** [air of resignation] **'Cause I remember some-**
17   **where around the shopping center,** [waver on "er" of "center"] **uh,** [pause;
18   next comes out stabilized, smoothly] **he took off with the van and I had**
19   **to run out there and catch it and everything.** [smooth segue into the following
20   request, during which he moves back from table and lifts his gaze
21   from edge to center of table] **Let me have another cigarette if I could.**
22   [pause] **God.** [soft; pause as adjusts handcuffs for mobility to take ciga-
23   rette] **I don't know all** [noticeable wavering in "all"] **of what happened.**

If we look patiently at the details of his conduct, the self-re-presen-
tational role of Martin's crying becomes clear. Martin first experiences
a fall and dramatizes his perception that he has been undermined with
an enactment of the hot-seat metaphor. Second, his talk shapes a new,
pitiful posture for himself. Third, crying emerges in the process of producing a new line of exculpatory talk. Retrospectively, Martin's crying
indicates a sense of lost power, but within the immediate interaction
and prospectively it is part of an effort to reestablish a basis for controlling his future. His crying, then, is not just cognitive or perceptual,
nor is it only a sign of being taken by the force of events. It functions
as an effort at narrative transcendence of his emergent dilemma.

Wiping the Slate Clean

A second episode even more dramatically shows the constructive narrative thrust of Martin's crying as it is linked to his self-pitying speech
and his gestural conjuring up of metaphor. At 1:26 P.M., the interrogation having continued virtually nonstop since 11 A.M., the police
substantially harden Martin's image by getting him to admit to a cold-
blooded attempt to kill a homeless man, Johnson, for his truck. Johnson was not in fact present when Martin kidnapped the woman, he
has by now conceded. Instead, after disposing of the woman's body,
Martin invited Johnson into the van in order to shoot him. The shot
missed and the homeless man ran off.

With this nailed down, at 1:27 P.M. the police give the focus of the
interrogation another dramatic turn. R asks, "Have you done anyone

else since then? Have you shot anyone else?" Martin now has the first indication that his murder of an elderly man in Las Vegas may be known by the police.³ There was no sign of emotional difficulty during the passages in which he admitted to the attempt on the life of the homeless man. This was, after all, just an attempted murder, a crime less serious than the one to which he had already confessed guilt. But the Las Vegas crime would make him a multiple murderer. Immediately Martin begins constructing a new theme of pathos that depicts him as a vulnerable being in the wild; he is scared, shivering, hopeless, an orphan cut off from his family. As he portrays himself as the victim of circumstances, his crying emerges.

```
 1  R:  [softly] Have you done anyone else since then? Have you shot anyone
 2      else?
 3  M:  Un-hnn. Nope. No no
 4  R:  I mean,—
 5  M:  I've just, I've just stayed hid out. I just stayed hid out and survived.
 6      Slept out in the cold and everything and, uh, it's, just a matter of
 7      time, but you know I couldn't call nobody [shoulder shrug, pause]
 8      'cause, you know [pause; shrugging segues to negative shaking of
 9      head, mouth opens and closes without speaking]
10      hell [pause],       you know I ain't
11                         ↑         ↑
12          [mumbled,    breaking voice]
13                  ↓    ↓    ↓    ↓
14      talked to non mah own people
15      ↑          ↑         ↖
16      ↑  [dropped syllable; choked down]
17      ↑
18      [gaze briefly up to R on right, then across chest down to left elbow
19      on table]
20
21      'cause they um [gaze front, down] they wouldn't understand. [gaze
22      up to S]. Nobody would. [gaze down from S to table in front,
23      negative shaking of head]
24
25      And I didn't know where to go, what to do [pause: precisely on
26      "do," M swings his gaze to his right, to the table, and he quickly and
27      in a small motion wipes the table edge with fingers of his left hand,
28      which is balled up to hold a tissue]
29
30      and, um, [lips open and close silently]
31          ↑
32          [negative shaking of head]
33
34  S:  Well, we let you talk with us 'cause we understand.
```

At lines 25–28, above, as Martin's crying reaches its most intense state in the interrogation, he silently produces a gestured metaphor. Martin wipes the table edge in a small motion as he declares his sorry state in being cut off from his family (figure 6.3); his family turned him in. The transcript portion reproduced below continues without a break from the portion above. It shows that Martin repeats the metaphor, this time in a more sweeping gesture (figure 6.4), at lines 7–11.

```
 1   [negative shaking of head]
 2        ↓  ↓
 3   M:  Nn uh uh. [lips silently opening and closing]
 4   S:          Maybe more so than the family can, huh?
 5   M:                  mmh mmm [soft, guttural; mouth "cry" compressed]
 6
 7   M:  Nna I ain't never gonna make more contact with my
 8        family. Hhehh [laugh changing to pained expression]
 9            ↑
10        [Within this sentence, M wipes the table at its near edge with his left
11        hand, in a long motion to his left. As his hand leaves table and he
12        turns his gaze to table center, he marks the ending with the laugh,
13        "Hhehh," which becomes a grimace.]
14
15   R:  Oh, sure you will. [casual, relaxed tone]
16
17   M:  Oh no. [thin, high, nasal; face in cry grimace, lower lip raised, upper
18        lip compressed downward, corners of mouth frozen] No. [pause] No.
19        [thin, high, nasal; pause] No.
20                        ↑
21   R:                  you know
22
23   M:  No, [mouth in cry grimace, upturned lower lip, jaw out and up.]
24        No I won't. [M looks up to R]
```

The precise meaning of the gesture is inherently ambiguous. It is tempting to translate it into a phrase like "living on the edge" or "wiping the slate clean," but the gesture is not implicated in any spoken expression. When, as in most of the interrogation, Martin talks smoothly, without signs of crying, words are enough, at least in the sense that, besides being accompanied by negative and positive head motions, they are not typically accompanied by such gestures.

Instead of presuming that language is most fundamental and reducing the gesture to words, we should appreciate that at least three interrelated corporeal processes are in motion. For one, Martin is

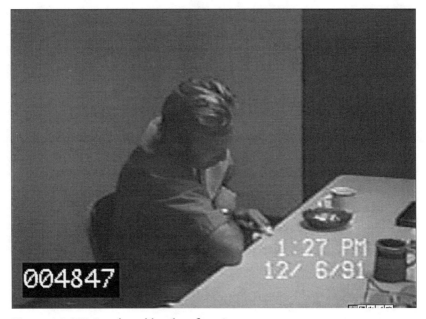

Figure 6.3 Wiping the table edge, first time

talking: his utterances, though challenged by emotion, are intelligible. Second, he is crying, albeit in a way that is perceptible to others (the police, the analyst of the videotape) only in and through his speech. And third, he produces two variations on a single kind of metaphoric gesture.

If, on the one hand, a translation of gesture into words is inherently risky, on the other hand the evidence points much more forcefully toward an attribution of meaning than to a characterization of these gestures as meaningless or meaningful in some way independent of the speech in progress. They are produced in a very precise and recurring relationship to a particular substantive line in intelligible talk. The two occur within a brief time span and in both instances Martin is talking about being alone in the world, cut off from his family. In the first instance he is depicting a family that would not understand his dilemma. In the second instance, he is depicting a family that has moved beyond his conceivable reach. The gesture indicates that there is something that Martin wishes to express for which his speech is inadequate, something that his speech is reaching for that is difficult to articulate.

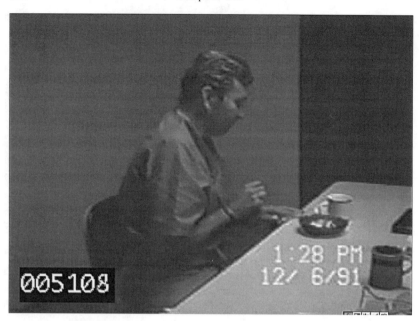

Figure 6.4 Wiping the table edge, second time. "I ain't never gonna make more contact with my family."

We have seen this thematically continuous relationship between gesture, language, and emotion before, in the shifting movements that occurred when Martin first realized that he might well be headed for a hot seat. The ambiguity of the gestured metaphors is part of Martin's tripartite corporeal effort to shift the collective focus to another story line, one in which he rather than his victim is the object of pity. As one part of the effort, the *metaphoric gestures* are flourishes that *set the stage* for the new narrative focus. Deployed either to cue or to summarize, they frame or bracket his speech and its related crying.

In a second part of Martin's narrative effort, his *language articulates* a narrow, specific, bleak *story line* about what the emerging, retrospective portrait of his life means for his future. And, in a third part of his struggle to alter what he is conveying, in the crying itself, Martin displaces the self that had been the object of police questioning. As he cries he moves out from being within and behind his speech, in the process *taking up the stance of a sympathetic observer of himself,* joining with the police-audience that he hopes to seat in a position of similar regard on his dismal fate.

To review: the first condition of Martin's crying is that it will emerge only after a narrative crisis and within an effort to rebuild his narrative project. Metaphoric gesture may come before or after crying begins, but impaired speech will be the context for crying. And overall, his crying emerges only when the stage is set for its role in re-presenting his fallen self. This professional suspect cries when he falls into narrative crisis and, through gesture, speech, and emotion, he struggles to shift the story line that is being dramatized.

2. Glossing Verisimilitude: Crying and the Interactional Struggle over the Embodiment of the Suspect's Speech

For James Martin, it made sense to participate in a police interrogation only if he was going to lie. On one level, his lies were about his responsibilities for murders. In reviewing his file, I came to the opinion that, on another level, he had long before become a creature of the criminal justice system and that the larger lie was that he wished to be free of its constraints. In any case, his working strategy in the interrogation was to pursue two tracks of sense making, one that he offered overtly to the police and another that he reserved for himself. And for their part, in order to set Martin up for conviction and execution, the police interrogators also operated on two interpretive tracks. They constantly understood Martin's utterances as they related more or less consistently to what he had said before; and, at another level, as statements that often did not fit with what they privately knew about the case.

The interpretive work is complicated on both sides of this interaction. In the first instance, the interactional power that the police have in interrogations comes from the asymmetry of this peculiar communicative relationship. The police gain power to force suspects to confess only because suspects are powerless to get their interrogators to tell all they know. The police and the suspect both pursue a double-tracked understanding of the proceedings even while they deny they are doing so, and each takes on dualistic interpretive work in the knowledge that the other is reading the proceedings on two levels. Martin's episodes of crying emerge specifically at those points at which the police reveal crucial evidence that they have had all along. At these moments the police demonstrate that they have been engaging in a pretense while they were eliciting what they knew were Martin's lies without reacting to them as such.

For Martin's work of sustaining his own double-tracked under-standing of the interrogation, such police revelations provoke a two-fold crisis. On the one hand, he has to reconstruct a self-protective version of events that now include facts that he had omitted or denied before. On the other hand, he is obliged to reconstruct a way of claim-ing authenticity for his new story in the wake of revelations that his prior story line had not been authentic. If the new story is delivered in much the same way as was the old, why should it be any more credible?

This second level of understanding, which is about the authentic-ity of the narrative being delivered, is engaged at a literally deeper, more fundamental level than is the interpretive interaction about narrative content. The police and Martin are engaged in a struggle over the embodiment of his speech. Martin underwrites his narrative with body glosses that attest to the truth of what he is saying. In the first section, we saw how, as a precondition of Martin's crying, the substantive text of his narration was undermined. Now we will see how the police, in an even earlier precondition to his crying, seize control of his embodiment of his narration. The loss of his control over the embodiment of his speech is a second condition of Martin's crying.

Bodily Glossing Verisimilitude

As Martin talks in the interrogation, he frequently moves his head affirmatively or negatively in patterns that comment on his own state-ments. Occasionally he will nod "yes" or "no" while the police are speaking, but usually he holds his head still when he listens. His positive and negative head motions are routinely associated only with his own speech. Such nods provide a gloss of verisimilitude for the substance of what he has to say. He typically gestures affir-matively and negatively in direct relationship to the thrust of his talk (figures 6.5 and 6.6). The basic pattern is that he begins gestur-ing agreement or dissent before and through his own speech, in ways compatible with the substance of what he says, and then fades or snaps to a still head position as one of the officers begins to speak. We can say confidently that Martin's head motions are habit-ually used to support his own speech rather than the speech of his inter-rogators.

Here is a representative passage from the interrogation. The police have just gotten Martin to acknowledge that he had planned to shoot the homeless man to get his truck. He is asked where he was headed and what he planned to do with the truck.

```
 1   M: [pause] I don't know. [very soft]
 2              ↑    ↑  ↑  ↑
 3              [negative shaking of head]
 4
 5   S: Were you gonna hang around Ventura any longer?
 6        ↑          ↑              ↑         ↑
 7   M:            [no head motion]
 8
 9   M: No. No.
10       ↑ ↑ ↑
11       [negative shaking of head]
12
13   S: Were you gonna leave him in the motor home and leave the
14      motor home there in the state park?
15       ↑      ↑          ↑        ↑
16   M: [no head motion]
17
18   M: Possibly, yeah.
19       ↑     ↑      ↑
20      [positive nodding, bowing; gaze is ahead, down to table]
21
22   R: Or would you take him out and dump him off some—
23        ↑                         ↑
24   M: [no head motion; gaze remains down, ahead, although R is to
25   right]
26   M: No. I wouldn't think so. I'd just've left him there down in
27      it.
28       ↑          ↑                        ↑
29      [negative shaking of head; minimized in the last phrase]
30
31   S: Yeahp.
32          ↑
33   M: [positive nodding]
```

It would imply too much self-conscious strategizing to suggest that Martin is deploying his head movements in this fashion in order to send discrete messages of authenticity to the police. His head motions are more accurately characterized as a familiar means of creating a sense of self from which speech can flow naturally. Instead of launching each phrase to stand on its own, he issues his statements from what he establishes as a base for the statement. Produced in this manner, *his statements, whether they are fabrications or are grounded in his personal history, emerge naturally,* from a preexisting home, *out of a background that indubitably, even palpably exists.*

I do not mean to imply that Martin moves his head in this fashion only or specifically when he lies, or that only Martin moves his head

Figure 6.5 "No. No." with negative (horizontal) head nodding

in this manner. The practice is common in the most innocent corners of everyday social life. If such movements imply self-doubt and an effort to transcend it, the doubt is existential rather than specific to the scrutiny of the criminal justice system. Indeed, the practice is commonly used by people when the recipient of their speech is not likely to be directly influenced by their head motions, for example when one is talking on the phone.[4] On the other hand, the recipient of speech, whether listening in face-to-face interaction or on the phone, makes distinctions between a correspondent's artificial and authentic utterances. Indirectly, head gestures, by corporeally realizing the direction of speech before or as it is issued, is a ubiquitous, interactionally useful means of providing an effective gloss of verisimilitude for speech. And whenever one is purporting to relate events that occurred in the past, head motions can create a real point of reference for the story, even if the only real historical resonance of the reference is in a past much more recent than the one claimed in the story being told.

If head motions are a widely used means of providing a gloss of verisimilitude for speech, this method of warranting talk is especially likely to be challenged in police interrogations. Underlying the struggle between Martin and his interrogators over the explicit text of his confession is a more subtle struggle over the control of Martin's body.

Figure 6.6 "Possibly, yeah."

Interrogators are oriented to the strategic control of many aspects of a suspect's sense of composure. The offering of cigarettes, breaks for lunch, opportunities to use the restroom; the stark and hard character of the interrogation room and its furniture; the implications for the regulation of the suspect's gaze of the positioning of the two officers vis-à-vis the suspect in the interrogation room . . .: these are textbook concerns of the police.[5] Such matters are understood to be useful in breaking down a suspect's story. More subtly, the control of the structure and dynamics of the corporeal interaction in the room also serves the interrogators' interests in developing their own energy and enhancing their sense of control, all to the end of creating a posture of irresistible power.[6] The regulation of the suspect's head movements in relationship to his speech is a natural part of the interrogator's working focus.

The suspect's positive and negative head motions enact an "other" who has already accepted the thrust of the speech to be uttered. For related reasons, the suspect's line of gaze is also critical. By avoiding direct contact with the police gaze, suspects avoid the perception of a contradictory, nonsupportive "other." On the other side of the table, it is common in interrogations for the police to demand that the suspect "look at me" or "look me in the eyes," and for turning points to occur at such moments. Such demands are based on an implicit appreciation that suspects have a powerful need to provide a corporeal grounding for their stories. The regulation of the interactional implications of Martin's body movements is a critical secondary drama underlying the primary record-making focus of the interrogation.

Turning points in this drama are significantly related to the natural histories of Martin's bouts of crying. Just preceding the two bouts of crying that we have reviewed, Martin's head gestures become confused and self-contradictory. In the first instance, both of the police interrogators demand and get control of Martin's head movements in various ways. Interrogator R turns the discussion to the lady in the van with a casually delivered request:

1 R: **Hey, uh, [pause] James, why don't cha**
2 M: [gaze up to R's eyes]
3 R: **tell us what happened with the old lady that had the motor home.**

Martin's shift of his gaze to the police when they speak is part of a pattern that runs through the interrogation. But now, when Martin moves his gaze away from eye contact to begin his talk, and when he uses head nods to gloss his speech, his interrogators interrupt him (figure 6.7; see line 9 of the first transcription on page 293).

Figure 6.7 "Let me interrupt you" pulls Martin's gaze up

1   M: [gaze down to table just before he begins talking] **That,** [slight pause
2   and slight horizontal-plane "no" head shake] **I don't know, they told**
3   **me, you know, I found out from my relatives thu-**
4   R: **James,** [sharp, direct]
5   M: [still shaking head "no"]
6
7   R: **wait, wait, wait. Let me,**
8
9   M: [stops horizontal head shake and gazes up to R]
10
11 R: **let me interrupt you for a second.**
12
13 M: **oh** [very soft; does a vertical 'yes' head
14   movement, but as a deferential bow, more downward with head and
15   eyes than upward]

Soon after Ray has interrupted Martin's talk and his head motion (at lines 7–11, above), Skehan will sharply grab control of Martin's head and gaze. Following the passage in the transcription above, Ray drops the bombshell of the witnesses to the kidnapping, and as Ray talks Martin's gaze is down. Martin now says he does not recall, shaking his head on a horizontal plane, "no." At the end of one such head shake, Skehan snaps Martin's gaze to him by calling him by name, "Jim." (See the transcription below.) Skehan implores, "Come on now" (and confess); Martin retracts his gaze and begins another negative head shake and starts speaking, "I don't." The battle for the control of Martin's fate is conducted by both officers, not only in the substance of their communications but in the way they aim to take over his body.

1   [M has just said, **I don't remember, I really don't,** and has been shaking
2   his head "no," looking down]
3   S: **Jim**
4   M: [snaps gaze to S] **Wheh**
5
6   S: **Come on now**
7   M: [gaze down, shaking head "no"] **I don't**
8
9   [passages not transcribed]
10
11 M: [head nod "no"] **I don't know-[at] all what happened.**
12   [head nodding "no" throughout the phrase]
13
14 S: **But you remember it vaguely. You've got a vague recollection of it.**
15   **You're not a stupid man, I've read your stuff.**
16   ↑
17 M: [head remains still; attentive expression]

```
18
19   M:  [head nod "yes" slightly, then "no" clearly] I know. I know that.
20       I know I'm not stupid but uhh [head nod 'no'] I don't know.
21       Ta          tu
22       ↑           ↑
23   S:  You know    You know how you got the motor home.
24
25   M:  [affirmative head nod] Yeah, I stoled it.
26
27   S:  Yeah. You didn't steal it the way you told us originally.
28       Right?
29
30   M:  Nnyeah,    basically, but uh
31       ↑          ↑
32       [affirmative nod] [negative head nod]
33                        ↑
34   S:                   Nonono. Not basically.
35
36   M:  Hmmm. [affirmative head nod and slight lift of torso up and back from
37       table]
38
39   S:  It didn't happen that way, did it?
40
41   M:  No. [negative head nod]
```

Martin does not give up easily. As he tries to right his story, he
continues trying to ground his position in moralized (positive/
negative) head motions. Skehan interrupts Martin's "I don't [recall],"
and, as a ploy to encourage Martin to acknowledge contact with the
van owner–victim, he now offers (in a passage not transcribed) that
"This is not you, normally" (i.e., You have always been a nonviolent
criminal), and that "Somethin' happened that could have been an accident." Martin nods "yes" very slightly during the latter statement.
Skehan goes on (lines 14–15): "But you remember it vaguely. You've
got a vague recollection of it. You're not a stupid man, I've read your
stuff." Martin's head is still, but at the conclusion of this statement,
Martin gestures "yes" slightly and then "no" clearly. Martin in effect
tries to weave his way through a difficult passage by leading with his
head motions. He tries to identify with the police, nodding "yes" when
their statements are innocuous, but he tries also to hold off confessing
on this key issue by shaking his head "no" about his memory and their
assertions that he had met the victim.

The police, however, are there to block his escape attempts. Hitting
him in rapid-fire fashion, they effectively turn him around. In the

following segment, which leads to his abandonment of his original account that he stole an empty van, his alternating positive and negative head motions become complicated to the point of confusion. Note the shifts in Martin's head movements throughout the following dialogue, and the quick shift at lines 30–32. In lines 30–32, Martin has nodded "yes" and shaken his head "no" within the same utterance, and in ways that are not clarified by their relation to the content of his speech.

Note that Skehan, at line 34, in effect expropriates Martin's negative head shake by using it as a kickoff point for his own "Nono-no" resistance to Martin's evasiveness. The emerging confusion in Martin's head movements indicates that he is losing his method of grounding his story in a bodily gloss of truth. With this crucial support gone, his story begins to collapse. His lifting of his torso up and back from the table, at lines 36–37, is the first of at least three such movements, leading up to the more elaborate enactment that I discussed earlier as being in the hot seat. He performs this unprecedented body movement directly after R's question, "You did, you did take it with the lady in it, right?" and immediately before his response, "Yeah." (See the first transcription on page 279.) Martin first starts crying in the process of trying to recover from this admission.

The way that Martin *stops* crying is also shaped critically by an interactional struggle over the regulation of his gaze and morally signifying head movements. When Martin is asked if he shot anyone else, he cries as he evasively depicts himself as virtually orphaned by his family, but he abruptly stops crying when he lifts his gaze to see how his sad story is being received. What he finds when he looks up is that the one interrogator on whom he might have counted to act as a sympathetic audience for his crying is no longer attending to his narrative line but is scanning his notes in order, it emerges, to draw Martin back to the "additional shootings" theme in a novel way (figure 6.8).

As long as Martin keeps his gaze down, he can be his own audience, providing morally expressive nods that corporeally ground the turns of spoken pathos in his story. But he takes a big risk when he abandons his own bodily accompaniment to his talk and looks up in search of embodied support from his interrogator. Martin's perception that Ray is preoccupied with his notes occasions a strikingly sudden end to what is Martin's most profound crying in the interrogation. The shift occurs between lines 17 and 20, below.

Figure 6.8 Martin sees that Ray is looking at his notes

 1   M: **Nna I ain't never gonna make more contact with my family.**
 2   **Hhehh** [laugh changing to pained expression]
 3
 4   R: **Oh, sure you will.** [casual, relaxed tone]
 5
 6   M: **Oh no.** [thin, high, nasal; face in cry grimace] **No.** [pause]
 7   **No.** [pause] **No.**
 8   ↑
 9   R: **you know**
10
11   R: [R inclines forward, looking down at his notes; M's gaze is down to
12   the table, directly in front of him, not up to R's eyes]
13
14   M: **No.** [mouth in cry grimice, upturned lower lip, jaw out and up] **No I**
15   **won't.**
16
17   M: [M looks up to R. R sweeps his head toward M and further right,
18   but R's gaze is down, so R catches M's eyes only grazingly if at all.
19   R's gaze sweeps right toward S and then back left and down to check
20   his notes; R clearly doesn't receive, hold and return M's glance.]
21
22   R: **Were you talking to uhh** [long pause; reading from notes] **to other**
23   **people about trying to kill, uh, Charles's wife** [pause] **because she**
24   **was going to testify against Steve.**
25   S: **Karen.**

26
27   M: **Oh I would've, yes.**   [pause] **I would've.**
28   ↑   ↑   ↑   ↑
29   [affirmative shaking of head]

Martin not only sees that Ray is not attending to his line of pathos about his isolation from his family, Martin sees that Ray has not been gazing at him for some time, but has instead been looking for material, either from his notes or from Skehan, to redirect the discussion. By offering "Karen," Skehan supports this impression by indicating that he understood that Ray, in looking at him and reading his notes, had been searching for this name. At this point, Martin's mood turns 180 degrees.

Steve and Charles are his brothers; Karen is Charles's wife. The matter on which Karen was to testify against Steve is unrelated to Martin's crimes. Perhaps because he never acted on the plan, he is downright enthusiastic to share it. With the rapt and bemused attentions of his interrogators, Martin dispenses with head movements and goes through a sequence of motions in taking and lighting a cigarette. Interpreting his interrogators' questions as signs of their respect for his cunning criminal knowledge, Martin's talk becomes lively. He explains his plan with the pleasure that a pedant might display on finding himself blessed with a captive audience.

1   R: **What were you gonna kill her with, the gun?**
2
3   M: **No. No. No. It's called pepperfidoxin** [*sic;* the word is "tetrodotoxin"]
4   ↑
5   [swings back in chair and front, beginning
6   sequence of taking cigarette from package on table; smiling; clear,
7   quick speech]
8
9   R: **It's who?**
10
11   M: **Pepperfidoxin. Did you ev, remember that term?**
12   ↑ ↑   ↑   ↑
13   [leaning forward, taking cigarette, smiling]
14
15   R: **No.**
16
17   M: **Puffer fish poison.**
18   ↑   ↑
19   [righting self in chair, putting cigarette to mouth]
20
21   R: **It's what?**
22   S: **What?**
23   ↑
24   [M gazes up to S]

25
26   M: **Puffer fish poison.**
27   ↑ ↑   ↑
28   [M inclines to S to take light at midtable, removing cigarette to say
29   this and then putting cigarette back into his mouth just after he
30   finishes the phrase]
31
32   R: **Puffer.   Fish.   Poison.** [articulating for verification]
33   ↑   ↑   ↑
34   [M takes light by dragging on the lighter's flame]
35
36   M: **Um-hmm.**

Martin makes it clear that he is proud of the self-presentation these remarks make. The police are interested in other uses he may have made of the gun, but he won't help them with that here, as his plan was "she just gets shot in the bet, uh, butt with a BB gun, and, uh, the BB had the poison on it." Asked where he was going to get this poison, Martin replies: "Uh, we had . . . I learned a few things in prison. I'm not totally, totally fuckin' ignorant, I'm just screwed up a lot." Continuing in a pedantic style, he explains that this poison is "210 times more powerful than curiare [*sic*]," and that it can be obtained easily from Japanese restaurants: "Just bullshit them and they'll give it to you . . . they boil the food so it isn't poisonous." Throughout this passage, Martin's voice is strong and steady. For a short while, he is in undisputed control of a stretch of talk. The police still understand him on two levels, but for now they are willing to give bodily support to what he says, providing their attentions and cigarettes for his corporeal preoccupations, while keeping in private reserve any thoughts that would undermine their collaboration with Martin in providing a gloss of credibility for this tale. The support they provide here will only make more forceful its removal at more crucial points in the interrogation.

3. The Fog in the Whirlpool: Taken by Metaphor in the Interrogation Room

We have reviewed two preconditions of Martin's crying. It emerges after the police undermine his tacit bodily practices for glossing his narration with verisimilitude; and in the midst of a crisis in his narrative, as he searches in speech and with metaphoric gesture to shift the drama by representing and thus beginning the transcendence of a self that is in the process of dissolution.

We must also appreciate that crying, like other behaviorally expressed emotions in everyday social life, is not just a two-dimensional, interactional pattern of conduct; it is also a three-dimensional phenomenon, a sensually and figuratively lived metamorphosis. In emotional behavior, the metaphoric vehicle of the self itself changes. It is not just that *the message* the person tries to convey becomes different. And it is not just *the responses of others,* realized or anticipated, that change. *It is also the locus of the grounding of action that changes.* The third condition of the suspect's crying is the rise of the transcendent force to which crying naturally, organically, seamlessly responds.

In analyzing Rachel's movement from whining to talking, we saw her take a kind of ontological leap from subjectivity to objectivity through a spate of coughing. She began coughing when still whining; she came out of the coughing already taken up by collaborative talk with her teacher. The criminal suspect goes through a similarly profound ontological transition as he falls into crying. When criminal suspects under interrogation figuratively find the bottom dropping out of their story, they often find themselves literally experiencing something morphologically similar.

I submit that the metaphor that best fits this experience is one of falling into a whirlpool. The suspect's subsequent crying is a fog-making activity with which he tries to scramble up and out of the threatening forces that swirl around. Perhaps the reader will think of a more apt metaphor, but what is critical is that the right description is not only a metaphor. It is the subject's experience and not the analysis that introduces the element of metaphor in the first place. What does one experience when one is caught? Thoughts may get confused but corporeally one realizes something quite distinct, that the bottom has fallen out. When the bottom falls out in a suspect's self-protective story, the suspect often feels something analogous in his or her stomach.[7] What naturally follows is a frenzied search for some fallback position. Where to look for safety is not clear; when interrogators are watching from above, with a video camera running, and they are personally observing intently from the left and the right, it will readily seem that dangers are all around. In order to understand the emergence of the suspect's crying under interrogation, we must see how the whirlpool becomes the metaphor that temporarily forms the troubled frame of the suspect's experience.

The Swirl of Pressures and Crying's Fog

For adults, crying often creates a kind of fog in the sense that, as we saw in a range of materials in chapter 4, it presents an interpretive puzzle. One might think that crying would be appealing very generally and constantly to criminal suspects because of its ambiguating quality. But suspects, perhaps especially suspects who, as career criminals, are always guilty of more than they are charged with, do not have the production of ambiguity as their main objective.

Suspects often want to make clear statements so that they can get clear confirmation that in some respects they are off the hook. The value of interrogations to the lifetime suspect may be difficult to appreciate for people who are not professional criminals or full-time paranoids. But even when a suspect is found to be guilty of a capital offense, he or she will have succeeded in getting away with some offenses that the police have not discovered or documented. Even when emerging from the interrogation essentially convicted, he or she will emerge scot-free on other offenses. That may not matter much to the police or the public, but it matters enormously for understanding the suspect's experience of the interrogation.

Career criminals often take for granted that they have a great deal to gain if they can speak fluidly in ways that make exculpating brush strokes over large segments of their lives or that inculpate them in some regards but motivate the police to credit their speech more generally.[8] The professional suspect will often be brought down just as he or she swings freely into dramatic narration. The diametrically opposite significances of his or her speech—one moment loosely delivered and seemingly inconsequential, then devastatingly inculpating the next—are essential features of the swirling pressures that may pull even the professional suspect into crying.

The constancy of pressure is also a causally relevant part of the environment. The suspect knows that his or her every gesture is under scrutiny. This scrutiny has a particular structure that helps explain why talk would be a necessary condition for eliciting his or her crying.

For James Martin, it is the very fatefulness of his talk as a socially consequential act—what he says is heard, recorded, held against him—that provides the objective power to provoke his crying. His thoughts do not matter nearly as much as does his talk, because they cannot be noted by others, made evidence, recalled at any future point by those who would judge him. But even as he attempts to talk with an air of casualness that would support his claim of authenticity for the substance of what he says, he knows that once he has said something it cannot be taken back. This taken-for-granted sense of consequentiality enables his thoughts-become-talk to resonate backward and provoke him to cry.

This may seem obvious, but speech is a precondition of his crying only because there is no easy "going back" in an interrogation.[9] Martin will have protested, again and again, some key fact of the police version of the case. For example, early in the interrogation he repeatedly claimed that, when he entered the RV on Ventura beach, no one was in it. And then he will say, yes, the middle-aged woman who was murdered was indeed inside when he entered the RV. The police may urge him to repeat the "admission" once or twice. Usually they will do this indirectly, by asking a question (like "How old of a lady was she?") that presumes the admission that he had met her. But what is striking is that his single admission will be enough for all to assume that the scores of denials he previously offered are now washed away. Everyone in the interrogation room rightly assumes that for the rest of the interrogation and for the trials to come, the matter has been settled. The suspect himself will collaborate in treating the previous denials as washed away, because if they remain alive in awareness, they will now just indicate that the deviousness of his criminal conduct has continued into the interrogation. (And indeed they will reappear in the penalty phase of the trial to support the prosecution's negative character portrait.) If the suspect is to go on with the interrogation, he must do so with an air of truth, and to that end Martin again and again treats earlier segments of his statements as exceptional and final acts of deception, never to be repeated.

The suspect, we may say, is faced with an asymmetry in the hermeneutic power of his speech. Denials of culpability may be repeated infinitely without achieving probative effect. Admissions, said once, are instantly and irretrievably effective. Speech much of the time means nothing for the suspect's fate as it emerges from his mouth. His speech often is as free, light, and worthless as air. At other times, it is hugely costly and unbearably heavy. A single word, once it jumps a matter of inches from his mouth to a recording tape, can change his life forever. For much of the interrogation, Martin spins out his story casually, elaborating with colorful details (e.g., the puffer fish business) that in style and substance gloss his speech with a veneer of truth. That cavalier practice of speech, itself a sign to police that they are dealing with a professional suspect, is also part of the framework that sets up the suspect's crying.

When Martin's crying occurs, it comes specifically in and through passages in which fateful turns are occurring in his confession. He doesn't begin to cry either at the start of the interrogation or at random points during its three hours, nor does he cry when the emerging narrative touches on the sufferings of his victims. Innocent people under interrogation often do that.[10] In the experience that police have of interrogations, witnesses and innocent suspects often cry extensively in

just such a random fashion, for example when they are giving their
name and address or when they are providing non-event-specific background information on their relationship to other parties associated
with a criminal event. In effect, *by not crying* when his participation
in the interview has no particular narrative consequence for his criminal case, the professional suspect helps construct the narrative consequentiality of his crying when it *does* occur. For then his crying is
not just a sign of personal breakdown, it is a sign that his story has
broken down. Occurring precisely at narratively significant points in
his story, Martin's cryings themselves threaten to stand as evidence
against him.

Indeed, the very way that Martin cries indicates his awareness of
the fatefulness of his utterances. His crying is detectable only as a wavering of vowel sounds, a truncation of phrases, a turning away of
gaze in a shamelike search for invisible walls for privacy, sometimes
accompanied by shielding hand gestures and foldings of his arms. All
of these aspects of crying impair the intelligibility of what he is saying. In the impaired way he speaks, the suspect indicates that these
are especially hard words to say. And they are, not only because of
the future consequences of the substance of what he will have to
say, but also because he will be retrospectively undermining what
he said before, and that will make more difficult his renewed efforts
to construct a new line of deceit within a compelling aura of credibility.

Slipping into the Whirlpool

One of the first indications that Martin's crying responds to a sense
of being pulled down by a whirlpool is the fact that just before the
crying begins, he slips huge distances. Shortly before James Martin
cries the first time, he has not only admitted meeting the victim, he has
admitted shooting her. His initial story is in the process of precipitous
collapse as he begins crying. In the crying itself, as he sees himself in
steep descent, he grabs for a branch that suddenly and for the first
time comes into view. Within his crying talk, he leaps at the idea that
a third person, a homeless man, was in the van and in control of the
situation.

The whirlpool metaphor is also useful for noting that, even when
the suspect emerges from the crying with a defensive strategy, he is
attempting to reestablish control over a sense of self that has gone into
free fall. That is, Martin is primarily dealing with emotional forces.
The police are behind those forces, but what the suspect confronts
immediately are the monstrous dimensions of his situation.

More clearly than a new defense, what the suspect's cryings articulate is a sense of drowning. Martin's crying comes out in the form that adult cry-talk often takes, a gasping through speech. "I don't, [voice cracking, grabbing breath] I don't all know. [voice cracking through last phrase] Got a big-ass argument [singsong]." The whirlpool sucks one's breath away as it sucks one in. The words one says when crying take on a power to attack, to overcome, to vacuum up one's breath. The throat constricts in response to the power that the words engender as they are spoken. The subject is no longer behind speech, pushing it out; as his speech is uttered, it becomes treacherous in a serpentine way, curling around and threatening to pull him down. Talk usually enhances respiration by promoting an extended exhale,[11] but when it provokes crying, talk threatens suffocation. Related to the gasping in cry-talk is the emergence of thin sounds as the voice is choked down. The experience is one of trying to thrust above the surface a helpful expression of self that can survive pressures toward drowning.

The difficulty that the criminal suspect faces is constituted in part by the inability simply to shed his or her prior self-definition. Part of what the suspect grasps for is an explanation of why his or her new versions of past events should now be believed. In a way, the suspect's crying is a lamentation for a self that is surely dead but cannot easily be buried.

So the suspect does not simply go down as in a pool of still water; he or she spins around, alternatively looking ahead for a way to build up a new story and looking to the past for a way to give some respect to the old self even as he or she tries to put it out of view. Words are especially hard to say because they must do double-duty. Martin turns to self-pity as he invokes a pathetic image of himself as orphaned by his family, alone in nature like an animal, with nothing to look forward to but the electric chair. . . . If he is going to continue without conceding everything, he must find some way to honor the shell of his abandoned story, and his imagery of pathos is a prayer delivered through invoking primordial images of family, his own death, and his existential isolation in the world. He sends these images, not only to the police in desperate hope of salvation but through the police to whatever powers might respond with inspiration for the next steps to take.

But the whirlpool has still more precise terrors. Crying as he talks, the suspect finds it difficult to give up his past self. In effect the suspect must solve the crime of the murder of his old self before he can find a new way to cover up his own murderous crime. Martin, who for most of his life has been preoccupied with framing fraudulent stories about himself in the face of authority,[12] has compelling reasons to be consumed by the spectacle of the destruction of his twenty years of posturing as a relatively harmless, jerk-type, petty property criminal. Can it be that an identity that he had been cultivating all his criminal career has been blown away in an instant, not by the murders he committed—it survived those challenges for months—but by these interrogators, just a moment ago? How did that happen? What did he do wrong to bring this about? Where in the development of his posture in this interrogation could he have avoided it? Like other mourners, Martin must be imaginatively hoping to take back the recent past even as he knows that the effort is futile. In this respect as well, he spins as in a whirlpool.

Like the forces of a whirlpool, police specialists suck in suspects during interrogations and then spit them out a shambles. A whirlpool has two fundamental parts, a vacuumlike center in which one is pulled down and swirling wet walls that hold one in. Drawn to the center of the whirlpool, there is no escape directly to solid ground but only the chance of grasping onto a saving limb as one is unwillingly embraced by the vortex. The well-known Mutt and Jeff or good cop–bad cop structuring of interrogation promotes the development of the whirlpool as the structure of suspects' experiences.

Delivered in a pointed fashion, the evidence against the suspect is especially hard-hitting. For Martin, it is those two boys and the gun: very simple, very specific, and introduced serially in a punchy one-two fashion. These provide the suspect with images of pinpoints to focus on at the center of the vortex that is closing around him.

Surrounding the introduction of these particular pieces of evidence is a showing of massive power and the possibility of an accepting embrace. Before particular pieces of evidence are cited, the overwhelming, transcendent power of the police will be dramatized. In Martin's case, as he develops his crying story about being abandoned by his family, Ray makes positive remarks to suggest that Martin won't be alienated from his family forever. Skehan, the tough cop in the interrogation, at times yells at Martin. In order to get Martin to put in his own words a description of his plan to kill the homeless man for his truck, Skehan paradoxically says in a voice that is loud and imperative, "I'm not telling ya, I'm asking ya." When Martin starts to cry, Ray provides words that would diminish his problems with his family. But Skehan sees another opportunity.

1 M: **And I didn't know where to go, what to do, and um—**
2 S: **Well, we let you talk with us 'cause we understand.**
3 M: **Nn uh uh.**
4 S: **Maybe more so than the family can, huh?**[13]

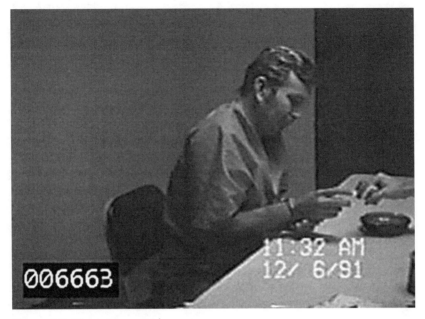

Figure 6.9 Cigarette control

For Martin the criminal justice system is his most loyal family, always ready to embrace him. His most pronounced crying occurs during this segment, when he is brought to address that fact directly.

From the start of an interrogation, the police routinely and in detail work to create an environment that the suspect will sense as overwhelming.[14] Holding the key to a wall switch, they may monopolize the power to turn the lights on and off; even if they leave a pack of cigarettes lying on the table, the suspect, hands in chains, will need their help to get a light (figures 6.9 and 6.10). From the police side, this is described as a matter of manufacturing and managing power. From the suspect's side, it is an ongoing confrontation with interactional walls that make the interrogation room a prison only for the suspect.[15] This is a kind of magic. The same place has a radically different meaning for those sitting on different sides of the same table. This meaning is not intellectualized by the participants; it is known as it is felt.

Because of the total control that the police exercise in an interrogation room as they punch holes in a suspect's story, the environment is dialectically structured for the suspect. The police often inquire into the suspect's sexual life. Martin is pressed on whether he had sex with

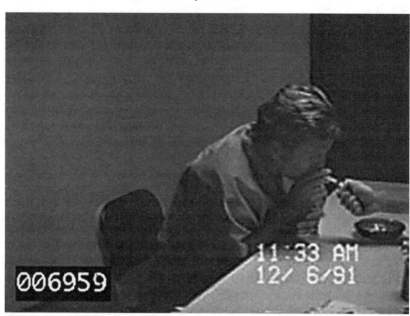

Figure 6.10 Cigarette lighting control

the van owner (her pants and underwear had been cut). Martin is also pressed to describe a sexual experience he had in the van, after the murder, with an apparently mentally deficient relative. In addition to specific strategic objectives (an admission that Martin had sex with the victim would aid the effort to send him to execution), inquiries into such intimate matters contribute powerfully to keeping alive a dialectical sense of the environment, one that is homing into the subject's center from all around, always mercilessly pressing in as it offers the prospect of a merciful embrace. The suspect moves into crying by absorbing the message: we are all around you as we do surgical operations on the center of your soul.

We might consider the juxtaposed thematic structure of pressures on the suspect as raising any number of holistic metaphoric pairs: nice guy and tough guy; mom's comforting embrace and dad's punch to the guts; the sacred (the matter of the suspect's future life or death is being worked out) and profane (the details focused on, the unremittingly mundane, plastic environment); even morality (the police as Authority) and immorality (the police, springing revelations on the suspect, reveal that they are his or her superiors in deceit as well).[16] All of these metaphors apply to a degree, but none is completely adequate. I prefer the whirlpool metaphor because its aesthetic character makes it more accurate empirically: the "whirlpool" keeps the analytic focus on the suspect's inability to focus on the dialectics swirling around.

Crying's Saving Grace

But why bother pushing the analysis to this length? For understanding the causal path that leads to the suspect's crying, the dialectical structure of the interrogation environment, as felt from his or her side of things, is essential to explain why the suspect's response is not some emotion other than crying. We have reviewed many forms of "fall" in this volume, various forms of experience in social life in which one finds the taken-for-granted, tacitly embodied foundations of one's conduct suddenly removed. Some lead to laughter, some to anger, some to shame. Here, a suspect receives something like a coup de grâce when the police introduce crucial pieces of evidence as within their possession. Suddenly the suspect's prior story is swept away; he is left naked; a face in which he has made extensive commitments has been disgraced. Why doesn't he just experience shame? Why cry?

For amateur criminals, especially those who have been led to detail private sexual activities, the police coup de grâce is commonly first a deeply shaming experience before it is an occasion for crying. Even for Martin, shame at losing his story line seems to be present. Recall the bizarre recovery he attempts to make after his second bout of crying, when, reaching for a cigarette, he puffs himself up to deliver a pedantic explanation of the properties of a fish poison with which he planned to kill his sister-in-law.

But these experiences don't stop at shame, they move quickly through shame to another form of emotional expression. They don't move to anger because that would imply turning the tables on the interrogators, and the police have created an ambience of power to keep that possibility from appearing on the horizon. The experience does not stay frozen in shame, although there is often a phase of shocked inaction as the suspect, wide eyed and expressionless, first absorbs the evidence and takes in the implication that, if it is true, the police have hidden it all along.

Crying emerges because the counterpoint of the punch to the center is a bearlike embrace: the suspect takes for granted that he or she must respond, that he or she cannot long indulge the fantasy often experienced in shame, which is one of the earth opening up and swallowing him or her.[17] There is no time out for the suspect here, even in fantasy, because the videotape is running. Here a nonresponse, held too long, is a response, an admission. He or she must enact some definition of self, and crying's mobilization of a self in the process of drowning is a metaphoric response that fits the whirlpool-like situation in a manner that is effective aesthetically, even if in the long run it proves to be not of much use practically. Artfulness, after all, may be essential for action, not for its inherent beauty but because, when one needs to ground a self caught in free fall, there is no other resource.

SEVEN

MUNDANE METAMORPHOSES

When we examine how people laugh, cry, become ashamed, or get angry, we find them routinely giving a finely nuanced significance to their behavior, even while their experience resonates with feelings of independently flowing, provocative forces. How can people so frequently and easily be both out of control and in control at the same time?

The enigma presented by socially shaped emotional life is an instance of a larger mystery. Even as people self-reflectively tailor the self that they present to others, they construct forces to move themselves in ways that are in some sense invisible to themselves. How can people be so finely self-reflective and, at the same time, so powerfully and colorfully moved by hidden aspects of their being?

The solution of the enigmas created by emotions as they course through social interaction depends on appreciating parallels with larger mysteries. In each of the prior chapters, I have pursued three lines of inquiry in order to explain how emotions emerge and decline in particular social situations. Each line of inquiry grows out of a long-standing tradition for comprehending the mysterious combination of subjective and objective dimensions in human conduct. Equipped with a unique vocabulary and taking a distinctive analytic focus, each tradition has been centrally preoccupied with what may be summed up as a common riddle: "What is it that, being itself invisible, produces all that is visible?"

Scholarly thought and professional research have produced solutions that may be compared with those that folk cultures and lay crafts have devised. Conjuring up mysteries and demonstrating a competence to solve them is the central work of sorcerers. Magicians generate appearances and disappearances by processes that remain invisible to the attentive audience. We in the audience never learn how the mystery

309

is solved, but we are shown proof that for us the mystery is obdurate and haunting, and that a hidden knowledge exists that can easily solve it. Perhaps there is also a kind of magic in the routine presentation of self in everyday life. Erving Goffman appreciated that we seem to have a craftlike understanding of how to produce personal identities that we know to be in one sense or another constructed, but that will appear to others to emanate from our nature rather than from our strategies.

The best-known solutions to the riddle invoke deities. Almost by definition, we think of religions as bodies of thought that have pinned their appeal on the haunting power of invisible forces that lie behind what is visible. Religions with gods commonly tell stories about the sacred sources of the contemporary environment—the Invisible that was behind the visible in primordial times—and they also explain why mankind cannot directly witness the god-creators who may still be at work. What should we make of the fact that religion was so important to the early sociologists and psychologists? Religion was a mystification to be set aside by Marx and Freud; for Weber, the fundament of both traditional and capitalist economies and societies; for Durkheim, the misplaced appreciation of the vividly sensed transcendence of society over the individual. Did they protest and project too much? Or might the social psychologist's work inevitably be much closer to theology than any professional sociology or psychology association would dare admit?

Another answer, one widely appealing outside of social-psychological research circles, directs attention to aesthetic processes. Many artists don't try to provide universally accessible references to things; they work to show how things appear under one or another condition of illumination. In a sense, what painters, photographers, and sculptors often try to convey is the creative power of light, gaze, and the embodied commitments that bring a perspective into focus. But they usually assume that they cannot depict the sources of appearance directly. So they try to capture light in its reflections and to represent the posture of the viewer indirectly, in the features, cast and assemblage of what is illuminated. Questions of the origin of the visible are commonly addressed in art through symbolic allusion. Instead of a figure of the Sun or a sketch of the observing artist, the color of the fruit and the slope of the table may be worked out to indicate the constituting power of a changing atmosphere and a mobile viewer. Still lifes become self-portraits; self-portraits become landscapes, revealing regions in perceptual apparatus and showing how light diffuses and thickens to become the textured background that sustains a personal outlook.

This variety of answers, some from tricksters, some that take sacred forms, some based on an aesthetic sensibility, indicates that the riddle is both ancient and still compelling. I want to suggest that the same mystery has structured what might be regarded as the major contributions to social and psychological thought in the twentieth century.[1]

Ancient religious beliefs often conveyed the warning that an attempt to look directly at the source of Being will lead to self-destruction, or at least would be sacrilege. It may seem that science should have no truck with such anxieties and, finding it easy to ignore religious restrictions, should make a direct and decisive assault on the targets of inquiry. Certainly the answer that religion provides is one that is soundly disdained in modern social-psychological research. But here are three twentieth-century sources of social and psychological thought that have shared in the primordial wonder of religion, magic, and art about the intrinsically elusive source of the visible facts of people's identities.

1. For Freud, the answer to the riddle was the subconscious. That Freud, in his disdain for religion, should have given new life to the sensibility of a religious hermeneutic even as it faced unprecedented threats by the confident rationality of his age, is one of the great ironies in the history of thought. As Paul Ricoeur brilliantly demonstrated, for Freud, as for religious consciousness, everything that has a mundane, everyday, practically rationalized meaning also has a second, more elusive meaning, one that dwells in the motivating regions of personal conduct.[2] Thus the story of Christ on the cross is both a simple narrative about historical events and a chain of ringing sacred symbols that carry transcendent meaning. And for Freud, the manifest content of dreams is always the product of subconscious forces that transcend the dream itself and can never be observed or described directly. So also, everyday emotions, such as the expression of humor and embarrassing slips, embody and address ongoing, hidden provocations in life even as they respond to observable situational exigencies.[3]

Heidegger's answer was not dissimilar.[4] In an unreflective manner, the individual copes with a succession of situated everyday challenges. The techniques one uses, the strategic postures one takes up, the skills one employs in using the equipment that one finds in different situations—all of that may be raised to conscious awareness, if not immediately then at least after the fact. But one also constantly acts on an understanding of the life being lived through one's daily succession of situational copings. Personal reflection on the transcendent course of one's life, being itself limited as a form of situational, culturally conditioned coping, is never quite adequate to the nature of what it addresses.

Note the parallel to the Freudian contrast between the preconscious (or tacit) and the subconscious (or "repressed" awareness) in Heidegger's thought. As Dreyfus explains, Heidegger discussed

> two kinds of covered-upness. The first is simply being *undiscovered*— "neither known nor unknown." This is the kind of covered-upness we find when we investigate the background of everyday practices. The second is being *buried over*. "This means that [the phenomenon] has at some point been discovered but has deteriorated to the point of getting covered up again." This happens when Dasein senses its unsettledness. Then Dasein attempts to pass off the phenomenon that has covered over the original phenomenon as itself the truth, in effect denying that anything has been covered up. Heidegger calls this cover-up *disguise,* which suggests that the covering up is motivated by not wanting to see the truth. . . . According to Heidegger, the *world* and Dasein's absorption in it . . . are so obvious as to be unnoticed in the course of our everyday activity; Dasein's way of being, however, is so unsettling that, just because it is constantly sensed, it is constantly covered up.[5]

In the preceding chapters, I have worked with a parallel contrast. On the one hand, I examine the tacit aspects of situation responsive conduct, an analysis that covers strategic aspects of interaction similar to those that Erving Goffman characteristically took up. On the other, I describe the larger resonance of how one is treated by and acts toward others, such as what it means to a family to create cross-generational laughter in a fun house while stranger-visitors impassively stand close by, or how a conflict among drivers over minor advantages in road position can take on life-threatening meanings. Even as people shape emotional expressions so that they will be seen by others to be a certain kind of person in a certain kind of situation, they address challenges that existed before they entered the immediate scene and that they know will persist after they leave each separate transaction. But the appreciation of the transcendent significance of situated conduct is grasped through a kind of sensual self-reflection that, from the standpoint of discursive self-reflection, typically appears disguised in the inspired resonance of anger, laughter, crying, etc.

2. For George Herbert Mead, the answer to the riddle was the process of interaction between self and other that shapes mind. In Mead's view, a view that has come to dominate the analysis of social interaction in American sociology, the only version of his or her identity that a person can examine is an objectified version, a representation of "me" that is shaped in anticipation of how I would be viewed from the standpoint of others. The self I present to others, while it is eminently visible, always in a way masks the process in which I define myself for others.

What I produce for others to see is the outcome of my anticipating how others will respond to alternative versions of my self. My unrealized foreshadowings of action are not routinely visible to others. My anticipation of others' responses occurs so quickly, and so much more through an experience of symbolic refraction than by anything rightly called thinking, that commonly it is not even subject to my own reflections, much less available to the others I face.

For their part, the others with whom I interact are not free to search for the "real" me behind the visible me. They are all the while involved in their own productions of self. In everyday life, the "I," or the "I/me" dialectical process, is always hidden somewhere just behind the appearance of personal identity, eluding observation even as it creates observable versions of self.[6]

When Mead's insight was picked up by Erving Goffman, the result was a description of the mechanics of self-presentation that unapologetically left out a portrait of the being behind the machinations.[7] Goffman shows people to be artful dodgers, always cunningly shaping versions of themselves that will in turn shape the responses of others, but people act, and Goffman wrote, for no reason narrower than that such manipulations are the stuff of social being. And Goffman threw in the following kicker. People know that everyone, being a master of dissembling, will suspect that everyone else is presenting an artificial self, i.e., that what is visible about one or another's identity, whether a true or a false version of intentions and interests, is necessarily also a cover-up. So people shrewdly cover up their covering up. People manage their conduct not only to give an impression of who they are but to give off the impression that they give. They present themselves such that indications of their intentions and interests seem innocently shed and thus reliable guides to personal disposition in its natural state.[8] In the final analysis, the doubly layered visibility of self only goes to show the haunting invisibility of the self.

3. For Maurice Merleau-Ponty, the invisible is in another sense the

ontologically hidden inner lining of the visible. Merleau-Ponty was fond of making his points by drawing on the painter's struggle. For some painters, the challenge is not to reproduce what anyone can see, but to capture the invisible processes that produce what everyone sees. The objective of an artist like Cézanne was not to create a landscape that anyone could instantly match with a patch of conventionally denoted geography as it is seen in a certain season, at a particular time of day, in specific weather conditions, and from a given standpoint. Such a painting would accept an assumption of ontological separation between viewer and viewed. In an alternative strategy that recognizes the interdependence of viewer and landscape, the painter might try to paint the coherence in the movements of the perceiver's body that brings a specific perception of a specific scene into view, that accounts for the highlights and shadows or varying intensities of color and shape in the perceptual experience, that gives rise to its symmetries and asymmetries, and so forth. This was quite a challenge, since, for one thing, a portrayal of either the viewer's body or the perceived landscape would miss the objective entirely, and for another, anything painted would instantly become stationary and held in a fixed frame.[9]

Transferred to people's everyday behavior, the challenge becomes one of trying to describe the embodied practices that produce visible conduct as its outer lining. Michael Polanyi issued a parallel call to inquiry.[10] In Polanyi's language, each of our effective actions requires that we disattend our body as we act, focusing away from the point at which our body intersects with the world. In writing, for example, if you watch how your pen creates the form of each letter, you soon lose your train of thought and stop writing. In speaking, if you persist in attending to how you express the sounds of the words you utter, your speech quickly loses coherence.

The appreciation of the indirect consciousness required for competent conduct leads quickly to an appreciation of the essential place of aesthetics in all behaviors, however mundane or esoteric. Writing requires an unselfconscious engagement of skills in shaping letters, thus writing is a kind of tacit drawing; talking, which requires a kind of disattended melody as the vehicle for evoking meaning, is a tacit singing; walking, a kind of dancing; and so forth. However rational and practically motivated the subject of one's writing, talking, or walking, in order to get things down on paper, to get things said comprehensibly to others, or to get around at all, one must be an aestheticized subject.

Polanyi and Merleau-Ponty invited us to start a new generation of research that would make visible what the individual must keep invisible, or outside of reflective self-awareness, in all conduct. *This invitation is especially relevant for social psychology, because the implication is that, in the most fundamental way, the individual depends on others in order to know him- or herself.* I see, hear, feel, and express myself through actions that in part always remain behind myself, always just beyond the reach of my self-awareness. *I must look to others to see myself, to know myself, literally to find myself.* It is only through the responsive actions of others that I can, for example, see my seeing. I can see *by* myself, but it is only in the presence of another that I can become aware of *my gaze,* i.e., that I am altering my vision in this way or that. Routinely I see *through* my seeing; preoccupied with what I see, I do my seeing transparently. I may know many landscapes, but for access to my idiosyncratic practices of constructing them, I must rely on designations about myself from others.[11] On this understanding, the ancient call to "know thyself" becomes an invitation to study social interaction.

The lines of inquiry emerging from each of these three breakthroughs in twentieth-century thought have flowed separately. It is not too much to say that between the analysis of (1) the subconscious or situation-transcending meanings of action, (2) the examination of face-to-face interaction in social life, and (3) the phenomenology of the body, when the scholar's attitude has not been one of studied indifference, almost all the intellectual action has been characterized by ridicule and disgust. But if we seek harmoniously to exploit central contributions of each tradition, we can comprehensively explain the rise and fall of emotions in the practice of everyday life, and in the process, point the way toward a comprehensive social psychology.

The analyses of the preceding chapters sought to demonstrate in detail the three ways that people, through processes that remain beyond their reflective grasp as they act, make visible the emotions of everyday social life. The first line of inquiry is interactionist. It focuses on how people perceive and anticipate the responses of others as they participate in social life. The second line of inquiry describes a double hermeneutics. It examines both the situation-specific and the situation-transcending projects that people pursue through their conduct. And the third is the study of incorporation, or how behavior is literally fleshed out. An inquiry into the incorporation of conduct is especially useful to reveal how emotions are metamorphoses of the embodied, sensual foundations of personal action.

1. Naturally Hidden Contingencies of Emotions in Everyday Social Interaction

Sociology has at least two long-standing ways of understanding that something invisible in social interaction underlies personal identity. George Herbert Mead, in an early version of the point, wrote of mind as the upshot of social interaction. Individual consciousness emerges and is sustained through a process of taking the standpoint of others on oneself. The identities of others, as anticipated or encountered, are from the start intrinsic to the shaping of one's own lines of action and of the self that is inscribed in them.

Mead's perspective always brings news because all cultures create ideas of individual identity that deny the collective basis of individual action. Thus in contemporary Western society we reward the prophetic individuals who can grasp and write down catchy tunes, and we reward entrepreneurs for imagining and developing products that work well, but the rewards flow to such individuals most heavily when the tunes and the products are instantly recognizable and widely marketable. Collective histories create the demand for the individuals' contributions, call out their innovations, and construct their talents by creating gaps they can fill. Cultures that honor individuality create diversions that routinely disguise the collective bases of individual identity.[12]

Another way to explain why an interactionist focus always brings news is to note that, as people act, there is no gap between taking the standpoint of others and responding. There is no time-out from life, no regular or universally available occasion for "perceiving" others' view of oneself, much less weighing the consequences of alternative paths of action, and only then responding. One's perception of others and one's response are of a piece; each is naturally hidden in the other. This thesis was clear to William James, who captured it in his example of someone fleeing in fear from a bear in the woods: one doesn't first see the animal and then decide it would be best to run away; one sees the bear with flying feet. One is always going through the woods in one state of anticipation or another, and the perception of a menacing bear is constructed by the gingerly manner in which one is already walking.[13] Put more in terms that would become familiar with mid-twentieth-century existentialism, the process of thinking, considering, or reflecting on how others will respond before one acts already responsively expresses a perception that the situation permits delay. Meanwhile, what could be gained by not pausing is lost and nondoing can become one's undoing.

Because there is no time out from expressive being, perception and response are naturally intertwined. Cultures deny this by sponsoring notions of personal competency, as such ideas generally deny the reality of intertwining by asserting an inherent state of response-ability. As the pragmatists understood, the ideas about abilities and disabilities that we attribute to individuals when we use essentializing nouns such as "smart" or "weak" or even "blind" disguise an active interaction between person and environment. In a world with no light, no one and everyone is blind.[14]

The preceding studies have focused on moments in everyday life when the natural intertwining of self and other, having become problematic, is raised toward visibility by an emotional response. The angry driver confronts the fact that his or her personal competency depends on the structure of interaction with other drivers. If they are blind, unaware or indifferent to ones intentions as signaled by the trajectory of one's car, then, willy-nilly, one becomes instantly dumb. Anger is at once the driver's way of *recognizing and denying the interdependence* of his or her identity on the conduct of others in social interaction. Cut off by an insensitive driver, one becomes sensitive to one's own impotence. The turn to anger brings vividly to life the interdependence of one's own and others' experiences, actions, and identities, and anger simultaneously and righteously denies the inevitability of interdependency by attributing the suddenly heightened awareness of interaction to the wrongdoing of another driver. In the mythical thinking that anger inspires, if one can get back effectively at the other and teach him or her a lesson, then perhaps one can afterward drive on in peace, reassured that one's identity will no longer be dependent on others' limitations.

Somewhat separate from the Meadian "symbolic interaction" tradition in sociology, a second tradition, one closer to European phenomenology than to American pragmatism, has nourished interactionist sociology. It has made a similar point about the invisibility of interdependent identities by referring to the dilemma of "intersubjectivity." Alfred Schutz, developing the sociological implications of Husserl's phenomenology, made clear that an individual's conduct with others routinely depends on a presumption of intersubjectivity.[15] In talking with you, I take for granted that we share a common ground for understanding each other's expressions, such that you will understand what I say from my standpoint. This assumption is as absurd as it is routine. No matter how closely we may have lived together, our biographies will have been so different as to ensure that the contexts and trajectories of the current moment carry fundamental differences. As a result, we must in a sense pretend to understand each other if we are to interact. This pretense usually works well enough that it goes unnoticed. It works "for all practical purposes," i.e., well enough, in the judgments that each of us makes, so that we let the reconciliation of perspectives remain imprecise, allow confusions to proliferate harmlessly, and get on with our lives.

The Meadian and the Schutzian traditions have different emphases, but for our purposes they amount to the same thing. Schutz's perspective blends easily with that of Hans Christian Andersen's self-confident child who knew that the emperor had no clothes. What is visible to the child is invisible to everyone who has a practical stake in the ongoing order of society, namely that authority, prestige, power—everything that makes society work—is a construction built on faithfully not seeing an absence. Doubt must remain invisible for social interaction to proceed routinely. Put most generally, social life would quickly move to a state of crisis if we really questioned whether we shared precisely the same understanding of what each of us is doing and saying.[16] Yet if we do not routinely demand of each other that we make explicit our presumptions about each other's understandings, we are not wholly unaware of the questions that we are passing over and the potential misunderstandings that we are content to treat from moment to moment as innocent.[17] Thus we can see institutions in social life that invite people to address presumptive intersubjectivity in a nonthreatening way. One is the theater of Eugene Ionesco.

Another is the fun house. Academics need fine-grained data and often use bizarrely distorted language to bring to the surface the routinely invisible practices of getting by in social life on presumptions of intersubjectivity, but the challenge is not for academics alone to appreciate. Every competent comedian knows it, and so do people who encounter halls of distorting mirrors in amusement parks. These are places for playing with the versions of self that one takes for granted as obvious, and for addressing the distorted versions of one's identity that are secretly held in other's understandings of oneself.

The study of laughter at what appears on funny mirrors indicates that the dilemma of reconciling the versions of one's identity as implied by self (one's actions toward others) and person (the actions of others toward oneself) are existential.[18] Everyone (above a minimal age), from any culture, can find funny mirrors funny. But this is one existential truth that is not full of pathos. Everyone knows how to interact with companions so as to enable the mirrors to bring intersubjectivity to the surface as a problem to be positively transcended. Laughter does not deny the problem of reconciling personal standpoints; it joyfully finesses the issue by tapping a visible corporeal bond, in this setting, most typically, family relations, to insist on a presumptively shared reality. Just as the driver, in labeling another stupid or an asshole, responds to something that is inherently invisible by making emphatically visible something else that is routinely and essentially hidden, so family members in the fun house overcome the challenge of the invisibility of intersubjectivity by manufacturing a new order of visibility. By shaking their bodies emphatically in a laughing response that is bounded by family units, they make visible a spirit version of that treasured, supposedly constant but mystically elusive entity, the family bond.

Of all the emotions, shame most directly reveals the interactive foundations of personal identity. In shame one stands naked in isolation from a sacred community. Note that in everyday experiences of shame, as reviewed in chapter 3 and as described in Genesis, the challenge is not to exist but to exist in some protective cultural clothing: the desire in shame is not for suicide but to flee to a place of covering, to a hiding forest, back to an undifferentiated place in the masses or, in many accounts ("I wished that the earth would open and swallow me up"), to a womblike place.[19] Without any need for reflection, the individual in shame knows instantly and vividly that his or her integrity depends on being folded into membership in a transcending community.

Significantly, the acceptance sought in shame is not personal in the sense of being idiosyncratic and intimate; the wish is for a kind of impersonal embrace. Mother's embrace is comforting in its very impersonality, at least when it is understood to be offered unquestioningly and rooted in a universal biological drive, and not offered for particularistic reasons that might hinge on contingent judgments of fault and merit. A related point has been made in various cultural and intellectual traditions: the individual in shame seeks clothing, a way to recover the anonymity of a role, an unselfconscious, taken-for-granted way of doing things, the behavioral vehicle of "das Man."

The rawness of shame, as revealed in the blush and more generally as an aspect of shame's discomfort, indicates the painful loss of the invisibility that is the vehicle for routinely smooth participation in social life. Shame registers the loss of social skin, the absence of a self-encasing, self-protecting, yet at the same time an instrumentally useful way of knowing others and making oneself known to others. Here is another form of the dialectical nature of individual identity as revealed by everyday emotions. The clothing that the individual painfully lacks in shame is one that hides as it expresses, that gives the individual a comforting invisibility only because it presents him or her as a visible instantiation of a known category of social participant.

The intertwining of personal identity and one's impersonal status in "community" is not an abstraction in these experiences. As analysts, we may raise endless questions about the evidence that "community," as a morally resonant, collectively coherent entity, exists, either in a particular instance or as a general matter. But to the individual in shame, the one thing that is not questioned is the reality of moral community. Its existence is acknowledged in an appreciation of its negation, in the excruciating awareness that the embrace of such a community has been lost. Community enables the individual to avoid shame by offering a cover, a disguise, an invisibility, even as it acknowledges, recognizes, and designates his or her individuality.

This paradox, that the individual becomes invisible so long as he or she is recognizable as a social type doing something ordinary or conventional,[20] is poignantly represented when people struggle to maintain modesty under the pressure of collective praise. When a ceremony places a person before the admiring gaze of an audience, the overt purpose is to celebrate the person's individuality, i.e., how he or she differs from the group norm. The moral embrace of the community then often threatens to become too powerful and personal. When people blush or cry as they receive an award, they are literally trying to create a new covering for the self, even as they recognize that the omniscience of the community, which they would not deny because it means that they have been rightfully singled out for praise, makes that impossible.

That the self, in its socially presented, expressed form, ironically relies on the maintenance of a layer of invisible involvement with others, is easier to state in the abstract than to document in individual cases. The idea of aiming research at portraying the invisible seems rather futile, but what saves the effort is a methodological paradox: that the very density of the interactive flow that maintains invisibility for the participants creates a window of opportunity for the observer. In two case studies, I tried to demonstrate the production of invisibility by working through thick data on crying.

The course of Rachel's whining elaborately revealed the emergence of corporeal invisibility in her movement out of crying and into emotionally unremarkable speech. Following Merleau-Ponty, I refer to this accomplishment as one of "effacing" the body, of rubbing away attention to the body even as the body is used to guide collective attentions elsewhere. Another phrase that makes the point would refer to the work of making the body transparent, using it as a kind of tool that is seen through as it guides people to stay together in social interaction.

In examining the production of invisibility as a routine task in non-emotional social interaction, we must always struggle with the artificial limitations created by our retrospective and indifferent perspective as observers. When we are talking with someone, we move constantly *through* our utterances. What we say does not exactly disappear after we say it; more accurately it fades away, gets tucked into the background, where it may persist, for moments or years, to be drawn upon as a reference. As we express ourselves interactively with others, we *push off from* our expressions, displacing them from our focal attentions even as we utter or gesture them into being. But when we analyze talk, we use devices that freeze and frame talk, devices like tapes and transcriptions that give speech an artificially obdurate, eternally present character. We create false invisibilities, typing spaces between letters and words that no one heard; and more unfortunately still, we create false visibilities that elide the essence of the interaction focus. In order to create a record of what was said and how it was said, we do things like underlining what was subtly emphasized by the participants, we put type into boldface to distinguish speech from gesture even though the relationship of the two was seamless during expression, and we insert icons for facial expressions that were never witnessed by the person whose face we try to represent. Much of the research work necessary to examine talk, or other forms of mutually responsive expression, is a struggle to create a reliable visible record of what transpired. But our analytical efforts to objectify and preserve expressions run precisely contrary to speakers' concerns to erase their expressions as they emerge. It is easy to forget the irony in this analytical process. But if we do, we lose sight of the constant effort by participants to create transparent expressions as they act collaboratively. The very essence of a conversation, its spirit, resides in just those places that our data cannot reach.

The effort is, however, not hopeless. If we persist we can discover that the production of invisibility, far from being an esoteric matter solely of interest to metaphysicians, is at the very heart of everyday social life. The invisibility of speech is brought into being through numerous carefully attended and meticulously executed processes.

In the case of Rachel's metamorphosis from crying into speech, her utterances remain audible but they become covered over and hidden in new ways. Here are but four.

1. *Sequence.* As she whines Rachel's utterances stand out as a repeated protest that is timed to be simultaneous rather than responsive

to the teacher's speech and instructive gestures. In speech, the child's utterances become collaboratively responsive as they emerge sequential to her teacher's spoken questions ("Which one is next?"). Ironically, when the child's utterances take the form of sequential questions ("This one?"), the teacher's pause for silent listening does not highlight the child's body, relative to what has gone before. On the contrary, the sequential positioning of the child's talk effaces the child's body by throwing attention back to the teacher even as each spoken phrase emerges. The question form spurs the sequential progress of the interaction, which in turn rapidly effaces the emergent body of each.

2. *Three-dimensionality.* As the child ceases whining, she gives up the resonant isolation of her own body. She opens her mouth to speak, letting sound out and reducing its echoing reverberations within.

3. *Gaze.* During whining, the child's gaze was often ahead, away from the teacher and the puzzle; and the teacher's gaze turned at times from the puzzle work to the child. During speech, the gazes of both turn away from either of the two bodies and toward the blocks that they are jointly moving into place.

4. *Mutual gifts of the instrumental body.* As the child and her teacher enter conversation, each lends the other her body. Their conversation emerges as a series of reciprocated gifts of the body of each to manifest the other's mind. This occurs as each uses her own speech and her manual movements of the puzzle's blocks to anticipate, to finish, and to confirm what is taken to be the other's intentions. Who is controlling whom, which body is the originator and which the agent of completion of the other's intentions, becomes blurred, indistinct, in a phrase, naturally invisible.

Whining, then, appears to be a way of stubbornly resisting the invitation in social interaction to ambiguate the relationship of identities. In whining, the child holds on to her body as a way of expressing her isolation from interaction.

It is, in a way, obvious that emotions are ways that people make visible to themselves and others what is otherwise hidden. There is an embodied practice of revelation in emotions: blushes, laughs, cryings, and anger emerge on faces and through coverings that usually hide visceral substrata. The doing of emotions is a process of breaking bodily boundaries, of tears spilling out, rage burning up, and as laughter bursts out, the emphatic involvement of guts as a designated source of the utterance.

Even as emotional expressions in social interaction make the invisible visible by removing covers that are routinely maintained, they retain a deeper layer of disguise. In my search of a range of shame experiences for the constant elements in the phenomenon, I found, as many analysts of shame had found before, that the theme of revelation was prominent. But what is revealed is a mystery. What does it mean that someone is ashamed of an ugly foot? Why would anyone be ashamed of that? What does such a shame imply? Certainly something more than a reluctance to take off shoes and socks in public. Similarly, when investigating the range of forms and situational expressions of crying, I found that crying is always a presentation of a mystery. When a president cries, his or her country will notice; but not all commentators will take for granted that something profound has been revealed. It is not easy to predict whether the crying will be taken to mean admirable sensitivity, deplorable weakness, or a shallow and manipulative performance. Who and what is being cried for are likely to stir some controversy.

In short, a variety of emotions in social life emerge in responsive recognition of the invisible dimensions that ground routine social interaction. Anger, as experienced by the enraged driver, at once acknowledges and protests the subtly invasive dependence of self on other. Other drivers provoke one's rage by frustrating the fantasy of symmetrical intersubjectivity, the fantasy that others who are ahead of oneself on the road will perceive one's intentions from one's own moving standpoint. Laughter, as developed by the fun house visitor, addresses the myth of an intersubjective, taken-for-granted belief in shared understanding, a myth without which social action would be impossible. But far from exploding the myth, laughter is reassuring just because it can play with the invisible foundations of personal identity. In shame, a person immediately launches a search that is frantic just because the grounding that is sought, a grounding of self in community, is not to be found in any visible place. For adults, crying most commonly arises either as silent tears that honor what is too sacred to capture in the conventionalized expressions of language, or as a choking down of speech. In either case, crying is not so much a defect of speech as it is formal evidence of what, in one's relations with others, speech cannot congeal.

2. The Dualistic Narrative Structure of Socially Situated Emotions

People work their way through a day's socially situated interactions as if stopping briefly on the separate stones that mark a path. They always know that what happens in each particular scene makes up only one of an infinite series of scenes, and that what transpires in a given time and place makes up only the most obviously divisible segments in their ongoing lives. But this transcendent perspective is always put somewhat in the background of awareness as people attend to the details of situated interaction. If sociologists are only willing to address the little maneuvers that people launch when they land on each stepping stone, the pictures of personal life that the discipline will produce may be interesting and insightful, but on the whole, they risk becoming a series of, at best, animated comic strip images of personal life.

The narrative dimensions of people's lives are easily neglected when socially situated interaction is analyzed. In the study of emotions, sociological research that neglects people's transsituational concerns often becomes a sterile examination of how people represent their emotions, express their dispositions and indicate what they are feeling. Such studies fail to address the origins of what is distinctive in emotional experience. This failure can be remedied if we examine not only what people are trying to do within the boundaries of given situations, but also how people shape their doings in each given situation to have meaning as they move among situations. We will then see that emotions are not only expressions that people emit with an eye to how they will be taken up and responded to by the others who are currently before them; they are also a double commentary on social interaction. Through their emotions, people comment, to themselves if not to others, on what the interaction that is occurring says about themselves in a given scene, and they also comment on the overall stories that they are constructing as they shape a path through life.

The study of emotions is an especially useful way to make visible the twofold narrative project that people are always pursuing in social life. This dualistic narrative task exists before emotional experiences begin to run their course. The twofold sense-making project *emerges* in emotional moments, not in an existential sense but in the sensual form of metamorphosis: the subject's ongoing narrative work becomes visible to self, to other, and to the analyst, as a distinctive incorporation of conduct.

Thus when a shopper becomes angry at another shopper who seems to cut the queue at the supermarket checkout counter, a usually invisible double storytelling springs toward the surface. When the checkout line goes smoothly, each shopper implicitly understands and participates in what he or she treats as a well-known collective project. People place themselves visibly "on line." Numerous mutual adjustments are made without averring to them, such as when someone volunteers to put a dividing bar in front of or behind his or her items, altruistically organizing the relationship between the product representations of his or her and another shopper's identities. Then a familiar sequence of interaction is engaged with the register clerk. All of this is recognizable as checking out, the performance of a little script, the unremarkable retelling of a little story that, while it is being enacted, is treated by all as having been known by all before each episode of dramatization. We may think of this strip of action as a distinguishable situational project or narrative. These are things that people do such that everyone can understand them to be checking out of the market.

But that is not the only story being constructed and told. A shopper may be comparing what he or she buys to what others are buying, and so getting some evidence of where he or she fits into the overall social order. Clothing and comportment are often read in similar ways. Whether things are going smoothly or not on a particular day is also commonly being registered. If the queue is seen as moving slow or fast, that appreciation grasps how the situation-bounded interaction of checking out is fitting into the ongoing course of one's day. The moments spent in a slow checkout line may carry a warning of trouble down the road, that other situations will not be entered on time. A fast line may carry the promise of a smooth connection among the various sets of others to be encountered later on; one generalizes easily; life seems "a breeze."

A sense that one is in a slow- or a fast-moving line is already an emotional sense, although usually one so minimal as to go barely noticed. But the emotionality of the sense, slow or fast, is in any case due to the problematic relationship between what is happening here and now in one's interaction with others on the scene and the implications in the current scene for one's relations to others in other times and places. It takes little more than being cut off by someone who is seen to be jumping the queue to spring the relationship between situational and transcendent meanings into a vividly explicit configuration. The offended party is likely then to snap to thoughts that transcend the current scene, for example to generalize about the nature of the rude party, to focus on worries about being late for some engagement, or, through reaching back days or years in memory, to associate the scene with other troublesome people and events that have been suffered.

Being cut off on queue or on the highway regularly gives rise to similar emotions. Why both cutoffs should have the same effect is not immediately obvious. But what they share is a communistic structure for interaction. The provocative character of this structure is worth some consideration because it highlights the existential nature of the narrative projects that fuel emotions in general.

Interactionally, the activities of driving on the highway and moving through a market checkout line are quite different in the access that others have to one's expressed intentions. Drivers must work hard to have their intentions recognized by drivers in front of them. They are often frustrated when their intentions, as implied in the course of their car's progress on the road, are ignored by cars ahead that do not move aside or that rudely cut in. In contrast, shoppers on queue are highly sensitive to the visibility of their merest expression. Even the regulation of their vision will be accountable. Hence the frequent use of magazines to provide a safe haven for one's gaze.

Thus it is not a common interaction structure that gives such ready rise to anger in both locations. It is, instead, the cultural communism that they share. By this I mean that no externally relevant status is routinely useful in the distribution of rights on the road or on queue. All differences in income, prestige, social power, and respectability are washed out on these quintessentially egalitarian turfs. Wealth, as indicated by cars or by clothes, surely provides no advantage. Commonly, it is only existential need and difference, such as may be represented by an ambulance siren or by a pleading of some universally recognizable and status-impartial difference (such as carrying a single item when approaching a queue of shoppers with full carts), that can justify a request for a privileged passage through the masses. Cars empower people with fantastic abilities to zip through space even as they strip people of any status advantages they may enjoy elsewhere. For people on the market queue and for drivers on the highway, only universal norms, like "first come first served," and universally available talents, like the shrewdness of assessing other customers and finding the quickest checkout line, or the cunning to develop reliable shortcuts around traffic, should determine one's relative position.

What is astonishing about these two everyday scenes is how quickly and effortlessly minor changes in one's position in a situation's interaction can be experienced as carrying the most general significance for one's overall life. Suddenly the shopper or the driver experiences a rude person as making a general statement about his or her identity, a statement on the order of: you are a fool, a nobody, someone who deserves no respect, who need not even be treated as existing. It is the nakedness of personal identity in these scenes that makes emotions so raw. It seems that capitalism and democracy have effectively created everyday public scenes in which personal status is essentially reduced to one's position in time and space. The result is the routine production of radical passions, but on a wholly individualized, micro scale.[21]

By stripping people of their externally significant status identities, cars and queues leave drivers and shoppers starkly facing the meaning of their lives vis-à-vis others who, confronted as strangers, they address as relatively blank templates. On queue and on the road, what is experienced as situational disrespect mushrooms without the buffers of extraneous status layers, often encountering no cultural resistance at all, with the result of suddenly taking on transcendent dimensions.[22]

It is facile to explain such outbursts as revealing deep-seated hostilities, universal aggressive drives, or angry forces that are built into people by some presumed character of their culture, for example by its competitive nature. Often the immediately preceding mood was a pleasant reverie, taking the form perhaps of a memory about a family celebration, a humming commentary on the unproblematic character of life, or a dwelling on the promise held in a passenger's thighs. Insofar as road rage indicates something negative as preceding and giving rise to anger, it points to the fact that people's lives do not make sense unless they give sense to them. We cannot stop making sense in two senses. We cannot help but construct a narrative understanding of what is happening within the situational horizons of the immediate interaction field ("I'm getting screwed by that dumb jerk"). And, condemned to an awareness that even when we are standing still, we are on the road to somewhere, we cannot escape telling ourselves a story about the fateful implications of what is transpiring here and now.[23]

All socially situated emotions are dualistic narrative projects. The transsituational message of anger usually is accessible only through autobiography or interview. But the transcendent meaning of laughter is sometimes visible in the sequential way it is done. In the study of families and funny mirrors, for example, we saw that parents often segue from a first to a second form of laughter. With the first, they might respond to a child's call to recognize a funny image in the mirror, or they might call a child to see the reflected image that the adult has designed. With a second form of laughter, which differs in the way it is corporeally delivered and in the way it alters the adult's availability for interaction responsiveness, the adult laughs about the experience of laughing with the child.

When, for example, one walks up to a distorting mirror with a young child, it is often a tricky matter to create an interaction that will display that a forty-year-old, six-foot adult, and five-year-old, three-foot child, are seeing and laughing about the same thing. And indeed, often such pairs do not manage to laugh together. Sometimes the child laughs wildly and the parent responds by restraining the child. Sometimes the parent uses a laugh to point out something funny in the mirror, and the child looks on unperturbed, or becomes afraid

and begins to cry. The achievement of joint laughter under these constraints nicely demonstrates the resolution of the dilemma of intersubjectivity. A sense of the difficulty of meeting that challenge can give
rise to a second wave of laughter in which the adult celebrates the
achievement of joint laughter, an achievement that appears as proof
that a common spirituality underlies family relations.

If the family is anything as a social unit with moral integrity and
substantive coherence, it must be a place where people have an especially intimate knowledge of you, a knowledge that offsets what people
outside think they know about you. When the trials of the distorting
mirrors go well for a family group, the laughter that emerges carries
the reassuring implication that the family contains a force capable of
correcting all the funny, distorted appearances that family members
may have when their identities are reflected in outsiders' eyes. As the
multigenerational family passes before fun house mirrors and laughs
while strangers look on impassively from the sidelines, it tells an ancient story about the family as hearth, as a place that warms by giving
off a light that at once makes faces visible to intimates in the inner
circle while creating shadows for those who wait just outside.

The specification of the transcendent meanings of emotions is made
problematic for observer-analysts, not just because what emotions address is something that is routinely invisible in social life, but also because people from an early age understand that emotional expressions
will be read for transcendent meanings, and they very quickly work
at controlling those readings in the situations in which they appear.
Here we may recall, from the materials that were examined in chapter
3, the crying of Little League baseball players.

In an examination of videotape showing the emergence of emotional expressions, I described eight-year-old batters who, anticipating
that initial cries would soon flower, invoked a situational, moral justification (a bad call by the umpire, a nasty remark by the catcher) or
a short-term physical problem (incapacity from a fall earlier on) for
their reaction. Here shame, with its generalizing implications about
essential incompetence, provokes the beginnings of crying (apparent
in trembling and compressed face), but before crying ripens, indignant
anger is invoked to give the emotional provocation a kind of middle-
range meaning.[24] Then when crying emerges more fully, the child will
have given it the gloss of meaning something more and something less
than it otherwise would. Complaining to coach or parent about an
unfair judgment or remark, the child invokes a situational frame for his
crying, one that goes just slightly beyond the game-defined situational
meaning of striking out. The complaint strategically invites a shift of

attention to the offending other and invites sympathy for some morally defensible harm, ethical or physical, that one has suffered.

Such emotional courses demonstrate the folk understanding of the theme of metamorphosis. Everyone knows that emotions tell a transcendent story of some kind, indicating something that is typically hidden about one's identity. Thus when one is aware that others are observing the flowering of one's emotions, one is likely to take care to shape the message about the typically invisible aspects of one's identity that will become visible. For the young baseball players, as shame sets off crying, the disturbance first is masked with some other emotion, offering observers the filters of anger or pain for understanding the tearful, sobbing course of crying that will emerge.

Emotions in everyday life are minidramas of change of state, often developing as a series of transformations of the body of conduct. As the embodiment of their conduct changes, people often struggle to provide a visible script, a cultural explanation that will make sense of what observers will see. Here we may recall how the murderer under police interrogation works on controlling the transcendent meaning of his crying as it emerges.

James Martin's crying appears when he realizes that his lines of defense are collapsing. In both cases, he cries for a lost self, seeking and to some extent getting demonstrations of sympathy from his interrogators. Martin's second crying stint is particularly useful for understanding how emotional expression makes visible a narrative theme that more often invisibly underlies his social life.

On this occasion, Martin indicates that his crying responds to his sense of a final break in his relationship with his family. As Martin sobs, an interrogator attempts to reassure him that his family (which turned him in) will become supportive of him again, and Martin repeatedly rejects this possibility, asserting that the breach is permanent. Through a direct question, Martin, who earlier confessed to one murder, has just been put on notice that the police know of a second murder. His crying, following this turn in the interrogation, might be regarded as growing from his anticipating another major breakdown in his posture of innocence. He now introduces the theme of his break from his family, in the process simultaneously provoking himself to cry and offering the alternative interpretation that what is disturbing him is the irrevocable destruction of his primordial family relations.

The toddler in preschool covers the transformation out of crying with a cough. The young boys playing baseball rush to transform shame into anger before it emerges as crying. The murder suspect in the police station transforms the meaning of crying from an indication that he has more to confess to a lament over the loss of family relations. Instead of challenging the interpretation of crying as a revealing moment, they work rapidly and with varying degrees of subtlety on the social understanding of what is revealed. Their attempt reflects a taken-for-granted assumption that crying will be understood as a manifestation of some abiding, usually masked theme in personal identities that reaches far beyond the situation in which they are crying.

In my attempt in chapter 4 to define what crying is, I argued that a comprehensive analysis requires a dualistic and dialectical understanding of crying's projects. A double hermeneutics is required to appreciate the narrative meanings of each of the four emotions taken up in this volume. It is striking that the analysis of emotions has systematically ignored one of the two forms that all the common emotions take. Crying is readily recognized as a response to the suffering of loss, but its form as a posture of gratitude for an awe-inspiring gift has been ignored or denied. Shame is treated endlessly in popular culture, popular psychology, and most of social psychology as something essentially negative that should be overcome, while the Nietzschean understanding that shame has a precious, indispensable role in life struggles to be heard. Hot anger is readily understood as the result of some deprivation or indignity, but the attractions of a cold resolve to be mean are ignored even though the ways of being mean virtually scream that they are inspired by spiritual commitments to nothing more or less valuable than giving life inspiring meaning. Laughter is often analyzed as something that is more or less subtly negative, an expression that overcomes gaps in relations with others and something done at someone else's expense. It has been much more difficult to appreciate how laughter works like an everyday Durkheimian "effervescence," celebrating bonds that are limitless and invulnerable to situational challenges, for example, when laughter serves as a vehicle for religious bliss.[25]

Social-psychological theory has generally seen only one of the two dualistic forms of emotions. It is not coincidental, I think, that the one side of each emotion that social psychology has been prepared to recognize is the negative side, the form of shame, laughter, anger, and crying that responds to something that is, respectively, unfortunate, pathetic, demeaning, or sad. But the implications for understanding contemporary culture of a one-sided perspective on emotions, the widespread self-mistrust and self-disgust that such a perspective may represent, is a task for another writing. Here I would be content to convince the reader that if we do not recognize the positive forms of emotions, we arbitrarily represent as univocal a human reality that is dualistic.

Emotions require an analysis that recognizes their dialectical dynamics as well as their dualistic cultural forms. In striking out angrily at another, one also bonds with the other.[26] Indeed, at the extreme, angry action seeks a bond that will be eternally fateful for aggressor as well as for victim. At the same time, angry aggression toward another is also a fight directed against oneself. In anger, people struggle against admitting something terrible about the self, often torturing themselves beyond what their would-be victim will in fact suffer. Anger is in the first instance self-martyring.[27]

And sad crying has positive implications by going beyond loss as a representation of loss. It will be tempting for some readers to regard such statements as a playful use of words that offers nothing more than the charm of paradox. But close attention to the facts of emotional experience grounds the point. The experience of trauma can be documented independent of evidence of crying, and thus the role of crying in subsequently going beyond trauma can be established. We can observe fallen toddlers in playgrounds, searching for eye contact with a parent before allowing a bout of crying to issue forth. Sad, self-pitying, or mournful crying, by putting suffering into a conventional social form, expresses a faith that culture can recognize and contain what had been experienced as horrible, just because it had seemed beyond anyone's reach.

Inversely with joyful crying. We can identify some instances of crying as joyful because they respond to what are regarded as positively transcendent events, moments that are precious, blessed, incalculably valuable. But the situational doings of such cryings are self-denigrating. If sad cryings are often loud, noisy projections of self, when people cry joyfully they almost always work to cry silently. It is common for joyful criers to experience shame when others detect their crying. They brush tears aside discreetly; they put hands over mouths to avoid intruding into a scene whose sacred character they fear they will pollute; and they may blush when they see others detecting their crying. The self is made humble; the body is treated as potentially contaminating something in the world that is pure. In joyful crying, something regarded as positively transcendent is recognized by a spontaneous dramatization of the self as small and insignificant.

The dialectical messages of crying point to a second answer that the study of emotions provides for the riddle of the invisibility that underlies what is visible in social life. There is an obscured narrative practice in everyday social interaction. However apparently immersed they may be in the interaction at hand, people never completely lose awareness that their lives transcend the current situation. But the individual's orientation to the transcendent meanings of situated interaction does not typically take the form of thoughts. The possibility of thought is offset by the effort to remain responsively engaged in the scene.

Instead of thinking about transcendent significance, the person registers the implications of the action in progress in a sensual appreciation. He or she has a comfortable or awkward sense of self, appreciates the strangeness or familiarity of the scene, has a feeling about how the action is going. One commonly *feels* situations. One feels that things are going fast or slow; that one's actions are difficult or easy; that the matter at hand is simple or densely complex; that what is being done with someone else is just like previous instances and unfolding as expected or is unprecedented and full of surprises; that what one is doing here and now is making one more separate from, or more connected to, other relationships; that the situation requires only habitual patterns of conduct, or calls for reaches into novel regions of the self. . . . These senses and feelings might be termed latent or incipient emotions.

Emotions do not *introduce* feelings and themes of transcendence into social action, they highlight them. Better, emotions are metamorphoses of themes of transcendence. Emotions give dramatically new and emphatically visible forms to the narrative themes that had been less visibly present in social life. The relationship between socially situated emotions and their less visible origins can be traced, but, because emotions are revelations through processes of transformation, they can be traced only with great difficulty. In a way, the understanding that emotions are in tension with reason, self-reflection, or thought exactly misrepresents what emotions are. Emotions are ways of turning back on the self, ways of reflexively amplifying and giving added resonance to the transcendent meanings of situated action.

3. Emotional Metamorphoses: Background and Foreground in the Embodiment of Conduct

The most distinctive aspect of emotional experience is its three-dimensional character. Perhaps because this point is so obvious, it has been thoroughly ignored in sociological and psychological research. When we begin to look at just how emotions are three-dimensional forms of experience and conduct, a world of phenomena, at once familiar and bizarre, opens up.

In many experiences of shame, others' eyes pierce through one's defenses, and an intolerable soullike feeling wells up from some indefinite source within. Similarly with anger, the catalyst is often the recognition of having been pierced by an insult, a recognition that may be met, instantly or after a period of simmering, with an explosive urge that leaps up and seeks to strike out with a penetrating blow, a cutting remark or a symbolic thrust that would break through the offender's defenses.

Consider also the three-dimensionality of humorous experiences. When comics cause audiences to laugh, they exercise a power to penetrate that is vivid, if surrealistic to describe. One person, standing before a large mass, inflects a gesture or drops a phrase, and the message ramifies through the audience, seemingly grasping listeners' backbones and shaking them fiercely from inside. The comic can easily understand him- or herself to be making a sexual conquest of the masses he or she entertains. At times the comic virtually rapes the audience, making them tremble in accordance with his or her whim, even against their manifestly resisting will ("no, stop, I can't take it!").[28]

Crying often involves collapsing feelings and unusually noisy projections. When crying registers a loss, the loss may be felt as a hollowness within. An internal floor to the self has been removed; feelings cycle downward even as one shouts out, seemingly in an attempt to reach infinity, projecting the same measureless quality that is present in the hopeless nature of the loss. When crying comes from joy, three-dimensional metaphors mix unproblematically in experience. Eyes well up and a single tear may emerge. One becomes overwhelmed in the spatial structure of the experience, which features chills shooting up the spine as one witnesses the spectacle that is unfolding up ahead.

Psychological analysis has long drawn on three-dimensional *ideas* to understand emotions. What could be more three-dimensional than the sexual metaphor? But it is one thing for the analyst to understand people's emotions by reference to internal mechanisms and images of sexual intercourse, and another to hone analysis to the evolving three-dimensional metaphors that describe emotional experience. Even when the target of analysis is three-dimensional ("sub"-conscious and "internal" drives), the facts of lived experience are treated in a two-dimensional, flat manner. Once they are glossed or coded into theoretical categories, the focus quickly turns to symbolic matters, the classic example being the analysis of dreams as an analysis of textual contents projected onto a screen. *Images* in dreams are examined for their association to *images* of places, people, and acts. Whether in the form of academic experimental psychology or depth-psychological analysis,

the language of understanding is far from sensual and richly phenomenological because analysis ignores *how the person bodily lives* the matters being analyzed. Nothing is more disappointing then reading Freud
on sex in hopes of an erotic experience. What we get are indicators
of forces that are not themselves observed, or readings of the mind as
texts produced by an author. If there is anything that distinguishes
emotional experience it is precisely a poetic resonance that the person
at once creates and witnesses. One would be hard pressed to find any
naturalistic poetry in academic or clinical psychological analysis.

In sociology as well, the three-dimensionality of emotions has been
elusive. Anyone who briefly glances at the last decade's literature of
social theory and interactionist sociology will see volumes of works
on "the body." But like the writings of both depth and academic psychology, this sociological work is overwhelmingly two-dimensional
and rationalistic. The focus is either on the body as represented and
read in culture (in ads, in movies and novels, in the content of talk
about the body, or more generally, in "discourse"), or the body as
manipulated to give off indications about the self or about one's place
in an emerging sequence of collaborative action. The body so regarded
is either a mannequin, a billboard, a neon sign, a puppet, or some
kind of symbolic text. The person is not seen as embodying a moving
comprehension of various depths and regions of self.

For sociology, the body tends to be surface, something read off by
others from outside. For psychology, the body tends to be a container
of needs and drives whose existence is posited as residing deep inside.
Equally missing from the major traditions of social and psychological
analyses is an examination of the travels that emotions make through
the various regional depths of the body.

Something else about the three-dimensionality of the body is even
more radically missing from traditional and contemporary social psychology. What we are looking for is not only a matter of feelings perk-
ing up, dying down, and spreading around territories and through levels within, it is also a matter of an interpenetration or an intertwining
with what social and psychological analysis usually regards as existing
outside the body. Simply addressing the tickling feeling of humor
within does not capture the special magic of emotions; we also must
grasp the invisible lines between the comic and the crowd he or she
moves. If we see a driver angrily responding to being cut off, we will
beg key questions about the causation of his or her anger if we refer
to him or her as "defining" and "perceiving" events that are occurring
out there. The metaphor of rational, thoughtlike action is misleading,
and it puts off the challenge of understanding the visceral nature of

the experience. What we need to understand is how a driver could naturally, unproblematically have felt that he or she existed corporeally out there, thirty feet beyond the front end of the car, such that he or she really was cut off.

Both the movements of feelings through the body and the interpenetration of the body and its landscape are generally invisible to psychological and sociological analysis. What is missing is an understanding of emotions as metamorphoses. As emotions ebb and flow in experience, the person is absorbed into and withdraws from given regions and features of the world. What he or she draws on as the vehicle for conduct changes. The one constancy in the metamorphoses that distinguish different emotions is a sensual turning of one's attention to regions of the body that, outside of one's own direct awareness, had been employed to construct behavior. The invisibility that creates all that is visible in social life is the three-dimensional body, and in emotional experience one turns, sensually rather than via thought, toward background corporeal foundations of the self.

Falling and Being Engulfed

In the genesis of the emotions that we have been examining, an experience of falling is a common event.[29] In the Bible "the fall" is a source of shame. But if all cultures know of falls that lead to shame, they also know of falls that are occasions for slapstick humor. There are also falls that lead to tears. Children keep this culture alive, using it to seek an embrace that will restore tranquility. And when falls are understood to be the consequence of being pushed, they may provoke anger and a counterattack.

After the experience of a fall, shame, anger, laughter, and crying often compete as directions of metamorphosis. It is not uncommon for a man to laugh as insults are delivered in playful rounds of exchange, and then to find himself, without hitch or impediment, transforming from laughter to anger. Female interviewees report that their crying often emerges as a transformation of an anger that they dare not express.[30] In observational field notes written several years ago, I described a toddler who, seated at the dinner table at a friend's house in anticipation of his first sleepover, first launched a fit of laughter that responded to a surprising remark. His laughter evolved into in a process of wildly erupting expressions, and then segued without hitch into a bout of seemingly boundless crying. Shame flirts around many of these transformations, providing the motivation to flee into shifting emotional forms and hues.

Why does one person laugh at a fall, another cry, another become stunned in shame, and another search paranoically for someone who pushed? We wish to know how personal biography and cultural context are reflected in the characteristic emotional guise in which people rise from falls. In the current studies I can only take up a less ambitious question, but one that is in any case a necessary preliminary. Why should the experience of fall be so common in the etiology of socially situated emotions? Clearly, falls do not necessarily lead to a particular emotion, but we might ask what physical and metaphoric falls have in common that makes them so often and so diversely emotionally provocative.

On the common route to each of the four everyday emotions examined in this volume, one falls out of a taken-for-granted incorporation of the landscape. The angry driver need not project him- or herself out into the highway in order to feel cut off by another driver. He or she was already out there, having extended him- or herself smoothly through foot pedals and steering wheel into a distal figure moving at some point ahead on the road. From out there, the driver adjusts proximate driving motions. If there is something surreal in this imagery, the fantastic nature of the scene is natural and essential to the mundane practice of driving through it. That we regard it as surreal is a result of presumptions about divisions between subject and object in what we conventionally refer to as visible reality when we, as analysts reviewing the events from a position outside of them, re-present the experience in our conventions of discourse. What makes the corporeal foundations of emotions invisible is our taken-for-granted mundane reasoning about what is real, visible, and conventionally obvious.[31]

Michael Polanyi's ideas about the relationship between what is proximate and what is distal in the organization of action give us another important clue to the process in which emotions arise.[32] Both the proximate and the distal are implicit or outside of direct awareness in personal conduct. We focus *from* our hands on the wheel and feet on the pedals *to* distant places up ahead and to the rear as we drive, often surprising ourselves as we come to a heightened awareness of cars approaching from the rear because we only then realize that we had been attending to our rearward projections and relationships all along. We manipulate the pedals and the steering wheel without a direct awareness of doing so. We don't routinely feel the point at which our hands and feet meet the car; instead we feel our bodies extended through the car to where the tires meet the road, and to the emerging relationships we are developing with other car-extended people. When we are cut off, our attention snaps in two directions, to the driver up ahead who has truncated our direction of travel, and to the point at which our hands and feet meet the car. As we feel amputated by something that happens many feet up ahead, we also feel the steering wheel with an awareness of our tightly gripping response. Indeed, it is the necessity to attend to the meeting of our feet and the pedals that often generates the sense of being cut off in the first place. The mere necessity of lifting one's foot slightly to reduce pressure on the gas pedal is sometimes enough to trigger a sense that one's car-body has been being cut off up ahead.

When a fall leads to an emotional response, there will have been not only a sudden withdrawal from one's incorporation of the landscape, there will also have been a turn of attention to a region of the body that had been tacitly employed to maintain routine conduct. This is what we saw happening again and again in the fun house. An image of oneself out there on the mirror throws off one's taken-for-granted sense of how one appears to the world. This "fall" may be taken as an occasion for a brief laugh, or it might be taken as the cause of an embarrassing moment, as may occur when one normalizes the mirror in order to correct a problem with personal appearance, for example that one's hair is out of place. In either case, a heightened self-consciousness gives rise to the emotion.

The sensual self-consciousness that arises with emotions was illustrated nicely with the example of Maman's two-stage laughter. After first "doing" laughter in order to call her son and husband to appreciate a humorous image of herself in the mirror, the woman found herself "done by" the spirits she had raised and forced to run off from the scene, almost crashing into her son as she made a hasty exit. What did her in was the emergent problem of keeping her body in the background of social awareness in order to point out what was laughable in the mirrors. In order to keep a collective experience developing with husband and son, Maman had to indicate to them what was provoking her laughter, but each designating movement would itself be reflected bizarrely by the mirror, bringing unexpected regions of her background body into focal attentions. Each attempt to use part of her body as an unseen device to point attention to another reflected part would itself be reflected, becoming unintentionally alive, causing new ridiculous appearances and compelling her to try to, in effect, chase her tail, a problem that was itself hilarious. Unable to divide her body into a tacitly used background region from which she would designate matters for attention on the foreground, Maman had become practically incompetent for interaction. As she began to laugh, Maman's gaze metamorphosed from transparency to a witnessable status: how she was regarding the mirror to see its humorous contents itself became visible.[33] With her seeing now visible, she could not practically maintain its use to see what was in the mirror.

We saw the reverse process occurring as Rachel, the toddler in preschool, moved from whining to emotionally unblemished speech. Entailed in the child's transition out of emotion was a process of making her body a transparent device for the creation of a collective body of action with her teacher. Through whining, she had emphatically marked her respiration, adding a crying sound to almost all of her exhales. So consistent was Rachel's practice that her teacher, who was attempting to wean her from whining, could appreciate a dramatic moment of decision building up during each silent inhale. The return of the whine on each exhale was understandable as another act of refusing to become involved in collaborative work.[34]

When Rachel's whining disappeared, so did her respiration. As she began talking with her teacher and acting out her teacher's intentions by manually moving puzzle pieces, and as her teacher guided and completed the child's movements with her own comments and hands, the line between intending and executing body became blurred. Who was doing the puzzle work became ambiguous, and the two entered emotionally muted, mundane social interaction. The emergent collaborative body of puzzle-solving activity eclipsed the visibility of the child's body. As the three-dimensionality of her own body became invisible in the interaction, her crying subsided.

In the case of James Martin's crying under police interrogation, we saw the professional manipulation of the issue we are examining. The police provoked Martin to cry and to confess by pushing him to fall out of his tacit practice of backing his statements with gestures and rocking motions of verisimilitude. Interrupting and confusing his tacit bodily grounding of his overtly spoken defense, the police shook him out of the exculpating lines that he had been maintaining. When Martin's crying emerged, his crying was a natural symbolic re-presentation of a self that had just been broken up in an eminently practical manner. His ability to participate unemotionally in his defense depended on maintaining an invisible bodily grounding for his talk.

Just before suspects break down, police interrogators often issue commands such as "look me in the eyes when you say that!" Suspects immediately become responsible for the meaning of their gaze. They are pushed toward a self-conscious awareness that their vision is being judged for its incriminating implications. In effect, the police press the test of the suspect's spoken posture of innocence more deeply into the suspect's body. At the same time, police interrogators also manipulate the suspect's lived landscape in order to throw him or her into the critical movements of self-doubt that produce confessions. The interrogation room is managed as a prison room, and, at key moments, the interrogators move physically in on suspects, limiting the boundaries of their experienced landscape.[35] The suspect's fall out of his or her defensive line is thus achieved by undermining his or her taken-for-granted grasp of the bodily background and the landscape of his or her expressions.

Something similar often happens on the route to joyful crying. A sunset or an eclipse creates a moving landscape on an infinitely embracing scale. Patriotic, wedding, or child recital music swells up and surrounds members of the audience. Sexual interaction reaches a moment of total ecstatic embrace. The experience is one of an extraordinary visibility of self, of community, and of nature. The individual is swept into joyful tears in a kind of epiphany in which something sacred, something awesome and routinely invisible has suddenly and briefly been fully revealed.

In the metamorphosis into everyday emotions, a new light is thrown in two directions and invisibility recedes on one or both of two horizons. Regions of the body that had been employed outside of self-conscious awareness are brought into collective attentions. And regions of the landscape that had been maintained as beyond the need for closely monitored attention are brought into exceptional focus: cars up ahead surprisingly slow down or move into the driver's lane, the Moon passes in front of the Sun, the body of an interrogator suddenly fills the suspect's vision. In emotional experience, the invisible becomes visible in two directions as the landscape rushes in and a region of the body emerges from its shadowy operations.

The Turn to Latent Bodily Resources for Emotional Expression

People become emotional by turning back on the ongoing resourcefulness of their bodies. When creating their emotions, they seize on resources that are immediately at hand. This turn is done so rapidly, and the resulting emotional behavior is itself so striking, that the process of exploiting invisible regions for resources that will make emotions socially visible often is itself invisible to self and other.

But in shame-related behavior, the searching process is relatively visible. Much conduct on the edge of shame is of a self-probing, self-picking, physically self-searching nature. When, for example, children resort to counting on their hands, the strategy ensures that they will not embarrass themselves by recording any wrong answers but it also guarantees that, at some stage of educational challenge, they will not record all of the required answers. Competency is invisible; understood as an essential feature of identity, it can never be established by any situated act or set of acts.[36] But the body, in the form of the fingers of the hands, is right there to rely upon. Thus it is the very tangible, visible, self-confirming reality of the body that gives it appeal as a reassuring source when competency is deemed to be at issue.

In crying and in laughter, the turn to the body for resources for emotional expression is more masked, but the socio-corporeal logic of the turn is equally coherent. Respiration is a universally accessible resource for marking one's break from the world because, in its emotionally unmarked state, respiration is an invisible, constant process of being interlaced with the world.[37] No other ongoing bodily process so clearly and yet so invisibly challenges analytical or folk-cultural perspectives that would distinguish subjects, on the one hand, and their environments, on the other. If we attend to respiration, people appear to be *essentially* intertwined with their environment. We cannot see a point in the respiratory cycle where the person ends and his or her surroundings begin. There is no unambiguous line separating outside air and personal mouth, or dividing air as it enters the respiratory tract and oxygen as it enters the bloodstream. Nor, seen in the other direction, is there any natural marking of the end of one's projection of self into the world through exhaling[38] (a fact, I suspect, that accounts for much of the attraction of smoking).[39]

The existential intertwining of person and world in respiration is universally, if implicitly understood. Thus, to construct expressions of laughter and crying that will respond to falls out of being interactively intertwined with others, people in widely differing cultures readily find in respiration a resource for marking their breaks from the social environment. Back to our riddle! Crying and laughter commonly emerge in social life through making respiration visible, marking that routinely invisible bodily process of intertwining with the world that is itself at the ongoing source of all that is visible in social life.

Note also how laughter and crying turn the body inside out. They not only show respiration, they also, in various forms, mark the guts and reveal the usually transparent fluid medium that makes vision possible. As people laugh, they elaborate on the corporeal social logic they encounter. Thus if initial laughs are polite bleats on the exhale, a subsequent phase of laughter that would demonstrate that now the person "can't take it" may be marked by laughter that invades the inhale phase of the cycle.

Such natural puns will not seem surprising if we appreciate that emotions generally entail a turning of consciousness toward the body to find resources to represent a break from being intertwined in the world. Because that intertwining is naturally invisible yet constantly known in an intimate, carefully monitored and managed way, it requires no new talent to produce the conventionally recognizable emotional expressions of laughter and crying. An American father of twins, visiting the house of funny mirrors examined in chapter 2, makes a simple, effective point by emitting a laugh for one daughter just as he begins to stop attending to her in order to meet the approach of his second daughter with a greeting. His gut-marking laugh extends a bridge to the daughter from whom he breaks even as he moves to extend a bridging gesture to the second child. With his laugh he gives the soon-to-be-abandoned daughter a little corporeally transcending gift that will emotionally patch over his momentary departure.

Corporeal three-dimensionality is, of course, a constant of human existence, but one's awareness of it is not. Indeed, in routine nonemotional (or, in acknowledgment of the continuous nature of the matter, we should perhaps say *relatively* nonemotional) social life, the three-dimensionality that is lived is that of a collective body, a body that is constructed in the ongoing interplay of conduct with others. The different bodies that are attended to and "worked" in emotional and in nonemotional social interaction are not inventions of analysis; they are different ways of three-dimensional being, different vehicles for conduct.

Not unlike the child's whining, adult crying is often meaningful essentially as a negation of speech. Adults, for example, finding themselves unable to go on with a line of talk, may just fall silent between phrases, and nothing more visible than their not-speaking at a particular moment will be instantly understandable as a kind of crying. For the child as for the adult, the provocation to crying comes from an awareness that in order to speak one must abandon contact with one's body and take up a collaborative body for action as the invisible vehicle for expression. But, in the case of a separation from Mommy or the loss of a loved one, the heaviness of one's body will often be the last tie to, the last sign of presence of the absent person. To speak is to take up an especially light body, one created by the symbols, mutually responsive acts and cultural places that form the habitus of speech. The would-be speaker can anticipate that in the lightness of speech, the weight of a relationship to a loved one will be cast off or the weightiness of an inspiring occasion will be belied.

Aesthetics of the Self

The close study of emotions in everyday social life brings out the artful elaboration of the self. People are revealed as exercising a nuanced sensitivity to the aesthetic possibilities in their bodily resources. The toddler, Rachel, is revealed to be adept in employing the classical dramaturgic device of a deus ex machina. Like a god descending to provide the moral that ends a human drama that cannot figure out its own ending, her cough comes to her. It works as a neat transition from whining to speech by providing a nonvolitional explanation for a metamorphosis in the control of her audible utterances. How can she manage to cough at just the precise position in the sequence from whining to nonemotional speech so that it will divert attention from her abandonment of bodily self-regard in crying and allow her to take up speech without appearing to abandon the loyalties that her whining sustained? Anticipating speaking, she raises the tension of self-regard onto the channel for producing talk and senses a tickle in her throat. Here, as always, the sensation of the tickle is the product of a focus on the thin line between doing and being done, between the body as lived from within and as acted upon from without, between the body given three-dimensional awareness through physical interaction and the body as effaced by its use in collective symbolic interaction.

If a child not yet three years old already knows the ancient aesthetic device of the deus ex machina, perhaps we should explore how much of the arts we can understand as a re-presentation of the democratically possessed aesthetic knowledge of everyday life. What else does the study of everyday emotions reveal about the artful talents of everyman? We reviewed finger flipping on the highway at some length. We saw that people know how to cast just the right finger in an aggressive role, how they understand the rules of histrionics that will allow them to send lightning bolts of insults effectively across great distances to pierce the dignity of their enemies, and how the merest of motions can produce the greatest of emotionally explosive effects.

And we saw why the magic of this common street theater works. A well-flipped finger effectively removes the sting of a received insult. For this metamorphosis out of anger and into joyful revenge to work so quickly and well, the finger flipper must be sensitive to the changing perspectives he or she has on his or her flesh. Being cut off, the angry driver is treated as an object and sees him- or herself from without, as a fool treated without decent regard by another. Throwing a finger back via a well-crafted gesture, and seeing the target perceive the motion, the driver, who just before had been in the position of an offended party acted upon as a dumb object, instantly shifts posture and becomes a member of the audience that can passively observe another getting a neat "up yours." As soon as the offended party witnesses his or her lightning bolt entering the other's perception, the sting of insult is removed from his or her bodily experience. The entire drama has the vengeful driver acting first on one and then on the other side of his or her own flesh.

I have insisted on the use of metaphors to describe emotional experiences in full awareness of the risk of hyperbole, because the risk is greater if analysis does not directly offer metaphors as descriptive. Something is happening in crying, for example, that goes beyond any strategic "work" that the person may be "doing" and that is not captured by discriminating the interaction "practices" the person's behavior demonstrates. Some sort of feeling arises. Between oneself and the world there is a new term, a holistically sensed, new texture in the social moment, and one relates to others in and through that emergent and transforming body for experience. A kind of metamorphosis occurs in which the self goes into a new container or takes on a temporary flesh for the passage to an altered state of social being. The subjects of our analysis in the first place own the poetic devices.

Specifically, I have suggested that adult crying often emerges as in a fog. Crying often is a mood that unexpectedly and quickly sweeps into experience, sometimes hovering briefly, sometimes settling down for an extended stay before slipping away. The humidity that can precipitate tears also offers a screen behind which one may find a private reserve for some strategic machinations. A child's crying, in contrast, is often like a fugue, and in two senses of the term. It suggests a musical form that conveys the potential for endless and systematically shaped variations that will always point back to a basic motif. And it suggests a kind of reverie in which one is captured by seemingly unending repetitions of obsessive concerns. When children lapse into silence between respiratory phases, their whining is patterned like thoughts that return uninvited, thoughts that are increasingly unwelcome as they show up again and again to distract one's attentions. But there is no need to read pathos into this form of crying. Unlike obsessive thoughts, whining bothers others more clearly than it signifies weakness in oneself. As an audible obsession, the child's whining is a finely disciplined and powerful tool for social interaction.

How can we explain how people universally can find the aesthetic genius to produce convincing emotional effects? A sociological understanding will always insist on the contributions of the community in making individual conduct possible. The magic is there for anyone to exploit, in the artfully collaborative work that makes individual bodies routinely disappear as people participate in mundane social interaction.

Three Concluding Notes

1. An image of conduct as artful is far more accurate than is the currently popular competing image of people at "work" or caught in the "machinery" of social interaction. Once we start to look closely at behavior in face-to-face interaction, we quickly see that everyone is always producing the most precisely shaped and sensitively placed complements to the actions of others. One minute of social life looks like an affair so burdensome as to give a headache not only to the reader of its transcription but to the subjects of its execution in the first place. That's not life. It is artfulness that keeps such exquisite interaction sensitivity doable. The saving virtue of art is pragmatic; it lies in the weightlessness that grace gives to action.

2. Why do emotions feel irresistible if they are artistic productions? Why are emotions distinguished by their paradoxical, dialectical tensions between carefully crafted doings and spontaneous inspiration? Because they are turns to the body that is always there to be found, always encountered as already there, and always to some degree still in the shadows. The person is indeed "thrown into the world," a phrase that is at base a reference to encounters with the bodily frame of being and with the landscapes people constantly create through their unselfconscious comportment. "I think therefore I am" arrogantly denies the existence of shadowy back regions. But no matter where one's gaze, or one's thinking, is turned, the turns are made by a head that guides and trails behind the outlook of regard, always securely hidden from the subject. Thus there is always something to be found when one falls out of involvement in the world and turns back on the three-dimensional body. There are always depths in which a probing drop into the dark will be met with a responsive resonance.

3. In societies that believe in myths, metamorphosis is a familiar and reassuring motif, a cultural form that helps people understand why things good and bad are as they encounter them. At some point in history, metamorphosis became a Kakfaesque nightmare, not a motif for understanding how people can act in a godly manner but one only useful for trying to grasp how people can become cockroaches, vampires, or werewolves, their bodies snatched by some evil, alien forces. If the culture that believes in divine as well as hellish spirits is dead to us, if we no longer can imagine heroes who are not bionic or folksy types, still a richer moral array of timeless visions remains with us on a micro level, densely masked in the lightning-fast, heavily disguised metamorphoses of our everyday emotions.

NOTES

1. Robert Solomon: "Apart from our passions, do we have any personalities at all?" "It is the web of our emotions that defines human subjectivity" (1983, 131, 133).

2. Biological explanations will not go far here, as biology is constant and all emotional expressions not only vary as to their emergence and staying power, but each type of emotion also varies enormously in its aesthetic dimensions from one expressive occasion to another. As an explanation for conduct, "biology" just restates the current question. The recent popularity of evolutionary and psychobiological ideas of "emotional intelligence" (Goleman 1995), while compatible with the studies that follow, has been relatively indifferent to the central concern here, which is specifying the situational conditions and processual dynamics of different forms of emotional conduct.

3. The six (now seven) emotions that Paul Ekman and Wallace Friesen identified as cross-culturally familiar (happiness, anger, fear, sadness, surprise, disgust, contempt) have been used over the last twenty-five years as stimuli for research subjects in hundreds of social-psychological studies of emotions (Ekman and Friesen 1976, 1986). The field virtually never questions how the facial expressions (of anger, happiness, etc.) are presented and perceived in everyday life. José-Miguel Fernández-Dols (Fernández-Dols and Carroll 1997; Fernández-Dols and Ruiz-Belda 1997) uses photographs of Olympic athletes to show that winners are sometimes crying and losers smiling. Viewers and viewed know that such tears and smiles are meaningful specifically because they show the opposite of what one might expect. It is a significant contribution to have found that all societies develop the same emotional masks, but quite another challenge to explain how they are used in contextualized interaction.

4. Perhaps the one way that academic psychology and social psychology have been loyal to the Freudian tradition is by investing prodigious energy in proliferating and distinguishing concepts. My failure to cite the large quantitative social-psychological research literature on emotions is not for lack of reading or trying. The general problem is that great and arbitrary leaps of inference are required to connect the stuff of emotions in the context and flow of every-

day life and the isolated dimensions addressed either in the psychology lab or through surveying respondents on their emotions.

5. This point has been made effectively by critiques of studies of "representations" of emotions and the body. See Lyon and Barbelet 1994; Lyon 1995; Coulter 1989.

6. Between the traditional misunderstanding in sociology that "science" somehow requires fixed methods and statistics, and much recent argumentation about how "reflexivity" blocks direct access to the subjects of study, social-science academics seem to have forgotten the Darwinian version of the scientist as naturalist, a kind of voyeur of nature who takes journeys, sometimes in familiar media, increasingly by traveling the paths of revelation that new instruments provide, essentially in service of a curiosity to see what has long been out there, or for astronomers, up there, or for microbiologists, in there. It is difficult to look at the history of psychological research on emotions and conclude that the scientific spirit had much to do with setting its basic direction. Freud had a profoundly scientific curiosity but he also was eager to make a living, and that meant that his data on emotions were constrained by what could be elicited in a psychiatry office and were skewed to the problems that would seem worth spending money to talk about in such a place. Emotions in everyday life offered Freud an entertaining way of presenting his ideas (see Freud 1960, 1989), but they were never deemed worthy of the serious effort he put into his analysis of dreams, clinical cases, and even of artists and literary figures. In finding subjects and devising methodology, academic social-psychological research has stuck similarly close to its practitioners' places of business. If the decision as to where and how to study emotions were to be governed primarily by a concern for gathering the highest-quality data on their nature and functioning (i.e., data that are precisely detailed, naturally contextualized, richly varying, and available to all for recurrent and replicable inspection), the therapist's office and the university psychology lab would not be the most obvious places to begin the search.

7. People familiar with Paul Ricoeur's work will know how deeply indebted I am to him (see, especially, Ricoeur 1970). My understanding of the doubly narrative significance of conduct has been shaped through numerous interchanges with, on the one side, the social psychologist Theodore Sarbin (see, e.g., Sarbin 1988) and on the other, the psychoanalyst Melvin Lansky (see, e.g., Lansky 1996).

8. The following studies indicate the variety of work in this tradition: Hochschild 1979; Cahill and Eggleston 1994; Thoits 1996; Clark 1997.

9. For a sense of the empirical focus required for such research, see Bermúdez, Marcel, and Eilan 1995; Bermúdez 1998, chap. 6.

10. Even by Sartre (1948), who gave new life to the Cartesian tradition he purported to fight when he defined emotions as a kind of magical thinking. Operating as comforting self-delusions, emotions perform a "magical comedy of impotence" that misrepresents unsolvable, real problems. Sartre's view sustains the denigrating perspective on emotions that he professed to resist. He missed how, through their emotions, people take an ironically self-reflective turn onto their ongoing being-in-the-world, a process that is frequently creative and pragmatically successful in finding new joys as well as new ways in

troubling circumstances. See Solomon 1981, 220: "the problem is that Sartre has retained *too much* of the traditional view of emotions . . . as irrational, disruptive, passive, and degrading." Concerned to reclaim personal responsibility for emotions, Sartre usefully stressed their intentionality, but in the process he lost access to what is distinctive about emotional experience. By implication, he saw nonemotional life as less mythological, more rational, down-to-earth, grounded, or mundane in a metaphysical sense. For an alternative view that points up the routine magic underlying what people take to be mundane reality, see Pollner 1987; and see Oatley 1990 on irrationality in nonemotional life.

11. Exceptions to the common assumption that these traditions are incompatible include, in philosophy, Paul Ricoeur's phenomenological reconstruction of Freudian analysis (1970); in sociological theory, Pierre Bourdieu's development of Heidegger's and Merleau-Ponty's thought for a critical understanding of symbolic interaction and ethnomethodology (Wacquant 1992, 20–21); and in microsociological analysis, Thomas Scheff and Suzanne Retzinger's psychoanalytically sympathetic effort to locate, not sex but that most sociological emotion, shame, at the motivational heart of numerous patterns of behavior, including aggression, conformity, and suicide (Scheff 1990; Scheff and Retzinger 1991). Merleau-Ponty's contribution deserves special emphasis, particularly his meditations on the relationship between the visible and the invisible (1968), a perspective useful for incorporating psychoanalysis into phenomenology. Little developed although pointing in a useful direction was his use of a phenomenology of the body to explain the child's imitation of the other as the upshot of a "coupling" within perception (1988, 1964b).

12. Becker 1958.

13. Hence the quotation from Whitehead (1958 [1938], 30) that begins this book. "[T]he body is . . . as much part of nature as anything else there— a river, or a mountain, or a cloud. . . . [I]f we are fussily exact, we cannot define where a body begins and where external nature ends."

14. On proprioception, the sixth sense, see Bermúdez 1998. Proprioception is one's sense of the interrelated volumes, pressures, movements and weights that shape posture and perspective. A primary resource in dance, proprioception is a common objective in figurative sculpture.

15. Over the last twenty years, the effort to grasp behavior without imposing a distinction between subjectivity and objective environment has led many investigators to risk other unconventional forms of description. This emerging movement in social and psychological research has produced numerous significant studies across countries and academic fields, but little awareness of their commonalities. Bruno Latour takes at once so seriously and so playfully the idea that people do not exist as beings independent of the environment in which they act that, following Michel Serres and trying to avoid a separation between "science" and "society," he treats microbes as equal participants in the story of Pasteur's success, which becomes the defeat of one parasite by a more powerful parasite (Latour 1988b, 39). In a more recent work (1996) he examines a transportation innovation, giving a speaking and thinking role to a kind of personalized subway car that has existed more in imagination than in production. David Sudnow's ethnomethodological studies of typewriting

and piano playing (1978, 1979) used diagrams of hand movements, musical scores, and a close reading of Merleau-Ponty's *Phenomenology of Perception* to try to get the reader to see what the competent practitioner knows only in an embodied way. Paul Stoller (1989) invites anthropology to capture "the taste of ethnographic things." He describes the tastes and sounds known by Songhay-speaking peoples of West Africa to show their epistemology; and, to make Songhay sorcery understandable, he describes his experience of illness in that culture, arguing that "profound lessons are learned when sharp pains streak up in our legs in the middle of the night" (Stoller 1997, 23). Arthur Kleinman (1995) writes "at the margin" between biomedicine and culture, challenging fundamental distinctions that are fiercely maintained by the disciplines. He addresses the "liminal" region ("the border as a threshold") between: what is symbolic and what is somatic; religion, professional medicine, and banal folk therapy; suffering as physical symptom and as the configuration of personal struggles with the pressures of large-scale forces of social change; pain as idiosyncratically personal and as the systematic result of political terror. William McNeill (1992), who confesses he is not quite sure what to call his subject, uses painstaking transcriptions and drawings that show body movement in order to examine the relationship between thought, speech, and gesture used when subjects are telling stories. And Andrew Meltzoff has for twenty-five years been developing a series of studies of newborns' ability to imitate adults' facial expressions, an ability that precedes not only the infants' ability to recognize that they have a face like the one they are "imitating," but the self-awareness that they have a face at all. The newborn is apparently naturally intertwined in the world, producing socially recognizable, culturally conventionalized expressions through interactive practices that will become the basis for language acquisition. But the description of how the infant manages to produce imitative expressions remains elusive. (Gallagher and Meltzoff [1996] find a contradiction between this body of work and their reading of Merleau-Ponty.)

16. Katz 1983.

17. Lindesmith 1947; Cressey 1953.

18. There are good (if not sufficient) reasons that sociology has become so difficult to read in the last twenty-five years. One is that a variety of methodologies have been developed to move beyond correlation analysis and address processual change. Historical writings make the description of social process eminently readable, but sociology is committed to the additional challenge of establishing patterns that cut across infinite historical instances. In quantitative sociology, the level of statistical complexity has geometrically increased since event history and time series analysis entered the field. In conversation analysis, the appreciation that the shaping and meaning of utterances depend on their location in interaction sequences has led to an unprecedented density and microanalytic focus in sociological writing. Ethnographic sociology has advantages for remaining more readable even when it addresses the significance of sequence in the natural history of a phenomenon (see, e.g., Emerson 1983, arguing that how a decision maker handles a case depends on whether it comes up the first, last, or in the middle of the workday). But in all cases, the analysis of recurrent patterns of behavior in their sequential social context

is likely to increase the burdens on readers, as compared to the analysis of the history of a given instance or the features of multiple cases considered atemporally.

19. Within the last twenty-five years, it has become common in many academic fields to use notions about reflexivity in the researcher's relations with his/her subjects, the cultural relativity of meaning, and the fact that definitions of social reality are historically contingent and politically interested to beg off the work of creating sets of data that can be presented to readers independent of the author's analysis. In works labeled as ethnography, authors may never quote from subjects or otherwise present subjects to the reader in anything but the author's own voice. In works labeled as historical essays, readers may be given no clear directions as to how to identify the time and place in which the matters analyzed supposedly occurred. In works with a "postmodern" flair, the reader is often given an interpretation of the meaning of representations without evidence of for whom, besides the author, the materials have had such meanings. Each of these styles of work compromises the reader's ability to see the target of inquiry except by going through the author's perspective. The reader remains dependent on the author to locate what the author is writing about, and thus to have a firm basis for critically examining what the author is saying about it. Privacy concerns will perhaps always limit the presentation of all of the underlying data in a qualitative study, and economic or practical concerns will impose additional limitations as long as the book remains the principal vehicle for presentation. But I can see no principled justification for abandoning the objective of constructing a triangular relationship, and the democratically enfranchising critical touchstone it provides, throughout the research act.

CHAPTER ONE

1. Goffman (1963, 87) alludes to what often happens when one is caught employing such tortuous tactics: "when a person takes advantage of another's not looking to look at him, and then finds that the object of his gaze has suddenly turned and caught the illicit looker looking . . . [t]he individual caught out may then shift his gaze, often with embarrassment and a little shame, or he may carefully act as if he had merely been seen in the moment of observation that is permissible; in either case we see evidence of the propriety that should have been maintained."

2. When gaze is sustained between pedestrians who are facing each other as they approach a passing moment, moral meanings, such as sexual interest or "character contests" (Wolfinger 1995, 335–36, following Goffman 1967b, 239–58) can quickly develop. Goffman refers to pedestrian blinders as "civil inattention." Using an automotive metaphor, Goffman (1963b, 84) describes the required "casting the eyes down as the other passes" as "a kind of 'dimming of lights.'" For the beginnings of a comparative analysis of the social interaction of pedestrian and vehicular movement, see Goffman 1971, 5–18. On contemporary American inner-city streets, pedestrians must weigh the alternative risks of not encumbering their vision enough, in which case they may be seen to emit a suspicious gaze that could be taken as racist (Anderson 1990); and encumbering their vision too much, in which case they become paranoid.

There are also now-significant gender-related power struggles over the regulation of gaze in public passings (Gardner 1995).

3. For other aspects of the incompetencies created for their drivers by cars, see McGrane 1994, 170–97. The variations in the structure of the competencies and incompetencies of pedestrians and drivers merit a more elaborate treatment than is justifiable in this volume. Each form of social interaction creates a distinctive ontology, a unique set of touchstones for shaping conduct, for the people who sustain it. The theme of the "embodiment" of social action is currently enjoying great popularity but the term is usually employed on the unjustified assumption that people incorporate different lines of action into constant bodies. Marcel Mauss (1973 [1935]) wrote of the "techniques of the body" in a seminal article in which he introduced the concept of *habitus*. Following his lead, we can search for the bodies that are produced by different technologies, thereby giving sensual and not just symbolic meaning to Goffman's (1967c, 3) directive to study "[n]ot, then, men and their moments. Rather, moments and their men."

4. Compare the concept as used, with no trace of irony, in a psychological study of driving: "Someone has said that a moron makes the best driver. From all the studies we have done, this is not correct. It would be more nearly correct to say that a person of about average intelligence makes the best driver. Apparently the job suits him well and fits his capacity." Lauer 1960, x.

5. The communicative efficacy of such messages depends on the assumption that the gesticulating driver and recipient will share the same symbolic universe, but it is not clear that all intended recipients live in social worlds where such gestures are familiar or recognizable. What is striking is not only that the gesticulators don't care, but that they do care to make an expression whose effective reception they don't care about. This enigma, about the personally compelling yet interactionally futile nature of insulting expressions, will be addressed at length in section 3 of this chapter.

6. The "backseat" driver situation in one respect inverts the interaction asymmetry we have been reviewing, as here the driver's motions are monitored closely and continuously by another who is situated outside of the driver's equally attentive reach. The "backseat" designation, understood as referring to the location of foreground and background regions of consciousness, may be phenomenologically accurate even when applied to a passenger in a front seat. The emotions provoked by the "nagging" irritation of the "backseat driver" may be equally or even more unpleasant than the anger occasioned when one is "cut off" by another driver. But the structure of the displeasure appears to be significantly different when the sense of asymmetrical awareness is a constant awareness of overattentiveness as opposed to a sudden realization of inattentiveness by the other. That drivers tacitly analyze the structure of social interaction to constitute their anger should be verifiable in the responses they make. One customarily "flips off" someone by whom one was "cut off," but one does not usually flip off a backseat driver. For that sort of irritation, the fitting response is a mood of ongoing, numbing rejection, i.e., being sullen, uptight, sarcastic, etc.

7. Polanyi 1966, 1962; Merleau-Ponty 1968.

8. With his development of Mauss's concept of habitus and with phrases like "the intentionless invention of regulated improvisation," Pierre Bourdieu (1990, 57) fights the distinction on a broad front in the history of social thought.

9. This occurs with a certain regularity in some settings, and the emergent emotional tone is instructive. As weekend sojourners return to Mexico City on Sunday afternoons, traffic may stop completely for an hour, and it is not uncommon for "a one-hour trip" to take five. Leaving their cars, drivers begin making direct contact with each other. They discover common acquaintances, share weekend experiences, and exploit unique interaction possibilities in the common dilemma. Someone pulls an inflated ball from his or her trunk and starts a trans-lane volleyball game. Others build a huge picnic table stretching over half a dozen cars. Strangers may work together to dismantle highway barriers in order to create a shortcut over a flat field. What such events bring out is the fact, usually hidden in the privacy of contemporary lives, that anger emerges from a falling out from community and is curable by the resurrection of community along other lines. Usually, the transcendent project that traffic cuts off is different for each driver. One is on the way to work, another to the market, another to a social event with friends. But for each the current trip is just one of several possible ways of linking an individual life into a communal order. On those rare occasions when everyone happens to be on the same biographical path (in this example, going home; in other examples, "going to the big game"), if a common dilemma develops and drivers are suddenly able to escape the communicative limitations of their automobiles, many motorists will prove ready to produce novel forms of community with enthusiastic creativity.

10. Certeau 1984.

11. Examples of how drivers play "the traffic game" are available in Berger 1993, 53 ff.

12. The railway journey was a powerful stimulant in the nineteenth century. Schivelbusch (1986, 77–78), recalls the sexual significance that Freud attributed to railway travel. Freud commented on dreams of missing a train as "dreams of consolation for another kind of anxiety felt in sleep—the fear of dying," an idea he applies to the dream "of a patient who had lost his father six years earlier" and who dreamed that his father "had been travelling by the night train, which had been derailed." Freud's own dream, known as "Count Thun" or the "revolutionary dream," grew out of an experience with a railway trip and featured railway experiences in multiple ways (Freud 1965, 241–52). On the prominence of cars and driving in contemporary dreams, see Berger 1993, 18–19.

13. John Brinckerhoff Jackson describes the evolution of the road's meaning. "The Navajo journey is . . . everyday existence ruled and protected by rites and precautions. He follows the paths his forebears followed. They lead to places where there are rare and special herbs. They avoid all places associated with death. . . . [I]n the seventeenth century . . . [t]he European metaphorical use of the words *road* or *way* or *path* emphasized the difficulties encountered by the average wayfarer in the course of his or her journey through life.

... But over the last century and a half, ... a third interpretation is taking shape: a multitude of roads, each with its own destination, obliges us to choose, to make decisions of our own; and the discourse of planning, of policy in the public realm, increasingly resorts to such road-associated phrases as *crossroads, dead ends, avenues of agreement, gridlock, collision course, impasse* and *bypass.*" Jackson 1994, 203–5.

14. Polanyi 1966. For the application to keyboard competencies, see Sudnow 1978.

15. For a particularly shrewd appreciation, see Arthur Leff's (1976) concept of "Calvinist causation."

16. The marketing of cars and watches has set up a kind of cultural competition between metaphors of space and time, and cars are now winning decisively in this struggle. Cars commonly have clocks in them that display time more visibly than can any wristwatch. And cars now contain other devices (phones, fax machines, CD players) that allow one to conquer time and space by maintaining several lines of actions and identities at once. So far, timepieces have not yet been made into mechanisms for moving their wearers.

17. As I began studying angry driving, I caught myself engaged in such maneuvers. What did I expect to find? I began to wonder. My search, I concluded, was for a sign to take out of the scene and use as a helpful prejudice elsewhere, something along the lines, "Ah yes, that's what these characters look like."

18. Those exceptions that do occur indicate that some rudimentary socialization is required to learn to interpret the gesture accurately. When I first arrived in Los Angeles, I frequently found middle fingers raised on hands projected out of drivers' windows. I initially took these signs as good Samaritan efforts to remind me that I had left something on the roof of my car, as indications that there was something above, perhaps a helicopter, that deserved my attention, as an odd turn signal, or as an offensive message that must have been directed at some other driver whose malfeasance had escaped me. The investigations leading to this chapter began as an effort to overcome my local cultural incompetence.

19. Note that with respect to the raised ring finger, the shaping of hand into balled fist adds little to the dramatic perfection of the gesture. Indeed, the initial result of such a maneuver is to give the finger to oneself. In contrast, the radical juxtaposition of the raised middle finger to the base hand is enhanced when thumb and index finger are joined into a testicle-suggestive closed round figure.

20. My thanks here to Melvin Lansky (1999), whose essay on Sophocles' *Electra* suggested thinking about the electric character of anger empirically. Sophocles' drama suggests that the cathartic success of revenge depends on a particular relational dialectic, a combination of personal distance from the target of anger and a personal leadership in directing the counterattack. When Orestes returns home after a seven-year absence, he is virtually a stranger to his family and thus is easily disguised. He can enact a drama of vengeance that will restore him to the throne and to his lands in triumph. (He kills his mother, Clytemnestra, and his stepfather, Aegisthus, who together killed his

father, Agamemnon.) In Sophocles' version of the story, revenge leaves Orestes relatively free of the furies of matricide. But Electra, who never left home, cannot take the same satisfaction from the revenge, although she fervently helps to arrange it. Having lived at home all the while, her emotional isolation continuously structured by multiple forces—by her brother's absence, by a prohibition on her marriage, and by a hatred for her mother and stepfather inspired by sexual envy of the liaison she must witness on a daily basis—her anger seeks a revenge that can never fully ground her passions. She is at once more fully involved in anger than her brother and, in the dialectic that defines her emotions, she is also more distant in the drama of revenge, reduced as a woman to shouting encouragement from the sidelines as Orestes personally slaughters the villains. That angry drivers are strangers to those who cut them off enables them to conjure up dramas that will effectively cleanse humiliation from their souls, but only if they personally mobilize revenge; thoughts about the miserable life the miscreant must live will not be enough because thoughts, when left as mere thoughts, emphasize distance from the offender.

21. There seems to be a natural impulse in road rage interaction to give a saga form to rounds of revenge in which the trading of insults comes to an end only when natural barriers to communication arise, as when one party follows the contours of an exit ramp. In small communities where feuding parties have no sure escape from the prospect of future contact, such as was the case in medieval Iceland, feud sagas must find other means of terminating, and even when the issue of revenge is about killing, alternatives to compensation in blood may be found. See Miller 1990, 263 ff. The paradox is that on contemporary roads, the very existential insignificance of drivers' conflicts, the fact that it is foreseeable that they will soon end, is a condition of their intensity. There is a rush to get revenge before the opportunity vanishes.

22. A contemporary version of an audible sigh that is popular among young female drivers in L.A. is an "oh well." With a light touch, "oh well" jettisons an embarrassment with a verbal shake of the head, instantly creating a gulf between a negative, down moment in the immediate past and an upbeat future that one glides into with newborn innocence. With the sociological insight that being is a situation-bounded phenomenon, this hard-working cultural creation by contemporary youth celebrates the freedom of plastic identities. "Life's a bitch" and "oh well" are alternatives to the currently popular philosophical statement displayed on bumper stickers and T-shirts, "Shit happens."

23. Southern California became infamous for "freeway shootings" in the summer of 1987, but in the fall of that year Saint Louis produced an even more disturbing rate (twenty-two "confirmed shootings" in two months); and "sprees" of shooting occurred earlier in other areas, for example in Houston in 1982. See Novaco 1991b, 237; and on the construction of this myth, Best 1991.

24. On awareness contexts, see Glaser and Strauss 1964.

25. An ethnographic study in Los Angeles documented the breakdown of this practice in what may be a culturally specific phenomenon, the "inverted smile." After a pedestrian makes a silent, smiling gesture to greet a stranger

and then finds that the gesture is seen but not reciprocated, he or she will often invert or compress the smile, indicating a moment of embarrassment. The behavior is one of attempting visibly to take back the profferred smile by swallowing it. Initial research indicates that the inverted smile is more likely to appear when strangers of putatively similar status pass each other in such public places as supermarkets and jogging trails (e.g., between joggers running on tracks in a public park but not between middle-class, white joggers and working-class Latinos picnicking by jogging trails). Lori Cronyn (1992) identified and videotaped the phenomenon, which grows out of the odd American urge to show another whom one does not personally know but is presumably "like" in some currently expressed sense (joggers, workers in the same building, shoppers in the same market) that one "likes" the other.

26. In a broader cross-cultural review, the cars of the poor would probably be the most highly differentiated vehicles of all. Models that when originally manufactured represented a limited number of types over time become increasingly idiosyncratic as they are substantially remade with the use of serendipitously available material and amateur labor. Since such drivers have personalized their vehicles by necessity, we might expect them to be especially likely to take it personally when they are cut off. But see the next note.

27. For some evidence that education and socioeconomic status are positively related to impatient/antagonistic driving habits in Southern California in the 1990s, see Novaco 1991a.

28. Trillin 1995.

29. Berger 1993. Visitors to L.A. seem to be kinder to the area's drivers than are the area's drivers. I have heard many Europeans echo the sentiments described by Paul Theroux (1995, 35–36): "I seemed to notice a Zen of driving: smooth merging, safe passing, full and complete stops at red lights. LA people groaned about the terrible driving, especially on the freeways, but I saw more courtesy displayed in a single day in California than I had seen in months anywhere else."

30. Advocates of Zen driving criticize drivers who treat their windshields as TV screens. But before computer screens, one does not sit "separate from what you are watching," nor, although everything in some sense *is* preprogrammed, does anything *seem* preprogrammed. (On interaction with computer games, see Sudnow 1983.) Zen counselors recommend a "samurai awareness" in which one attends to "what is taking place inside of you" and to one's "surrounds," but while the surrounds include the eyes of other drivers, one should not look to what may be going on behind them. One interacts with other drivers, but by remaining within one's own subjectivity, not on a presumption of intersubjectivity. Quotes are from Berger 1988, 42–43, 126–27, 146.

31. Some minor exceptions were found in research on drivers' interactions conducted in the 1970s: "an institutionalized code of communication via lights and horns" that imply guildlike relations among truck drivers; Corvette and Porsche owners treating each other like "enlightened brethren"; salutations acknowledging fraternal relations among drivers of "low-priced sports cars"; patterns of derision directed from big cars to small cars and vice versa; age- and gender-specific competitive solidarities among "drag" racers; and the infinitely

multiplying allegiances to cultural communities displayed through bumper stickers. Dannefer 1977, 34.

32. On the rapid shift between 1970 and 1990 from ethnic homogeneity to heterogeneity, see Waldinger and Bozorgmehr 1996.

33. In many of the accounts of angry drivers in L.A., small-town life is used as a background to highlight the hassles of driving in big cities. For example, Max from "mellow Cucamonga," whose truck stuck out like a sore thumb when drivers and pedestrians in Beverly Hills would not accommodate his efforts to make a turn, "felt that these actions by these people just show how selfish people in Los Angeles are, especially when it comes to driving. . . . He feels very strongly that everyone in Los Angeles is like this." Residents of less densely populated areas often say something analogous about drivers in New York, Paris, Rome, etc.

CHAPTER TWO

1. Freud 1960.

2. "It is natural . . . to find embarrassment and joking together, for both help in denying the same reality." Goffman 1967a, 112 n. 10.

3. Coser 1960. On laughter as a kind of political agreement, see Emerson 1969.

4. Jefferson, Sacks, and Schegloff 1973, 1987.

5. Characterizations of family relationships were imputed by French and American preschool teachers.

6. Transcription conventions: Capital letters indicate increased volume. Plus and minus signs indicate changes in pitch. Exes stand for a crunching sound. Ellipses indicate truncated words. Curly brackets contain pauses and sounds not transcribed phonetically.

7. When people find themselves laughing alone, they often realize that perhaps they had not been alone. So an isolated reader in laughing may appreciate that he or she had been found out, that the author, when writing, had already read the reader, in the sense of knowing intimate features of the reader's life.

8. The boy's riff of laughter appears to respond to PaPA's motion toward tickling, beginning *before* PaPA actually makes contact with the tickle target. Adults commonly employ the logic of tickling to convey humor to children. Tickling creates an untenable juxtaposition between the inside and the outside of one's body. It attacks the skin's role as a secure metaphysical divide between one's subjectivity and the outside world. As a form of metaphysical play, tickling shares the strategy of erotic interaction, which enables an envisioning of the idea to make the body sensible even before touch is realized.

9. For an analysis of how telling jokes conveys to recipients a challenge to get it, see Sacks 1974, 346: "Jokes, and dirty jokes in particular, are constructed as 'understanding tests.' " Laughter shows not only that you got a particular "it" but also that you have the competence to get such things. But not laughing at such times is not necessarily an admission of incompetence. Done in a manner that conveys understanding but not agreement, not laughing can be a powerful, pointed offense. See Paperman 1995.

Sometimes laughter itself is used as a summoning and designating device, a way of calling a companion to grasp a referenced "distortion" in the mirror.

If perceived, a designating-summoning laugh makes the companion's gaze accountable. He or she need not laugh in response, but either way the companion's gaze will have become palpable, emotionally alive as a basis for accountability. If the companion does not show he or she got it and is "with" the summoning party in a shared experience, some other account, perhaps rudeness or callous indifference, will appear on the horizon. In these instances, the laughter itself sets up the tension.

10. Laughter and other performative emotions are ways of bringing into social awareness the three-dimensionality of the body, most commonly by marking the process of respiration. Effective language, in contrast, requires what Merleau-Ponty (1973) referred to as the "effacing" of the body that is its vehicle. In order to keep attentions on an emerging collective line of talk, participants must listen through utterances and keep in the background the audibly breathing bodies that are talk's vehicles.

11. In this respect, contemporary cultures that preserve such ritual devices as handshakes and dispassionate kisses as ways of beginning and ending interactions may be understood as guarding corporeally deeper mechanisms of emotional expression, such as laughter, from "artificial" uses. If modern cultures cannot avoid drawing a line between artificial and authentic aspects of the self, they can still determine where in bodily practice that line is drawn.

12. This makes the transcription of laughter a near-hopeless ambition. Conventions have been developed for the transcription of extraordinary levels of subtlety in conversational interaction, with special devices for tracing alterations of gaze, regions of body posture, and some hand gestures. Laughter, and emotionally resonant conduct in general, is lived and perceived in three-dimensional forms that cannot be reduced economically to a two-dimensional page. Moreover, because the embodied character of laughter is not only its vehicle but also a key part of its message, and because bodies are idiosyncratic, laughs (again like emotionally resonant conduct in general) are misrepresented in deeply flawed ways by any transcript conventions, which to work must claim priority of conventional form over expressed substance. The distinction between transcribing and glossing data, so important to the study of conversational interaction, makes little sense in application to conduct like laughter, which exists fundamentally in aesthetic contrast to language.

13. The motif of raised arms becomes a serendipitous and subtle resource elaborated by father and son to maintain their bond. F. inadvertently raises S.'s arms to a crucifixion position as he lifts the boy by his armpits. F., in his similar posture, in effect imitates S.'s initially unintentional gesture. Then S. imitates F.'s gesture by flapping his arms. F.'s call to his wife and daughter then becomes a joint summons from F. and S., at least in its gestural aspect. By keeping his arms raised, F. can stay with S. even as he directs his attentions to the missing members of the family. The subtle, improvised intimacy of the relationship between F. and S. indicates the forces being applied to manifest a bond. That commitment of energies becomes the background for the explosive celebration of four-part family unity that soon follows.

14. My thanks to Melvin Pollner for a suggestion along these lines at an early stage of my work on laughter.

15. My thanks to Emanuel Schegloff for making available the transcript

and a copy of the audiotape. The "orchid/organ" passage had been referred to in Jefferson 1985.

16. Speech is not only especially compatible with the exhale phase of respiration, it actually enhances it, producing a greater volume of expelled air, upping the average volume, in one study, from 0.5 to 3.5 liters (Levelt 1989, 422). In contrast, speech restricts the volume of air inhaled.

17. A full-scale study comparing demonstrative and spontaneous laughter has not yet been attempted. For research on voluntary and involuntary aspects of smiles, see Ekman and O'Sullivan 1991, 172–74, on the "enjoyment" or "Duchenne" smile.

18. See Scheff and Retzinger 1991, 46–49.

19. This is one way to state the central thrust of ethnomethodology. See Garfinkel 1967a; Cicourel 1964. In Garfinkel's early work, he established that interpersonal gaps, addressed as the Schutzian problem of "intersubjectivity," are ubiquitous. He then called for studies of how the gaps are papered over. The current volume aims to bring out the aesthetic, interactional, and tacit interpretative techniques by which emotions bridge existential separations between personal lives.

20. My thanks to Elena Cielak for this observation.

CHAPTER THREE

1. Until recently, it was easy to discount efforts to go beyond the looking glass image of the self as trips to a wonderland where facts could not be distinguished from imagined realities. But the search for a three-dimensional analysis of personal experience has become increasingly accessible for sociological analysis with the advent of cheaply acquired and easily reviewed videotaped data. Technical and economic limitations on using filmed data had for many years limited naturalistic researchers to audiotapes and to the position of in situ observer. Reviewers of audiotapes were limited to hearing from the correspondent's standpoint. But the reviewer of a videotape gains a third perspective: the analyst can ground claims about what A is doing with B on endlessly reviewable evidence about aspects of A's conduct that neither A nor B can directly witness. Both because the analyst can slow down and replay conduct that people must live immediately and one-time-through, and because the analyst can see regions of the actor's body that exist in the shadows of his own perceptual abilities and beyond the reach of his respondent's perspective, videotape gives the analyst an unprecedented vantage point for a three-dimensional examination of personal conduct. (See the pioneering work of Adam Kendon [1981].) Before the cheap video camera, data on three-dimensional identity was available primarily through Proustian fiction, phenomenological philosophy, and studies of filmed movement that were principally of interest to art audiences (on the last, see Fondation Maeght 1992), sources that served more as haunting reminders of what social science could not reach than as data useful for testing explanations.

2. "Almost every version of social theory insists that we *act* to produce social life. Karl Marx and George Herbert Mead both thought that, but their followers' syntax often betrays that theory." Becker 1986, 80.

3. Nobody seems to like this awkward term. Used originally by Blumer

(1937), it has become unstoppable in sociology ever since it was adopted as a convenience for the title of an influential collection of Blumer's essays (1969).

4. Whitehead [1925] 1960.

5. Neonate studies have for years now been documenting newborn-mother imitative interaction that seems to contradict Meadian notions of the self as emergent only as one becomes able to see oneself from the perspective of others. Newborns can imitate their mothers' facial expressions virtually at birth, certainly long before they can recognize their own faces. See Meltzoff and Moore 1994. I think the only way to understand such findings is to carry forward the insight that Merleau-Ponty developed in his philosophy and art commentary, that every perceived landscape is in effect already sculpted by the movements of the perceiver's body and that, in consequence, every landscape is a self-portrait. The newborn already imitates the mother in the process of seeing her, and what we observers see as the imitative actions of the infant are the elaborated articulations of the proprioceptive configuration of the infant's visual experience. Also ignored in the explanation of infant imitation is a prior point. That the infant has a tongue to stick out when he sees the mother's tongue sticking out at him is possible because the infant is, of course, already an imitation of the mother, who in turn has already in effect imitated the infant's body by sticking out something that the mother presumes can be imitated by the infant and that corresponds to an already active part of the infant's body.

6. Also inadequate is the traditional understanding of emotion as opposed to reason or self-reflection, which, by failing to appreciate the sensual self-regarding in emotions, risks getting it exactly wrong. It is not emotions that are nonreflective parts of our being or identity; emotions present us with corporeally enlivened, sensually captured aspects of the nonreflective practices that we had been engaging. This volume is intended as a step in clarifying the relationships among the self-reflective and the corporeally known self. The point has recently been argued in a philosophical context by José Luis Bermúdez (1998).

7. I am not arguing that we drop the language of "social construction" or experience as a "project." Indeed, one of the three analyses I undertake in each of the substantive chapters in this volume is to see how emotions are projects of creating narratively bounded episodes of experience. I do not think there is or can be any single descriptive perspective that will permit us to grasp what is occurring in social interaction. We should be prepared repeatedly to shift between the active and the passive voice in order to describe the dialectical processes in which people shape their action and find their experience shaped.

8. Goffman 1967a. In what is offered as a powerful critique of Goffman's analysis of embarrassment, Christian Heath (1984) argued that the behavior that Goffman would code as embarrassment is far from a necessary indication of shame; it may be explained as a strategic effort to avoid the eruption of shame rather than as a response to it.

9. Lynd 1958.

10. Lewis 1971.

11. Schneider 1992.

12. Broucek 1991.

13. Scheler 1987.

14. Updike 1985.

15. On shame in shoplifting, see Katz 1988, chap. 2.

16. John Braithwaite has found this pattern, which he has generalized into a universal anticrime strategy, in his studies of adolescent crime in Australia (1989).

17. In the humiliating police investigation that required that he take off all his clothes, Dmitri (Mitya) Fyodorovitch Karamazov, "[f]eeling intolerably ashamed," was especially degraded by the command to take off his socks, as he "had thought both his big toes hideous. He particularly loathed the coarse, flat, crooked nail on the right one, and now they would all see it." "It's like a dream, I've sometimes dreamed of being in such degrading positions." Dostoyevsky 1950, 587.

18. Sartre 1956, 221–22.

19. See also Mann 1985.

20. Jahoda, Lazarsfeld, and Zeisel 1971, 63.

21. Ricoeur 1969.

22. Scruton 1986.

23. The atmosphere in "boiler rooms" is richly described in Stevenson 1998.

24. Morris 1975. See also Du 1995, on the romance of love-pact suicides.

25. Another instructive source is Jean Baechler's (1979) study of French suicides. Several of his cases were unrelated to personal fault and appear to have been ways of avoiding rather than exiting from shame. See case 37, the suicide of a mayor who, with eighteen years of official tenure and an unofficial career as the soul of his town, was suspended after thirteen people died in an accident. See also case 42.

26. Goffman 1952.

27. The rape trauma syndrome has a prolonged phase in which "the victim has the recovery task of restoring order to his or her lifestyle and re-establishing a sense of control in the world." Burgess 1983, 100.

28. Cf. Lewis 1971, 15–16.

29. Hollonbeck and Ohls 1984.

30. See, e.g., Isherwood 1986.

31. Cf. Broucek 1991, 118.

32. Goffman 1967a, 98.

33. Lindsay-Hartz 1984.

34. Lindsay-Hartz 1984.

35. "Shame causes a person to look at the ground to avoid the glance of the other. The reason for this is certainly not only because he is thus spared the visible evidence of the way in which the other regards his painful situation, but the deeper reason is that the lowering of his glance to a certain degree prevents the other from comprehending the extent of his confusion. The glance in the eye of the other serves not only for me to know the other but also enables him to know me." Simmel 1924, 358.

36. Salman Rushdie's *Shame* (1983) revolves around the relationship between Omar Khayyam Shakil, a man born of three mothers and no identifiable father, who is immune to shame, and Sufiya Zinobia Hyder, a woman who

was born blushing when her parents, expecting the reincarnation of a dead infant son, insisted that her genitalia were male. He has never left the womb; she was born through the denial of her own womb.

37. Lindsay-Hartz 1984, 692.

38. Lewis 1971, 41.

39. In this respect too, shame may be distinguished from guilt. People not uncommonly nourish and take pride in cultivating their guilt. Shame—but not the posture of modesty that would avoid shame—is terrifying in the chaos it embodies. Pagels offers the provocative observation that "were it not that people often *would rather feel guilty than helpless*—I suspect that the idea of original sin would not have survived the fifth century." Pagels 1988, 146.

40. Lewis 1971, 37.

41. Lynd 1958.

42. Lansky 1995.

43. For a sampling of current work, see Lansky and Morrison 1997.

44. Scheff and Retzinger 1991.

45. American culture is distinctive in favoring sports that, by isolating the individual before a mass, become shame games. As Arthur Leff observed (1977), what is necessary to make a sport a huge commercial success in the United States is the possibility, in the structure of the game's competitive interaction, of a moment in which one player can stand out from the team and suddenly and decisively change the collective fate. A contrast with soccer is instructive. Apart from penalty shots, players are rarely set up for isolated disgrace. It may seem that an offensive soccer player has "beaten" a defensive player, but the interaction may retrospectively be understood as a set-up that works to the advantage of the defensive player's team. Or the defensive player may have followed a signal from a teammate who has the real responsibility for the move. In baseball, a strike is almost never good for a batter; when a ball is hit in the air a fielder will almost never do the "right" thing by dropping it; and a throw to first base should be five feet over the first-baseman's head only in the rarest of circumstances. The baseball field is a relatively unambiguous terrain for celebrating or ridiculing individual performance.

46. This is not unlike the sequence of silent tears followed by tortured smile and muffled chuckle that I have found on videotapes of people who are moved by awesome moments (e.g., among parents at children's music recitals), except that the sequence is reversed. In the face of failure, the boys show a tortured smile and then cry. In the face of precious innocence, adults find their eyes tearing and then smile/laugh in a self-deprecating manner, as if their tears might distract from rather than honor the moment. Such experiences are discussed in the next chapter.

47. Contemporary American parents in middle-class Little League audiences work diligently to discourage nasty comments, presumably to avoid what they anticipate would be the boys' feelings of shame. They appear not to appreciate that rough language between opposing teams provides each player with a ready shield against shame by creating an ongoing, vivid moral solidarity with teammates. The social structure of the game makes shame inevitable. What is variable is whether the player will turn to peers or to parents for cover.

48. Lewis 1971, 40.

49. Simmel focuses on the imputation of essential character in shame in order to suggest the structure of relationships in which shame is more and less likely. Others' perceptions of given acts are relatively unlikely to elicit shame where the others are either intimate associates or bare strangers. In the former case, the other has far richer sources for constructing one's character than an isolated act; in the case of the stranger, the other has little basis to presume how characteristic the act is. In Simmel's time, this helped explain the surprising openness of people who would meet for the first and presumably last time when they shared a train compartment: "[T]ravelling companions, who were unknown to one another until an hour ago, and who will not see one another again an hour later, are often prepared to entrust one another with intimacies." He expected that shame would be most likely in relationships that were, in these terms, of the middle range. Gerhards 1986, 907.

50. Reisman 1979.

51. Cf. Morano 1976, 79.

52. Lynd 1958, 39.

53. Scheler 1987.

54. Gregory 1964, 43–46.

55. Goffman 1952.

56. Bourdieu 1990, 105.

57. Morano 1976, 79.

58. Johnson 1993, 21. Contrast the more familiar perspective that creative achievement is a strategy against personal shame. An entertaining example is John Cuddihy's (1974) somewhat facile argument that Marx, Freud, and (by extension) Goffman worked to undermine different anti-Semitic stereotypes of Jewish motivations (money, sex, interpersonal manipulation) by generalizing them to everyone.

59. Updike 1985, 50.

60. Goffman 1959, 2.

61. For an application of this line of argument to piano playing, see Sudnow 1978.

62. On sex, see Broucek 1991.

63. See Katz 1988, chaps. 1 and 3.

64. The McMartin prosecution in Los Angeles was perhaps the single most famous such case. After seven years of investigation and two trials, during which one defendant was incarcerated for five years, no confessions or guilty pleas were obtained and all charges were dropped. Eberle and Eberle 1993.

65. For a close examination of how the popular culture of child abuse entered the psychoanalysis of a patient, temporarily providing a screen against more painful personal issues, see Prager 1998.

66. Mecca, Smelser, and Vasconcellos 1989.

67. Braithwaite 1989.

68. Scheff and Retzinger 1991; Scheff 1994, 1997.

69. Bakhtin 1968.

70. This is not to say that we are ever lacking in emotions or that one's natural state is some form of being undisturbed by the urgings of emotion. It is to say that there is no one emotion that primarily underlies conduct. The

falls that we experience are commonly falls out of being taken by the scene in one way or another. Recall the variety of immediately prior dispositions— frustrated, complacent, euphoric, aggressive—from which drivers become pissed off.

CHAPTER FOUR

1. Bruner 1983.

2. For an appreciation of the musical evolution of preverbal vocal activity in infancy, see Loewy 1995. For a call to extend Bruner's perspective and study the "cry interaction sequence," see Gustafson and Deconti 1990: crying "initiates primitive 'social dialogues' of the sort thought to facilitate social and communicative development during infancy" (47).

3. For evidence of the gender difference, see Lombardo et al. 1983; Ross and Mirowsky 1984. It has been suggested that women's anger more often bursts out in spates of crying than does men's anger. See Crawford et al. 1992, 171–76: "crying out of anger serves two purposes, one which is not obvious to the person who cries, and one which is not obvious to the person who witnesses it. The person who cries believes that it is . . . a signal of the righteousness of her anger along with the strength of the hurt. The person who witnesses it sees . . . a sign of sorrow . . . and a signal that his anger is no longer appropriate" (176).

4. Williams and Morris 1996.

5. It is not easy to clarify causal ordering. For a qualified endorsement of a negative finding, see Hubbard and IJzendoorn 1994.

6. Brazelton 1990.

7. Brazelton, Robey, and Collier 1969; Barr et al. 1991.

8. But see Barr 1990, calling for "qualitative behavioural studies of the 'crying act' " (360); and Zeskind, Parker-Price, and Barr 1993.

9. E.g., Stein and Brodsky 1995. But see the "Cry Research, Inc." system for mechanically describing dimensions of the acoustics of infant cries, in Huffman et al. 1994.

10. Stroebe and Stroebe 1987, 36. Arthur Kleinman (1995, 233–34) writes: "It is a telling comment on the interest of anthropologists that the huge corpus of ethnographies of social mourning practices has so little to say about the social experience of bereavement." The particular work he is reviewing, and by extension the field he is criticizing, "ends up unable to examine the emotional response of real people to real losses. . . . Grief, for all its deeply resonant subjectivity, is handled largely as a source of powerful cultural symbols."

11. E.g., Dessureau, Kurowski, and Thompson 1998.

12. But see the sketches in Acebo and Thoman 1992, 1995.

13. Plessner [1950] 1970.

14. Frey 1985. Yet this finding poses a new mystery. At the end of *All's Well that Ends Well*, Lafeu responds to the lovers' reconciliation: "Mine eyes smell onions; I shall weep anon." The similar experience of an emotionally and a physically provoked stinging sensation, long recognized in folk cultures, still calls for explanation.

15. Plessner [1950] 1970, 133.

16. "In my opinion, we never weep directly over pain that is felt, but always only over its repetition in reflection . . . *weeping is sympathy with ourselves.*" Schopenhauer 1969, 376–77.

17. From observational field notes and an interview in the Rijksmuseum, Amsterdam, 1990. Michael Polanyi (1970) defines painting in a way that fits nicely with this crying viewer's appreciation of Vermeer. The viewer is moved, not in a suspension of disbelief nor by neglecting the practical brushwork in favor a gestalt of the image, but through a subsidiary awareness of the artifices that have been used to create the focal image. The observer's eyes fill as she witnesses, in her here and now, what is taken to be the same miraculous transformation that the artist crafted over three hundred years earlier.

18. Westwood 1985, 96.

19. A practical problem of not being able to be in two places at once is at the center of William F. Whyte's (1949) classic explanation of why waitresses cry. The impossible demand comes up when waitresses are caught in cross-pressures between customers and food preparation staff in the kitchen. Interestingly, given the argument made below that crying embodies what language cannot contain, Whyte's solution was a communication device, the spindle that enables waitresses to avoid face-to-face interaction when leaving orders for cooks.

20. References to parents crying at children's music recitals are based on field notes and videotapes of several Yamaha music school recitals in Los Angeles the early 1990s.

21. My thanks to A. Saa Meroe for guiding me to Unity Church in 1997.

22. On the latter, Roth 1963.

23. On the repression of crying among Holocaust children, see Gampel 1992.

24. Crying, I am arguing, arises to embody what speech cannot contain. By the time a child can whine, it makes sense to consider that he or she cries as a sensed alternative to speech. But I do not in this volume make more than passing references to "crying" in the life cycle before two years of age. Admittedly, it would be difficult to argue that neonate crying is produced in an appreciation of what speech cannot embody. But that we, adults, understand neonates as "crying" is itself a topic for investigation. From the adult perspective, neonate crying may well be incomprehensible other than as an alternative, defective form of speech. Certainly adults speak to newborns, even, these days, fetuses in the wombs of highly educated women, as if they are conversational partners. The thrust of research on early interaction is that much if not all of adult interaction with infants is from the start, intentionally or not, an effort to shape, even seduce them into speech. See, for example, Bruner 1983. To avoid a sterile debate over whether crying evolves or emerges as speech is acquired, we need a broader understanding and richer conceptualization of interaction as embodied by the infant and the young child.

25. Speculation along this line is emerging in evolution research. See Lummaa et al. 1998.

26. Infant research tentatively suggests that crying shortens memory, in effect washing away a past self. Singer and Fagen 1992.

27. It is in one sense true, as a Hollywood rabbi confided in bemused re-

flections, that it would seem to make more sense, in order to ease the reconciliation of family and friends, to stress the negative aspects of the deceased's
personality, thus minimizing the estimation of what has been lost. But this is
one of those cute truths that will only be enacted in Hollywood by comedians.
All officials in the rabbi's position understand that, were they in fact to specify
the ways in which the deceased was, as he put it, a "son of a bitch," the participants would turn from the deceased to the clerical official, and from tears to
shock and anger. The essential point of the ritual, to define loss, would be
undermined.

28. Friedman 1992, 18–19.

29. Count Tolstoy's social circle seems to have based its aristocratic privi-
lege on a claim of sensibility manifested through a seemingly infinite ability
to produce tears. I found 157 instances of crying in *War and Peace,* mostly
but not all by women, before I gave up the effort to be more rigorous in measuring such watery stuff. That figures to be at least one bout of crying for each
five pages of communal life.

30. Retirement celebrations clearly can evoke crying independent of the
perceived worth of the retiring person and on the basis of appreciating the
value of crying in manifesting how precious the community itself is. I recall
a tear-evoking primary school assembly in which children of various ethnicities
expressed their affections for an African-American woman who had served
for years in the front office as the first line of comfort for students who missed
the bus, forgot their lunch money, became injured in the school yard, etc. I
mention the racial configuration because in contemporary U.S. cities what is
sensed as transcended, when such celebrations inspire widespread tears, is often far more than individual-level matters. Many of the adults who cried as
the woman was honored had nothing but stereotypes before them, because
the ceremonial moment was their only familiarity with her.

31. My thanks to Linda Van Leuven for this material.

32. Folk cultures understand this meaning of crying as signifying the abandonment of one bodily ground of experience for another. In her ethnographic
research on weddings in Romanian villages, Gail Kligman (1988) finds that
brides are supposed to cry, and if one is not prepared to do so, older women
will help by holding an onion near her eyes. Crying is morally required to
authenticate that a metamorphosis is occurring in both sexual and power
terms. The young woman is supposed to be moving out from the limited auton-
omy she has in her own family to become subject to the domination of her
husband and his family. The fact that the women of the community are prepared to stage a narrative of this transformation is an indication that the metamorphosis, in which tears signify a joyful holistic abandonment of a prior
version of self, may not be complete.

33. Sociologists who do not themselves work with qualitative materials
sometimes find it convenient to think that dialectical analyses are just facile
ways of playing with ideas. "Sure, look at something positive and you'll
imagine some associated phenomenon that's negative; and vice versa." The
effort is neither so easy nor so trivial. Phenomenological claims are empirical
propositions, in this case propositions about feelings. The prediction here
is that people can identify whether crying is sad or joyful based on their

narrative understanding of the context of the behavior, and that within the event itself, they find comfort in sad crying (which they often report with an awareness of the irony) and discomfort in the process of joyful crying (which they often show in shamelike gestures of attempting to hide their tears).

34. This seems to be the reason that the bittersweetness of joyful crying is familiar to adults but unknown to most children. The age at which death becomes a personally grasped reality, as opposed to a romanticized image of what happens to others, demands study, not only by students of emotions but also by gender scholars (my interviews suggest it is much earlier for females), as well as for those who would explain such age-related patterns as the decline of violent crime in the life cycle.

35. In chapter 2, I analyzed laughter in similar fashion, as a way of using the body to demonstrate a bridge between two logically inconsistent perspectives. But where laughter, by representing the need for a bridge, conveys, "I got it!," crying dramatizes an alternative range of responses to the risks of a fall, from taking a lonely, outsider's stance at the shaky edge of a chasm to dropping freely into the gap. This range will be reviewed in the next two chapters, and in the concluding chapter I will return to compare the analyses of the various emotions treated in this volume.

36. Frey 1985, 95.

37. The *New York Times,* 27 April 1996, A33, col. 2, reported that the Chicago police had investigated charges "that Mike Tyson had spoken to her inappropriately and groped her," and found "no evidence" against Tyson.

38. "Leo Buscaglia said it well: 'You can never understand someone else's tears. Tears are very lonely and very private. You can't say "I know *exactly* why you're crying." ' " Frey 1985, 133.

39. This point is detailed in the case studies of crying in the next two chapters. In chapter 5, a child's whining, done as an extended, audibly varied crying, is seen to be an extraordinarily rich device for coordinating interaction. Although the whining child and the responsive adult seem to know exactly what is going in their relationship, the adult only asks the child directly why she is crying in a moment of frustration, after the child has finally started talking and then begins whining again. The child's response is, from the standpoint of logical reasoning, pointedly absurd. In chapter 6, we see how the crying of an adult under interrogation works as a strategy to withdraw temporarily from a conversation. Here crying produces a brief fog, under which the suspect tries to find a new route for escape.

40. Garot 1997.

41. My thanks to Stacy Burns for the opportunity to review this tape.

42. The press conference was televised on April 8, 1992, on *International Hour* (CNN).

43. Langer 1942.

44. Reading the painter's and donor's names and the date of the work and the donation is good emotional insurance. It wisely anticipates conversations in which shame might follow an inability to defend the quality of one's education by conventionally identifying what has been seen. People often enjoy movies, get absorbed by books, become inspired by music, are moved when wit-

nessing a dance, respond to architecture and sculpture, even recite bits of poetry without knowing the names of the directors, performers, sculptors, and authors. We need to study how the emotional lives of different forms of art are shaped by the social conventions for relating practically to them. Are not paintings given distinctively mean spirits by being hidden within sealed spaces that can be accessed only by practically manifesting deference to rich contributors and institutional authorities, and by a culture of refinement that interposes an obligation to identify the artist as a condition of responding to the work?

45. Joe Buissink, a Los Angeles–based photographer who for several years has been hired to work unobtrusively at weddings in search of naturally occurring emotions, reports that the most predictable cry-provoking moments in the ceremony occur when the words "I do" are spoken. He has learned to swing his lens quickly from the marrying couple to the first two rows in the audience in order to capture the unsettling, decompositional effects of this self-committing, relation-constructing little phrase.

46. In writing about another emotionally powerful social form, Erving Goffman (1967b, 166) noted that "action" is a time when "an act becomes a deed." In the context of bank robbery, sex, and gambling, what is in a mundane sense an unremarkable act, the mere turn of a hand, can start a getaway car, turn on a sexual partner, or place a bet.

47. Brinley 1995.

48. Many of the materials in this chapter were upshots of casual conversations in which acquaintances, after asking what I was working on, volunteered descriptions of recent instances of crying.

49. It may be noted that in this case, the problem was not that of the "second shift," at least not simply in the sense of a woman carrying the major family responsibilities both economically and domestically (Hochschild 1990). The "shift" problem here is a also matter of the necessity of going through a kind of existential shock as one migrates from, on the one hand, mundane work environments that are treated by everyone as demanding twelve-hour workdays and virtually twenty-four-hour telephone accessibility, and, on the other hand, a sphere of private life that is regarded, when work demands let up, as properly carrying more transcendent significance than made-for-TV movies are likely to convey. Crying and other emotional ramifications emerge out of such shifts because of an absence of language, an inadequacy not in the narrow sense of particular words or phrases but in the larger sense of a lack of a cultural recognition that, issues of equity aside, many people find it hard to make sense of these daily migrations. We don't yet have a culture that encourages women to laugh off the absurdities encountered in the transition from high-pressure, profit-maximizing work settings to the quietly transcendent concerns of home life. For men such cultural resources are deep, ranging from regular late-afternoon squash partners, to after-work drinking, to seventy-five years of *New Yorker* cartoons that have humorously depicted men as continuing an elite lifestyle at home, acting absurdly as business executive, lawyer, doctor, etc., with wife, child, or dog.

50. Schwalbe 1996, 63.

51. Davis 1979, 7: "why is it . . . that when someone tells me of a friend

who is 'feeling nostalgic' I know generally that the friend is neither elated nor in bleak despair, that his mood is more contemplative than active, that the echoes, if not always the actuality, of tears and laughter alternate more vividly in him at such a time than they do at other times?"

52. Kaplan 1993, 213.

53. Many other sensed expression gaps are part of Kaplan's experience, including some that are implied in the metamorphosis of a struggling student changing into an accomplished colleague. The student's surprising success in articulating the strategy of the text came in moving juxtaposition to the struggles toward articulation that a good teacher must often witness in students without direct commentary. And Kaplan's experience also registered a kind of unspeakable pedagogical fraud that underlies much university teaching, that inspired instruction depends on remaining as another student among students who unwittingly become one's own teachers.

54. Srinivas 1997.

55. Canetti 1979, 226.

56. Dan Marks, *My Crasy Life* (documentary film), 1992, Department of Anthropology, University of Southern California.

57. Callace was released from prison on October 6, 1992.

58. Buckley 1995–1996, 46.

59. The narrative structure of death appears to be so powerful that it can provoke tears when the death is only simulated in situational and temporary endings of relationships. In 1980, in Mexico City's airport, I observed from a distance as a woman and two children became apparently overwhelmed by the emotions of sending off the man of the family. When I asked my companions, who knew the family well, what tragedy had befallen them, they responded with surprise at the question, and the information that the husband-father was off to Monterrey for a routine weekend business trip. With a bit more investigation, it became apparent that the airport was overflowing with such dramas.

60. For a review of such studies and a discussion of the controversy as to whether crying is universal in bereavement, see Stroebe and Stroebe 1987.

61. As documented in Robert Siegel, "Murder, Punishment and Parole in Alabama, Parts I and II," *All Things Considered,* National Public Radio, 26 and 27 April 1996 (tape and transcript available from NPR). I wish to clarify that I am not attempting to debunk the parole opponents as artificially dramatizing the victim's spirits. The issue is much too complex to be handled so easily. As I argue in the next chapter, in everyday life we routinely lend and borrow bodies with our conversational respondents. And in family relationships, we unwittingly, even unwillingly speak in the accents and with the phrases of our parents long after face-to-face conversation is over.

62. *Morning Edition,* National Public Radio, 20 March 1992.

63. As the visitor proceeds into the cemetery, signs of a more mundane variety soon appear (one warns that cars should be locked because burglaries are common, another directs visitors to keep off the grass), and then one reads the curt phrase, "Silence and Respect." A consistent reading of the theory of these messages would be that noise, talking, and crying all share the defect of dishonoring the dead by projecting expressions that the dead cannot appreci-

ate. If a cemetery is a home of the dead, then visitors are guests and they will be rude if they continue to express themselves in ways their hosts cannot understand. In what many regard as the paramount literary act of listening to the dead, Rilke's *Notebooks of Malte Laurids Brigge* (1983), much loud and sustained wailing happens on and around deathbeds, but there is much more silence in the multitude of ways that death and the dead remain present in life.

64. Staples [1986] 1996, 74.

65. The logic of the argument enables negative predictions (crying will not occur without the stipulated conditions) and what might be termed retrodiction. The objective is not to predict when people will cry, but neither is it mere definition. When one of the three conditions is removed, crying should end (see chapter 5 for an example of crying ending as speech begins). When one finds an instance of crying, it should be the case that the crying was shaped in these three ways.

66. In other places, subgroups may be deputized by authorities to cry publicly on behalf of the community. Islamic clerics have criticized women for inadequately mourning the death of the martyrs. See, e.g., Ameed 1974. In Romanian villages, brides are obligated to cry to dramatize the correct relationship of power in gender and kinship relationships. See Kligman 1988.

67. Froemke, Dickson, and Maysles 1996.

68. Put another way, we are always tacitly monitoring how what we touch touches us and how we incorporate the world as we enter it. Thus, without ever having looked, and clearly before my foot hits the ground, I know that I have misgauged the number of steps left to descend on the staircase. Realizing that the next step should already have announced its presence to my foot, or, conversely, that something is responding to my step before it should, I turn my gaze to the floor just in time to right myself. The experience gives us rare evidence that we were constantly shaping our body to the contours of the environment, all the while tacitly monitoring invisible dimensions of our embodiment of the scene.

69. Earlier I argued that there is an intrinsic hermeneutic mystery in crying. This is a different point. Crying often makes a speaker's utterances especially clear, as a matter of what is heard by a recipient, even while it makes exceptionally clear that the recipient cannot grasp all that is moving the speaker. Thus crying can be an especially effective way of saying "I need that" without clarifying *what* "that" is, much less *why* "that" is deemed so important. Crying is especially well suited for demonstrating to another person that he or she cannot reach the crying person's concerns. Crying often makes a vivid and power-enhancing display of an internal murkiness.

70. "People constantly produce a fluid called 'basal' or 'continuous' tears, which keeps the surface of the eye moist and helps prevent infection. With each blink of the eyelid a tear film bathes the surface of the eye with a bacteria-fighting fluid secreted by the main lacrimal gland and by accessory lacrimal glands located in the eyelids. And when the surface of the eye is irritated, the main lacrimal gland in humans and a similar gland in other animals produce additional tears, called 'reflex' or 'irritant' tears." Emotional tears are different in chemical structure from irritant tears. Frey 1985, 4.

71. Frey 1985, 7–8.

72. On crying as religious behavior, see Csordas 1994, 111–33.

FOG AND FUGUE

1. The most famous textbook on police interrogation states: "Crying is an emotional outlet that releases tension. It is also a very good indication that the suspect has given up and is ready to confess." Inbau, Reid, and Buckley 1986, 164.

2. As a basis for developing a specification of the interactional contingencies of crying, we can identify a series of work settings in which it is in the interest of a professional to reduce the crying of a client or patient. Nurses working with the elderly, for example, tend to become stressed when their clients cry, especially when they cry continuously (Chappell and Novak 1994). So do public assistance case workers. See Garot 1997; Miller 1991, 77. Studies of how people manage others' emotions are reviewed in Thoits 1996.

3. Interrogators take pride in their ability to bring suspects to tears. " 'They think they're so good at lying, they think, "I can pull this off," but I've had the toughest of them in here crying' and admitting guilt. . . . 'They're big, they're all buffed out, but they'll pucker up and cry on you.' " Detective Carolyn Flamenco, on bringing a murder suspect to a tearful confession by reminding him of his desire "to be a good role model" for his twelve-year-old son. *Los Angeles Times,* 21 September 1995, A29. Psychological counselors treat the eruption of crying by their clients as a measure of success when they take the crying as indicating breakthroughs and the emergence of repressed materials. See, e.g., Mills and Wooster 1987.

4. Arresting officers, for example, often want a suspect to "act like a man" and not make their work difficult by crying, at least not until he is in custody and under interrogation. See McClenahan and Lofland 1976, 268–69.

CHAPTER FIVE

1. The episode analyzed here is a single clip from a larger set of staff- and researcher-recorded videotapes of day care and preschool children in Dijon, France, and in southern California. My thanks to the staffs, children, and families involved, and to Eric Rivera for making available clips from his research in the San Diego area.

2. Merleau-Ponty 1973. This is a convenient point at which to acknowledge the very general utility of Leder's (1990) essay on the "absent body" for my treatment throughout this volume of the appearance and disappearance of the body in social interaction.

3. Treitler 1993, 46.

4. If the emotional response to music is through a resonance of the structure of emotional experience and the structure of music, the audience's response will not necessarily reflect the same emotion as is contained in the music, as understood by the composer and performers. The fierce debate over whether the emotions that listeners' experience are "in" the music or shared by the composer or musicians does not quite address this issue because it does

not look closely enough at the structure of comportment in playing. See, e.g., Kivy 1989.

5. My approach differs from paralinguistic analyses in that I focus on patterns used as resources for shaping the course of interaction, not on emotional expressions as objects examined out of the context of their use. The description of what might be termed "objective" dimensions of emotional expressions overlaps with the current treatment. See, for example, the description of laughter in Poyatos 1993.

6. The transcription of length of whine elements, phrases, and subsections of phrases was not done in a standardized manner, for example by using a stopwatch. Instead length was transcribed to describe its interactional significance, for example to clarify whether two or more people were producing utterances and body motions that were starting and/or ending simultaneously or whether one began or ran on beyond the other.

7. Peaks appear cross-culturally in infant whines. Barr et al. 1991.

8. In newborns, prolonged "bouts" of crying exhibit acoustic features of a "basic" or regular cry. Green, Gustafson, and McGhie 1998. The pitch of a burst of infant crying rises early and falls sharply at the end. Stark 1989. See also the investigation of the "temporal morphology" of crying, Zeskind, Parker-Price, and Barr 1993, 322.

9. See Levelt 1989, 413–54.

10. In this sense, whining is a way in which the child him- or herself can carry on what Nancy Chodorow (1978), in a macrosociological and theoretical perspective, refers to as the "reproduction of mothering."

11. A study of the distinctive interactional skills that define the competence of a seasoned preschool teacher would highlight such practices of keeping more than one child simultaneously at the foreground of the teacher's attentions. The challenge for the teacher is not simply to keep in touch with the situated experience of multiple children, it is to sustain the sense among multiple children that each is within the ongoing awareness or fabric of concern, if not direct attention of the teacher. The children themselves help sustain the teacher's miraculous ability to be in more than one social place at a given time. Here, for example, Rachel is not unaware that her teacher is talking to Gina, but by keeping her focus on the teacher's hand movements in disassembling blocks as this talking goes on, Rachel contributes to keeping the teacher at the foreground of her attentions.

12. Goffman 1963, 43.

13. Because the meaning of behavior in social interaction is created prospectively and retrospectively, still images, which usually fail to express the temporal horizons of action, can be critically misleading. A still photograph or video frame taken from X's continuous alteration of gaze from A to B and back to A might suggest an abandonment of attention to A, ignoring a continuity of movement that, within the situation, is laboriously arranged just to fight that local interpretation.

14. These would be Goffman's "creature releases" (1963, 68–69).

15. Indeed, coughs are common in children's crying. In research on infants, coughs are said to appear because of the glottal closures and voiced inspiratory sounds in crying. But, interestingly, coughing is seen as a way the infant begins exercising will over reflexes; in effect, coughing is a first step in playing or

working with crying. "The elaboration of coughs" in crying is part of the "modification of reflexive behaviour in the first stage of sensorimotor development. . . . It may reflect increased ability to manage respiration" in crying. Stark 1989, 133–34. I would suggest that the stream of respiration, which is a naturally occurring intertwining of the inside and the outside of the body, is the first field for the emergence of will and personality.

16. Near the start of the episode, Rachel emitted a single note that may have been either a hiccup or a cough.

17. Responsively paired turns in talking have been analyzed as "adjacency pairs" (hi/hello; question/answer; bye/see ya). Alternating turns at talk define conversations, and a pair of sequentially adjacent utterances done by two people, in which each calls for or responds to the other's turn, is commonly enacted to begin conversations. I.e., people do a ritualized and especially emphatic version of the processual structure of conversation as a way of moving into conversations. Sacks 1992, 521–22: "there's this thing that I call '*overall structural organization of conversation*,' which is the means whereby parties get into conversations and out of them. And it turns out that at the precise points of getting into them adjacency pairs are used." More clearly than coherence in topics, it is the maintenance of such interlocked, sequential turn taking that gives conversations their coherence (Schegloff 1990).

18. To review: When the teacher returns, Rachel has assembled the blocks into a cube. The teacher celebrates, "This is beautiful, Rachel." Then she quickly disassembles the blocks, placing them randomly on the table as she simultaneously says, "Now, let's try to put it back in the box." Rachel now stops crying and completes five units of interaction with her teacher.

In order to fit the blocks into the box, they must be placed in either progressively larger or smaller order. When she had assembled the cube, Rachel had worked from the smallest to the largest block, and had ended by placing the largest block as the cube's top.

Now Tamara asks, "How do you think it goes?" As Rachel coughs, she selects the largest block and moves it to the storage box in a horizontal position. The teacher takes the block from her in midair, moves the block into a vertical position, and places it in the box. This is the first unit of action in the episode in which the two work together.

In the second unit of coresponsive sequential action, the teacher asks Rachel to select the next block to go into the storage box, Rachel chooses a small block, and the child asks for confirmation of her choice. In the third unit, the teacher verbally and demonstratively guides the child to a different block, a large block that is the next smallest to one already put into the box; the child picks up the designated block; and the teacher explicates the progression they are following ("Now we're going from the biggest to the smallest"). In the fourth unit, the teacher asks Rachel to choose the next block and the child picks up another small block, again not the next in the progression. Next the teacher makes a comment, "Okay, keep on trying. [pause] What else?" This comment ends the fourth and begins the fifth unit of paired action. The teacher comments on the prior move without confirming it or defining the child's choice as wrong, and she also urges the child to chose another block. Rachel responsively chooses another (too) small block, and again asks for confirmation. The next statement is from Alan and it provokes a renewal of Rachel's whining.

19. A phenomenology of this nature is needed to complete an understanding of the interactional dynamics of the mother-infant bond. Cf. Stern 1985.

20. In my view, this analysis builds directly from work on the ontogenesis of speech acts that stresses how language articulates interactional processes already mastered in the relationship of mother and child (Bruner 1983). Perhaps because the pioneers of the interactionist understanding of language acquisition were cognitive psychologists, the infant's body remained essentially invisible in their analyses. Treating language as an intellectualized activity and the child as challenged "to grasp concepts embodied in language" (Bruner 1975, 8), researchers neglected not only crying but the general issue of how language releases the child's grasp of his or her body.

21. Over the school year, parents also change, becoming less anxious when dropping their children off and picking them up. Research on parental behavior and crying by preschool children suggests that a child is more likely to cry if a parent sneaks off without a parting ritual, but also that the more a parent explains his or her departure, the more likely that his or her child will cry. Field et al. 1984.

22. For example, among the Kaluli of Papua New Guinea, "[o]lder children have been observed to be relentless in their torment of younger children, provoking them to crying tantrums." Schieffelin 1986, 171.

23. Merleau-Ponty 1973, 19.

CHAPTER SIX

1. The facts as reported in this chapter reflect points of agreement between Martin and the police. I became familiar with the videotape, transcripts, and police records in the case after issues of fact were settled, when I was asked by Seymour Weisberg, of the public defender's office of Santa Barbara, to assist in the defense of Martin at the punishment phase of his trial for the California murder. I thank Mr. Martin for his cooperation and Mr. Weisberg for guiding me through the large record and correcting errors on a draft of this chapter.

2. Pierre Bourdieu's development of the concept of the *habitus* is doubly applicable to this case. "The *habitus* is a spontaneity without consciousness or will" (1990, 56). The police target and at crucial moments take away Martin's spontaneity. Indeed, the interrogation room is generally an attractive setting for novelists, philosophers, and sociologists because it is a place where people assume that they cannot be seen to think up their selves if they are to remain effective. A second aspect of habitus, that of an interpenetration of self and operative field, is equally important for understanding Martin's fate. As some of the details of the interrogation will reveal (especially in part 2 of this chapter), Martin is fascinated with being a criminal and eager to brag about his exploits, just up to the point of acknowledging that he has been violent. He is content, at times manifestly happy, to be a suspect, just not a murder suspect. A creature of the system he has sought to deceive for most of his life, Martin has often been charged with pretending to be a police officer. He reminds us of David Matza's (1969) powerful analysis of how the operations of the criminal

justice system can sustain an image of society as Leviathan, an image that makes possible criminal lives lived in the privately celebrated heroics of endless evasions and cunning deceptions.

3. In this, perhaps the most cruel irony in his short saga of violent criminality, Martin apparently did not realize that the man was blind. Because he was blind, the victim did not turn on lights when he heard a disturbance. Unable to appreciate his immunity from identification, Martin apparently took a gratuitous shot in the dark, striking the victim in the chest.

4. For reviews of research on how speech is grounded in bodily movements, a growing and newly contentious area of research, see Rimé and Schiaratura 1991, 241 ("with the gestures and bodily movements of the speaking person, we are faced with embodied thinking"), and the contrasting perspective of Kendon 1994 and 1997.

5. Inbau, Reid, and Buckley 1986, 159–61.

6. Like others who have studied police interrogations, I have been struck by the police tactic of inventing pseudoscientific evidence that supposedly links a suspect to a crime. I do not think that the only value of inventing the "Neutron Proton Negligence Intelligence Test" (Ofshe and Leo 1997, 1033) and the like is solely for the *substantive* value in deceiving suspects. Interrogators have a lot of fun conning suspects with outlandish pretexts that express the police position in moral stratification, simultaneously mocking the suspect's uneducated status and the popular belief that scientific knowledge is relevant to the solution of real issues of good and evil in the world. That working joy, in turn, adds to the incomprehensible atmosphere of self-confident control that the suspect confronts in the police station. It is the ineffable power of context, not only particular substantive deceptions, that lubricates confessions.

7. I previously came across such experiences when reviewing autobiographical accounts of adolescent shoplifters who were caught by store detectives. Katz 1988, 65.

8. Erving Goffman (1969, 20) wrote of the spy's strategy to admit to some form of domestic illegality in order to provide a cover for anxiety rooted in a role in international espionage.

9. Watson 1990; Leo 1996a.

10. For documentation on this point, I am grateful to Richard Leo who allowed me to review a set of videotapes of interrogations in a northern California police station, many of which featured cryings by witnesses and relatives of suspects.

11. Levelt 1989.

12. One of his idiosyncrasies was the use of policelike disguises in his everyday transactions, even for innocent actions like routine consumer purchases. He would try to talk with regional accents that were not his, suggest that he was part of an espionage or international policing agency, gratuitously offer descriptions of his travels, carry multiple forms of identification, etc. Several times he was charged with impersonating a police officer. This is a man who, within or outside of confinement, always lives deep in the belly of Leviathan.

13. Nabokov (1989) vividly portrayed this dynamic.

14. Inbau 1985.

15. On the significance of space in interrogations, see Lebaron and Streeck 1997.

16. That the police are skilled in deceit helps explain why, after the *Miranda* decision required the police to inform suspects that what they said would be held against them, suspects continued to confess unsuspectingly in high numbers (Leo 1996b). The police thus emerge as con men, beating criminals at their own game, demonstrating their dominance at playing on either side of the walls of moral authority that empower and contain them.

17. See text at page 162, where this metaphor is discussed.

CHAPTER SEVEN

1. And sociological thinking more generally. "The prime insight of sociology has always been that there are forces out there in the world that give shape and direction to human behavior . . . something in the nature of social life that induces people to behave in an orderly way at least some of the time. . . . Sociologists tend to regard (and to speak of) those forces as *things*. One cannot see them or touch them, of course, but we study their properties by observing what happens to the people caught up in them." Sociological "eyes are for the most part trained on the *spaces between* intersecting individuals—on the shape of their conversation, the architecture of their transaction, the way the words spoken and the gestures enacted form a pattern that is altogether independent of the personalities and intentions of the persons who contributed to it" (Erikson 1997, 3–4, 9).

2. Ricoeur 1970.

3. Freud 1960, 1989.

4. Taking advantage of my license as a pragmatic sociologist, and following the spirit of Ricoeur's reading of Freud, I brashly run Freud, Ricoeur, and Heidegger together here. It is easy to highlight the enormous differences among these thinkers, but it will be enormously useful to read their perspectives as forming a common line of inquiry into the doubly hermeneutic character of personal action in social situations.

5. Dreyfus (1991, 33) has been as invaluable for my understanding of Heidegger as has Ricoeur for my understanding of Freud.

6. At least in face-to-face interaction. Note that when I present myself in a congealed form, as in a writing, others are relieved of the pressure to respond, but then what they see of me is two-dimensional and superficial, a thin, disembodied, easily manipulated version of who I am.

7. For a classic critique of Goffman's hollow image of the social actor, see Messinger, Sampson, and Towne 1962.

8. Goffman 1959.

9. Merleau-Ponty 1964a, 1964c.

10. Polanyi 1962, 1966.

11. This is the sense in which Merleau-Ponty would write that the artist doesn't see the landscape, he sees himself seen by the landscape. Here is the point in one of his more social-psychological passages. "As soon as we see other seers, we no longer have before us only . . . the plate glass of the things with that feeble reflection, that phantom of ourselves they evoke by designating a place among themselves whence we see them: henceforth, through other eyes we are for ourselves fully visible; that lacuna where . . . our back, lie[s]

is filled, filled still by the visible" (1968, 143). Thus, as the painter portrays his perception of the landscape, not through a self-portrait in the conventional sense but by painting a landscape that "designates" his place and perspective in it, so "we are for ourselves fully visible" not in what we can see directly of our embodied action but only in what we see of others' comportment.

12. Howard S. Becker has devoted much of his career to the endless socio-logical work of showing the culturally hidden collective basis of what are re-garded artificially as individual attributes (Katz 1994). Thus, in his work on art worlds (Becker 1982), he effectively debunked the notion of artistic genius in much the same way that in earlier work he debunked the idea that deviance is a quality of the individual (Becker 1963). What is constant is a description of how the activities of organizationally separate, often mutually unaware peo-ple, fit together to construct the practical dimensions and the social definitions of artistic or deviant acts.

13. "Common-sense says . . . we meet a bear, are frightened and run. . . . The hypothesis here to be defended says that this order of sequence is incor-rect . . . , that the bodily manifestations must first be interposed between, and that . . . we feel . . . afraid because we tremble. . . . Without the bodily states following on the perception, . . . [w]e might then see the bear, and judge it best to run . . . but we should not actually *feel* afraid. . . ." (James [1890] 1950, 449–50). Seeing a dark form moving in the woods, before any articulate idea of danger takes shape, a person catches his breath and senses an irregular heartbeat.

Writings that trace the implications of Mead's thought have done bet-ter in appreciating how perception sets up response than in appreciating how response constructs perception. A deep fault line opened when Her-bert Blumer brokered Mead's thought to American sociologists. Blumer de-scribed the interactional nature of the social act as a process in which people weigh alternative lines of action as they anticipate alternative responses from others (1969, 69, 109, 111). The model underneath this image is that of delib-erative thought. In the ongoing, pressing flow of social life, thinking is not what people usually do, even, indeed, especially when they are working at their most accomplished level. A more accurate model is the knowledge in the hands of the piano player (Sudnow 1978). By separating out "non-symbolic interaction" ("An unwitting response to the tone of another's voice illustrates non-symbolic interaction": Blumer 1969, 66) as less worthy of sociological consideration, Blumer made an artificial dichotomy of what is a continuum and severely compromised the depth of social research on "symbolic inter-action."

14. Katz 1975.

15. In American sociology, Schutz, and his emphasis on the problem of intersubjectivity, was a source for the development of "ethnomethodology" and its progeny, which have been primarily studies of artistic action, conversa-tion analysis, and the work of scientists. The best review is Heritage 1984b. Ethnomethodogy developed in resistance to Blumer's teaching at Chicago and Berkeley and to Goffman's influence over the analysis of social process.

16. As Harold Garfinkel, a mid-twentieth-century academic incarnation of Andersen's troublemaking child-hero, demonstrated by putting Schutz's pro-vocative idea to the test in his famous "experiments" (Garfinkel 1967b).

17. These confusions are not, however, innocent. They give rise to the apprehensions, ill feelings, senses of power, and so on that infiltrate the ongoing streams of emotional life. Only on relatively rare occasions do they burst out in socially situated emotional expressions. Here we see how the empirical perspective of situational social-psychological analysis opens without any mystical legerdemain onto the traditional topics of psychological therapy.

18. It is significant that Erving Goffman (1971, 340–41), and before him Kai Erikson (1957), developed an appreciation of the contingent integration of the two sides of personal identity, self and other, in studies of people defined as mentally disturbed. This conception of personal identity has flourished in contemporary culture far beyond academic circles. Recently, a "narrative" emphasis, one that privileges language and suggests too much self-discourse to be quite right, has taken up the idea. "What we call 'I,' the self that we spend a lifetime making and remembering, is really a story that we tell ourselves and that is reflected back to us by the world. When both versions of this narrative are more or less in synch, you have sanity; when they aren't, you have madness" (Lahr 1994, 104).

19. I have elsewhere written of the numerous, detailed parallels between the structure of shame as indicated by the myth of Adam and Eve and the structure of emotions in everyday life (Katz 1996b). The phenomenology of shame, particularly the wish to flee from Yahweh to Gaea, back to Earth as it was lived before the encounter with the father figure, also suggests other, perhaps more ancient mythical traditions.

20. A category that includes culturally recognized "exceptional" or "wow" events. See Sacks 1984.

21. The fate of queue culture in formerly communist Central European nations calls for study before we can determine whether capitalism or communism has bred a nastier version of this social institution. West Germans, who themselves have a reputation among Europeans for being outrageously pushy in public interaction, attribute the allegedly barbarous manners of East Germans to their experience under communism. And some observational evidence in formerly socialist countries cuts the other way, indicating a sentimental attachment to the egalitarianism of queue culture. In supermarkets around Prague almost a decade after the Velvet Revolution of 1989, a shopper may be required by a private guard to obtain a cart before he or she will be allowed to enter the food aisles. By requiring customers to obtain a cart before moving beyond the cash registers into the store, and by limiting the number of carts, the market can easily control the number of customers in the store and thus assure each shopping party the minimal amount of private space that the cart provides. What is curious is that the practice is still authoritatively maintained in some markets even when they are virtually empty. In winter, people sometimes queue up for carts, waiting patiently in long lines that may leave numerous shoppers outside the doors in subzero temperatures, and some locals say that they are fond of the custom out of nostalgia for the solidarity that the successful management of queue tensions once allowed them to display on a routine basis. For some Czechs, everyday shopping life under capitalism is now disappointingly apolitical. Orderliness is vanishing as a manifest social achievement as the "invisible hand" or differential pricing sorts out supply

and demand. Now if a shopper is seen violating egalitarian queue norms, he or she is indicating something about him- or herself personally rather than challenging the communal regime as a whole.

22. Anger of course frequently arises at work and at home, at times with fatal consequences. The point is not to explain the frequency or intensity of anger but to clarify its dualistic narrative structure. That is easier to see in road rage and queue anger because within these bounded communistic settings, the transcendent meaning that fuels anger springs up in an especially sudden manner. When anger arises at home, it typically rises through what is seen as disrespect for the honor or deference that a sibling, parent, or spouse should receive. Ongoing status characteristics are implicated, and tensions will also often be diffused across situational encounters of family members and coworkers. It is easier to see the transcendent themes in queue and drivers' anger, not only for the analyst but also for the people involved, just because what happens in the market and on the highway is otherwise so clearly of such minimal relevance to the rest of one's life. Much of the data in this volume is indeed about trivial, everyday matters, and thus the methodological strategy here is precisely the opposite of that which Freud took up to understand emotions. His subjects emphasized traumas, diffusely troubled personalities, classic narratives, and the accomplishments of great men. Does it not make more sense initially to try to figure out how emotions work by studying the simplest, most isolated, and most widely accessible experiences, i.e., the stuff of everyday life?

23. It is virtually irresistible for social scientists to assume that there must be something negative behind anger. But if there is anything negative that gives force to drivers' and shoppers' anger, it does not help much to argue that aggression is inherent in human being, since anger springs up only when the interaction situation is appropriately structured. Nor are there any grounds in these data to assume that anger is a transformation of some prior experience of shame that was repressed. The appeal of becoming pissed off when driving is too widespread for ideas of repression to be very useful. The person who is cut off is presented with a pristine challenge to make sense of a situation, to create a new narrative meaning. As Hollywood has shown us, anger and violence are universally accessible, readily constructed narrative lines. Just as it is practically easier to make a movie about anger and violence than about the emotionally diverse evolution of interpersonal relations, so it is easier for drivers to make up little dramas of anger than to reflect about their expectations, their limited knowledge of others, how the current moment fits into their past and future, how others might react to the same challenge, etc. On the big screen and in the little scenes of everyday life, anger is a cheaply produced emotion that is especially attractive when, for practical reasons, some sort of show must be put on quickly. What is perhaps most amazing in both settings is the size of the audiences that find such dramas so consistently compelling.

24. This would be an example of what Thomas Scheff (1990, 86; 1997), following Helen Lewis (1971), has analyzed as "unacknowledged" and "bypassed shame."

25. In the course of writing this volume, I have spoken with people who have declared themselves routinely suspicious of laughter because they assume it must be somehow cruel, an act more or less viciously directed at someone.

Academic social psychology can hardly be held responsible for this pathos in popular culture, but it does little to fight it.

26. Simmel (1964) understood this at the level of collective conflicts.

27. The frightening power of anger is rooted in its self-martyring nature. If the angry person is his or her own first victim, this provides a powerful defense against feeling guilt for what he or she is willing to do to others.

28. My thanks to Melvin Pollner for offering this memorable image in casual comments made years ago.

29. The following text draws some phrases from Katz 1996b.

30. See Crawford et al. 1992, discussed at chapter 4 note 3.

31. The study of emotions in everyday life is a complement to the study of mundane reason (Pollner 1987), just as Harold Garfinkel's "breaching experiments," which produced a range of emotions (including anger, shame, crying, and laughter) in the people unwittingly subject to them, were, considered in one light, an opening toward a sociology of emotions and, as more commonly considered, an introduction to the study of the routine sense-making practices of everyday social life.

32. Polanyi 1962.

33. Compare Goodwin 1996, 376–98, who writes about vision as "transparent" when a set of people interact on the assumption that they are all seeing the same thing in the same way. In his context, that of airport ground traffic controllers watching monitors, exclamations on the order of "Oh, Jesus" and brief outbursts of laughter imply that everyone in a setting may ignore differences in perspective on what is perceived, even when such differences are real and potentially consequential. Vision is transparent when interaction keeps a collective focus practically trained on a presumptively shared landscape and away from highlighting how individual lines of regard idiosyncratically construct what each sees.

34. Part of the teacher's strategy in her attempt to lure the child into speech was, after an initial hug, generally not to look at the child as she whined and not to comment on the whining. "Normalizing" the interaction as she continued with a demonstration of the puzzle work, the teacher in effect willfully conferred a mantle of invisibility onto the child's body (which the child as willfully threw off). When, after having stopped whining and speaking, the child started to whine again, the teacher ended her effort to keep the child invisible. As a sign of her frustration, the teacher then looked directly at the child and uttered what she had left unspoken during about five minutes of whining, the direct (and predictably unproductive) question, "Why are you crying?"

35. Recall the double entendre of the interrogator thrusting his gun-shaped, pointing finger at Martin as he asked him to confirm that the police had found the gun he used in a murder (figure 6.2).

36. Katz 1975.

37. The link between respiration and crying has subtleties far beyond those investigated here. It is said that one can produce tears at will by gently stirring the hairs inside one's nostrils (Peck 1987, 38–39). The social logics of emotions may well be elaborations of the structures of bodily practices that work beneath the normal reach of awareness.

38. Nor is there a natural dividing point in the ongoing flow of food into the body, through the digestive process, and out as excretion. The culturally enforced invisibility of the digestive intertwining of person and world sets up the emotional consequentiality of turning awareness to particular points in the process, creating a universally exploited substratum of resources not only for humor but also for building religious consciousness on notions of the sacred and the profane (Douglas 1972), and for building psychological theory on notions of repression (Freud 1958).

39. For decades, photographers used this fact to suggest the reach of writers' personalities. The subtle and nuanced character of the smoke that curls out from a cigarette, and its capacity to overcome resistance and become diffused as a feature of any environment, would do proud any writer who could permeate his or her writings with such qualities.

REFERENCES

Acebo, Christine, and Evelyn B. Thoman. 1992. "Crying as Social Behavior." *Infant Mental Health Journal* 13:67–82.

———. 1995. "Role of Infant Crying in the Early Mother-Infant Dialogue." *Physiology and Behavior* 57:541–47.

Ameed, Syed Mohammad. 1974. *The Importance of Weeping and Wailing.* Karachi: Peermahomed Ebrahim Trust.

Anderson, Elijah. 1990. *Streetwise: Race, Class and Change in an Urban Community.* Chicago: University of Chicago Press.

Baechler, Jean. 1979. *Suicides.* New York: Basic Books.

Bakhtin, Mikhail. 1968. *Rabelais and His World.* Cambridge: MIT Press.

Barr, Ronald G. 1990. "The Normal Crying Curve: What Do We Really Know?" *Developmental Medicine and Child Neurology* 32:356–62.

Barr, Ronald G., Melvin Konner, Roger Bakeman, and Lauren Adamson. 1991. "Crying in Kung San Infants: A Test of the Cultural Specificity Hypothesis." *Developmental Medicine and Child Neurology* 33:601–10.

Becker, Howard S. 1958. "Problems of Inference and Proof in Participant Observation." *American Sociological Review* 23:652–60.

———. 1963. *Outsiders.* New York: Free Press.

———. 1982. *Art Worlds.* Berkeley and Los Angeles: University of California Press.

———. 1986. *Writing for Social Scientists.* Chicago: University of Chicago Press.

Berger, K. T. 1988. *Zen Driving.* New York: Ballentine Books.

———. 1993. *Where the Road and the Sky Collide: America through the Eyes of Its Drivers.* New York: Henry Holt.

Bermúdez, José Luis. 1998. *The Paradox of Self-Consciousness.* Cambridge: MIT Press.

Bermúdez, José Luis, Anthony Marcel, and Naomi Eilan. 1995. *The Body and the Self.* Cambridge: MIT Press.

Best, Joel. 1991. " 'Road Warriors' on 'Hair-Trigger Highways': Cultural Resources and the Media's Construction of the 1987 Freeway Shootings Problem." *Sociological Inquiry* 61:327–45.

Blumer, Herbert. 1937. "Social Psychology." In *Man and Society,* edited by Emerson P. Schmidt, 144–98. New York: Prentice-Hall.

———. 1969. *Symbolic Interactionism.* Englewood Cliffs, N.J.: Prentice-Hall.

Bourdieu, Pierre. 1990. *The Logic of Practice.* Trans. R. Nice. Stanford: Stanford University Press.

Braithwaite, John. 1989. *Crime, Shame, and Reintegration.* New York: Cambridge University Press.

Brazelton, T. Berry. 1990. "Crying and Colic." *Infant Mental Health Journal* 11:349–56.

Brazelton, T. Berry, J. S. Robey, and G. A. Collier. 1969. "Infant Development in the Zinacanteco Indians of Southern Mexico." *Pediatrics* 44:274–90.

Brinley, Maryann Bucknum. 1995. "Software Tells You What to Expect When You're Expecting a Baby." *HOMEPC,* October, 121.

Broucek, Francis. J. 1991. *Shame and the Self.* New York: Guilford Press.

Bruner, Jerome. 1975. "The Ontogenesis of Speech Acts." *Journal of Child Language* 2:1–19.

———. 1983. *Child's Talk.* New York: Norton.

Buckley, Christopher. 1995–1996. "Dedicated Lines." *New Yorker,* December 25, 1995/January 1, 1996, 46.

Burgess, Ann Wolbert. 1983. "Rape Trauma Syndrome." *Behavioral Sciences and the Law* 1:97–113.

Cahill, Spencer E., and Robin Eggleston. 1994. "Managing Emotions in Public: The Case of Wheelchair Users." *Social Psychology Quarterly* 57:300–312.

Canetti, Elias. 1979. *Auto-Da-Fe.* New York: Seabury Press.

Certeau, Michel de. 1984. *The Practice of Everyday Life.* Berkeley and Los Angeles: University of California Press.

Chappell, Neena L., and Mark Novak. 1994. "Caring for Institutionalized Elders: Stress among Nursing Assistants." *Journal of Applied Gerontology* 13:299–315.

Chodorow, Nancy. 1978. *The Reproduction of Mothering: Psychoanalysis and the Sociology of Gender.* Berkeley and Los Angeles: University of California Press.

Cicourel, Aaron. 1964. *Method and Measurement in Sociology.* Glencoe, Ill.: Free Press.

Clark, Candace. 1997. *Misery and Company: Sympathy in Everyday Life.* Chicago: University of Chicago Press.

Coser, Ruth L. 1960. "Laughter among Colleagues." *Psychiatry* 23:81–95.

Coulter, Jeff. 1986. "Affect and Social Context: Emotion Definition as a Social Task." In *The Social Construction of Emotion,* edited by Rom Harre, 120–34. Oxford: Basil Blackwell.

———. 1989. "Cognitive 'Penetrability' and the Emotions." In *The Sociology of Emotions: Original Essays and Research Papers,* edited by David D. Franks and E. Doyle McCarthy, 33–50. Greenwich, Conn.: JAI Press.

Crawford, June, Susan Kippax, Jenny Onyx, Una Gault, and Pam Benton. 1992. *Emotion and Gender: Constructing Meaning from Memory.* London: Sage.

Cressey, Donald Ray. 1953. *Other People's Money: A Study in the Social Psychology of Embezzlement.* Glencoe, Ill.: Free Press.

Cronyn, Lori. 1992. "The Inverted Smile: An Embodied Metaphor of Shame in Public Places." Department of Sociology, University of California at Los Angeles.

Csordas, Thomas J. 1994. *The Sacred Self: A Cultural Phenomenology of Charismatic Healing.* Berkeley and Los Angeles: University of California Press.

Cuddihy, John M. 1974. *The Ordeal of Civility: Freud, Marx, Levi-Strauss, and the Jewish Struggle with Modernity.* New York: Basic Books.

Dannefer, W. Dale. 1977. "Driving and Symbolic Interaction." *Sociological Inquiry* 47:33–38.

Davis, Fred. 1979. *Yearning for Yesterday: A Sociology of Nostalgia.* New York: Free Press.

Dessureau, Brian K., Carolyn O. Kurowski, and Nicholas S. Thompson. 1998. "A Reassessment of the Role of Pitch and Duration in Adults' Responses to Infant Crying." *Infant Behavior and Development* 21:367–71.

Dostoyevsky, Fyodor. 1950. *The Brothers Karamazov.* New York: Random House.

Douglas, Mary. 1972. "Deciphering a Meal." *Daedalus,* winter, 61–81.

Dreyfus, Hubert L. 1991. *Being-in-the-World: A Commentary on Heidegger's Being and Time, Division I.* Cambridge: MIT Press.

Du, Shanshan. 1995. "The Aesthetic Axis in the Construction of Emotions and Decisions: Love-Pact Suicide among the Lahu Na of Southwest China." In *Social Perspectives on Emotions,* edited by Michael G. Flaherty and Carolyn Ellis, 199–221. Greenwich, Conn.: Sage.

Eberle, Paul, and Shirley Eberle. 1993. *The Abuse of Innocence: the McMartin Preschool Trial.* Buffalo: Prometheus Books.

Ekman, Paul, and Wallace V. Friesen. 1976. "Measuring Facial Movement." *Journal of Environmental Psychology and Nonverbal Behavior* 1: 56–75.

———. 1986. "A New Pan-Cultural Expression of Emotion." *Motivation and Behavior* 10:159–68.

Ekman, Paul, and Maureen O'Sullivan. 1991. "Facial Expression: Methods, Means, and Moues." In *Fundamentals of Nonverbal Behavior,* edited by R.S. Feldman and B. Rimé, 163–99. Cambridge: Cambridge University Press; Paris: Editions de la Maison des Sciences de l'Homme.

Emerson, Joan P. 1969. "Negotiating the Serious Import of Humor." *Sociometry* 32:169–81.

Emerson, Robert M. 1983. "Holistic Effects in Social Control Decision-Making." *Law and Society Review* 17:425–55.

Erikson, Kai T. 1957. "Patient Role and Social Uncertainty: A Dilemma of the Mentally Ill." *Psychiatry* 20:273–274.

———. 1997. "Prologue: Sociology as a Perspective." In *Sociological Visions,* edited by Kai Erikson, 3–16. Lanham: Rowman and Littlefield.

Fernández-Dols, José-Miguel, and James M. Carroll. 1997. "Is the Meaning Perceived in Facial Expression Independent of Its Context?" In *The Psychology of Facial Expression,* edited by James A. Russell and José-Miguel Fernández-Dols, 275–94. Cambridge: Cambridge University Press; Paris: Editions de la Maison des Sciences de l'Homme.

Fernández-Dols, José-Miguel, and Maria-Angeles Ruiz-Belda. 1997. "Spontaneous Facial Behavior during Intense Emotional Episodes: Artistic Truth and Optical Truth." In *The Psychology of Facial Expression,* edited by James A. Russell and José-Miguel Fernández-Dols, 255–74. Cambridge: Cambridge University Press; Paris: Editions de la Maison des Sciences de l'Homme.

Field, Tiffany, Jacob L. Gewirtz, Debra Cohen, Robert Garcia, Reena Greenberg, and Kerry Collins. 1984. "Leave-Takings and Reunions of Infants, Toddlers, Preschoolers, and Their Parents." *Child Development* 55:628–35.

Fondation Maeght. 1992. *L'Art en Mouvement* (exhibition catalog). St. Paul-de-Vence, France: Fondation Maeght.

Freud, Sigmund. 1958. *Civilization and Its Discontents.* New York: Anchor.

———. 1960. *Jokes and Their Relation to the Unconscious.* New York: W. W. Norton.

———. 1965. *The Interpretation of Dreams.* New York: Avon.

———. 1989. *The Psychopathology of Everyday Life.* New York: W. W. Norton.

Frey, William H. 1985. *Crying: The Mystery of Tears.* Minneapolis: Winston Press.

Friedman, Jennifer. 1992. "The Process of Interconnected Status Passages: An Illustration with Mother-Daughter Relationships." Paper presented at American Sociological Association meetings, Pittsburgh.

Froemke, Sisam, Deborrah Dickson, and Albert Maysles. 1996. *Letting Go: A Hospice Journey.* Documentary film. Home Box Office.

Gallagher, Shawn, and Andrew N. Meltzoff. 1996. "The Earliest Sense of Self and Others: Merleau-Ponty and Recent Developmental Studies." *Philosophical Psychology* 9:211–33.

Gampel, Yolanda. 1992. "I Was a Shoah Child." *British Journal of Psychotherapy* 8:390–400.

Gardner, Carol Brooks. 1995. *Passing By: Gender and Public Harassment.* Berkeley and Los Angeles: University of California Press.

Garfinkel, Harold. 1967a. *Studies in Ethnomethodology.* Englewood Cliffs, N.J.: Prentice-Hall.

———. 1967b. "Studies of the Routine Grounds of Everyday Activities." In *Studies in Ethnomethodology.* Englewood Cliffs, N.J.: Prentice-Hall.

Garot, Robert. 1997. "Emotions and Human Service Work: Anger and Tears in a Section 8 Housing Office." Department of Sociology, University of California at Los Angeles.

Gerhards, Jurgen. 1986. "Georg Simmel's Contribution to a Theory of Emotions." *Social Science Information* 25: 901–24.

Glaser, Barney G., and Anselm L. Strauss. 1964. "Awareness Contexts and Social Interaction." *American Sociological Review* 29:669–79.

Goffman, Erving. 1952. "On Cooling the Mark Out: Some Aspects of Adaptation to Failure." *Psychiatry* 15: 451–63.

———. 1959. *The Presentation of Self in Everyday Life.* Garden City, N.Y.: Doubleday.

———. 1963. *Behavior in Public Places: Notes on the Social Organization of Gatherings.* New York: Free Press.

———. 1967a. "Embarrassment and Social Organization." In *Interaction Ritual,* 97–112. Garden City, N.Y.: Anchor Books.

———. 1967b. "Where the Action Is." In *Interaction Ritual,* 149–270. Garden City, N.Y.: Anchor Books.

———. 1967c. Introduction to *Interaction Ritual,* 1–3. Garden City, N.Y.: Anchor Books.

———. 1969. *Strategic Interaction.* Philadelphia: University of Pennsylvania Press.

———. 1971. *Relations in Public.* New York: Basic Books.

Goleman, Daniel. 1995. *Emotional Intelligence.* New York: Bantam.

Goodwin, Charles. 1996. "Transparent Vision." In *Interaction and Grammar,* edited by Elinor Ochs, Emanuel A. Schegloff, and Sanda A. Thompson, 370–404. Cambridge: Cambridge University Press.

Green, James A., Gwen E. Gustafson, and Anne C. McGhie. 1998. "Changes in Infants' Cries as a Function of Time in a Cry Bout." *Child Development* 69:271–79.

Gregory, Dick, with Robert Lipsyte. 1964. *Nigger: An Autobiography.* New York: Dutton.

Gustafson, Gwen E., and Kirsten A. Deconti. 1990. "Infants' Cries in the Process of Normal Development." *Early Child Development and Care* 65:45–56.

Heath, Christian. 1984. "Embarrassment and Interactional Organization." In *Structures of Social Action: Studies in Conversation Analysis,* edited by J. M. Atkinson and J. Heritage, 136–60. New York: Cambridge University Press.

Heritage, John. 1984a. "A Change-of-State Token and Aspects of its Sequential Placement." In *Structures of Social Action,* edited by J. M. Atkinson and J. Heritage, 299–345. Cambridge: Cambridge University Press.

———. 1984b. *Garfinkel and Ethnomethodology.* Cambridge: Polity Press.

Hochschild, Arlie Russell. 1979. "Emotion Work, Feeling Rules, and Social Structure." *American Journal of Sociology* 83:551–75.

———. 1990. *The Second Shift.* New York: Avon.

Hollonbeck, Darrell, and James C. Ohls. 1984. "Participation among the Elderly in the Food Stamp Program." *Gerontologist* 24:616–21.

Hubbard, Frans O. A., and Marinus H. van IJzendoorn. 1994. "Does Maternal Responsiveness Increase Infant Crying? Replication of the Baltimore Study." In *Reconstructing the Mind: Replicability in Research on Human Development,* edited by Rene van der Veer, Marinus H. van IJzendoorn, and Jaan Valsiner, 255–70. Norwood, N.J.: Ablex Publishing.

Huffman, Lynne C., Yvonne E. Bryan, Frank A. Pedersen, Barry M. Lester, John D. Newman, and Rebecca del Carmen. 1994. "Infant Cry Acoustics and Maternal Ratings of Temperament." *Infant Behavior and Development* 17:45–53.

Inbau, Fred Edward. 1985. *Criminal Interrogation and Confessions.* Baltimore: Williams and Wilkins.

Inbau, Fred E., John E. Reid, and Joseph P. Buckley. 1986. *Criminal Interrogation and Confessions.* Baltimore: Williams and Wilkins.

Isherwood, Robert M. 1986. *Farce and Fantasy: Popular Entertainment in Eighteenth-Century Paris*. New York: Oxford University Press.

Jackson, John Brinckerhoff. 1994. *A Sense of Time, A Sense of Place*. New Haven: Yale University Press.

Jahoda, Marie, Paul F. Lazarsfeld, and Hans Zeisel. [1933] 1971. *Marienthal: The Sociography of an Unemployed Community*. Chicago: Aldine Atherton.

James, William. [1890] 1950. "The Emotions." In *Principles of Psychology*, 442–85. New York: Dover.

Jefferson, Gail. 1985. "An Exercise in the Transcription and Analysis of Laughter." In *Handbook of Discourse Analysis*, edited by Teun A. van Dijk, 3:25–34. London: Academic Press.

Jefferson, Gail, Harvey Sacks, and Emanuel Schegloff. 1973. "Preliminary Notes on the Sequential Organization of Laughter." Center for Urban Ethnography, University of Pennsylvania.

——. 1987. "Notes on Laughter in the Pursuit of Intimacy." In *Talk and Social Organisation*, edited by Graham Button and John R. Lee, 153–205. Clevedon, England: Multilingual Matters.

Johnson, Galen. 1993. *The Merleau-Ponty Aesthetics Reader: Philosophy and Painting*. Evanston, Ill.: Northwestern University Press.

Kaplan, Alice Yaeger. 1993. *French Lessons: A Memoir*. Chicago: University of Chicago Press.

Katz, Jack. 1975. "Essences as Moral Identities: On Verifiability and Responsibility in Imputations of Deviance and Charisma." *American Journal of Sociology* 80:1369–90.

——. 1983. "A Theory of Qualitative Methodology." In *Contemporary Field Research*, edited by Robert M. Emerson, 127–48. Prospect Heights, Ill.: Waveland.

——. 1988. *Seductions of Crime: Moral and Sensual Attractions in Doing Evil*. New York: Basic Books.

——. 1994. "Jazz in Social Interaction: Personal Creativity, Collective Constraint, and Motivational Explanation in the Social Thought of Howard S. Becker." *Symbolic Interaction* 17:253–79.

——. 1996a. "Families and Funny Mirrors: A Study of the Social Construction and Personal Embodiment of Humor." *American Journal of Sociology* 101:1194–237.

——. 1996b. "The Social Psychology of Adam and Eve." *Theory and Society* 25:545–82.

Kendon, Adam. 1981. "The Organization of Behavior in Face-to-Face Interaction: Observations on the Development of a Methodology." In *Handbook of Methods in Nonverbal Behaviour Research*, edited by Klaus R. Scherer and Paul Ekman, 440–505. Cambridge: Cambridge University Press.

——. 1990. "Behavioral Foundations for the Process of Frame-Attunement in Face-to-Face Interaction." In *Conducting Interaction*, 239–62. Cambridge: Cambridge University Press.

——. 1994. "Do Gestures Communicate?: A Review." *Research on Language and Social Interaction* 27:173–200.

——. 1997. "Gesture." *Annual Review of Anthropology* 26:109–28.

Kivy, Peter. 1989. *Sound Sentiment: An Essay on the Musical Emotions.* Philadelphia: Temple University Press.

Kleinman, Arthur. 1995. *Writing at the Margin: Discourse between Anthropology and Medicine.* Berkeley and Los Angeles: University of California Press.

Kligman, Gail. 1988. *The Wedding of the Dead: Ritual, Poetics, and Popular Culture in Transylvania.* Berkeley and Los Angeles: University of California Press.

Koestler, Arthur. 1964. *The Act of Creation.* New York: Macmillan.

Lahr, John. 1994. "Losing the Plot." *New Yorker,* June 13, 104.

Langer, Susanne. 1942. *Philosophy in a New Key: A Study in the Symbolism of Reason, Rite, and Art.* Cambridge: Harvard University Press.

Lansky, Melvin R. 1996. "Shame and Suicide in Sophocles' Ajax." *Psychoanalytic Quarterly* 65:761–86.

———. 1999. "The Stepfather in Sophocles' Electra." In *Stepfatherhood: Creating and Recreating Families in America,* edited by S. Cath and M. Shopper. Hillsdale, N.J.: Analytic Press. In press.

Lansky, Melvin, with C. R. Bley. 1995. *Posttraumatic Nightmares: Psychodynamic Explorations.* Hillsdale, N.J.: Analytic Press.

Lansky, Melvin, and Andrew Morrison. 1997. *The Widening Scope of Shame.* Hillsdale, N.J.: Analytic Press.

Latour, Bruno [Jim Johnson, pseud.]. 1988a. "Mixing Humans and Nonhumans Together: The Sociology of a Door Closer." *Social Problems* 35: 298–310.

Latour, Bruno. 1988b. *The Pasteurization of France.* Cambridge: Harvard University Press.

———. 1993. *We Have Never Been Modern.* Cambridge: Harvard University Press.

———. 1996. *Aramis, or, The Love of Technology.* Cambridge: Harvard University Press.

Lauer, A. R. 1960. *The Psychology of Driving.* Springfield, Ill.: Charles C. Thomas.

Lebaron, Curtis D., and Jürgen Streeck. 1997. "Built Space and the Interactional Framing of Experience During a Murder Interrogation." *Human Studies* 20:1–25.

Leder, Drew. 1990. *The Absent Body.* Chicago: University of Chicago Press.

Leff, Arthur. 1976. *Swindling and Selling.* New York: Free Press.

———. 1978. "Law and . . ." *Yale Law Journal* 87:989–1011.

Leo, Richard A. 1996a. "Inside the Interrogation Room." *Journal of Criminology and Criminal Law* 86:266–303.

———. 1996b. "*Miranda*'s Revenge: Police Interrogation as a Confidence Game." *Law and Society Review* 30:259–88.

Levelt, Willem J. M. 1989. *Speaking: From Intention to Articulation.* Cambridge: MIT Press.

Lewis, H. B. 1971. *Shame and Guilt in Neurosis.* New York: International Universities Press.

Lindesmith, Alfred R. 1947. *Opiate Addiction.* Bloomington, Ind.: Principia Press.

Lindsay-Hartz, Janice. 1984. "Contrasting Experiences of Shame and Guilt." *American Behavioral Scientist* 27:689–704.

Loewy, Joanne Victoria. 1995. "The Musical Stages of Speech: A Developmental Model of Pre-verbal Sound Making." *Music Therapy* 13:47–73.

Lombardo, W. K., G. A. Cretser, B. Lombardo, and S. L. Mathis. 1983. "For Cryin' Out Loud—There Is a Sex Difference." *Sex Roles* 9:987–95.

Lummaa, Virpi, Timo Vuorisalo, Ronald G. Barr, and Liisa Lehtonen. 1998. "Why Cry?: Adaptive Significance of Intensive Crying in Human Infants." *Evolution and Human Behavior* 19:193–202.

Lynd, Helen Merrill. 1958. *On Shame and the Search for Identity*. New York: Harcourt, Brace.

Lyon, Margot L. 1995. "Missing Emotion: The Limitations of Cultural Constructionism in the Study of Emotion." *Cultural Anthropology* 10: 244–63.

Lyon, Margot L., and J. M. Barbelet. 1994. "Society's Body: Emotion and the 'Somatization' of Social Theory." In *Embodiment and Experience: The Existential Ground of Culture and Self*, edited by Thomas J. Csordas, 48–66. Cambridge: Cambridge University Press.

Mann, Kenneth. 1985. *Defending White-Collar Crime*. New Haven: Yale University Press.

Matza, David. 1969. *Becoming Deviant*. Englewood Cliffs, N.J.: Prentice-Hall.

Mauss, Marcel. [1935] 1973. "Techniques of the Body." *Economy and Society* 2:70–88.

McClenahan, Lachlan, and John Lofland. 1976. "Bearing Bad News: Tactics of the Deputy U.S. Marshall." *Sociology of Work and Occupations* 3: 251–72.

McGrane, Bernard. 1994. *The Un-TV and the 10 MPH Car*. Fort Bragg, Calif.: Small Press.

McNeill, David. 1992. *Hand and Mind: What Gestures Reveal about Thought*. Chicago: University of Chicago Press.

Mecca, Andrew M., Neil J. Smelser, and John Vasconcellos. 1989. *The Social Importance of Self-Esteem*. Berkeley and Los Angeles: University of California Press.

Meltzoff, Andrew N., and N. Keith Moore. 1994. "Imitation, Memory, and the Representation Of Persons." *Infant Behavior and Development* 17: 83–99.

Merleau-Ponty, Maurice. 1964a. "Cezanne's Doubt." In *Sense and Non-Sense*, 9–25. Evanston, Ill.: Northwestern University Press.

———. 1964b. "The Child's Relations with Others." In *The Primacy of Perception*, edited by James Edie, 96–155. Evanston, Ill.: Northwestern University Press.

———. 1964c. *L'Oeil et l'Esprit*. Paris: Gallimard.

———. 1968. *The Visible and the Invisible*. Evanston, Ill.: Northwestern University Press.

———. 1973. "Science and the Experience of Expression." In *The Prose of the World*, edited by Claude Lefort, 9–46. Evanston, Ill.: Northwestern University Press.

———. 1988. *Merleau-Ponty à la Sorbonne: Résumé de Cours, 1949–1952.* [Grenoble]: Éditions Cynara.

Messinger, Sheldon L., Harold Sampson, and Robert D. Towne. 1962. "Life as Theater." *Sociometry* 25:98–110.

Miller, Gale. 1991. *Enforcing the Work Ethic.* Albany: State University of New York Press.

Miller, William Ian. 1990. *Bloodtaking and Peacemaking: Feud, Law, and Society in Saga Iceland.* Chicago: University of Chicago Press.

Mills, C. Kingsley, and Arthur D. Wooster. 1987. "Crying in the Counseling Situation." *British Journal of Guidance and Counselling* 15:125–30.

Moore, Barrington, Jr. 1966. *Social Origins of Dictatorship and Democracy: Lord and Peasant in the Making of the Modern World.* Boston: Beacon.

Morano, Donald V. 1976. *Existential Guilt: A Phenomenological Study.* Atlantic Highlands, N.J.: Humanities Press.

Morris, Ivan I. 1975. *The Nobility of Failure: Tragic Heroes in the History of Japan.* New York: Holt, Rinehart and Winston.

Nabokov, Vladimir. 1989. *Invitation to a Beheading.* Translated by Dimitri and Vladimir Nabokov. New York: Vintage.

Novaco, Raymond W. 1991a. "Aggression on Roadways." In *Targets of Violence and Aggression,* edited by Ronald Baenninger, 253–326. New York: North-Holland.

———. 1991b. "Automobile Driving and Aggressive Behavior." In *The Car and the City,* edited by Martin Wachs and Margaret Crawford, 234–47. Ann Arbor: University of Michigan Press.

Oatley, Keith. 1990. "Do Emotional States Produce Irrational Thinking?" In *Reflections on the Psychology of Thought,* vol. 2, *Skills, Emotion, Creative Processes, Individual Differences, and Teaching Thinking,* edited by Kenneth J. Gilhooly, Mark T. G. Keane, Robert H. Logie, and George Erdos, 121–31. Chichester, England: John Wiley and Sons.

Ofshe, Richard J., and Richard A. Leo. 1997. "The Decision to Confess Falsely: Rational Choice and Irrational Action." *Denver University Law Review* 74:979–1122.

Pagels, Elaine. 1988. *Adam, Eve, and the Serpent.* New York: Random House.

Paperman, Patricia. 1995. "L'absence d'émotion comme offense." In *La Couleur des Pensées: Sentiments, Émotions, Intentions,* edited by Patricia Paperman and Ruwen Ogien, 175–96. Paris: Éditions de l'École des Hautes Études en Sciences Sociales.

Peck, Stephen Rogers. 1987. *Atlas of Facial Expression: An Account of Facial Expression for Artists, Actors, and Writers.* New York: Oxford University Press.

Plessner, Helmuth. [1950] 1970. *Laughing and Crying: A Study of the Limits of Human Behavior.* Evanston, Ill.: Northwestern University Press.

Polanyi, Michael. 1962. *Personal Knowledge: Towards a Post-critical Philosophy.* Chicago: University of Chicago Press.

———. 1966. *The Tacit Dimension.* Garden City, N.Y.: Doubleday.

———. 1970. "What Is a Painting?" *American Scholar* 39:655–69.

Pollner, Melvin. 1987. *Mundane Reason: Reality in Everyday and Sociological Discourse.* Cambridge: Cambridge University Press.

Poyatos, Fernando. 1993. "The Many Voices of Laughter: A New Audible-Visual Paralinguistic Approach." *Semiotica* 93:61–81.

Prager, Jeffrey. 1998. *Presenting the Past: Psychoanalysis and the Sociology of Misremembering.* Cambridge: Harvard University Press.

Reisman, W. Michael. 1979. *Folded Lies: Bribery, Crusades, and Reform.* New York: Free Press.

Ricoeur, Paul. 1969. *The Symbolism of Evil.* Boston: Beacon.

———. 1970. *Freud and Philosophy: An Interpretation.* New Haven: Yale University Press.

Rilke, Rainer Maria. 1983. *The Notebooks of Malte Laurids Brigge.* New York: Random House.

Rimé, Bernard, and Loris Schiaratura. 1991. "Gesture and Speech." In *Fundamentals of Nonverbal Behavior,* edited by Robert S. Feldman and Bernard Rimé, 239–81. Cambridge: Cambridge University Press; Paris: Editions de la Maison des Sciences de l'Homme.

Ross, Catherine E., and John Mirowsky. 1984. "Men Who Cry." *Social Psychology Journal* 47:138–46.

Roth, Julius A. 1963. *Timetables: Structuring the Passing of Time in Hospital Treatment and Other Careers.* Indianapolis: Bobbs-Merrill.

Rushdie, Salman. 1983. *Shame.* New York: Knopf.

Sacks, Harvey. 1974. "An Analysis of the Course of a Joke's Telling in Conversations." In *Explorations in the Ethnography of Speaking,* edited by Richard Bauman and Joel Sherzer, 337–54. London: Cambridge University Press.

———. 1984. "On Doing 'Being Ordinary.' " In *Structures of Social Action,* edited by J. Maxwell Atkinson and John Heritage, 413–29. Cambridge: Cambridge University Press.

———. 1992. *Lectures on Conversation,* vol. 2. Oxford: Blackwell.

Sarbin, Theodore R. 1988. "Emotions as Narrative Employments." In *Interpretive Investigations: Contributions to Psychological Research,* edited by Martin J. Packer and Richard B. Addison, 1–31. Albany: State University of New York Press.

Sartre, Jean-Paul. 1948. *Emotions: The Outline of a Theory.* New York: Philosophical Library.

———. 1956. *Being and Nothingness: An Essay on Phenomenological Ontology.* New York: Washington Square Press.

Scheff, Thomas J. 1990. *Microsociology: Discourse, Emotion, and Social Structure.* Chicago: University of Chicago Press.

———. 1994. *Bloody Revenge: Emotions, Nationalism, and War.* Boulder: Westview Press.

———. 1997. *Emotions, the Social Bond, and Human Reality.* Cambridge: Cambridge University Press; Paris: Editions de la Maison des Sciences de l'Homme.

Scheff, Thomas J., and Suzanne M. Retzinger. 1991. *Emotions and Violence: Shame and Rage in Destructive Conflicts.* Lexington, Mass.: Lexington.

Schegloff, Emanuel A. 1990. "On the Organization of Sequences as a Source of 'Coherence' in Talk-in-Interaction." In *Conversational Organization and Its Development,* edited by Bruce Dorval, 51–77. Norwood, N.J.: Ablex Publishing.

Scheler, Max. 1987. "On Shame and Feelings of Modesty." In *Person and Self-Value: Three Essays,* translated by M. Frings, 1–85. Hingham, Mass.: Martinus Nijhoff.

Schieffelin, Bambi B. 1986. "Teasing and Shaming in Kaluli Children's Interactions." In *Language Socialization Across Cultures,* edited by Bambi B. Schieffelin and Elinor Ochs, 165–81. Cambridge: Cambridge University Press.

Schivelbusch, Wolfgang. 1986. *The Railway Journey: The Industrialization of Time and Space in the 19th Century.* Berkeley and Los Angeles: University of California Press.

Schneider, Carl D. 1992. *Shame, Exposure, and Privacy.* New York: W. W. Norton.

Schopenhauer, Arthur. 1969. *The World as Will and Representation.* New York: Dover.

Schwalbe, Michael. 1996. "The Mirror in Men's Faces." *Journal of Contemporary Ethnography* 25:58–82.

Scruton, Roger. 1986. *Sexual Desire: A Moral Philosophy of the Erotic.* New York: Free Press.

Simmel, Georg. 1924. "Sociology of the Senses: Visual Interaction." *Introduction to The Science of Sociology,* by R. E. Park and E. W. Burgess, 356–61. Chicago: University of Chicago Press.

———. 1964. *Conflict, and the Web of Group Affiliations.* New York: Free Press.

Singer, Jayne M., and Jeffrey W. Fagen. 1992. "Negative Affect, Emotional Expression, and Forgetting in Young Infants." *Developmental Psychology* 28:48–57.

Solomon, Robert C. 1981. "Sartre on Emotions." In *The Philosophy of Jean-Paul Sartre,* edited by Paul A. Schilpp, 211–28. La Salle, Ill.: Open Court.

———. 1983. *The Passions.* Notre Dame, Ind.: University of Notre Dame Press.

Srinivas, Lakshmi. 1997. "Ethnography of Hindi Film Audiences." Department of Sociology, University of California at Los Angeles.

Staples, Brent. [1986] 1996. "A Brother's Murder." *New York Times Magazine.* April 14, 74.

Stark, Rachel E. 1989. "Temporal Patterns of Cry and Non-Cry Sounds in the First Eight Months of Life." *First Language* 9:107–36.

Stein, Lawrence B., and Stanley L. Brodsky. 1995. "When Infants Wail: Frustration and Gender as Variables in Distress Disclosure." *Journal of General Psychology* 122:19–27.

Stern, Daniel N. 1985. *The Interpersonal World of the Infant.* New York: Basic.

Stevenson, Robert Joseph. 1998. *The Boiler Room and Other Telephone Sales Scams.* Urbana: University of Illinois Press.

Stoller, Paul. 1989. *The Taste of Ethnographic Things: The Senses in Anthropology.* Philadelphia: University of Pennsylvania Press.

———. 1997. *Sensuous Scholarship.* Philadelphia: University of Pennsylvania Press.

Stroebe, Wolfgang, and Margaret Stroebe. 1987. *Bereavement and Health.* Cambridge: Cambridge University Press.

Sudnow, David. 1978. *Ways of the Hand: The Organization of Improvised Conduct.* Cambridge: Harvard University Press.

————. 1979. *Talk's Body.* New York: Knopf.

————. 1983. *Pilgrim in the Microworld.* New York: Warner Books.

Tangney, June Price, and Kurt W. Fischer. 1995. *Self-Conscious Emotions: The Psychology of Shame, Guilt, Embarrassment and Pride.* New York: Guilford.

Theroux, Paul. 1995. *Translating LA: A Tour of the Rainbow City.* New York: W. W. Norton and Company.

Thoits, Peggy. 1996. "Managing the Emotions of Others." *Symbolic Interaction* 19:85–109.

Treitler, Leo. 1993. "Reflections on the Communication of Affect and Idea Through Music." In *Psychoanalytic Explorations in Music,* 2d series, edited by Stuart Feder, Richard L. Karmel, and George H. Pollock. Madison, Conn.: International Universities Press.

Trillin, Calvin. 1995. "What's the Good Word?" *New Yorker,* May 15, 102.

Updike, John. 1985. "At War with My Skin." *New Yorker,* September 2, 39–40, 43–44, 46–57.

Wacquant, Loïc J. D. 1992. "Toward a Social Praxeology: The Structure and Logic of Bourdieu's Sociology." In *An Invitation to Reflexive Sociology,* Pierre Bourdieu and Loïc J. D. Wacquant, 1–59. Chicago: University of Chicago Press.

Waldinger, Roger, and Mehdi Bozorgmehr. 1996. *Ethnic Los Angeles.* New York: Russell Sage Foundation.

Watson, D. R. 1990. "Some Features of the Elicitation of Confessions in Murder Interrogations." In *Interaction Competence,* edited by George Psathas, 263–95. Washington, D.C.: International Institute for Ethnomethodology and Conversation Analysis and University Press of America.

Westwood, Sallie. 1985. *All Day Every Day: Factory and Family in the Making of Women's Lives.* Urbana: University of Illinois Press.

Whitehead, Alfred North. [1925] 1960. *Science and the Modern World.* New York: Macmillan.

————. [1938] 1958. *Modes of Thought.* New York: Capricorn.

Whyte, William Foote. 1948. *Human Relations in the Restaurant Industry.* New York: McGraw-Hill.

————. 1949. "The Social Structure of the Restaurant." *American Journal of Sociology* 54:302–10.

Williams, D. G., and Gabrielle H. Morris. 1996. "Crying, Weeping, or Tearfulness in British and Israeli Adults." *British Journal of Psychology* 87:479–505.

Wolfinger, Nicholas. 1995. "Passing Moments: Some Social Dynamics of Pedestrian Interaction." *Contemporary Ethnography* 24:323–40.

Zeskind, Philip S., Susan Parker-Price, and Ronald G. Barr. 1993. "Rhythmic Organization of the Sound of Infant Crying." *Developmental Psychobiology* 26:321–33.

INDEX

Page references to figures appear in italics.

active voice, 142–44
Adam and Eve, 148, 149, 150, 160,
    161, 162, 376n. 19
adults: bodily presentations in social
    interactions, 255–56; corporeal aes-
    thetics of crying of, 212–22; crying
    by, 176, 181, 192–210, 299, 341,
    343; responding to whining child,
    273. *See also* adults before a fun
    house mirror
adults before a fun house mirror: body
    part presented to the mirror, 110; em-
    bodied tension created in children
    by, 110–11; generational differences
    in interaction narratives, 125–30;
    guiding child through a series of ref-
    erences, 98–99, *101;* guiding small
    children to grasp that the image is
    of them, 105; introductory guidance
    provided for children, 100–104,
    102, 104; laughing at fun house mir-
    rors, 92, 327; lifting a child off the
    ground, 97–98, *99,* 110; losing com-
    posure, 127–28; needing children to
    make sense of acting silly, 139; with
    other adults, 105–6, *106;* teaching so-
    cial competence to children, 134–39;
    touching child's head, 98, *100*
African-American drivers, 55
age: learning to enact, 170; in stereotyp-
    ing offending drivers, 23, 54, 56, 58
Alabama, spirit of the dead in legal pro-
    ceedings in, 208, 367n. 61
All's Well that Ends Well (Shakespeare),
    362n. 14

altruism, 51
analytic induction, 11–12, 76
Andersen, Hans Christian, 318, 375n.
    16
anger: as central metaphor for social psy-
    chology, 173; and community, 351n.
    9; as cross-cultural, 345n. 3; crying
    contrasted with, 15; defining a provo-
    cation by responding to it, 144–45;
    as dialectical, 15, 330, 331; as dualis-
    tic, 15, 330, 377n. 22; electric charac-
    ter of, 66, 353n. 20; after a fall, 335;
    game theory for understanding, 71;
    gender differences in, 362n. 3; at
    home, 377n. 22; a "piercing insult"
    as catalyst of, 333; public expression
    of, 80–81; self-martyring nature of,
    378n. 27; and self-reflection, 146,
    312; and sex, 173; social-science ex-
    planations of, 327, 377n. 23; after
    striking out, 164; two forms of, 171.
    See also road rage
animals, language gap with, 202
Anna Karenina (Tolstoy), 167
art: Cézanne, 314; construction of artis-
    tic genius, 375n. 12; crying in re-
    sponse to, 198, 365n. 44; origins of
    the visible in, 310–11; Vermeer, 182,
    183, 363n. 17. *See also* music
Ashe, Arthur, 194–95, 216
Asian drivers, 54–55
asymmetrical interaction: in driving, 24–
    31, 78; in police interrogation, 287
audience segregation problems, 203–4
"backseat drivers," 350n. 6

393